JUSTICE AND THE PRESS

BY *John Lofton*

BEACON PRESS
Boston

Library of Congress Card Catalogue Number 66-23788

Published simultaneously in Canada by Saunders of Toronto, Ltd.

Beacon Press books are published under the auspices
of the Unitarian Universalist Association.

Printed in the United States of America

For the right to quote pertinent material, the author expresses grateful acknowledgment to the following parties for the indicated selections: the *St. Louis University Law Journal,* for permission to reprint portions of the author's article, "Justice and the Press—Communication Inside and Outside the Courtroom," which appeared in the Fall 1961 issue; *The Nation,* for permission to adapt portions of the author's article, "Trial by Fury," which was published in the November 25, 1961, issue; *The New York Times* and Dr. Ralph Banay, for permission to reprint in the latter part of Chapter 7 an excerpt from an article, "Why the Prison Alarm Sounds," by Dr. Banay in the July 26, 1959, issue of *The New York Times Magazine* (© 1959 by The New York Times Company. Reprinted by permission.); Little, Brown & Co., for leave to quote the verse in Chapter 10, from the poem "Period Period," in the Ogden Nash book, *Verses From 1929 On,* (Copyright © 1954, by Ogden Nash), which originally appeared in *The New Yorker.*

TO WILLIAM BLOCK, PUBLISHER OF THE PITTSBURGH POST-GAZETTE, WHOSE PROFOUND RESPECT FOR THE PRINCIPLES OF FREEDOM AND JUSTICE IS CLEARLY REFLECTED IN HIS NEWSPAPER'S EDITORIAL SUPPORT FOR ALL OF THE GUARANTEES OF THE BILL OF RIGHTS, INCLUDING FREEDOM OF THE PRESS AND FAIR TRIAL.

ACKNOWLEDGMENTS

OF ALL THE PEOPLE who helped me bring this book to fruition, a few deserve special mention: William Block, publisher of the Pittsburgh *Post-Gazette,* who encouraged and aided me in many ways, including the granting of paid time off from my regular duties; Wilbur Schramm, director of the Institute for Communication Research at Stanford University, who provided valuable guidance during the initial months of work; Chilton R. Bush, Clifford F. Weigle, Nathan Maccoby, Richard F. Carter, and M. E. Samuelson, all of the faculty of Stanford's Department of Communication and Journalism, who read portions of the manuscript and made useful suggestions; Herbert L. Packer of the Stanford Law School and Joan McCord of the Stanford Department of Sociology, who, along with others, constructively criticized the proposed outline of the book; Attorneys Thomas M. Kerr, Jr., and Marjorie Hanson Matson of Pittsburgh, who read parts of the manuscript and gave me the benefit of their incisive legal insights and their keen appreciation of the Bill of Rights; Professor Henry H. Foster, Jr., of the New York University School of Law, for giving the valued guidance of a concerned lawyer who recognizes the essential role of freedom of the press; Professors Thomas S. Checkley and William F. Schulz, Jr., of the University of Pittsburgh School of Law, for locating and cheerfully making available hard-to-find research materials; my colleagues at the *Pittsburgh Post-Gazette,* including Editor Frank N. Hawkins, former Editor Andrew Bernhard, and others, for providing the daily working forums so important to the shaping of practical views on hard problems; Judy Klimowski, who earned my thanks as a decipherer of handwriting and a conscientious typist; Beacon Press Editor William E. Dennen, for his skillful, tireless, and understanding contribution to an improved final manuscript; my wife, Anne, who patiently and helpfully shared my years of effort and was a vital source of inspiration.

Though all of these people—and others too numerous to name—won my gratitude, none of them deserves any blame for any errors of fact or for my expressions of opinion.

CONTENTS

INTRODUCTION

FEW INSTITUTIONS, when their interests clash, exhibit such combative proclivities as the press and the bar. In castigating a lawyer for his proposal to ban certain disclosures to the news media in advance of criminal trials, Alexander F. Jones, former president of the American Society of Newspaper Editors, exclaimed that he would guess the author to be Goebbels.[1] Commenting on newspaper handling of sensational cases, Clarence Darrow said, "It is a species of mob law more insidious and dangerous than ordinary mob law."[2]

In view of the belligerent inclinations of the two sides, productive discussion between them has been difficult to promote. And yet such discussion is now more important than ever.

One of the incidental results of the assassination of President John F. Kennedy was a great awakening of national interest in the performance of the press in reporting crime news. The Warren Commission roundly rebuked the newsmen on the scene, the Dallas police, and the district attorney for their irresponsible dissemination of information on the suspects in the world-shaking crime and concluded that "it would have been a most difficult task to select an unprejudiced jury, either in Dallas or elsewhere."[3]

Not since a joint committee of newsmen and lawyers took up the same question in connection with the Lindbergh kidnapping trial thirty years ago have members of the two professions been so stirred up as they are today over the competing claims of freedom of the press and fair trial.[4] After a review of the Lindbergh kidnapping case, a group representing the American Bar Association, the American Newspaper Publishers Association, and the American Society of Newspaper Editors declared: "The trial of Bruno Richard Hauptmann [the kidnapping defendant] . . . exhibited, perhaps, the most spectacular and depressing example of improper publicity and professional misconduct ever presented to the people of the United States in a criminal trial." [5]

In the years between the Lindbergh kidnapping and the Kennedy assassination, the subject of justice and the press has been dealt with in sections of numerous books, in literally hundreds of articles in legal and journalism periodicals, and in countless numbers of the nonspecialized magazines. It has been a topic for discussion at scores of meetings of lawyers, meetings of newsmen and at symposiums made up of members of both groups. Despite all of the recent effort to reach an accommodation, the varying points of view have seldom been reconciled.

Lawyers usually emphasize the constitutional right of criminal defendants to be presumed innocent until proved guilty in a fair trial. They claim that, without some curb on prejudicial publicity, the accused may be unfairly convicted on the basis of published allegations about him which are not substantiated or which have nothing to do with the crime and which would not be allowed as evidence at the trial.

Newsmen, on the other hand, usually emphasize the constitutional right of freedom of the press and claim that any curb on news about criminal cases may interfere with justice by shielding law enforcement officers and the courts from press criticism and from public criticism based on press reports.

But if the opposing viewpoints of the bar and the press are still far apart, the pressure for some kind of resolution of their differences is perhaps greater today than ever before. The Warren Commission asserted that the "experience at Dallas . . . is a dramatic affirmation of the need for steps to bring about a proper balance between the right of the public to be kept informed and the right of the individual to a fair and impartial trial." Not only has this comment prompted fresh reviews of the issue by the same organizations that studied the Hauptmann trial, but the United States Supreme Court in recent years has forced a reconsideration of the subject by a series of decisions reversing convictions which appeared to have resulted in part from prejudicial publicity.[6]

Since the current broad examination of justice and the press promises to bring about a new relationship between the press and the courts, it is important that any change be keyed to a proper appreciation of the roles of the institutions on both sides of the dispute. The courts and the press both perform tasks which are given high priority under our constitutional system—the courts, the function of insuring justice for individuals; the press, the function of securing for the public an independent scrutiny of the operation of governmental institutions, including the courts.

When the press performs properly, it helps to promote the right to due process. And on their side, the courts are the means of upholding and implementing the rights of a free press. Why then is there a conflict? Why do lawyers often take the position that the law enforcement agencies can do their job best with a minimum of interference from the press—at least in the pretrial stage? Why do newsmen often argue as though the agencies of justice can do their work properly only with a maximum of uninhibited reporting in the press?

The answer is that, despite the theoretical commitment of both the press and the courts to the allied causes of justice and freedom, history and experience have given both sides ample cause to distrust each other. The skirmishes of the last generation are only the latest in a history of press-court conflict going back at least 300 years. The press, on the one hand, has in many ways infringed the individual's constitutional right to due process. And the courts, for their part, have frequently curbed the press and denied it access to legitimate news. The courts on many occasions have also been responsible for injustices in which the press had no role, except perhaps in pointing out where judges erred. This too has led to conflict.

Whatever the circumstances of their conflict, however, it is clear that the roles of the press and the courts are so interrelated that the two institutions cannot be walled off from each other. A better approach would be for each side to seek a better understanding of the function of the other and to try to promote the proper exercise of that function.

One aim of this book is to examine how newspapers flout the rights of due process. Another aim is to note how the courts themselves abuse the rights of due process and obstruct the rights of a free press. The final objective is to suggest under what circumstances and in what ways the individual right to due process should take precedence over the collective public right to know and, conversely, when the right to know should take precedence.

The book will perform a useful service if it induces some agreement on rules and objective standards of conduct under which both the press—particularly newspapers—and the courts can perform their rightful missions more effectively. But it will not have been written in vain if it merely arouses a realization on each side that it is no purer than the other. Mutual recognition of fault should be the first step toward reform.

John Lofton

PART ONE

Free Press v. Due Process—Historical Preface to a Problem

CHAPTER ONE

WORDS ON TRIAL

IF SOME EDITORS TODAY seem hypersensitive on the subject of freedom of the press, their attitude is inherited as a part of the mystique of their calling. It is grounded in the history of words on trial. Man's written record of his ancient past tells of prosecutions and persecutions for words that incurred the displeasure of the rulers of the community. Though the same record also tells of undaunted defenses of free expression, the principle has never been easy to uphold. For words are the vehicles for dispute and challenge as well as the tools for reason and reconciliation.

GREECE

The ancient Athenians recognized the value of unfettered expression. Pericles defended freedom of speech as he delivered his famous oration (431 B.C.) in memory of the first Athenian soldiers to fall in the Peloponnesian War. Yet the Athenians had their limits and their weaknesses. Solon (594 B.C.) had forbidden evil speaking of both the dead and the living. Later Diopithes sponsored a decree authorizing the indictment of "those who disbelieve in divine things or teach theories about what goes on in the sky." Several well known Athenians were accused and tried for their spoken beliefs. And in 399 B.C. Socrates was condemned to death as one of history's outstanding martyrs in the cause of free speech.

Socrates was accused by his enemies and brought to trial before a jury of 501 Athenians, charged with corrupting the youth by teaching them to make "the worse appear the better reason," and with not recognizing the gods recognized by the state but introducing "new divinities." Spurning an opportunity to save himself, Socrates, as reported by Plato, made one of history's immortal exhortations for a free mind:

> If you offered to let me off this time on condition that I am not any longer to speak my mind in this search for wisdom, and that if I am caught doing this again I shall die, I should say to you, "Men of Athens, I shall obey the God rather than you. While I have life and strength I shall never cease to follow philosophy and to exhort and persuade anyone of you whom I happen to meet. For this, be assured the God commands. . . ." And, Athenians, I should go on to say, "Either acquit me or not; but understand that I shall never act differently, even if I have to die for it many times."

Rome

In another part of the ancient world, the Bible exalted the power of speech. It also contained examples of dissenters in difficulty: Jesus being tried and condemned for seditious preaching and St. Paul being called before King Agrippa (Acts 25:23). Though freedom of thought and religion was ostensibly a policy of Rome until near the close of the fifth century A.D., Rome, too, had its cases of suppression. Besides the early Christians who suffered martyrdom for their beliefs, Greek writings came in for condemnation.

From the Roman Empire to the Reformation, Western thinkers exhibited little concern for freedom of thought and speech, at least in the realm of politics and other secular subjects. On the subject of religious thought, St. Augustine, as early as 410 A.D., objected to free expression for heresy, thus displaying the common human trait of intolerance for opposing views. Once in positions of power, Christians were as harsh toward spokesmen for unorthodox doctrines as their oppressors had once been toward them. The Inquisition originated with Pope Gregory IX in 1233 A.D. and was continued in one form or another into the nineteenth century, with perhaps its most severe manifestations occurring in fifteenth-century Spain, where judicial torture was an accepted feature of heresy trials. It would be "better a hundred innocent should suffer than one guilty person escape," said leaders of the Spanish Inquisition.[1]

Europe in the Reformation

The ferment of the Protestant revolt gave history some of its most impassioned champions of freedom of conscience. Their appeals, however, were usually in behalf of religious liberty, especially liberty for their own brand of sectarian expression. Savonarola burned the works of Dante and was in his own turn burned together with his books. In 1553 John Calvin, the Protestant reformer, ordered the Unitarian Michael Servetus tried and burned. As the condemned heretic stood at the stake, "around his waist were tied a large bundle of manuscript and a thick octavo printed book." Bibles in versions of almost all sects have been burned or suppressed.[2]

Limited as were the pleas for tolerance during the Reformation, it was in this era that the mechanical as well as the doctrinal basis was laid for what were to become the modern concepts of freedom of speech and of the press. The Reformation gave birth to the idea of freedom for the individual to question and to interpret scriptural authority for himself, and this intellectual quest—encouraged by the rise of scientific inquiry—led to the assertion of the right to question and challenge political authority. The permanent printed word provided the best means of communicating such questions and challenges. Printing from movable type was invented in the fifteenth century, with the Mazarin Bible, printed by Johann Gutenberg about 1456, believed to be the first book so produced in Europe.

In time the printed newspaper was to become the most accessible medium of popular intelligence. Though the "newspaper" had existed in ancient Rome in the form of handwritten daily notices posted in public places and in T'ang Dynasty China (618–907 A.D.) in the form of a court gazette, wider distribution of news organs became possible only with the development of movable type.

From the beginning, newspapers encountered opposition from the political authorities. The first English papers were restricted to foreign news. James I (King of England, 1603–1625) forbade the publication of national news, calling it "lavish and licentious talking in matters of state . . . which the common people know not how to understand."

As the art of printing spread, licensing became the weapon of control. Publication without the imprimatur of the licensing authorities brought hardship and punishment and was a more effective means of suppression than sporadic criminal prosecutions for heresy and sedition. Systematic censorship of pamphlets and books existed in most of Europe during the early history of printing.[3]

England

The experience of England is a matter of special importance to Americans, since the United States inherited both its legal and its journalistic systems from the English. With Caxton's first use of the printing press in England in 1476, this method of disseminating unacceptable thoughts became an object of concern to the sovereign. Henry VIII (King of England, 1509–1547) perceived the political importance of printing and not only limited the privilege of keeping a press but also required previous inspection of the matter by a licenser. Under Henry VIII, the king's power of proscription was made practically absolute by a broadening of the definition of the crime of treason to have it encompass even the thoughts of men, who should by words, writing, imprinting, or any other exterior act, directly or indirectly, judge or believe contrary to the royal pleasure.

As early as 1566 the Star Chamber strictly regulated printing. Made up of members of the king's Privy Council and some judges, this court met in a room of Westminster Palace with stars painted on its ceiling. The name of its chamber became a synonym for an arbitrary tribunal. It exercised wide civil and criminal jurisdiction, sat in secret without a jury, acted often on mere rumor, and applied torture when it saw fit. In 1586 the Star Chamber issued an ordinance providing that no printing was to be done in any place except London, Oxford, or Cambridge; the Archbishop of Canterbury and the Bishop of London were to decide the number of presses needed and were to license all books (except law books and a few others).

Though the Long Parliament in 1641 abolished the hated Star Chamber, this did not end licensing or censorship. Instead Parliament took over the task on the pretext that the revolutionary Puritan government needed protection from the royalist press. Licensing acts were renewed from time to time under both parliamentary and monarchial rule, and were not finally allowed to expire until 1695.

Even the termination of licensing in England, and soon afterward in the American colonies, did not prevent efforts to control the written word. It nevertheless had a significant bearing on freedom of the press, for it meant there was no longer any prior official restraint on the printed matter that reached the public. Newspapers sprang up in greater numbers. The absence of licensing in England led writers like Voltaire to publish in that country.

Meanwhile, however, the government still had the formidable weapon of criminal prosecution of authors, editors, and printers for treason and for seditious libel. Ever since the time of Edward III (1312–1377), treason had been defined to include imagining the death of the king, the queen, or their eldest son and heir, or the levying of war against the king or the giving of aid and comfort to his enemies. Proof of traitorous conduct required a showing of some overt act, and for this purpose, words written or printed by the accused were sufficient.

Some of the most notorious trials for seditious libel occurred prior to the expiration of licensing. After such a proceeding against William Prynn in 1633, a work by him became the first book to be burned by the common hangman. The author was charged with seditious libel and tried in the Star Chamber. He was sentenced to be imprisoned for life, fined 5,000 pounds, deprived of his Oxford degree, disbarred as a lawyer, and set in the pillory, where both his ears were to be cut off; all copies of his book that could be found were to be burned so close to the pillory that the prisoner could smell the smoke from his offensive writing. Prynn was later released by the Long Parliament and, ironically, became the prosecutor of Archbishop Laud when the latter was tried and condemned to death in 1645.

John Lilburne had the distinction of offending both the Royalists and the Puritans by his publishing. In 1637, accused of having Puritan books printed in Rotterdam, he was brought before the Star Chamber, where his steadfast refusal to testify against himself made him not only a champion of a free press but also of the right against self-incrimination. He was sentenced to be whipped along the Strand to the Palace Yard and then placed in the pillory. Later—having joined Oliver Cromwell's forces and moved to the side of the democratic Levellers in the army—Lilburne incurred the displeasure of the Cromwellians and was imprisoned; his pamphlets were burned.

With a royal government back in power under Charles II, John Twyn in 1663 was indicted for high treason for imagining the death of the king. At Twyn's trial in Old Bailey, passages from a book, of which he was the printer but not the author, were entered in evidence to prove that the people had been inspired to believe that the supreme magistrate was accountable to them, that they were incited to take up arms against the king, to take over the management of the government from him, and to put the king to death. Found guilty, Twyn was sentenced to be hanged, drawn, and quartered.

One of the leading eighteenth-century cases on freedom of the press was that of John Wilkes (1727–1797), the English political leader who sympathized with the American colonies and sought parliamentary reform. In 1762 he founded the *North Briton* in opposition to the *Briton,* a progovernment paper edited by Tobias Smollett. For daring to publish in the *North Briton* an article commenting upon a speech of George III and suggesting that royal pronouncements were as open to criticism as any other speeches, Wilkes was convicted of seditious libel, sentenced to twenty-two months in prison, and ordered to pay fines totaling 1,000 pounds.

Convictions in sedition prosecutions remained relatively easy in eighteenth-century England as long as two potent legal doctrines were in force: (1) the doctrine that true as well as false statements about government could be punished (on the ground, as the courts put it, that "the greater the truth the greater the libel"), and (2) the doctrine that the judge, who was a crown appointee, rather than the jury was empowered to decide whether the printed matter was seditious. Not until 1792, with the passage of the Fox Libel Act, was the freedom of the press placed under the protection of the jury, which from that time was empowered to determine what constituted criminal defamation. Not until Lord Campbell's Act of 1843 was truth made a defense in a prosecution for criminal libel.

At the same time the common law courts were trying citizens for seditious libel, Parliament, too, was prosecuting for the same offense. Though it acted on the theory that the accused had been contemptuous of its authority, the proceedings—in which either house might function as prosecutor, judge, and jury—were instituted for objectionable words which were said to reflect on the members or on the government generally.

Eloquent as were such seventeenth- and eighteenth-century English spokesmen for liberty as John Milton, John Locke, and others, they did not change the common law doctrine of seditious libel. That doctrine, which held sway in both England and the colonies during the eighteenth century, was summed up by Sir William Blackstone in 1769:

> The liberty of the press is indeed essential to the nature of a free state; but this consists in laying no previous restraints upon publications, and not in freedom from censure for criminal matter when published. Every free man has an undoubted right to lay what sentiments he pleases before the public: to forbid this, is to destroy the freedom of the press: but if he publishes what is improper, mischievous or illegal, he must take the consequences of his own temerity.

While the liberals of Blackstone's day urged that juries be empowered to decide what was seditious and contended that true publications could not be libelous, they did not challenge his fundamental theory, under which words having the "bad tendency" of lowering the government in the public's esteem or of disturbing the peace might be adjudged criminal. The elastic "bad tendency" test, though it was finally rejected as a concept by nineteenth-century libertarians, was to keep reappearing in cases as late as the twentieth century.

Ultimately when the liberal eighteenth-century propositions were translated into law, the supposed beneficiaries were to discover that they were not fully protected by pleading truth as a defense or by entrusting their fate to juries with the power to decide the whole question of libel. Truth of opinions, as soon became apparent, was not a matter susceptible of proof. One man's truth is another man's falsehood. As for juries, they could only be relied upon to support as unseditious the latitude of press expression acceptable to public opinion.[4] Clearly the press, under such theories, had no warrant for unfettered criticism of government.

Colonial America

The English colonies, where many sought escape from the orthodoxies of Europe, had not long been established in the New World when censorship came to American shores. In Puritan Massachusetts in 1634 the public hangman burned a number of books and pamphlets to keep them from being read by the settlers. The first printing press in the American colonies was set up at Harvard College in 1638, and a year later a Massachusetts law gave this press, which the Puritans controlled along with the college, a monopoly on all printing in the colony. Some years later a licensing system was set up in Massachusetts.

In Virginia the authorities were no more friendly to freedom of the press than in Massachusetts. In 1671 Sir William Berkeley, for thirty-eight years Governor of Virginia, wrote to his superiors in London:

> But, I thank God, we have not free schools nor printing; and I hope we shall not have these hundred years. For learning has brought disobedience and heresy and sects into the world; and printing has divulged them and libels against the government. God keep us from both.[5]

The prevalent view on the part of government that the printing press was a dangerous machine cropped up as soon as an attempt was made to establish the first American newspaper. At Boston on September 25, 1690, Benjamin Harris brought out what was intended to be the first of a series of issues of *Public Occurrences Both Foreign and Domestic*. It was to be "furnished once a month (or if any Glut of Occurrences happen, oftener)." But only four days after the paper's publication, the governor and council declared that it had been published "Without the least Privity or Countenance of Authority." Charging "that therein is contained Reflections of a very high nature: As also sundry doubtful and uncertain Reports," they proclaimed their "high Resentment and Disallowance of said Pamphlet, and order that the same be Suppressed and called in; strictly forbidding any person or persons for the future to Set forth any thing in Print without License first obtained." So ended the first American newspaper, after only one issue.

At the time of the next venture in colonial newspaper publishing fourteen years later, the publisher was not so bold as to ignore the authorities. The Boston *News-Letter,* founded by John Campbell in 1704, carried a line under its nameplate attesting that it was "Published by Authority," which meant that the governor or his secretary commonly approved the contents of the paper before it was printed. Yet even the weekly *News-Letter,* which was to be the first continuously published American newspaper, suffered governmental rebuke.

In supposedly liberal Pennsylvania, the press and the authorities were in conflict soon after the founding of the colony in 1682. William Bradford, the province's first printer, found himself in trouble in 1686 at the time of his initial publication, an almanac. It was censored while still in manuscript and he was warned "not to print anything but what shall have Lycence from ye Council." In 1690 Bradford's press was seized by the colonial government and he was thrown into jail on a charge of seditious libel because he had printed a number of tracts written by a separatist Quaker faction. In what was perhaps the first criminal trial in America involving freedom of the press, Bradford stoutly defended himself and succeeded in gaining a deadlocked jury. But he nevertheless spent many months in jail awaiting a first trial and then a second, and the case ended only when he was released at the request of the governor of New York in order to set up a printing press there.

After William Bradford moved his press from Philadelphia to Manhattan Island in 1693, he was content for many years simply to be the official printer to the New York Council. Not until 1725 did he found New York's first newspaper, the *Gazette.* That journal printed chiefly stale foreign news, state papers, ship entries and clearances, and generally reflected its publisher's subservience to the royal government. Though Bradford got along with the authorities, this did not mean that speech was unrestricted in New York. Between 1706 and 1720, for example, there were four prosecutions of New York citizens for seditious reflections on the Assembly.

But political protest was in due time to take a daring form in New York. In 1733 the popular or opposition party was in the midst of a bitter dispute with the royal executive, William Cosby, when its members persuaded Peter Zenger, a German immigrant printer, to start an antigovernment newspaper. On November 5, 1733, Zenger, who had served his apprenticeship in Bradford's shop, brought out the first issue of the New York *Weekly Journal.* Bradford's *Gazette* spoke for the Governor. In his first number, Zenger published an article on freedom of the press with particular allusions to Governor Cosby. Other attacks on the Governor followed, with references to arbitrary interference with the judiciary and to citizens' loss of liberties. Cosby condemned the paper's "Scurrilous, Scandalous, and Virulent Reflections" and ordered several issues publicly burned.

When the enraged royal officials were unable to get the grand jury to indict Zenger or to get the Assembly to act, the Governor and the Council themselves charged him with "tending to raise Factions and Tumults among the People" and, by-passing the grand jury, initiated a prosecution for seditious libel by an information filed by the attorney general.

Arrested in November 1734 and denied reasonable bail, Zenger remained in jail for ten months. Meanwhile the paper was brought out by his wife and political supporters, one of whom was James Alexander, the talented lawyer who was both editor of the *Journal* and the mastermind of Zenger's defense. Disbarred in the initial stage of the case for daring to accuse the presiding judge of bias, Alexander helped to persuade Andrew Hamilton, the noted Philadelphia attorney, to act as Zenger's defense counsel and supplied Hamilton with a detailed brief for an argument to be used in court.

As the trial opened in August 1735 royal officials were ranged on the side of the court, which was in reality their instrument. But the common people, who packed the courtroom, were on Zenger's side. Opposing the common law rule, Hamilton argued that the jury should be allowed to decide whether the condemned *Journal* articles were true and, if they were so found, to acquit the defendant. Overruled on this point by Chief Justice James deLancey, Hamilton nevertheless contended eloquently that the only matter at issue was "the Liberty—both of exposing and opposing arbitrary Power (in these Parts of the World, at least) by speaking and writing Truth." Reviewing the history of political tyranny, he upheld the importance of open political discussion as an antidote to despotism. After hearing a brief and confused charge by the chief justice in which he referred to the dangers of allowing writers to speak unkindly about officials, the jury quickly returned a verdict of "not guilty," thus deciding the main issue on its own initiative.

Despite the Zenger trial's repudiation of the common law rules that truth is no defense against a libel charge and that the jury may only decide the question of whether the defendant published the alleged seditious matter, the New York outcome did not in fact change the law as it applied in future to other publishers and editors or even to Zenger himself. Zenger and Hamilton had won a rhetorical and moral victory, whose chief value was its inspiration for others to carry on an important cause.

Though the Zenger trial has been memorialized as a climax in a widespread and continuing struggle between the freedom-loving American colonists and the tyrannical royal judges, it was in fact an isolated phenomenon. Except for two rather obscure cases, one ending in an acquittal, it was the last common law prosecution for seditious libel under the royal judges. Between 1700 and the Zenger trial, only four persons had been convicted in the royal courts for seditious utterances under the common law of libel, and one of these convictions was reversed on appeal. Even in the preceding century, the defendants in the two most notable cases before royal judges had not been convicted. In America the number of common law prosecutions for seditious libel was negligible in contrast to the number in England where there were perhaps hundreds during the seventeenth and eighteenth centuries.

In the colonies, far more effective instruments of suppression were the governors (acting with their councils in a quasi-judicial capacity), and, most severe of all, the popularly elected assemblies. Emulating the House of Commons, which needed no grand jury to indict and no petty jury to convict, the provincial legislatures summoned, interrogated, and fixed criminal penalties against scores of colonial citizens who had supposedly libeled their members or the government generally by spoken, written, or printed words. Legislatures' punishment of verbal offenders, by jailing, pillorying, or otherwise, began in 1620 with the Virginia House of Burgesses, the first assembly to meet on American soil, and continued through the colonial period.

The history of American colonial and revolutionary experience suggests that on neither side were those in positions of power prepared to be magnanimous about freedom of expression for their political opponents. In 1735 William Bradford, who had himself suffered suppression in Pennsylvania, condemned Peter Zenger for publishing "pieces tending to set the province in a flame, and to raise sedition and tumults." In 1722 and again in 1729 one of the members of the Pennsylvania provincial Council, which penalized Andrew Bradford, son of William, for publishing derogatory material about the government, was the same Andrew Hamilton who later defended Peter Zenger in his trial for sedition. In 1775 in New York the leader of a band of armed men which smashed a Tory publisher's press was Alexander McDougall, a man who in 1770 had been mercilessly persecuted for seditious libel by the New York Assembly. In 1774 the Continental Congress, in an address designed to influence the inhabitants of Quebec, extolled freedom of the press in the interests of advancing truth. But in 1776 Congress urged the states to enact legislation to prevent people from being "deceived and drawn into erroneous opinion." By 1778 all of the states had enacted legislation designed in one way or another to suppress disloyalty and seditious utterances.[6] It should be noted, however, that a time of war has never been regarded as an appropriate period for completely unfettered expression.

The United States

Of the original thirteen states, nine incorporated guarantees of freedom of the press in their first constitutions: Georgia, South

Carolina, North Carolina, Virginia, Maryland, Pennsylvania, Delaware, Massachusetts, and New Hampshire.[7] But it seems likely that none of the nine, with the possible exception of Pennsylvania and Virginia, meant to do any more than to guarantee the press against previous restraints, leaving it subject to subsequent prosecution for seditious or licentious publications.

When the federal Constitution was drafted, it did not contain any provision for freedom of the press. And of the twelve states to ratify the Constitution before the First Amendment was drawn up in Congress in 1789, only Virginia, North Carolina, and New York sought to protect the expression of opinion from violation by the new national government. As it was worded and as understood when first adopted, the First Amendment imposed limitations only upon the national government. It contained no federal restraint against state violations of freedom of the press.

Although we cannot now establish with certainty what kind of restriction the framers meant to impose on the federal government, a serious scholar in the field, Professor Leonard W. Levy, has recently concluded that they intended only to outlaw prepublication restrictions, leaving the common law of seditious libel in force. In Dr. Levy's revisionist view, a broad libertarian theory of freedom of speech and press did not emerge in the United States until the Jeffersonians, when a minority party, were forced to defend themselves against the Federalist Sedition Act of 1798. Up to that time Americans did a great deal of talking about freedom of expression without clearly formulating any legal concept to replace the repressive common law, which still left the press largely at the mercy of the government. Obviously a publisher or an editor who might be jailed afterward for what he printed was not likely to feel free to express unpopular opinions even if he did not need a government license to do so.

But the passage of the Sedition Act less than seven years after the ratification of the First Amendment forced Americans of that time to consider what freedom of speech and of the press really meant. That statute, enacted during tension over expected war with France, made criminal "any false, scandalous and malicious" writings, utterances, or publications against the government, Congress, or the President, with intent to defame them, bring them into contempt or disrepute, or excite against them the hatred of the people. A defendant in any prosecution was permitted to give in evidence the truth of the matter charged as a libel, and the jury was empowered to determine the law and the facts of the case. By allowing evidence of truth to offset the charge of libel and by permitting the jury to decide the whole issue, the act contained the reforms advocated by the libertarians of the eighteenth century.

Yet both Americans and Englishmen were soon to discover that the elimination of the worst features of the common law on seditious libel provided an empty safeguard for unfettered expression.[8] In the United States a campaign of politically inspired and partisanly conducted prosecutions for seditious libel followed the enactment of the Sedition Act of 1798. There were some twenty-five arrests under the act itself, fifteen indictments, and eleven trials. Despite the new law's supposed bulwark of freedom in the form of a jury, only one verdict of "not guilty" was returned in Sedition Act trials. During the trial of Dr. Thomas Cooper, Federalist Judge Samuel Chase said, "The traverser must prove every charge to be true: he must prove it to the marrow." Cooper, a refugee from England and a scientist, lawyer, and publicist, was convicted, fined $100, and thrown into prison for six months for calling President Adams an incompetent in the Reading *Weekly Advertiser.*

Faced with the prospective attempt of the Adams administration to silence political criticism, the Jeffersonians began to evolve a broader legal formula to insure freedom of the press. In the congressional debates on the sedition bill, Congressman Albert Gallatin of Pennsylvania attacked its constitutionality, asked how the truth of opinions could be proved by evidence, and pointed out that a jury sympathetic to the administration would not hesitate to judge his opinion as "false and scandalous." He insisted that, under the First Amendment, Congress could not enact any law effecting any degree of restraint on speech or press and asserted that the federal courts had no jurisdiction over seditious libel. In 1800 James Madison—addressing himself more comprehensively to the question of freedom of the press than he had during the debates over the adoption of the Bill of Rights—declared that the Sedition Act was unconstitutional, that the United States had no jurisdiction over common law crimes (some of the sedition prosecutions of the period had been under the common law), that a free, republican government could not be libeled, that the first amendment was intended to supersede the common law on speech and press, and that the freedom guaranteed by the amendment was absolute so far as the federal government was concerned.

Republicans in Congress were able to block the extension of the Sedition Act beyond its expiration date of March 3, 1801. And the next day, in his first inaugural address, President Jefferson provided a standard for what has come to be the modern libertarian concept: freedom of expression even for those thoughts which are unpopular with the public.

> If there be any among us who would wish to dissolve this Union or to change its republican form, let them stand undisturbed as monuments of the safety with which error of opinion may be tolerated where reason is left free to combat it.

Jefferson in effect apotheosized the apocryphal aphorism, ascribed to Voltaire, that he wholly disapproved of what Helvetius said but would defend to the death his right to say it. The President also pardoned all those convicted under what he called the "unauthorized" Sedition Act of 1798, though no case under the act was ever passed upon by the Supreme Court.

The Jeffersonians, however, were not as pure in practice as they had been in preachment. Like so many others whose principles have weakened when they become the target for attack, the Jeffersonian Republicans, once they were in power, did not take kindly to continuing lampooning by Federalist publications. In 1803 a Jeffersonian official in New York obtained a common law indictment for seditious libel against Harry Croswell, editor of the Federalist newspaper, the *Wasp*. Croswell's crime was that he had accused Jefferson of paying James T. Callender to denounce Washington as "a traitor, a robber, and a perjurer" and Adams as "a hoary-headed incendiary." Croswell was convicted by a jury in a trial presided over by a Jeffersonian judge who overruled the defendant's contention that evidence of the truth of alleged libel should be allowed. Arguing the Croswell case on appeal to the highest court of New York, Alexander Hamilton, Jefferson's foremost opponent, championed the cause of freedom of the press, declaring that it consisted of "the right to publish, with impunity, truth, with good motives, for justifiable ends, though reflecting on government, magistracy, or individuals." Though the New York Court of Errors, by an equally divided vote, upheld the conviction, Hamilton's argument was so persuasive that shortly afterward the New York legislature passed a statute making it possible to introduce truth, as a defense in a criminal suit when it was published with good motives for justifiable ends.[9]

Jefferson's view of the Croswell prosecution is unknown. But the President is known to have written a letter in 1803 to his political supporter, Governor Thomas McKean of Pennsylvania, in which he suggested that "a few prosecutions of the most eminent offenders would have a wholesome effect in restoring the integrity of the presses." Some time later the arch-Federalist Joseph Dennie, editor of the *Port Folio,* was indicted in Pennsylvania for seditious libel against both the state and national governments after he published an essay calling democracy "contemptible and vicious" and predicting that it would bring the country to civil war, despotism, and anarchy. The case did not come to trial for more than two years, at which time a Federalist judge instructed the jury that the safety and happiness of a free people would be aided by a full examination of the system of government under which they lived. The jury acquitted.

The next year (1806) six defendants were indicted in the federal courts of Connecticut for the common law crime of seditious libel of President Jefferson. Jefferson later wrote that these prosecutions were instituted without his knowledge and that he ordered them discontinued when he found out about them. The government withdrew the prosecutions against four of the defendants. The case of the other two was appealed to the Supreme Court before trial for a decision on the question of whether federal tribunals possessed jurisdiction over the common law crime of seditious libel. In 1812 the high court handed down a ruling against federal common law jurisdiction. Since the cases of the early 1800's, there have been no federal prosecutions for the particular crime of seditious libel, though similar actions in the field of sedition have occurred. But state courts during the first third of the nineteenth century were forums for many libel cases, both prosecutions for criminal libel and private suits for damages.

In time, all of the states were to have constitutional guarantees of freedom of the press. Like the federal government, the states, ostensibly, were adhering to the libertarian principle that utterances by the press should be subject to a minimum of interference from public officials. Yet neither the First Amendment's restraint on the federal government nor the state charters' limits on state governments were to mean that the press would be free from official efforts to suppress minority opinion. A century and a quarter were to pass before the United States Supreme Court dealt significantly with the First Amendment's meaning for the press.

One way of controlling or penalizing the press for what were considered its aberrations was to cut off or limit its access to news. The galleries of the Senate itself were closed to the press until 1794 when complaints by editor Philip Freneau of the Philadelphia *National Gazette* resulted in passage of a resolution to allow newspaper representatives to hear and report on debates on the public business. Even so, the Senate restricted its reporters to those representing local papers until 1846. Though the House had "unofficially" admitted reporters prior to 1794, it continued for years to impose capricious restrictions for "misrepresentation" of its debates or for other reasons. Both houses of Congress and many state legislatures still reserve—and from time to time have invoked—the right to hold secret sessions.

In time of war the press has suffered from both official and vigilante repression whenever the sentiments it expressed were not stormed the printshop, wrecked the presses, and tore down the in keeping with popular opinion. During the War of 1812 a mob building of the *Federal Republican* in Baltimore.

Long before the Civil War, public controversy over slavery led to both official and unofficial repressive actions against the abolitionist press. During the Jackson administration Postmaster General Amos Kendall called antislavery papers "most flagitious" and privately advised Southern postmasters to intercept all such matter in the future and to deliver it only to those who would come forward and identify themselves as bona fide subscribers.

The chief weapon against abolitionist freedom of expression, however, was private intimidation, often officially condoned. William Lloyd Garrison was attacked by a mob in Boston in 1835. That same year the office of the Utica *Standard and Democrat* was sacked. James G. Birney's *Philanthropist,* another abolitionist paper, was driven out of Kentucky. He moved it to Cincinnati, where it was mobbed three times in the late 1830's.

Alton, Illinois, in 1837 was the scene of one of the worst outrages against the abolitionist press. The Reverend Elijah P. Lovejoy had engaged in journalism in St. Louis, had entered the Presbyterian ministry, and then established the *Observer,* a religious newspaper with antislavery leanings. As a border slave state, Missouri at the time was often gripped by mob psychology generated in those areas by the slavery question. Lovejoy deplored the disregard for law. In 1836 he quarreled editorially with Judge Luke E. Lawless of St. Louis over the latter's condoning of mob violence against a Negro.[10] Shortly afterward he moved his press across the river to Alton, Illinois, where he hoped to find greater liberty to oppose slavery. But mobs in the free state of Illinois destroyed his press and threw it in the river three times in one year.

Meeting under the chairmanship of the attorney general of Illinois, the citizens of Alton proclaimed their "sacred regard for the great principles contained in our Bill of Rights." Yet in the same resolution they warned Lovejoy to give up his press and leave town. The editor responded that he would stay in Alton and "insist on protection" in the exercise of his rights. If the civil authorities refused to protect him, he said: "I must look to God, and if I die, I have determined to make my grave in Alton." On November 7, 1837, he was attacked and killed by a mob as he defended a new printing press that had just arrived. He died in Alton, as he had pledged, a martyr in the cause of freedom of the press and of abolition. Abolitionist papers continued to speak out and to suffer the consequences of popular retribution as long as slavery lasted.

During this period the Mexican War sparked a good deal of criticism, which apparently was suffered with a fair amount of tolerance, perhaps because the critical comment was mostly in the North where the war was not popular.

Like earlier wars, the Civil War brought extraordinary restrictions on the press, some of them justifiable in the interest of military security, some of them an unnecessary curb of free expression in the name of rooting out disloyalty. Much of the repressive activity of the Civil War was not based on law but purely on the President's authority as commander-in-chief, a power which during the war was never successfully challenged in the Supreme Court. Military officers, acting without warrants and often on the thinnest of suspicions, arrested thousands of citizens all over the North. Sometimes they were subjected to drumhead courts-martial. Often they were never tried but simply locked up in forts or military prisons for an indefinite period. United States marshals, state, and local authorities also rounded up suspected subversives and lodged them in civilian prisons. The estimated number of political prisoners during the war ranged up to 38,000, with more than 13,000 being held in military lockups.

The atmosphere of free discussion was further clouded by the War Department's institution of censorship over telegraphic communication and the Post Office Department's denial of the use of the mails to newspapers deemed disloyal by the Postmaster General. Always in the air was the threat of mob action against dissenting voices. Gangs of soldiers and civilians demolished printing plants in smaller towns of a dozen states from New Hampshire to Iowa. After the war James Ford Rhodes, an admirer of Lincoln, wrote that the arbitrary arrests and interferences with freedom of the press in states outside of the theater of war were "inexpedient, unnecessary and wrong."

In the South, as in the North during the years 1861–1865, the behavior of leaders and people reflected the typical human reaction to wartime conditions. Not only did the Confederate government impose military censorship but it also sought to suppress dissenting opinion.

The cessation of military conflict did not necessarily mean peace for the press. In the South during the Reconstruction era, newspapers on both sides were manipulated by pressure, forced to speak softly or suspend. During the 1880's labor organizational activities and printed pleas for better wages and working conditions brought harsh interference with what was then an unfamiliar voice. When workers held meetings, marched in picket lines, distributed literature, or otherwise exercised their constitutional rights of freedom of speech and of the press, they were frequently met with injunctions and, if they persisted in their activity, they were thrown into jail without jury trials.

During the Spanish-American War military censorship was unusually lenient, though a censor was appointed in New York and tried to curb the disclosures of some of the correspondents. General William Shafter on one occasion banished all Hearst men from captured Santiago.

While official and collective private attacks on the press might have been most prevalent during periods of war and tension, individual assaults with the club, the horsewhip, or the dueling pistol came at many unexpected times, especially during the first part of the nineteenth century.

Editors in the South and West were frequently involved in man-to-man fighting over the contents of their papers, a phenomenon which led Mark Twain to write his sketch of "Journalism in Tennessee." In it he portrayed the old editor, who has just shot one man and leaves his new assistant in charge of the office with the following instructions:

> Jones will be here at three—cowhide him. Gillespie will call earlier, perhaps—throw him out of the window. Ferguson will be along about four—kill him. That is all for today, I believe. If you have any odd time, you may write a blistering article on the police. The cowhides are under the table, weapons in the drawer, ammunition there in the corner, lint and bandages up there in the pigeonholes. In case of accident, go to Lancet, the surgeon, downstairs. He advertises; we take it out in trade.[11]

By the opening of the twentieth century, the American press was well established in terms of numbers of newspapers, the power of metropolitan dailies, and the diversity of smaller sheets. Yet this development did not always insure the preservation of unfettered expression. In 1909 President Theodore Roosevelt was angered by stories in the New York *World* and the Indianapolis *News* hinting that an American syndicate, including Attorney General William Nelson Cromwell, had made a corrupt profit in connection with the purchase of Panama Canal rights. He ordered the Justice Department to bring common-law suits against the two newspapers for criminal libel, the first libel actions by the federal government since the prosecutions under the Sedition Act of 1798. Federal judges quashed both indictments on constitutional grounds.

In 1911 a federal statute was enacted making it a crime to publish "matters of a character tending to incite arson, murder, or assassination," with the Postmaster General being empowered to bar from the mails papers containing such material. Under this provision, many alleged Communist and anarchist papers have been suppressed. The law's constitutionality has been judicially sustained.

Beginning in 1902, with the enactment of a law by the New York legislature, the states moved to curb discussion by anarchists and others whose political and economic views were distasteful to the majority of citizens. As defined by new state statutes, the offense of "criminal syndicalism" consisted of violence or the advocacy of violence or other illicit means to bring about political change. Publications inciting to violence and the overthrow of government were thus made criminal. Laws against criminal syndicalism multiplied during and immediately after World War I until some thirty-three states had them, with many of the acts being uniform in wording. Chief targets of criminal syndicalism prosecutions were members of the Industrial Workers of the World and others who, under the intolerance of wartime emotion, were deemed guilty of radical, socialist, or "bolshevik" tendencies. The Kentucky law provided that the mere expression of radical opinion constituted evidence of a plot to overthrow the government. Thus the states in effect joined forces with the federal government in the effort to stamp out sedition. While criminal syndicalism acts soon became a dead letter in most states, California continued to enforce its law. In the five years after its enactment in 1919, 504 persons were arrested and held for bail of $15,000 each, and 264 were actually tried. When juries eventually began to refuse to convict, the California attorney general secured a court injunction under which

IWW organizers could be tried for contempt of court without juries for merely soliciting new members.[12]

Although there may have been some danger of sabotage from IWW incitement, some state prosecutions went far beyond a reasonable effort to curb speech creating a risk of illegal activity. The United States Supreme Court upheld earlier convictions under state statutes but later began to hold the acts unconstitutional as applied.

The biggest club against free speech in the history of the nation was given to the United States Government by Congress through the passage of the Espionage Act of 1917 and the amending Sedition Act of 1918. The first law gave the Postmaster General authority to ban seditious material from the mail and provided for heavy fines and imprisonment for anyone who "shall wilfully cause or attempt to cause . . . disloyalty . . . or shall wilfully obstruct recruiting," and made publications guilty of such acts unmailable. The 1918 act imposed heavy fines and imprisonment for the writing or publication of "any disloyal, profane, scurrilous, or abusive language about the form of government of the United States, or the Constitution, military or naval forces, flag, or the uniform of the army or navy of the United States," or any language "intended" to bring these things "into contempt, scorn, contumely, or disrepute."

During the first year of the Espionage Act, more than seventy-five newspapers were affected by it. Many retained their mailing privileges only by agreeing to print no discussion of the war question. Of these, nearly fifty were socialist papers. Such well known dailies as the New York *Call* and Victor Berger's Milwaukee *Leader* had their mailing privileges withdrawn. The *Call* lost its appeal to the Supreme Court in 1923 and went out of existence that year.

The 1917 Trading with the Enemy Act created a Censorship Board and authorized the censorship of all messages abroad. This agency, made up of representatives of the War, Navy, and Post Office Departments, the War Trade Board, and the Committee on Public Information, occasionally exercised its censorship power: for example, an entire mailing of the El Paso *Herald* was held at New

Orleans because the paper carried a story about a strike for higher wages. But for the most part newspapers invoked voluntary censorship under rules suggested by the Committee on Public Information, a war propaganda agency created by presidential proclamation. Some papers, which did not see eye to eye with the administration, were branded disloyal by the CPI and suffered popular proscription.

During World War I more than 1,900 prosecutions and other judicial proceedings involving objectionable speeches, newspaper articles, pamphlets, and books were undertaken. By June 30, 1919, 877 persons had been convicted for speaking and publishing. At least thirty-five persons were sentenced to prison for twenty years, while fifty-eight were sentenced to terms of fifteen to twenty years.

In 1919 the United States Supreme Court, in *Schenck v. United States,* upheld the constitutionality of the Espionage Act against a challenge that it violated the First Amendment. The defendant had been convicted in a federal district court on a charge of circulating antidraft leaflets among members of the armed forces. In his opinion upholding the conviction, Justice Oliver Wendell Holmes said for a unanimous court that the right of free speech had never been absolute in peace or in war. He went on: "Free speech would not protect a man in falsely shouting fire in a theatre and causing a panic." But when a nation is at war, he asserted, "many things that might be said in time of peace are such a hindrance to its effort that their utterance will not be endured so long as men fight," and "no court could regard them as protected by any constitutional right." Significantly, however, the Schenck case was the one in which Holmes borrowed from the rule of "proximate causation" to create the "clear and present danger" test for speech, a libertarian doctrine which (though it was forgotten during the remainder of the World War I period) was to be revived in 1937 to give greater latitude to critical expression. As Holmes put it:

> The question in every case is whether the words used are used in such circumstances and are of such a nature as to create a clear and present danger that they will bring about the substantive evils that Congress has a right to prevent. It is a question of proximity and degree.[13]

In the case of *Abrams v. United States* in 1919, the United States Supreme Court had its first opportunity to decide the constitutionality of the Sedition Act of 1918. The defendants, a group of young men and a girl, had been convicted and sentenced to terms ranging from fifteen to twenty years for throwing out of a window handbills denouncing the landing of United States troops in Russian ports at a time when the United States was not at war with Russia. The leaflets condemned the "capitalistic" government of the United States, called on Allied armies to "cease murdering Russians," and urged a general strike of workers to bring about the policies it advocated. Though a Supreme Court majority upheld the convictions and the statute, Justices Holmes and Louis D. Brandeis dissented, saying that nobody could suppose that the publication of the leaflet in question "would hinder the success of the government arms. . . ." In one of history's most moving defenses of freedom of expression, Holmes went on:

> But when men have realized that time has upset many fighting faiths, they may come to believe even more than they believe the very foundation of their own conduct that the ultimate good desired is better reached by free trade in ideas—that the best test of truth is the power of the thought to get itself accepted in the competition of the market, and that truth is the only ground upon which their wishes safely can be carried out. That at any rate is the theory of our Constitution. It is an experiment, as all life is an experiment. Every year if not every day we have to wager our salvation upon some prophecy based upon imperfect knowledge. While that experiment is part of our system I think that we should be eternally vigilant against attempts to check the expression of opinions that we loathe and believe to be fraught with death, unless they so imminently threaten interference with the lawful and pressing purposes of the law that an immediate check is required to save the country.[14]

Ignoring the Holmes dissent in the Abrams case and the Holmes "clear and present danger" test, advanced for the majority in the Schenck case, the Court, in *Pierce v. United States* (1920), reverted to the old "bad tendency" doctrine for speech. This case, the last of a series arising out of the Espionage Act, involved a prosecution for a Socialist pamphlet attacking conscription and the war. Justice Mahlon Pitney, speaking for the majority, said the pamphlet might "have a tendency to cause insubordination, disloyalty, and refusal of duty" in the military forces.[15] In 1921, three years after the close of the war, the Supreme Court upheld the Post Office's exclusion of seditious newspapers from the mails.

With the pretext of wartime military security no longer plausible, Attorney General A. Mitchell Palmer early in 1920 nevertheless used the presence of Communists and aliens to fan a national Red scare. In raids on hundreds of places where radicals were known to meet, Justice Department agents made dragnet arrests of everyone they found, including chance passers-by. Without the authority of arrest or search warrants, the agents hauled their victims off to jail, where many of them were held incommunicado and without bail. All literature, books, paper, and pictures in the raided meeting places were ordered seized. In all, more than 6,000 men and several hundred women were rounded up. Hundreds of aliens were summarily deported without even having the opportunity to notify their families. Press reports at the time told of a Justice Department discovery of a great conspiracy against the government, with a quantity of bombs having been found in New Jersey. Later reports, however, revealed that only three pistols had been found in the countrywide raids and no explosives at all. Many of the raided meetings had actually been held at the behest of government agents who had infiltrated the radical groups as members in order to facilitate the planned arrests.[16]

With the advance of the third decade of the twentieth century, the Red fright subsided. In 1925 the nation's highest court announced one of its landmark decisions on freedom of speech and press. The case of *Gitlow v. New York* raised the question of the constitutionality of New York's Criminal Anarchy Act of 1902, under which Benjamin Gitlow, a left-wing Socialist, had been convicted for publishing a pamphlet based on Marx's 1848 *Communist Manifesto*. While the Gitlow decision upheld the constitutionality of the New York statute, the Court for the first time said that "freedom of speech and of the press—which are protected by the First Amendment from abridgment by Congress—are among the fundamental personal rights and 'liberties' protected by the due process clause of the Fourteenth Amendment from impairment by the states." [17]

Six years later the Supreme Court, in *Near v. Minnesota,* actually declared a state law unconstitutional because it unreasonably restricted freedom of speech and press and thus violated the Fourteenth Amendment's guarantee against state deprivation of liberty without due process of law. The case arose in Minneapolis as a result of publication by a newspaper known as the *Saturday Press* of a series of articles stating that a Jewish gangster was in control of gambling, bootlegging, and racketeering and charging gross neglect of duty on the part of law enforcement officials, including the county attorney, the chief of police of Minneapolis, and others. Invoking a 1925 state statute providing that "malicious, scandalous and defamatory" newspapers and periodicals could be suppressed by injunction as public nuisances, the county attorney got a court order forbidding the publisher, J. M. Near, to publish or circulate any further defamatory matter. After the injunction against him was upheld by the Supreme Court of Minnesota, the defendant appealed to the United States Supreme Court, which reversed the state court decision. Chief Justice Charles Evans Hughes, writing for a 5-to-4 majority, pointed out that libel laws afforded redress for wrongs committed by publication and that censorship by injunction was contrary to the Bill of Rights.[18]

The late thirties brought further manifestations of the Supreme Court's willingness to protect speech and press against state abridgment. In 1936 the Court, in *Grossjean v. American Press Co.,* unanimously held that a Louisiana 2 per cent tax on gross income from advertising in large newspapers was unconstitutional. Levied in 1934 at the behest of Huey Long, whose political machine was being criticized by newspapers, the tax was said by the high court to be "a deliberate and calculated device . . . to limit the circulation of information to which the public is entitled by virtue of the constitutional guarantees." [19]

In 1937 the Supreme Court decided the case of *De Jonge v. Oregon.* Three years earlier the Communist Party had organized a public meeting in Portland, advertised by handbills, for the purpose of protesting against the shooting of striking longshoremen by the police and against police raids on workers' halls and homes. De Jonge, one of the speakers at the meeting, was later indicted under an Oregon statute for advocating the doctrine of criminal syndicalism and sabotage, though at the trial no evidence was introduced to show that he had urged any unlawful conduct. The meeting had been conducted in an orderly manner and the speakers had done no more than talk on the announced subjects and ask the audience to do more work in obtaining members for the party and to purchase Communist literature sold on the premises. This literature did not advocate unlawful conduct. The prosecution relied on Communist literature found somewhere else to buttress its claim that the defendant advocated criminal syndicalism. In a unanimous decision, the United States Supreme Court reversed De Jonge's conviction. Drawing on the general philosophy of constitutional liberty rather than any specific legal doctrine, Chief Justice Hughes said for the Court: "Peaceable assembly for lawful discussion cannot be made a crime." The conviction, he concluded, had been a violation of the defendant's rights of freedom of speech and assembly.[20]

In another case decided that year, the high court specifically invoked the "clear and present danger" doctrine enunciated by Holmes in the 1925 Schenck case. Angelo Herndon, a Negro organizer for the Communist Party, was tried and convicted in Georgia under a statute originally written to prevent the incitement of slave insurrections and updated after the Civil War simply by deletion of references to slaves. Herndon's crime was proved by a showing that he had in his possession a pamphlet advocating an independent Negro state in the South. The Supreme Court invalidated the conviction, with Justice Owen J. Roberts pointing out that the state had not shown any attempt to bring about insurrection either immediately or within a reasonable time. As construed, he asserted, the statute punished mere "bad tendency" and made possible a "dragnet which may enmesh anyone who agitates for a change in government." As applied in this case, he said it was "an unwarrantable invasion of the right of free speech."[21] The Herndon decision was one of a series in which the Court curbed state action when there was deemed to be no "clear and present danger" of a substantive evil which the state had a right to prevent.

With the beginning of World War II in Europe in 1939, war tension again rose in the United States, and in 1940 Congress enacted the Smith Act, the first peacetime sedition law since the drastic Sedition Act of 1798. It contained practically everything that Attorney General Palmer had asked for at the height of his "crusade" against the "Red Menace." This statute made it unlawful "to knowingly or willingly advocate, abet, advise, or teach the duty, necessity, desirability, or propriety of overthrowing or destroying any government in the United States by force or violence." It also forbade the publication or distribution of printed matter "advising or teaching" the overthrow of the government. And another section prohibited conspiracies to commit any of the previously mentioned outlawed activities, thus adding another category to the list of proscriptions against seditious utterance.

The next year found the United States at war. As Lincoln and Wilson had done before him, President Franklin D. Roosevelt took an expansive view of his war powers as commander-in-chief. Like Wilson, he created by executive order a vast mechanism for the conduct of the war, including offices with power to restrict freedom of the press. In December 1941 the Office of Censorship was established by executive order. Byron Price, executive news editor of the Associated Press, was appointed director. He immediately formulated rules and suggestions for both press and radio. While there was no specific law authorizing domestic press censorship, a 1938 act allowed restrictions to be put on the dissemination of certain pictures, photographs, maps, and designs portraying military installations. The First War Powers Act of 1941 authorized censorship over foreign communications. The order setting up the Office of Censorship had instructed the director to establish a voluntary self-censorship system for the domestic press and radio. In 1943 the code of wartime practices for the press was revised to request the suppression of all war information which might reveal military movements in advance or otherwise help the enemy. In general censorship in World War II was readily accepted by both newspapers and radio, although there was sharp criticism from numerous papers to the effect that censorship was too strict and that it was being used to cover up administrative mistakes.[22]

As in World War I, the Post Office Department during the second world conflict undertook to keep suspect publications from using the mails. Though the department interfered with both Father Charles Edward Coughlin's *Social Justice* and with the Trotskyite *Militant,* no case involving postal restrictions of this kind reached the Supreme Court during the war. In 1946, however, the Court ruled in the *Esquire* case that Congress had not authorized the Postmaster General to deprive a magazine of second-class mailing privileges because he found its contents not sufficiently elevating. A similar view was taken by the Court in other cases some years later.

Wartime actions affecting freedom of speech and press were not, however, in the province of the executive branch alone. The courts were also involved. In 1941 the government under the Smith Act, successfully prosecuted a small group of Minneapolis Trotskyite Marxists, who were strongly anti-Stalin and anti-Soviet. From 1943 to 1944, invoking both the Espionage Act of 1917 and the Smith Act, the government unsuccessfully tried to convict twenty-eight alleged Nazi sympathizers on charges that they sought to impair the morale of servicemen. Neither of these cases ever reached the Supreme Court.[23] But in *Hartzel v. United States* the Court reversed the conviction of the defendant under the Espionage Act for distributing pro-Nazi, anti-English, and anti-Roosevelt material.[24]

Though the states were not as zealous in suppressing alleged sedition in the World War II era as they had been in the First World War, some cases occurred. In Mississippi two defendants were indicted under a state sedition act which made it a felony to encourage disloyalty to state and national governments. They were convicted for preaching that all modern nations, including the United States, were in the grip of demons. Their convictions were reversed by the United States Supreme Court in *Taylor v. Mississippi* (1943) on the ground that the statute, as construed, made it "a criminal offense to communicate to others views and opinions respecting governmental policies and prophecies concerning the future of our own and other nations." Yet, said the Court, there was no clear and present danger to American institutions or government.[25]

For a time in the thirties and forties the high tribunal followed the doctrine that First Amendment rights had a "preferred position" as against state regulation—that is, that the burden was on the states to buttress the constitutionality of their legislative, administrative, and judicial measures interfering with First Amendment guarantees.[26] But after 1949, the year in which Justices Frank Murphy and Wiley Rutledge died, the influence of Justices Felix Frankfurter and Robert Jackson became dominant and the high bench, no longer according freedom of speech and press and other First Amendment rights a preferred position, instead sought to balance the guarantees in question against the wisdom and reasonableness of the regulation being challenged.

After the onset of war in Korea, Congress enacted the Internal Security Act of 1950. The law declared that a world Communist conspiracy existed, an objective of which was to establish a Communist dictatorship in the United States. Stating as a finding of fact that American Communists constituted a "clear and present danger" to the security of the United States, the act required, among other things, that "Communist-action" and "Communist-front" organizations must register and list their officers and members with the new Subversive Activities Control Board. In a veto message, which Congress overrode in order to pass the act, President Truman called the registration provisions of the law "the greatest danger to freedom of speech, press and assembly since the Sedition Act of 1798," mainly because the standards for classifying an organization as Communist were to be based solely on the identity between the organization's position on public questions and those of the Communist movement. The result, said Truman, might well be to "open a Pandora's box of opportunities for official condemnation of organizations and individuals for perfectly honest opinions which happen to be stated also by Communists." After years of litigation over the government's attempt to enforce the 1950 statute, the registration effort foundered on the Supreme Court's refusal to order compliance unless the government proved that some individual, acting for the Communist Party, was willing to register the organization and run the risk of self-incrimination.

While Congress was reacting to the Cold War by investigating and passing new laws against subversion, another case under the Smith Act was wending its way through the courts. In 1948 the Department of Justice had procured the indictment of the eleven principal officers of the Communist Party on charges that they had conspired to form groups advocating the overthrow of the government and had conspired to teach and advocate the necessity or desirability of overthrowing the government. The defendants were not accused of an actual plot to forcibly upset the government or of teaching the technology of violence—how to make bombs at home or steal guns from military warehouses or how to assassinate public officials. Yet, in the ensuing trial and appeals, the case was treated as though a direct conspiracy to destroy the government were involved. All eleven defendants were found guilty and the conviction was sustained on appeal by the United States Court of Appeals and by the Supreme Court in *Dennis v. United States* (1951). In his majority opinion accepting the constitutionality of the Smith Act, Chief Justice Fred M. Vinson virtually set aside the clear and present danger doctrine by saying that speech may be restricted if there is a probability of its producing at some time—not necessarily immediately—a relatively serious danger. In instances in which the theoretical ultimate harm was very great, the Court was in effect substituting "possible and remote" for "clear and present" as the test by which the objectionable speech was to be judged.

Justices Hugo Black and William Douglas dissented vigorously, Black declaring that the Smith Act was "unconstitutional on its face" and that the conviction of the Communist leaders was "a virulent form of prior censorship of speech and press, which . . . the First Amendment forbids." Douglas thought it impossible to believe that the Communist Party constituted any real menace such as would justify suppression. Observing that the Soviet Union banned free speech entirely, he said, "our concern should be that we accept no such standard for the United States."[27]

Six years later, in *Yates v. United States* (1957), the high court modified the doctrine of the Dennis case in a decision setting aside the convictions of fourteen second-string Communist leaders who had been charged with conspiring to advocate the overthrow of the government. Speaking for the majority, Justice John Marshall Harlan said a distinction must be made "between advocacy of an abstract doctrine and advocacy directed at promoting unlawful action." Those "to whom the advocacy is addressed," he explained, "must be urged to *do* something now or in the future, rather than merely to *believe* in something." Applying this doctrine, the Court ordered outright dismissal of the charges against five of the defendants on the ground that there was no evidence at all to show that they had engaged in incitement to action. As for the other nine defendants, the court said they might be retried under its newly enunciated rule.[28] Following the Yates decision, the government lost its zeal for prosecuting under the Smith Act. Of the 114 convictions of Communist leaders scored by the end of 1956, many were set aside and new trials granted. The Justice Department itself dropped a considerable number of prosecutions, including that of the nine remaining defendants in the Yates case, on the ground that the accused could not be convicted on the evidence required under the Yates rule.

Before the Yates ruling, the Supreme Court had already begun to tighten the free rein it had been giving to sedition prosecutions. In the 1956 case of *Pennsylvania v. Nelson,* the high court invalidated Pennsylvania's sedition act under which Communist leader Steve Nelson had been convicted and sentenced to twenty years in prison in a 1951 trial which stressed the dangerous character of Communist literature. The ground of the Supreme Court decision was that Congress, by passing the Smith Act and related statutes, intended to "occupy the field" of sedition.[29] Because the Nelson holding had the effect of setting aside antisubversive laws of some forty-two states, there was an immediate outcry from state officials and from some members of Congress.

As the 1960's advanced and tension with the Communist world receded, the pressure for conformity in America relaxed. At the same time the Supreme Court, with new justices on its bench, was taking a more libertarian view of the Bill of Rights, including the

First Amendment. In 1964 the high court handed down one of its most significant recent decisions on freedom of the press. As a result of a civil rights advertisement endorsed by a number of Negro ministers and published in 1960 in the New York *Times,* the police commissioner of Montgomery, Alabama, had sued the *Times* and four Negro clergymen and won a $500,000 libel judgment against them on the strength of a claim that the advertisement had falsely accused the Montgomery police of improper action. Though the *Times* admitted that the ad was erroneous in minor respects, it pointed out that the plaintiff was not even named in the publication, and he himself admitted that he had not suffered actual damage. The Supreme Court held that a public official cannot recover libel damages for criticism of his official performance unless he proves that the statement was made with deliberate malice. In his opinion for a unanimous bench, Justice Brennan said that libel actions of this kind had to be judged in the light of "a profound national commitment to the principle that debate on public issues should be uninhibited, robust, and wide-open, and that it may well include vehement, caustic, and sometimes unpleasantly sharp attacks on government and public officials." [30]

By the seventh decade of the twentieth century, the United States had already had more than 170 years of experience with the first article of the Bill of Rights, the one that is often held to be first in importance. Jefferson had written: "Were it left to me to decide whether we should have a government without newspapers or newspapers without government, I should not hesitate to prefer the latter." Justice Hugo Black would prefer to grant free speech absolute protection. Philosophical support for freedom of speech has been given by many of the world's great thinkers and writers, from Socrates to Milton, from Thomas Hobbes to John Stuart Mill. Under the First Amendment, the press of America has at times had remarkable latitude to criticize and to report. At times profound respect has been shown for the libertarian standard that verbal expression should be free up to the point at which it comes close to inciting crime or bringing about an imminent threat to public security. In the United States the press has flourished and grown strong.

Yet even today freedom of speech enjoys no impregnable protection. Regardless of philosophical tributes to freedom of expression, regardless of the laudable restraint which government has on occasion observed, it is nevertheless true that the verbal guarantee of the First Amendment cannot prevent weapons that still exist from being used to stringently curb the press. And they have been used even in our own time when some official wielder of power felt threatened or felt that his concept of the social order was being attacked. In times past the courts were often the official organs for suppressing speech and writing that was deemed to be too free. Today the courts are the agencies that are often called upon to exert restraint on the excessive use of censoring authority. Yet juries and courts, in deciding cases involving freedom of expression, can be, and are, often swept along by the tide of popular opinion. In the light of their long and harsh experience with words on trial, editors can hardly be blamed for seeing freedom of the press as an embattled right. As the defenders of one embattled right, however, they sometimes—as will be shown—exhibit a paradoxical blindness toward attacks on other rights.

CHAPTER TWO

MAN ON TRIAL

JUST AS EDITORS have found through the history of words on trial that freedom of the press has not been easily won and cannot be easily maintained, so concerned lawyers are aware from the history of men on trial that the rights of due process (fair treatment) have evolved only with painful slowness and are never immune from violation. At first the only right of the accused was such minimal restraint on mob action as was contained in primitive law.

ORIGINS OF CRIMINAL LAW

Since ancient times man has attempted to systematize methods of dealing with individuals who committed acts deemed harmful to their communities. As early as the third millennium B.C., the Sumerians had laws covering delinquent conduct.[1] The Code of Hammurabi (c. 1947–1905 B.C.), who was called of the gods to "make justice prevail," contained provisions on crimes of sex and personal violence, a law against sorcery, and a scale of penalties for specified offenses. Though a primitive form of society was suggested by the harshness of its penalties, by the commonness of capital punishment for relatively minor crimes, and by the use of the ordeal by water in trials for some offenses—a recognizable advance over primitive justice was manifested in the code's substitution of judicial settlement for the law of blood revenge and in its evident objective of protecting the weak against the strong. The prescribed punishments, though they were severe, may actually have been intended as maximum penalties to be inflicted only in the most flagrant cases. However it was applied, the Code of Hammurabi (282 laws promulgated in 8,000 words) was an example of an elaborate early effort to regulate human conduct. Adopting and revising for their own use the Babylonian laws codified by Hammurabi, the Assyrians, perhaps as early as the fourteenth century B.C., also aspired to more civilized forms of justice.

In another part of the ancient Mediterranean world, the Athenians were to develop a criminal code that lifted their law above the level of blood feuding. In the seventh century B.C., Draco systematized legal procedures and created courts of justice under responsible state officials. While the harshness of an earlier primitive law was carried over in the imposition of the death penalty for petty theft, Draco's code reflected an advance in legal thinking by making distinctions between offenses such as voluntary and involuntary homicide. Solon (c. 639–c. 559 B.C.) gave Athens the popular court elected by universal suffrage and open to all citizens. It was the final court of appeal from decisions of the aristocratic chief magistrates and was the beginning of the popular jury system.

The ancient criminal code that is probably most familiar in Western countries, however, is the Mosaic Law of the Old Testament. Though its biblical context has given this law the aura of an original promulgation, it actually stemmed from the precedent of the Babylonians under Hammurabi. There were some thirty-five points of contact between the Code of Hammurabi and the fifty laws in the old Hebrew Book of the Covenant (Exodus 20:23–23:33). The two codes were remarkably similar in their prohibitions against theft, kidnapping, sorcery, incest and other sex irregularities, bribery, false witness, and perjury. Both codes put property above human life, emphasized capital punishment, and legalized the principle of revenge.

Though the Mediterranean area was the fount of Western civilization and the source of its law, a system of organized justice also emerged early in China. As far back as the reign (961–906 B.C.) of King Muh, enlightened directions were promulgated for those who presided "over criminal cases throughout the empire." Yet in

China, as in other areas, the family-blood feud persisted, and was sanctioned even by Confucius.

In ancient lands of both East and West, surprisingly modern insights sometimes were exhibited both in substantive law and in modes of trial. As early as 200 A.D., Rome's way of dealing with suspected offenders presaged some of the familiar protective features of modern justice.

The history of criminal justice, however, is a continuing story of cruelty and superstition always battling with attempts to insure accuracy and humanity in the mechanism for dealing with proscribed conduct. Whether in Babylon, in Athens, in Rome, or in Western Europe, the fate of men on trial rested, until modern times, almost entirely on the wisdom and compassion of their judges. While there were ancient laws on forbidden conduct, there was no well developed body of procedural rules to guide the administration of criminal justice in the interest of the accused as well as of society.

Early in man's social development he realized, however, that unless the impulse for revenge against the supposed malefactor were controlled, it could lead to communal self-destruction, since the culprit might have friends who would side with him to do battle against his pursuers. Hence came the organization of a kind of tribunal to hold something comparable to a hearing and pronounce a judgment that would be acceptable to the community.

In the early stage of development in Greco-Latin communities, the tribunal consisted of the whole tribal group. It dispensed justice in disputes between families or clans or between members of different families or clans. But it left intrafamily or clan squabbles to be settled by the head of the respective group.

As the community became more elaborately organized, the tribunal was administered by the individual ruler or a person or group deputed to act in his place. However it was set up, the primitive tribunal—whether popular or autocratic—reached its decisions by its own mental processes, without the aid of advisers. In time elders or other specially designated advisers came to be relied on to guide the judgments. The use of such advisers, who were versed in the traditions of the community, had emerged in the Greece of Homer's time and in early Rome, though neither early Greece nor republican Rome developed an elaborate trial system. After the legal adviser, the rise of the partisan advocate was a natural development. In classical Greece, the accused was allowed to read a speech written by a professional advocate. Despite the appearance of these ancient predecessors of the lawyer, the accused's right to be aided by counsel was not recognized in law for many centuries.

The establishment of guilt or innocence by well defined rules of evidence was a late development in law. While some evidentiary rules were devised in Rome and later in Europe, the early tendency in most jurisdictions was for the tribunal to consider whatever the parties might say or produce by way of proof. In the history of almost every society, the accused was subjected to one of the endless forms of "ordeal," through which the deity was supposed to intervene and provide a sign of the sufferer's guilt or innocence. Grounded in popular superstition but sanctioned by the church sometime after 400 A.D., the ordeal in Europe took five or six forms. In an elaborate ceremony, with priests participating, the defendant might be put to the test of the hot iron or boiling water or fire. If he emerged, presumably through divine intercession, in the prescribed condition, he was deemed innocent. In time the public lost confidence in the ordeals. And in 1215 Pope Innocent III forbade their use in church tribunals. In 1219 King Henry III outlawed the ordeals in England.

In medieval times the culpability of an accused was sometimes determined through trial by battle, in which he fought with his accuser, or trial by compurgation, in which kinsmen or neighbors took an oath that they believed he was telling the truth in proclaiming himself innocent. Such trials were still being held in the fourteenth century.

One of the earliest instruments of the trial process was the jury, though it was not used at first to hear evidence. It derived from the primitive popular tribunal and was adapted by the Germanic tribes as a more specialized vehicle of taxation and law enforcement. The king's representatives would summon a body of leading citizens and take from them a statement as to the taxable wealth of the community, the condition of public order, and the nature of offenses against the king and his laws. The group was called the *jurata* and its report to the king, a *veredictum*. The Normans took the system to England in 1066. And a century later, at the historic Assize of Clarendon, the grand jury took definite form as varying numbers of country gentlemen were summoned before a royal deputy and questioned as to what they knew about persons accused of crimes in their neighborhood. So that the jurors need not be too fearful of retribution by some powerful violator, at least twelve of them had to agree on the accuracy of the report. For a time the grand jury acted also as a trial jury. But by the middle of the fourteenth century the trial (or petit) jury became a separate body. By 1600 the jury was the usual mode of trial in the common law courts of England, though not for another century did the jurors begin to decide cases on the basis of testimony of witnesses presented under rules of evidence, rather than giving a verdict based on their own knowledge.[2] At first the only witnesses summoned were those for the prosecution, and the defendant was at a decided disadvantage in this respect, as he was in so many other ways under early methods of trial. Gradually, however, he acquired the right to call witnesses and to testify in his own behalf. The popular jury, tenaciously preserved through nearly ten centuries, is one of the oldest instruments of the judicial process.

Judges at first were royal clerks (often men of the cloth because of their peculiar opportunities for learning) who held commissions for various assignments from the king and who held office at the king's pleasure. The monarch might at any time mount the bench himself, instead of leaving the administration of justice to his deputy. Under these circumstances, the judges were hardly free to decide cases contrary to the wishes of the king.

In the reign of Edward I (King of England, 1272–1307) England's first great judicial scandal came to light. As a result, a majority of the judges of the King's Bench and the Common Pleas were removed. This was while the judiciary was still largely manned by clerics. By the fourteenth century the practice of naming professional lawyers to the bench became more common.[3]

Until comparatively modern times, once a case was heard, a quick decision was demanded as a result of the emotion of the community and the insistence of the injured party on prompt redress.

The possibility of error and the value of delayed deliberation were given little weight. In England, as late as the 1700's, only a week elapsed in some criminal cases between perpetration and execution. And the appeal as a matter of course in criminal cases did not come into the law until the end of the 1800's.

While the judgment was oral among primitive peoples, some communities began the practice of recording such decisions as soon as the art of writing developed. The preservation of written judicial records led naturally to the formation and observation of a body of precedents in law.

Punishment through the centuries has been symptomatic of man's baser side. In primitive times, when crime was mainly attributed to the influence of evil spirits, the chief purpose of punishment was to placate the gods. The wrongdoer was at times ceremonially killed by the whole clan. The punishment of private crimes was sometimes left to a blood feud between private parties, with a murderer, for example, escaping unscathed unless the victim's immediate relatives took up the cause and settled the score with the offender—sometimes by inflicting a greater wrong. In twelfth-century England a man who killed another by falling upon him from a tree might himself be killed in precisely the same manner by a relative of the deceased. But a system of compensation was sometimes substituted for the blood feud, with fines or money payments providing restitution for individual wrongs. As the concept of sin was absorbed into the criminal law, restitution was no longer accepted. By the fourteenth century in England, murder, robbery, and rape were no longer regarded as torts which could be settled by compensation, but as offenses for which penance was required.

As the notion of sin took hold and crimes came to be regarded as the voluntary acts of free moral agents, society retaliated with punishment designed to deter such willfully perverse challenges to God. The eye for an eye concept was considered effective in preventing the offender from repeating his crime. In medieval times spies had their eyes gouged out, perjurers had their tongues torn out, rapists were castrated, thieves had their hands cut off. Though the death penalty was prescribed in Western Europe for many offenses, including robbery and petty crimes, it could not be employed for everything. Some offenders were assigned to toil on galleys. When the sailing vessel replaced the galley, this place of forced labor was removed. Authorities began shipping criminals to faraway places to perform disagreeable work. France sent convicts to Devil's Island. England sent them to the American colonies and to Australia.[4]

With the decline of the guilds in Europe and with the breakup of the feudal system, accompanied by the disbandment of mercenary armies, the number of idlers increased and so did crime. To meet the problem of beggars and paupers roaming the streets, London established a workhouse in 1557. While the workhouse served an economic purpose in that work was extracted from the inmates, an element of punishment was also involved. Whippings, restrictions of diet, and torture were employed. Though dungeons and other prisons have existed for thousands of years, systematic confinement as punishment for crime is a relatively modern development in many countries. Jails have been used for many centuries as places of detention for those awaiting trial and unable to obtain bail. Later they came into use to hold petty offenders sentenced to short periods. But the prison, as a place of restraint for those convicted of violating the law, did not come into general use until the eighteenth century.

While jails and prisons were theoretically institutions of the monarch, most of them in the early days were in fact maintained by private keepers who were subject to little or no control by the crown. Prisons were often dark, cramped, airless, disease-ridden places providing wretched food and living conditions. Innocent persons might be detained in them for long periods awaiting trial and then, after acquittal, be subject to continued imprisonment because they were unable to pay the jailer the cost of their keep.

During the eighteenth century an Englishman, John Howard (1726–1790) made the cause of improving miserable prison conditions an international personal crusade. He traveled through his own country, to Europe and the Middle East and visited prisons wherever he went. In 1777 and 1789 he published accounts of his findings. His reports of torture chambers, the degradation of prisoners, and general barbarous treatment[5] helped to spark a movement for more humane care of institutionalized persons.

One of the burdens of prison life in the 1700's was the ordeal of being held up to public scorn. Many jailers derived an income from fees charged to citizens for looking through the windows and observing the sorry state of the inmates. In 1724 the keepers of Newgate Prison were reported to have collected more than 200 pounds from crowds of people who flocked daily to the place and paid four shillings each to see John Sheppard, a notorious house-breaker and jail-breaker. When Sheppard was brought out to be hanged, an estimated 200,000 people lined the route from Newgate to Tyburn. Public humiliation, on the hurdle, in the pillory, or otherwise on exhibit, was one form of punishment. (Some modern proponents of newspaper publicity see news coverage as a form of public humiliation which deters crime.)

The popular sense of justice was slow in historical development even in civilized societies. The full manifestations of this sense—as signified by the creation of a disinterested tribunal, the allowance of adequate time for the uncovering of evidence and the preparation of the case, the granting of help to the accused in presenting his side—are only being registered in modern times. Though the philosophical roots of justice run deep into the past, the practical fruits have ripened and become generally available only with the growth of democratic and more affluent societies.

The Constitutional Guarantees

RIGHTS ON ARREST AND SEIZURE OF EVIDENCE

Most of the various rights of the accused that have come to be familiar in the United States were first enunciated in English law. Their application begins with the time of arrest. In the England of several centuries ago, arrest could be calamitous. An accused could be taken into custody by private, grudge-bearing persons. Lodged in jail, he might spend months or even years there awaiting trial. The need for protection against arbitrary action became apparent. The answer was the warrant, a written order by a judge or other official authorizing the seizure of the person or papers of the accused.[6]

In common law, a general rule evolved prohibiting search warrants and warrants of arrest which did not describe in detail the places to be searched and the things or persons to be seized. Parliament, however, authorized two exceptions, allowing the use of general search warrants or so-called writs of assistance for seizing goods that were contraband under the acts of trade, and permitting general warrants to be used for the search and seizure of libelous publications and the arrest of offenders against the sedition laws.

The use of general warrants by crown officials to enforce the acts of trade was one of the grievances that led to the break between the British government and the American colonies. Beginning in 1776, the new states—with Virginia first and then Pennsylvania, Delaware, Maryland, North Carolina, Vermont, Massachusetts, and New Hampshire—inserted in their constitutions guarantees against unreasonable searches and seizures.

The Fourth Amendment to the United States Constitution, of course, contained a similar guarantee with respect to the federal government, providing that no warrant should issue "but upon probable cause" and requiring that it should particularly describe the place to be searched and the persons or things to be seized. The United States Supreme Court has on the whole liberally interpreted the constitutional prohibition against unreasonable searches and seizures, ordering the return of property illegally seized and preventing its use as evidence against its owner. The rule against the introduction by federal prosecutors of illegally seized evidence, in effect since the 1914 Weeks decision, was extended to the states in the 1961 *Mapp v. Ohio* case by application of the due process clause of the Fourteenth Amendment.[7]

While constitutions and court decisions impose strict warrant requirements, there are circumstances under which law enforcement action may be taken without a warrant. Under the common law, now largely replaced by statutes, a private individual may make an arrest without a warrant when a felony or misdemeanor has been committed in his presence and he knows or has reasonable grounds to believe that the person arrested committed the crime. However, most arrests today are made by policemen, and their authority is usually covered by state statutes, which ordinarily provide that an officer may make an arrest without a warrant for all offenses committed in his presence, including misdemeanors which are not breaches of the peace. The policeman is usually given the authority to make an arrest without a warrant whenever he has reasonable ground to believe that a felony has occurred and that the arrestee committed it. He also is often given authority to arrest on sight when he has been notified that another state peace officer has a warrant for a wanted person.

The power of peace officers is more strictly limited than is generally understood. Although arrest on suspicion in order to conduct an investigation is illegal, it is a common occurrence. While policemen may search a person after arrest for weapons and evidence of crime, they have no authority in most states to frisk people without first arresting them.

PROTECTION AGAINST FORCED CONFESSIONS

A familiar maxim in modern criminal cases is that a prisoner in the custody of the police cannot be compelled to talk. Anglo-American revulsion against coerced confessions goes back at least as far as the reign of Charles I when "Freeborn John" Lilburne in 1637 won popular acclaim by refusing, despite severe beatings, to confess to offenses of which he was accused. English prisoners could be legally tortured by license of the king as early as the reign of Henry II (1154–1189), and the rack was in the Tower by the time of Henry VI (1421–1471). Torture as a means of forcing an accused to confess was actually used in England until the late 1600's, and its use to compel a defendant to plead innocent or guilty was not abolished in that country until 1827. Though torture was not generally permitted in the American colonies, it was allowed as a means of extracting confessions in some trials for witchcraft.

While the legal concepts on involuntary confessions and on self-incrimination are similar, their development has been separate. The protection against forced confessions has been established by court interpretation of the requirements of due process, whereas the guarantee against compulsory self-incrimination was spelled out in some of the early charters of the colonies and was included in the Fifth Article of the Bill of Rights (see later section on self-incrimination). The purpose of the confession rule is to exclude statements that are false, whereas the right against self-incrimination operates to exclude statements that may be true.[8] Confessions obtained by mental as well as physical duress have been held by the United States Supreme Court to be violations of due process required of the states by the Fourteenth Amendment.

In the 1966 case of *Miranda v. Arizona,* 34 U.S. Law Week 4521, (decided as this book went to press) the Supreme Court in effect merged the concepts of involuntary confession and self-incrimination. It held that the Fifth Amendment's privilege against incrimination comes into play as soon as a person is within police custody and that at that point the suspect must be warned of his right to remain silent, and his decision to do so must be respected by the police as an element of the due process required of the state. Before it can introduce any purported confession obtained during police interrogation, the prosecution, said the high court, has the burden of proving that the defendant knowingly waived his rights.

RIGHT TO COUNSEL

While persons charged with misdemeanors had been allowed to have counsel as early as the fourteenth century, the right of felony defendants in general to be aided by lawyers was only gradually recognized by English judicial decisions in the eighteenth century. And despite earlier pleas from such eminent jurists as Blackstone, the right was not guaranteed by statute in felony cases until 1836.[9]

Meanwhile in the American colonies, Massachusetts in 1641 and Pennsylvania in 1682 granted defendants the right to be represented by individuals serving without pay or by their friends. When the states adopted their first constitutions, the right to counsel was covered in those of New Jersey, New York, Pennsylvania, Delaware, Maryland, Vermont, Massachusetts, and New Hampshire. The same right was included in the Sixth Amendment to the federal Constitution and the original Judiciary Act of 1789. It is now contained in the constitution of every state except Virginia, whose Supreme Court has nevertheless construed that state's basic law as requiring it.

The existence of constitutional mandates, however, has not necessarily insured the full effectiveness of the right to counsel. Historically, the right did not extend to preliminary proceedings; and even when it was applied in court, it did not extend to all cases. Moreover, it might be considered as having been waived by the defendant. The scope of the right has been broadly applied in federal cases, since the Sixth Amendment provides for it in "all criminal prosecutions."

While statutes in all states provide for the appointment of counsel in capital cases and those of more than thirty states require such appointment on request in noncapital felony cases, many state courts for years took the position that, in the absence of explicit statutory direction, there was no constitutional duty to supply counsel to indigent defendants in noncapital cases, particularly when the accused was deemed old enough and experienced enough to look after himself.

Not until 1932 in the Scottsboro boys case (*Powell v. Alabama*) did the United States Supreme Court get around to saying the right to counsel was of such a fundamental character that its denial by a state, at least under some circumstances, constituted a violation of the due process of law guarantee of the Fourteenth Amendment.[10] Thirty-one years later, in the famous case of *Gideon v. Wainwright,* the Supreme Court held that due process obligated the states to provide counsel in all but petty cases, and the next year, in *Escobedo v. Illinois,* it by implication extended the right to counsel to preliminary proceedings in state cases by indicating that convictions would be reversed if defendants lacked counsel and compromised themselves without having been advised of their right to remain silent.[11] Finally in June 1966 the high court ruled in the case of *Miranda v. Arizona* and in three other cases decided the same day (34 U.S. Law Week 4521) that a suspect has a right to a lawyer during the process of interrogation by the police and that, if he desires an attorney and cannot afford one, police questioning must stop unless a court-appointed lawyer is provided.

RIGHT TO PRELIMINARY HEARING

Once the police have arrested a man, they have the right to interrogate him but not to compel him to say anything. Policemen are not judges and do not decide whether anyone is guilty of a crime.

Though the preliminary hearing is a modern device and is not provided for in the federal Constitution, this step is now called for by federal statute and by the constitutions and statutes of a number of states. The general pattern among the states is like that of Rule 5 of the Federal Rules of Criminal Procedure, which requires anyone who has made an arrest to take the arrested person "without unnecessary delay" before the nearest available commissioner, magistrate, or other committing officer for a preliminary examination for the purpose of deciding whether there is probable cause to hold the accused for trial. The commissioner or magistrate may discharge the accused or, if he deems that the police have enough evidence which, if not contradicted, will prove guilt, he may bind him over for indictment by the grand jury or prosecuting attorney.

In recent years the Supreme Court has sought to prevent the holding of suspects for inordinate lengths of time without a preliminary hearing by reversing federal convictions (as in the Mallory case, 1954) based on confessions obtained during a period when the accused was entitled to be brought before a magistrate.

RIGHT TO BAIL

Even if the evidence is considered sufficient to bind the accused over, he is entitled to bail in many cases. Imprisonment being costly and troublesome, the right to bail was early recognized in English law and practice. The ancient common law extended bail in all cases. Parliament, during the reign of Henry VI (1444), required sheriffs and other officers to "let out of prison all manner of persons upon reasonable sureties of sufficient persons." A reasonable bail was one deemed large enough to prevent evasion of the law by flight but still not beyond the means of the prisoner.

But exceptions to the right to bail were gradually introduced. During the reign of Charles I (in 1628) Englishmen complained that prisoners were being committed at the king's command and held for trial. The 1641 statute abolishing the Star Chamber provided that the courts of King's Bench and Common Pleas must decide within three days whether persons committed were entitled to bail. While James II was king (1685–1688), subservient judges sought to evade the law by requiring prisoners to provide bail in amounts they were unable to afford. This led to the inclusion in the English Bill of Rights of 1689 of the proviso that excessive bail should not be required.

But in Blackstone's day (1765) the number of nonbailable offenses had grown to about 160 capital crimes. Only a few offenses were bailable. By this time a jail system for holding accused persons had developed.

Among the English colonies, Massachusetts recognized the right to bail in its 1641 Body of Liberties and Pennsylvania, in its 1682 Frame of Government. After 1776 most of the new states provided for the right to bail in their original constitutions. A guarantee against the requirement of excessive bail was included in the Eighth Amendment to the federal Constitution and is also contained in the constitutions of all but one of the states.

The United States Supreme Court, in a leading modern case, has explained the importance of bail to fair procedure. The right to freedom before conviction is in keeping with the law's principle of presumption of innocence; it avoids the infliction of punishment by imprisonment of an accused who might be acquitted; it enables the accused to take a fuller part in the preparation of his defense.[12]

As provided for in United States statutes and described in Rule 46 of the Federal Rules of Criminal Procedure, the allowability of bail before and after conviction is differentiated. In the case of a person arrested for, but not yet convicted of, an offense not punishable by death, the rule says he *shall* be admitted to bail. But in the case of a convicted person whose appeal has not finally been disposed of, the rule, as lately revised, says bail *may* be allowed unless it appears that the appeal is frivolous or taken for delay. A similar pattern of law prevails in the states, with bail being regarded as a matter of right in noncapital cases before conviction but as a matter of discretion after conviction, though it is frequently allowed in noncapital cases pending the outcome of an appeal.

RIGHT TO ADEQUATE NOTICE

The requirement that the accused be given adequate notice of and a definition of the offense with which he is being charged, one of the indispensable elements of due process, had a clearly discernible origin in the quarrel between Charles I and his nobles. In the *Five Knights' Case,* men of some of the most influential families in England complained to the Court of King's Bench that they had been imprisoned at the king's command without any cause being expressed to them. The court nevertheless returned the prisoners to jail. Thus, in the Petition of Right of 1628, the first great English constitutional document since Magna Carta, one of the liberties which the monarch was called upon to recognize was the specification of causes for the detention of prisoners.

Closely related to the giving of adequate notice was the procedure of indictment by a grand jury. This requirement was specified in a fourteenth-century statute, which in turn derived it from Magna Carta's idea that a man must be judged by his peers and by the law of the land. The purpose was to prevent unjust accusations by the king or his subordinates. Grand jurors were neighbors of potential defendants, and they met in secret and thus could not be easily called to account for not following orders of the crown.

The right of an accused to be informed of the nature and cause of an accusation against him was spelled out in most of the original constitutions of the first thirteen states. The same right was incorporated in the Sixth Amendment to the United States Constitution. And the Fifth Amendment provided that no person should be held to answer for a capital or otherwise infamous crime except on indictment or presentment of a grand jury. Most of the older states, those east of the Mississippi, require grand jury action for major offenses, while in the newer states most accusations are filed by the public prosecutor in the form of an information. Even in these states, however, the grand jury is available at the discretion of the prosecutor. Before an information is filed, there must have been a preliminary hearing before a magistrate.

The reason for requiring that the accused be informed of the precise nature of the charge against him is, of course, that he must have this information in order to be certain that his alleged wrongful act is forbidden by law and to be able to prepare his defense.

As once conceived, the requirement of indictment by a grand jury was a protection for citizens, since the indicting body, consisting of twelve to twenty-three members, had to agree in secret on the validity of the charge and approve the indictment by a majority vote. But as the institution has evolved, it has for the most part become an instrument for the prosecutor and follows his lead in the overwhelming majority of cases. The grand jury, of course, makes no determination of guilt or innocence. All it hears is the prosecution's side, and its only function is to decide whether the evidence presented would, if true, warrant a conviction.

RIGHT TO A TRIAL

One of the paradoxes of law is that many of the intended legal safeguards of the accused—protection against arbitrary arrest, against unreasonable search and seizure, against the third degree and, finally, the protection of an attorney's advice—are most valuable to him in the preliminary stages of a proceeding against him; and yet they cannot be effectively invoked until he gets into court, at which time the inadequacy of the protection may not be easily substantiated. Provision for a fair hearing in open court is nevertheless a basic right.

A criminal trial is an inquiry aimed at ascertaining the facts and prescribing the legal consequences of a particular crime. Who committed it? What was the nature and degree of the offense? And if the defendant is determined to be the offender, what should the law require of him? Under our American system, the jury (still used in most trials for serious offenses) is supposed to determine the facts; the judge applies the law.

One of the law's primary protections of an accused person is the right to have his case decided on the basis of evidence produced at a trial. This essential element of due process, recognized by state and national governments, has historic antecedents going back to Magna Carta and the Petition of Right. And yet it has been one of the most precarious rights to maintain, being threatened by official as well as mob action.

PROHIBITION OF BILLS OF ATTAINDER

Among official devices for avoiding a court hearing, one of the most common in English history was the bill of attainder, a measure by which Parliament tried, convicted, and disposed of an offending citizen without regard to rules of evidence, thereby punishing him and attainting his blood so that he could not inherit property nor have his children inherit from him. Despite a provision against attainder in the charter of Edward III (King of England, 1327–1377), bills of attainder were passed by Parliament during the time of the Tudors (1485–1603) and during the reign of Charles I (1625–1649) and in 1690, during the reign of William III and Mary.

Bills of attainder were also employed in America during the colonial period. Being familiar with English history and convinced of the injustice of the method, the framers of the federal Constitution wrote into the first article of the document prohibitions against the use of bills of attainder by either the federal or state governments. Nevertheless, the procedure has continued to crop up, making it necessary for the Supreme Court to rule against bills of attainder in the Test Oath cases of 1866–1867 and the Lovett case of 1946.[13]

PROHIBITION OF EX POST FACTO LAWS

Like the bill of attainder, an *ex post facto* law is a form of arbitrary legislative punishment. A retroactive or *ex post facto* statute (after the deed or fact) is one which (1) makes a criminal offense of what was innocent when it was done, or (2) makes an offense greater than it was when committed, or (3) inflicts greater punishment than was prescribed at the time the crime was perpetrated, or (4) alters the rules of evidence to make conviction easier, or (5) in effect deprives the accused of some right to which he had become entitled.[14] The principle involved is that no one should be penalized under a law which he had no notice of.

In England agitation against retroactive legislation was one of the activities of the Leveller party during the seventeenth century. William Walwyn, in one of a series of Leveller tracts (1647–1653) entitled "The Bloody Project," declared that Parliament should have no power to punish any person "for doing that which is not against a known declared Law." During the eighteenth century Blackstone recognized the injustice of retroactive statutes.

Delaware in 1776 was the first state to adopt a prohibition against *ex post facto* laws. Others which followed were: Maryland (1776),

North Carolina (1776), Massachusetts (1780), New Hampshire (1784), Pennsylvania (1790), and South Carolina (1790). But the founding fathers were not as much in agreement on this right as they were on others. The convention which framed the Virginia Bill of Rights in 1776 rejected a prohibition against *ex post facto* legislation. In the federal constitutional convention of 1787, such men as Gouverneur Morris and James Wilson of Pennsylvania and Oliver Ellsworth of Connecticut opposed a prohibition on the ground that such laws were void of themselves and therefore a ban was unnecessary. The convention, however, wound up by putting into the Constitution (Article I, Sections 9 and 10) a barrier against the enactment of *ex post facto* laws by either the federal government or the states.

In 1798 in the leading case of *Calder v. Bull* [15] the United States Supreme Court ruled that the *ex post facto* clauses applied only to criminal legislation and not to retroactive civil statutes, thus settling one of the arguments that had engaged the founders. In further interpretations of the clauses, the Supreme Court has indicated that they refer only to the making of laws and not to their construction by the courts. However, the prohibition reaches every form in which the legislative power of the state is exercised, whether by constitutional provision, statute, municipal ordinance, or administrative rule or regulation.

RIGHT TO A SPEEDY AND PUBLIC TRIAL

The principle of a prompt trial is one of the most ancient in law. The Magna Carta recognized the injustice of delay. The foes of Charles I protested against the injustice of being forced to remain in prison for unconscionable periods awaiting trial. The Sixth Amendment to the federal Constitution and many state constitutions contain a guarantee of a "speedy" trial. Rule 48(b) of the Federal Rules of Criminal Procedure authorizes the judge to dismiss an indictment if there has been "unnecessary delay" in presenting the charge or bringing the defendant to trial. In the Provoo case the United States Supreme Court in 1955 upheld the dismissal of a treason indictment because the government delayed a first trial for more than two years after the defendant's arrest and then brought a second indictment (following a reversed conviction) some five years after the arrest.[16]

Along with the right of the accused to be tried without undue delay goes the right to a public trial. Long established in the common law of England, this right stems from the English revulsion against the tyrannical secret proceedings of the Court of Star Chamber. The Sixth Amendment assures the accused of "a speedy and public trial" in all criminal prosecutions. And the constitutions of more than forty states also guarantee a public trial. Statutes and court decisions secure the right in the remaining states. In 1948 the United States Supreme Court ruled in the Oliver case that the due process requirement of the Fourteenth Amendment imposes on the states a barrier against secret proceedings. The court said it could find no record of a secret criminal trial in any American federal, state, or municipal court or in any English court after 1641. It noted the advantages of publicity as being an effective restraint on the possible abuse of judicial power, the serving of notice to witnesses unknown to the parties, the education of the public on the functioning of the judicial system.[17]

While secret trials have been forbidden, the judge has considerable discretion in excluding some people from the courtroom in the interests of health, public order, and the avoidance of a public airing of some kinds of testimony. The guarantee of a public trial is for the benefit of the defendant, however, and therefore it has been held that he is the one entitled to invoke the right to have friends and relatives or the press present.[18]

RIGHT TO CONFRONT WITNESSES

Once the trial has started, an opportunity for the accused to confront witnesses against him is vital to his defense. Denied such an opportunity, he cannot cross-examine his accuser. During the reign of Henry VIII (1509–1547) the Duke of Somerset, on being tried for treason, demanded to be confronted by witnesses but was refused. After Edward VI (King of England, 1547–1553) came to the throne, a statute was enacted providing that no one should be convicted of treason except on the testimony of two lawful witnesses who should be brought in person before the accused. But during the reign of James I (1603–1625) Sir Walter Raleigh was condemned to death on the written testimony of a single witness who later recanted his accusation. Early in the seventeenth century a rule was established in common law that an accused was entitled to confront witnesses against him. (The requirement of two witnesses in treason prosecutions—dating from the time of Edward VI and reaffirmed in the English Treason Act of 1661—was incorporated in Article III, Section 3, of the United States Constitution as part of a strict procedure specified for securing convictions on charges that could be politically motivated.)

By the time of the American Revolution, the right of confrontation was valued highly enough so that it was recognized in the first constitutions of Virginia, Pennsylvania, Maryland, North Carolina, Massachusetts, New Hampshire, and Vermont. It was, of course, also included in the Sixth Article of the Bill of Rights. In interpreting this provision, the federal courts have held that in a criminal case the government cannot decline to identify the accusers on the ground that they are informers or because they are privy to state secrets.[19] Not until 1965 in the Pointer case did the Supreme Court squarely rule, however, that the right to confront witnesses and cross-examine them is one of the requirements of due process imposed on the states by the Fourteenth Amendment.[20]

RIGHT TO SUMMON WITNESSES

Closely related to the matter of confrontation is the accused's right to summon witnesses in his favor. Long unrecognized in common law, this right was urged by Sir Edward Coke as necessary to justice. In 1696 Parliament granted defendants in treason trials the right to call witnesses, and in 1702 the right was extended to all defendants. Meanwhile in America, the Pennsylvania Charter of Liberties in 1701 guaranteed the right of the accused to call witnesses. One of the subjects of dispute between the crown and the colonies at the time of the American Revolution was the matter of trying Americans in Britain, which would make it difficult for the defendants to summon witnesses in their defense. Most of the new state constitutions specified the right to call witnesses or produce evidence in favor of the defendant; the Sixth Amendment to the federal Constitution spelled out the right. In most state constitutions, in statutes, and in common law pronouncements the right to have compulsory process for obtaining witnesses is assured today, though the Supreme Court has not held it an obligation of the states as a part of federally guaranteed due process.

RIGHT TO A JURY TRIAL

Of the various mechanisms in the trial process designed to insure a just weighing of the evidence, perhaps the most respected is the jury. Whatever its defects, this feature has held its place in popular regard for centuries. From ancient times the parties were bound to accept its verdict. Though the exact origin of the rule that the jury must decide cases by a unanimous vote is not known, it is thought to date from a ruling in a 1367 case, which held unacceptable a verdict agreed on by only eleven jurors. The right of jurors to reach their decision freely without pressure from the judge or other governmental authority was established in Bushell's case in 1670.

In colonial America the colonists came to value the jury trial as a right of local self-government. When Parliament extended the jurisdiction of admiralty courts beyond their ancient limits so as to try colonists for various offenses without a jury, the colonial Declaration of Rights in 1765 proclaimed that "trial by jury is the inherent and invaluable right of every British subject in these Colonies." In another manifesto nine years later the colonists reaffirmed that they were entitled to "the great and inestimable privilege of being tried by their peers of the vicinage." The Declaration of Independence condemned George III for depriving the colonists "in many cases of the benefits of trial by jury." So dearly did Americans hold trial by jury that the right was provided for in both Article III, Section 2, of the original federal Constitution and in the Sixth Amendment.

As far as federal jurisdiction is concerned, the Supreme Court in a leading case has said that the Constitution requires a jury of twelve members, under the supervision of a judge and rendering their verdict unanimously.[21] But since the high court has not made the federal formula applicable to the states under the due process clause of the Fourteenth Amendment, the states have had latitude to experiment. And some of them have authorized juries of fewer than twelve and verdicts that are less than unanimous in certain types of cases. In federal and in many state courts defendants are allowed to waive a jury trial.

While both the Sixth Amendment and most state constitutions grant the accused the right "to an impartial jury," modern interpretations of the meaning of impartiality differ from Lord Mansfield's 1764 definition: "A juror should be as white paper, and know neither plaintiff nor defendant, but judge of the issue merely as an abstract proposition upon the evidence produced before him. He should be superior even to a suspicion of partiality." Chief Justice John Marshall once rejected the argument that jurors must be "perfectly indifferent and free from prejudice." Distinguishing between those with "light" impressions and those with "deep" ones, he said a juror of the first type "may fairly be supposed to yield to the testimony," while the second type "will close the mind against the testimony," which would be sufficient reason to reject him. In determining whether an admission of bias should disqualify a prospective juror, courts take into account both the source and the strength of the prejudice. It is common for veniremen (members of a panel from which jurors are drawn) to express opinions based on rumor, general sentiment, or newspaper reports, and these sources have been held to be not sufficiently reliable to disqualify without reference to the strength of the opinion.[22]

Though a jury does not have to be exactly representative of every facet of the district in which it sits, the Supreme Court has said it cannot, on the other hand, be "the organ of any special group or class."[23] Nor can the members of any group or class be arbitrarily excluded from jury service. Our tradition, the court has said, "contemplates an impartial jury drawn from a cross-section of the community."[24] Recognizing that in some areas Negroes might not be included in juries, Congress in 1875 stipulated that no citizen should be disqualified by reason of race for service on grand or petit juries in either federal or state courts, and officials who excluded or failed to summon jurors for such a reason were made subject to fine. Though the constitutionality of the statute was upheld in 1880 under the authority granted to Congress in the Fourteenth Amendment to insure "equal protection of the laws,"[25] direct federal prosecutions of state officials to discourage discrimination against Negroes have been extremely rare. The Supreme Court, however, has dismissed indictments or set aside convictions of Negroes who were prosecuted in state courts that practiced such discrimination.[26] In a 1950 case, reaffirmed by implication in 1964, the court said "an accused is entitled to have charges against him considered by a jury in the selection of which there has been neither inclusion nor exclusion because of race."[27] Discriminatory treatment of other substantial racial or ethnic groups in the community has also been held to be a violation of the equal protection of the laws guarantee.[28]

RIGHT TO A LOCAL TRIAL AND LOCAL JURY

Not only does the law aim to secure an impartial jury but also a local jury and a local trial, except in cases where this is impractical, as when the offense was committed on the high seas. Colonial Americans came to treasure local trials as a result of harsh experience. In 1769 Parliament enacted a law providing for trial in England of persons accused of treason in Massachusetts. Other parliamentary acts authorized the trial of revenue cases by vice-admiralty tribunals located outside the colony where the offense occurred. And trials for some offenses against the king's property could be held in England. The colonists protested. Not surprisingly, therefore, the founders of the nation put a guarantee of a local trial in the main body of the Constitution.

During President Grant's administration (1873) a court refused to grant a warrant for the transfer of an editor from New York to the District of Columbia in order that he might be tried there for libel. The ground was that such a removal was forbidden by the Constitution. In a similar case during the administration of Theodore Roosevelt a federal district court at Indianapolis blocked the government's attempt to transport editors from that city to the national capital for the purpose of trying them for criminal libel. Thus the jury guarantee was a shield for a free press.

In interpreting the Sixth Amendment's requirement of a "jury of the State and district wherein the crime shall have been committed," the courts have held that jurors cannot be drawn from outside the federal judicial district, though they need not be drawn from the whole district. Most state constitutions have jury of the vicinage provisions today, and this guarantee has been held to require that jurors be drawn from the county or parish or judicial district.

PROTECTION AGAINST ILLEGAL EVIDENCE

Though ideally the citizen should be able to avail himself of certain constitutional rights before he is ever haled into court, he may not in actual practice have the opportunity until a trial has begun. Thus the constitutional safeguards against unreasonable searches and forced confessions may not become operative except through exclusionary rules on evidence. Sometimes illegal activities of the police can only be discouraged by rulings to the effect that ill-gotten evidence may not be admitted. While such decisions by the courts may occasionally free a guilty defendant, they also help to protect the innocent citizen from abuse by law enforcement authorities. They tend to equalize the contest between the weak individual and the all-powerful state.

RIGHT AGAINST SELF-INCRIMINATION

Another evidentiary rule which by design operates to put the state at a handicap is that which enables the defendant to refuse to testify against himself. The technique of compelling suspects to testify against themselves was originated by special courts whose mission was to root out religious heresy and political subversion. During the thirteenth century ecclesiastical courts devised the *ex officio* oath as a means of inducing persons not under formal charge to give testimony about themselves. The judge, by virtue of his office—that is to say, *ex officio*—put the suspected enemy of the church under oath and proceeded to interrogate him. Since in that religious age, oaths were taken very seriously, the device was effective. In 1487 the Court of Star Chamber, which specialized in inquiring into political subversion, was authorized by statute to examine defendants under the oath *ex officio*. In common law courts a defendant was not put upon his oath until he was formally charged, unless he was under strong suspicion.

Opposition to the special courts' practice of forcing men to answer questions on any subject, however incriminating, began to develop in the seventeenth century. One of the earliest objections was made in 1604 when Parliament petitioned James I asking that "the oath *ex officio,* whereby men are forced to accuse themselves, be more sparingly used." After Sir Edward Coke became Chief Justice of thte Court of Common Pleas in 1606, he held in several cases that the ecclesiastical courts could not examine persons charged with crime by the oath *ex officio*. These decisions did not, however, affect the Court of Star Chamber. Revolt against the tyranny of Charles I led Parliament in 1641 to abolish the Court of Star Chamber and the Court of High Commission, which was the tribunal for eradicating religious subversion. Thereupon the oath *ex officio* disappeared. The statute doing away with the High Commission expressly forbade ecclesiastical courts to require persons to confess or accuse themselves of any crime or any other matter whereby they might be exposed to criminal penalties.

Though the common law courts did not examine defendants under oath, the judge did question the accused freely about criminal activities and press them to answer. With the passing of the special or so-called prerogative courts, opposition to wide-ranging questioning of defendants in the common law courts began to grow, particularly among the Levellers. By the end of the reign of Charles II (1660–1685), the privilege against self-incrimination was probably recognized in all courts when claimed by a defendant or a witness. Yet important as this protection was, and though finally it was firmly established in English law, it was not one of those rights specifically mentioned in Magna Carta, the Petition of Right, or the English Bill of Rights.

In the New World, Americans expressed explicitly their opposition to inquisitorial methods. The Massachusetts Body of Liberties of 1641 and the Connecticut Code of 1650 contained provisions against compulsory self-incrimination. In Virginia as a result of Governor Berkeley's reign of terror following Bacon's rebellion, the legislature adopted a statute declaring that "noe man shall compell a man to sweare against himself in any matter wherein he is lyable to corporal punishment." In all of the state declarations of rights adopted prior to the United States Constitution, the privilege against self-incrimination was specified in one form or another. The same protection was incorporated into thte Fifth Article of thte Bill of Rights. Today all but two state constitutions include provisions securing the privilege against self-incrimination. And in the other two states (New Jersey and Iowa) the courts have held that the privilege is nevertheless a part of existing law.

In a 1964 case (*Malloy v. Hogan*), the United States Supreme Court explicitly held that the Fifth Amendment guarantee against self-incrimination was made applicable to witnesses in state proceedings by the due process clause of the Fourteenth Amendment.[29] And the next year in *Griffin v. California,* the high court ruled that, if a defendant refuses to testify at his trial, neither the judge nor prosecutor can refer to his silence as in itself incriminating.[30] The court thus counteracted the laws of those states still permitting a judge and prosecutor to comment adversely on a defendant's failure to speak.

The constitutional guarantee against self-incrimination protects a person against having to reveal a criminal fact in any kind of proceeding, whether in civil or criminal courts, in grand jury or legislative investigations, or in administrative inquiries. It may be invoked by a witness as well as an accused. But it provides a safeguard only against prosecution which may lead to criminal penalties. It does not excuse a person from giving testimony merely because to do so would expose him to public ridicule or disgrace or would bring him into disrepute.[31]

A defendant or a witness may explicitly waive the privilege against self-incrimination or he may lose it by failing to invoke it. Or a witness may be compelled to give incriminating testimony under a statute which grants immunity from prosecution. Congress and some of the states have enacted immunity laws. The federal Immunity Act of 1954 has been upheld by the Supreme Court as constitutional.[32]

PROTECTION AGAINST DOUBLE JEOPARDY

In any catalogue of historic rights of the accused, one of the most important is the guarantee against being twice put in jeopardy for the same offense. Though occasions for invoking it today do not arise as often as they once did, its roots run deep into Greek and Roman history when there was a popular fear and abhorrence of the sovereign's power to try people twice for the same conduct. By the thirteenth century the rule against double jeopardy seems to have been firmly established in England. Under the common law rule, the defendant was not considered to have been placed once in jeopardy until the case had reached final judgment.[33] Hence a second prosecution for the same offense could occur unless a previous prosecution had actually been concluded with a verdict. The English rule developed as a barrier against—and was generally limited to—repeated crown prosecutions for capital felonies, a practice that had occurred during the reign of the Stuarts.[34]

In America the protection against double jeopardy was extended beyond capital offenses but the English requirement of a prior final verdict was maintained. Massachusetts had a safeguard against double jeopardy in its 1641 Body of Liberties. New Hampshire's was the first state bill of rights to include a stipulation against a defendant's being twice put in jeopardy. Today the constitutions of all but five states have double jeopardy clauses, and in those states without constitutional provisions the courts apply common law rules against double jeopardy.

The Fifth Amendment to the federal Constitution contains the somewhat ambiguous provision: "nor shall any person be subject for the same offense to be twice put in jeopardy of life or limb," by which the framers probably meant only to bar reprosecution after a verdict. But judicial decisions have broadened the rule.

With jeopardy interpreted to mean the danger of conviction, the general rule has come to be that in a nonjury trial jeopardy attaches when the first witness is sworn or when the court has begun to hear evidence; in a jury trial jeopardy attaches when the jury has been impaneled and sworn. Yet there are situations in which the judge may discharge the jury before it reaches a verdict without thereby barring a second prosecution. The discharge of a hung jury, for example, need not operate to prevent a second trial. When a mistrial is declared because of newspaper stories which may have prejudiced the jury, double jeopardy does not necessarily bar a new proceeding.[35]

The double jeopardy rule does not prevent a federal prosecution for an act for which the defendant has already been tried in a state court[36] or a state prosecution after a trial in a federal court.[37] Though it is settled law in the federal courts that the government has no right to appeal from an acquittal in a criminal case,[38] the same rule does not necessarily apply in state courts. In *Palko v. Connecticut,* the United States Supreme Court refused to read the double jeopardy concept of the Fifth Amendment into the due process required of the states in the Fourteenth Amendment. In that case the state had given the prosecution the right to appeal on questions of legal error.[39]

While the double jeopardy guarantee has its limitations, its main purpose is clear: to save a defendant from the harassment of repeated criminal prosecutions as well as multiple punishments imposed by a number of sentences stemming from the same verdict. Although the Constitution speaks of jeopardy of "life or limb," the guarantee has been held to apply to minor offenses as well as felonies. Both federal and state courts have applied the double jeopardy concept more stringently in recent years.

THE WRIT OF HABEAS CORPUS

If a defendant fails to get an injustice corrected by any other means, the writ of habeas corpus may be his salvation. Professor Zechariah Chafee, Jr., called it "the most important human right in the Constitution," the one that safeguards most of the others. The writ of habeas corpus is a legal process by which one may vindicate summarily his right to personal liberty when he is being detained illegally. Though the historical roots of "the great writ of liberty" are not easy to trace, the writ is thought to have grown out of Section 39 of Magna Carta, which provided that "no free man shall be taken or imprisoned or disseised or exiled or in any way destroyed except by the lawful judgment of his peers or by the law of the land." The first use of the writ as a constitutional remedy against the crown in behalf of men committed to jail is believed to have occurred during the reign of Henry VII (1485–1509).

By the time of Charles I the writ of habeas corpus had become established as a remedy for arbitrary justice by agents of the monarch. But it was during the reign of Charles I that the case of the five knights revealed a need to strengthen the writ. On being jailed by order of the king because they refused to make a forced loan to the crown, the knights questioned the legality of their imprisonment in a proceeding in the Court of King's Bench brought under a writ of habeas corpus. Despite the lack of an indictment, the prisoners were refused the right to bail and were remanded to jail. The case led directly to the Petition of Right (1628) which complained of the king's failure to honor many rights, including the writ of habeas corpus. In 1641 the act abolishing the Star Chamber specifically authorized the writ to test the validity of a commitment on order of the king or the Privy Council.

In a few years, however, it became apparent that the writ of personal liberty was still not firmly guaranteed. Few judges could issue it and those who could were unwilling to do so during the six months of the year when their courts were not in session. When Francis Jenkes, a London trader, had difficulty getting his freedom on bail after his arrest in 1679 for making an allegedly subversive speech, Parliament was induced to adopt the landmark Habeas Corpus Act of 1679. Its chief objective was to provide for a prompt inquiry by a judge into the legality of a petitioner's imprisonment on a criminal charge and for a speedy trial on the charge. In England the writ was strengthened still further by judicial decisions and by another statute in 1816.

The American colonies showed an early appreciation of the writ of liberty, several of them incorporating the British Habeas Corpus Act into their colonial law. When the Continental Congress in 1774 appealed for support from the people of Quebec, it listed habeas corpus as one of the great rights enjoyed by Americans. Seven of the revolutionary state constitutions contained habeas corpus provisions, and in the main body of the new United States Constitution (Article I, Section 9) the command was that the writ should not be suspended "unless when in Cases of Rebellion or Invasion the public Safety may require it." Most state charters have a similar guarantee, though only a few prohibit any suspension. Congress, in its first law dealing with courts, the Judiciary Act of 1789, empowered all federal tribunals "to grant writs of habeas corpus for the purpose of an inquiry into the cause of commitment."

In 1807 Thomas Jefferson vainly sought to persuade Congress to suspend the writ during the Burr conspiracy. Without waiting for any congressional authorization, Lincoln early in his term arbitrarily suspended the writ to meet the crisis of the Civil War. Since the Constitution was not clear on who was empowered to suspend habeas corpus, the issue was hotly debated, with Chief Justice Roger Taney, sitting as a circuit judge, contending that only Congress could act. In 1863 Congress granted the President the power to act at his own discretion.

Suspensions of the writ of habeas corpus by presidential action occurred again in 1871 in South Carolina during an uprising by the Ku Klux Klan, in 1905 in the Philippines during the revolt there, and in 1941 in Hawaii as World War II began.

The first great expansion of the coverage of the federal writ of habeas corpus came with the enactment of the 1867 Judiciary Act, designed to aid the enforcement of the Reconstruction statutes. This law made federal habeas corpus available to state as well as federal prisoners in all cases in which any person may be deprived of his liberty in violation of the Constitution or treaty or law of the United States. But the most significant broadening of the scope of habeas corpus has occurred through the action of the Supreme Court in connection with federal review of petitions filed by state prisoners incarcerated in accordance with the judgments of state courts. Applying the due process clause of the Fourteenth Amendment, federal courts have often examined the legality of the proceedings under which such prisoners have been sentenced.

As the writ of habeas corpus has evolved, it has become a method for judicial inquiry into various ways by which a person may be restrained, whether he is in jail, in the custody of police following an arrest, being held by authorities for extradition, being held in a mental institution, in the hands of military authorities, or being detained by immigration officials for deportation. A proceeding on the writ is summary, since it requires the immediate production of the person detained. It may be issued by any judge in chambers. A prisoner's right to petition for the writ, in person or through his agent, never lapses, since the right to personal freedom from illegal restraint never expires. The effect of the writ, when there is a finding of unlawful restraint, is to free the petitioner promptly.[40]

PROTECTION AGAINST CRUEL AND UNUSUAL PUNISHMENT

Law acts not only to protect an accused against unjust conviction but also to prevent mistreatment of the defendant after he has been found guilty. Section 20 of Magna Carta provided that: "A free man shall not be fined for a small offence, except in proportion to the measure of the offence; and for a great offence he shall be fined in proportion to the magnitude of the offence." The principle that punishment should not be disproportionate to the offense was set forth in an English statute in 1553. The English Bill of Rights of 1689, stemming from burning and whipping and other cruel treatment during the reign of James II (1685–1688), declared that excessive fines should not be imposed "nor cruel and unusual punishments inflicted."

But even after the passage of the Bill of Rights, penalties involving torture and mutilation were still legal in England in cases in which such punishments were considered proportionate to the crime. Some of the cruel and degrading punishments included the dragging of the condemned through the streets to the place of execution, hanging and public dissection of the prisoner (sometimes while he was still alive), mutilation by cutting off the hands or ears or slitting the nostrils, branding on the face or hand, whipping, and confinement to the pillory.

The fact that the early American colonists had begun to react against brutal punishment is suggested by provisions in the 1641 Massachusetts Body of Liberties:

> No man shall be beaten with above 40 stripes, nor shall any true gentleman, nor any man equall to a gentleman be punished with whipping, unless his crime be very shamefull, and his course of life vitious and profligate. . . .
>
> For bodilie punishments we allow amongst us none that are inhumane Barbarous or cruel.

This stricture did not, however, prevent Massachusetts from providing by law in 1711 that highway robbers should be burned on the forehead or hand, should be imprisoned for six months, and render treble damages to the person robbed. Later the death penalty was authorized for the same offense. Punishments inflicted upon criminals in the American colonies during the eighteenth century were in general probably just as severe as those common in England. Yet by the end of the century, six of the first state constitutions had specific guarantees against cruel punishment[41] and two others had provisions against excessive punishment or fines.[42]

Despite these signs of progress, a proposal to condemn cruel punishment in the federal Bill of Rights nevertheless stirred debate in Congress. In due course, however, the Eighth Amendment's prohibition against excessive fines and cruel and unusual punishments was adopted. Similar clauses are contained in the constitutions of every state but Vermont and Connecticut. In Vermont the state's highest court has ruled that excessive punishment is barred by the common law.

The basic question involved in interpreting the prohibition against cruel and unusual punishment has often centered on whether the ban applies only to the mode of punishment or also to the severity of punishment. While some courts have taken the position that the constitutional barrier affects only the method, the weight of authority, including that of the United States Supreme Court, is on the side of a court inquiring into the severity of the sentence; and sentences which seemed clearly excessive have been held to constitute cruel and unusual punishment.[43]

The habitual offender laws of many states have been sustained against the claim that their prescribed heavier penalties for third or fourth felony convictions amount to an imposition of cruel and unusual punishment. State appellate courts have shown a reluctance to invalidate criminal statutes on the claim that the punishment they authorize is excessive, preferring to act on a presumption that they are constitutional and that the legislators are best able to determine what is proper. But courts in reviewing individual cases have held the following punishments to be cruel and unusual: thirty years in jail at hard labor for burglary without weapons or tools on the part of a man without a previous criminal record; twenty-one months in jail for bigamy when the convicted man remarried in the innocent belief that he had been divorced from his former wife; banishment from the state for a period of years or permanently for various offenses.

Questions of cruel and unusual punishment arise not only with respect to penalties prescribed by legislatures and imposed by judges but also with regard to the kind of treatment prisoners receive in confinement. Complaints of cruel treatment in prison have frequently arisen in connection with extradition proceedings, which are themselves held at the command upon the states by the United States Constitution (Article IV, Section 2) to deliver fugitives from justice to the state having jurisdiction of the crime. The competing claims of extradition as against the right to asylum, as a form of freedom from cruel and unusual punishment, were extensively litigated in the federal courts after the escape in 1943 of some 175 Georgia convicts, many of whom said they were mistreated on chain gangs. Though the United States Supreme Court, when one case finally reached that tribunal, did not rule out federal relief, it held that the petitioner had to exhaust his state remedies first.[44] And in an Alabama case decided not long after, the high court indicated that the fugitive had to exhaust the remedies of the demanding state rather than the asylum state, which seemed to offer scant hope to those fleeing Southern prisons.[45] Few imprisoned men have the knowledge or resources to seek relief from cruel treatment.

Despite its negative decisions in the extradition field, the Supreme Court has indicated that the infliction of a cruel and unusual punishment by a state would violate the due process guarantee of the Fourteenth Amendment.[46]

RIGHT TO DUE PROCESS

In addition to the specific procedural guarantees enumerated in the United States Constitution, both the Fifth and Fourteenth Amendments contain the general requirement that the citizen must be accorded "due process of law." The phrase comes from an English statute of 1355, which reads: "No man of what state or condition he be, shall be put out of his lands or tenements nor taken, nor disinherited, nor put to death, without he be brought to answer by due process of law." And this law harked back to Magna Carta's provision for judgment according to the law of the land. Sir Edward Coke, in Part II of his *Institutes,* equated the term "by the law of the land" with "due process of law." And the American founding fathers derived their understanding of the terms from Coke.

The Fifth Amendment requirement of due process, of course, applies to the national government and the Fourteenth Amendment provision, to state governments. The phrase in both places has been invoked against arbitrary action by the executive, legislative, or judicial branches. It adds up to a requirement of governmental fair play. The Supreme Court has said that a legal proceeding, in order to provide due process, must conform to the guaranties contained in the Constitution and to other guaranties that have come to Americans through the adoption of the laws of England.[47] Interpretation of rights of due process, however, is a broad and complex field in which concepts are changing. In recent years the Supreme Court has been applying the phrase to impose stricter procedural requirements on the states in criminal cases in order to protect the accused from arbitrary treatment.

CHAPTER THREE

THE ACCUSED IN THE PRESS

Chronicles of Crime—No Modern Phenomenon

Avid popular interest in crime extends back to the biblical tale of Cain and Abel and down to the modern television melodrama. Through the centuries, crime and punishment have engaged the talents of the world's writers—dramatists from Euripides to Eugene O'Neill, novelists from Victor Hugo to Robert Penn Warren, and "whodunit" authors from Edgar Allan Poe to Erle Stanley Gardner.

More than 200 years ago Horace Walpole wrote: "You cannot conceive the ridiculous rage there is of going to Newgate, the prints that are published of the malefactors, and the memoirs of their lives set forth with as much parade as Marshal Turene's."

Newspaper writers quickly took a place among the narrators of adventures in crime. Sensing the public's latent appetite for this, newspaper publishers, almost from the beginning of their trade, were not hesitant about striving to satisfy, and even to create, popular demand. English papers of the early eighteenth century devoted considerable space to the drama of the criminal courts. Obviously the historical roots of the problems of justice and the press run deep. A chronological survey of journalistic treatment of crime will show that many of today's press practices are no modern phenomenon.

EARLY UNITED STATES PRESS PRACTICES

The American press at the beginning of the nineteenth century put so much stress on crime news that it prompted complaints. Fisher

Ames in 1801 protested against the rampant sensationalism of the time, declaring:

> Some of the shocking articles in the paper raise simple, and very simple, wonder; some terrour; and some horrour and disgust. Now what instruction is there in these endless wonders? . . . do they not shock tender minds and addle shallow brains? They make a thousand old maids, and eight or ten thousand booby boys afraid to go to bed alone. . . . Yet there seems to be a sort of rivalship among printers, who shall have the most wonders, and the strangest and most wonderful crimes.[1]

The Burr Case

Even in this early day newspapers were prone to dwell on questions of guilt or innocence long before the issues reached the courtroom. Months before Aaron Burr's trial for treason in 1807, the *Western World* of Frankfurt, Kentucky, openly charged that there was a plot in the making to combine Indiana, Ohio, Kentucky, Tennessee, Louisiana, and the Floridas under an independent government. While pointing out that a majority of the conspirators wanted to call a convention and obtain the consent of Congress, the newspaper went on to say that a considerable number wanted to achieve their purpose by force of arms. This report, based on pure speculation, was nevertheless picked up and widely republished in the East. Not only did the *Western World* speculate on the separatist movement but it also directly linked Burr and others with the conspiracy.

As the Burr trial approached, Jeffersonian and Federalist newspapers showed their colors by the way in which they viewed the proceedings—the Federalist press seeking to discredit the charges and the Administration press supporting the prosecution. On the Federalist side the Virginia *Gazette and Daily Advertiser* had cast aspersions on members of the grand jury which brought in the indictments and later attacked the honesty of the prosecution's witnesses. The *National Intelligencer* in Washington and the *Enquirer* in Richmond joined the fray on the side of the prosecution. While promising to refrain from "impassioned representations" and to present the facts "without any regard to the party whom they favor," the *Enquirer,* before the trial began, nevertheless republished a categorical statement from the *National Intelligencer* saying it could not be denied that "Aaron Burr has formed a treasonable plan leveled at the destruction of every ingredient of our felicity."

The *Enquirer,* not altogether without justification, chided Federalist Chief Justice John Marshall, the presiding judge at the Burr trial, for attending a dinner party at which the defendant was also a guest. Carrying its support of the government further, the same paper championed the prosecution's star witness, General James Wilkinson, and attacked the character of Luther Martin, a lawyer for the defense. Another example of how partisan editors were deeply immersed in the case was the visit of William Duane, editor of the Philadelphia *Aurora,* to Harman Blennerhassett in prison. The main purpose of Republican Duane's call on Blennerhassett was to get the prisoner to betray his associate, Burr.[2]

The Vesey Case

With regard to another type of conspiracy—that involving insurrectionary activity among slaves—the American press, especially in the South, was much more circumspect during this period of its history. The reason for the unusual exhibition of restraint, as in the case of the Denmark Vesey plot in South Carolina in 1822, was that the editors and authorities feared that publicity might have the effect of fueling the interest of other would-be insurrectionists. Hence, the state's action against slave rebels might move from arrests through trials and executions with scarcely any notice in the press.

Era of the Penny Papers

Early in the nineteenth century the press recognized the popularity of stories of homicide. When a clergyman was tried for murder in Newport, Rhode Island, in 1833, the New York *Evening Post,* then edited by William Cullen Bryant, used its entire front page for an account of the proceedings.

The most active news vehicle in playing up sensational criminal cases was the penny press, which was given its real impetus by the founding of the New York *Sun* in 1833. Designed to meet the tastes of uneducated draymen and porters—in contrast to the professional and mercantile subscribers of the six-cent dailies—the penny papers specialized in police reports. They sent their men at four o'clock in the morning to observe the drama of the police courts and to report on the wife-beaters, vagabonds, sots, and street-walkers who had been dragged in by policemen during the night.

HOMICIDAL FARE

When James Gordon Bennett entered the penny-press field with his New York *Morning Herald* in 1835 he increased the appeal of crime news by unabashed pandering to public curiosity over sex and murder.

Robinson-Jewett Case

Bennett helped to make the 1836 Robinson-Jewett case perhaps the first overplayed murder story in the United States press. Helen Jewett, a prostitute, was found murdered in her room. When a young clerk named Robinson was charged with the crime, Bennett devoted many columns to the story despite the fact that in this case, unlike those usually publicized at that time, neither party had any social standing. Once the trial began, the *Herald* printed scarcely anything else. Other penny papers in Philadelphia and Boston followed its example. Having done some detective work on the case himself, Bennett became convinced of the defendant's innocence. And when Robinson was acquitted, the publisher was exultant, not only because of the outcome but because his paper's circulation had tripled during the run of the story.[3] In Philadelphia the *Public Ledger,* which also gave much space to the Robinson-Jewett case, directed editorial barbs at the judge, jury, counsel, and witnesses during the course of the trial.

The Webster Case

While the American press, led by the penny papers, continued during the pre-Civil War era to give elaborate coverage to crime news, it was the reporting of the Webster case in 1850 which probably set the record for the period. The case began in 1849 with the mysterious disappearance of Dr. George Parkman of Boston. Lurid interest in the event mounted when dismembered parts of Parkman's body were found in the laboratory of John W. Webster, professor of chemistry and mineralogy at Harvard. In March 1850 Webster was put on trial for the murder of the doctor, who had been his creditor. Press interest in the case became nationwide. In Boston the *Transcript,* the *Daily Mail,* and the *Journal* each printed nearly 100,000 words on the proceedings. Intense public interest continued after Webster was found guilty and condemned to death. At the site of the execution in August 1850 the scene was almost as tumultuous as that in the courtroom had been. A mob broke into a nearby locked house in order to reach the roof and gain a better view of the gallows. More than 250 persons, including some 125 policemen, were admitted as witnesses to the hanging.[4] After the commotion had subsided, no sensitive Boston editor could have reflected on the riotous events without wondering about the role of the press in fanning an inflamed atmosphere for justice.

The Sickles Case

In 1859 the press sensed another titillating story when swashbuckling Daniel E. Sickles (later to be a Union general) publicly shot Philip Barton Key, U.S. attorney for the District of Columbia and the son of Francis Scott Key. Sickles accused Key of being Mrs. Sickles' seducer. The New York and Washington press especially gave full coverage to the trial of Sickles for murder, devoting concentrated attention to the sensational aspects. The defendant, then a member of the U.S. House of Representatives, was acquitted. The Sickles trial illustrates the apparent maxim of American justice that—even when a case is pursued by a prying press and panting public—a special leniency is reserved for outraged husbands implicated in crimes of revenge against rival lovers.

The Civil War Period

During the cataclysm of the Civil War neither the press nor the courts were careful about the niceties of justice when national loyalty was in dispute. Horace Greeley's New York *Tribune* boldly called for the court-martialing and hanging of men it deemed to be traitors.

ASSASSINATION PROSECUTIONS

Lincoln's assassination and the ensuing political upheaval led to some of the most sensational episodes in the history of American justice. John Wilkes Booth complained of press suggestions of cowardice in his conduct. "I struck him boldly," he was reported to have said, "and not as the papers say; I walked with a firm step through thousands of his friends; was stopped but pushed on."

After Booth was shot dead, eight of his alleged accomplices were brought to trial before a military commission despite protests from legal authorities and some newspapers that their case should have been heard by a competent civilian court. The press told the shocking story as the prisoners, chained and hooded, were brought into the courtroom on the opening day of the trial. Each day's lurid testimony was reported in the columns of the *National Intelligencer* and the *Evening Star*. Wild stories were relayed and embellished to be eagerly read by a curious public. At the conclusion of the clamorous and irregular proceeding, highlighted by reports of coached and perjured testimony, four of the defendants were condemned to die and four others sentenced to life imprisonment. Among those who were hanged was Mary Eugenia Surratt, keeper of a Washington boarding house where Booth had stayed.

In 1867, in another of the train of scandalous trials that came in the wake of the assassination, Mrs. Surratt's son, John Harrison Surratt, Jr., was brought to trial for the murder of Lincoln. Again the Washington press gave copious coverage to the event. The trial ended with a hung jury.

OUTRAGE AGAINST AN ENEMY LEADER

In this year of 1867, feeling on the war was still highly volatile. There was a storm of public outrage when Horace Greeley joined other reputable citizens in agreeing to underwrite a $100,000 bail bond for Jefferson Davis, who had been in prison without a trial for two years. While Greeley stoutly defended his action in the columns of the *Tribune,* the paper was swamped by abusive letters and thousands canceled their subscriptions.[5] When the accused (Davis) being aided by Greeley was deemed a traitor, the editor was in effect punished for upholding the Bill of Rights, which guaranteed a speedy trial and protection against excessive bail.

THE TRIAL OF A PRESIDENT

The next year the impeachment of President Andrew Johnson by the House of Representatives led to one of the great trials of history. Newspapers did not hesitate to pronounce judgments on the President's alleged offenses. As the historic drama unfolded before the jury of senators from March 5 to May 16, popular interest was focused intently on reports of the event. When six Republican senators indicated at a party caucus part way through the trial that they did not think the evidence so far introduced was sufficient to convict, their attitude was denounced by the Philadelphia *Press.* "Infamy," screamed the paper. The Republic, it exclaimed, has "been betrayed in the house of its friends." As the proceeding progressed, newspapers were channels for threats of violence against doubting Republicans. The unmistakable message in many papers was that a vote for "not guilty" would bring retribution against senators so voting.

The invective did not cease with the conclusion of the trial and the acquittal of the President by one vote. The New York *Tribune* called the verdict "tainted," and impugned the motives of the seven Republicans who had been unwilling to hold Johnson guilty. The Philadelphia *Inquirer* said these senators "had tried, convicted and sentenced themselves" and that for them there could be "no allowances, no clemency." Speaking of Senator Edmund G. Ross, whose vote against conviction had been crucial, a Kansas newspaper cried: "Poor, pitiful, shriviled wretch, with a soul so small that a little pelf would outweigh all things else that dignify or ennoble manhood."[6] Had the *Inquirer* and other papers gotten their way, a President would have been convicted on preposterously prejudicial grounds and the United States would have been plunged into perhaps the most cataclysmic political crisis of its history.

Decades of Journalistic Change

By 1869 the press was not so preoccupied with alleged plots of assassination, treason, and presidential scheming. Ordinary homicide again found a place on the front pages that year as a result of the shooting of the famous war correspondent, A. D. Richardson, by Daniel McFarland, whose wife had recently divorced him and was accepting the attentions of Richardson. As Richardson lay wounded in the hospital, his marriage to Mrs. McFarland was presided over by the Rev. Henry Ward Beecher. The bridegroom later died. During the trial of McFarland, his ex-wife's signed story appeared on the front page of the *Tribune,* the paper in which Richardson had won his fame.

THE PRESS AND CORRUPTION

In the prevalent corruption of the post-Civil War era newspapers played both a noble and an ignoble role. By robbing New York City of some $200 million, the Tammany machine headed by William Marcy Tweed set a record for graft. The Tweed Ring laid out great sums of hush money to newspapers, much of it in payments on fat advertising contracts. So extensive was this largesse that a contemporary writer remarked that there were eighty-nine papers on the payroll of the Ring, "of which twenty-seven so depended on this plunder for subsistence that when the Ring was broken they gasped and died." While many of the kept papers were weeklies owned by Tammany politicians, some were dailies. A labor paper called the *Star,* the *Evening Express,* the old *Commercial Advertiser,* and the Albany *Evening Journal* were Ring voices.

Though the New York *Evening Post* and the *Tribune* attacked Tammany in a lackluster manner, the *Times* beginning in 1870 won a place of honor in journalism by turning the attack into a crusade. After the *Sun* had declined to make use of incriminating records when they became available to it, the *Times* in 1871 laid bare the scandal. By analyzing city finances and presenting on its front page documented evidence of millions of dollars in graft, the *Times* goaded law enforcement officials into action. At one point *Times* publisher George Jones had spurned an offer of five million dollars not to print the records, remarking as he did so: "I don't think the devil will ever make a higher bid for me. My answer still stands." As a result of the exposé, Boss Tweed was tried, convicted, and sent to prison in a proceeding that probably would not have taken place if the *Times* had not persisted.[7]

VARIETY IN CRIME FARE

Political corruption, however, was not the most important item in the crime fare offered by the press. Beginning in 1866 newspapers told of the depredations of the James and Younger gangs as they robbed and murdered in a series of attacks on banks and trains throughout the central states. (Later—in the 1890's—the outlaw activities of the Dalton gang were also to get lively attention from the press.) The 1874 kidnapping of Charley Ross, never solved, was another big crime story of the period. In 1875 the trial of the Rev. Henry Ward Beecher, after accusations of adultery against him by Theodore Tilton, was one of the most sensational domestic scandal cases in American history. Beecher was acquitted.[8]

CRIME IN THE WORLD

Joseph Pulitzer's rejuvenation in 1883 of his newly acquired New York *World* marked the beginning of another fresh era in journalism comparable to the stir which accompanied James Gordon Bennett's entry into the penny press field in the 1830's. Bringing in a new managing editor and new reporters, Pulitzer encouraged them to scour the city for "human-interest" news, including scandal and gossip. By the clever use of the headline as a device for enticing readers, Pulitzer greatly increased the drawing potential of crime news.

The *World's* circulation shot up, and other papers imitated its gossip-crime play. In New York, the *Herald* and the *Sun* readily adopted the new sensational style, for which they already had predilections anyway. The *Tribune* and the *Times* were also affected. Across the country the Cincinnati *Enquirer,* the Chicago *Times,* and the San Francisco *Examiner* capitalized on the lurid treatment of crime. When he heard criticism of the press for its emphasis on such news, Charles A. Dana of the New York *Sun* once remarked: "I have always felt that whatever the Divine Providence permitted to occur I was not too proud to report." In Chicago, Melville E. Stone of the *Daily News* employed the newspaper detective technique to gain exciting, exclusive news. On one occasion he followed an absconding bank president, suspected of embezzling one million dollars, to Canada. After trailing the man to England, he lost him. He again picked up the trail by following an associate of the banker to England where, after threatening the second man, he was able to trace the suspected embezzler to Germany and confront him.[9]

SPEED IN SERVICING CRIME STORIES

During the latter part of the nineteenth century mechanical improvements in newspaper production were making it possible for publishers to get their product to more readers and to get it there more quickly. Linotype machines did away with the necessity for the laborious setting of type by hand. Flatbed presses were superseded by far faster rotary presses. Printing from single revolving type cylinders gave way to printing from multiple stereotyped plates. The installation of folding and cutting mechanisms made it possible for presses to perform a series of functions in one operation. Compared to a speed of 2,000 impressions an hour in the 1830's, presses by the beginning of the twentieth century were able to deliver 144,000 papers an hour.[10] All of these mechanical improvements helped to broaden and quicken the impact of crime news on the public and presumably to hasten and intensify the public pressure on justice.

CONTINENTAL REACH FOR CRIME

The transmission of news by telegraph had begun in the late 1840's and had been greatly expanded during the Civil War. The opening of the Atlantic cable in 1866 made rapid overseas transmission of news possible. The press could now reach across the ocean for crime sensations. When a mysterious assailant called Jack the Ripper murdered and mutilated some twenty women in London in 1888, the crimes were quickly and vividly reported in United States papers.[11] In 1889 the trial in England of Mrs. Florence Maybrick for the poisoning of her husband became an international news story, and cabled accounts were sensationally played in the New York *World* and other papers. In the same year, the Chicago *Herald* carried illustrated accounts of the murder trial which followed the killing of Dr. P. H. Cronin, the Irish Nationalist leader.[12] Using increasingly efficient techniques for the rapid printing and distribution of news, American newspapers by the end of the nineteenth century were able quickly to convey choice criminal cases from the United States and Europe to a reading public that could become in effect an unofficial national jury.

ECONOMICS IN THE JUDGMENT OF CRIME

The events associated with the 1886 Haymarket riots in Chicago highlighted the diverging points of view between the big metropolitan dailies and the small papers published by anarchists and other radicals. The radical sheets advocated violence against the affluent, and the Chicago *Tribune* urged violence against striking laborers. In 1886 a mass meeting of laborers had been called in Chicago. It was to be addressed by two anarchists, Albert Parsons, editor of the *Alarm,* and August Spies, of the *Arbeiter-Zeitung*. Three days before the meeting the Chicago *Mail* trumpeted editorially that the two speakers didn't have "an honest aim nor an honorable end in view," and continued: "Mark them for today. Keep them in view. Hold them personally responsible for any trouble that occurs. Make an example of them if trouble does occur." At the subsequent meeting in Haymarket Square a dynamite bomb exploded, killing seven Chicago policemen and wounding more than sixty persons, including policemen and other members of the crowd. After the explosion many papers throughout the country printed bloodthirsty editorials calling for the execution of labor leaders and anarchists.[13] Spies, Parsons, and others were charged with conspiracy to murder. A reporter for the Chicago *Times* contradicted the story of one prosecution witness. But his report had no effect. Spies, Parsons, and a number of codefendants were convicted in a notoriously unfair trial which was highly inflamed by popular passion. The Chicago *Tribune* cheered the verdict. After Governor John Peter Altgeld pardoned those defendants who had not been executed, he was condemned by the New York *Sun* and other newspapers.[14]

In 1891 a crowd of Hungarian workmen at a steel plant in Braddock, Pennsylvania, rioted over working conditions. During the melee Michael Quinn, a furnace boss, was beaten and later died. The Pittsburgh *Press* declared editorially: "Had the Hungarian laborers not raised the disturbance Quinn would most likely be alive today. This surely establishes the responsibility for his death, no matter who may have been the individual that struck the fatal blow." Andrew Toth, a recent Hungarian immigrant, was indicted and convicted. Long afterward it was shown that Toth had been mistakenly identified. He was released after twenty years in prison. (In fairness to editors at that time, it should be noted that they joined in urging the legislature to make reparation to Toth for his wrongful conviction.)[15]

FIRST ELECTROCUTION

New York in 1891 was the first state to electrocute a man for murder. Though this event went unreported, a change in the law the next year permitted newspapermen to be present as witnesses of an execution, and six reporters, including Arthur Brisbane of the New York *World* and Charles Edward Russell of the New York *Herald,* wrote the first news stories of a legal electrocution.[16] With the introduction of the electric chair, the public had a new instrument for vicariously visiting its rage upon malefactors, and the press had a gruesome subject for appealing to extraordinary public curiosity.

UNCERTAINTY WAS INTOLERABLE

As with so many criminal cases today, the press in the nineteenth century could not tolerate uncertainty. A failure to prosecute and to convict somebody was unacceptable even when evidence as to the identity of the criminal seemed insufficient or unreliable.

The Lizzie Borden Case

Among the mysterious cases that aroused editorial demands for answers during this era was a bloody slaying in New England involving questions of wealth and filial devotion. On a hot August morning in 1892, wealthy Andrew Jackson Borden and his wife, Abbie, were murdered by an ax-wielding assailant in their home in Fall River, Massachusetts. Though the authorities had meager positive evidence to go on, they added up suspicious circumstances and charged the dead couple's daughter, Lizzie, with the murder. The case became a national mystery story. When Lizzie went on trial in 1893, newspapers, including the Fall River *Globe* and the Boston *Globe,* joined in pointing the finger of guilt. The Fall River *News* maintained a record of greater fairness than its rival in the same city.[17] Despite the jury's acquittal of the defendant, the public continued to harbor notions of guilt, and Lizzie became a dark figure of legend, which the press no doubt had a part in building.

HEARST AS HOMICIDE HOUND

The year 1895 marked the pyrotechnic entry of William Randolph Hearst into the New York newspaper field with his acquisition of the *Morning Journal.* He had already proved himself on the West Coast as a master of what was then called the New Journalism. Using the San Francisco *Examiner,* which his father had put under his management in 1887, young Hearst, then twenty-four, began experimenting with the techniques he was to try successfully in New York. In the New York *Journal* he used copious illustrations and emphasized crime, scandal, and disasters. Meanwhile, in the same year that Hearst made his New York journalistic debut, his home base in San Francisco was the scene of a historic case of trial by newspaper. William Durrant, a church librarian, was tried and convicted of the murder of Blanche Lamont, whose naked body was found in the belfry tower of the church. The press was excoriated by a judge for its role in the case, but the conviction was affirmed.[18]

As the *Journal* continued its bid for supremacy in New York, Hearst in 1897 became a self-appointed agent for detecting criminals. The "Guldensuppe mystery" provided one of the first occasions for the *Journal's* enterprise. The discovery in the East River of the headless, armless, legless torso of a man, wrapped in oilcloth, made the first horror story in a series. Succeeding installments were built on the finding at various places on the East Side of one dismembered part of the corpse after another, each wrapped in oilcloth. By offering a $1,000 bonus to the reporter who identified the body, Hearst succeeded in producing another exciting installment in the series. He then had color prints made of the oilcloth pattern and sent thirty men out to find where the material had been bought and who bought it. By such procedures, two suspects—a former mistress of Guldensuppe and her new lover—were charged and convicted. Hearst later claimed that *Journal* reporters made up "a detective force at least as efficient as that maintained at public expense" by New York "or any other city." [19]

In the same year that Hearst was pumping out stories on the "Guldensuppe mystery" in New York, Chicago was the scene of another sensationally covered murder, that of Mrs. Luetgert, wife of a sausage manufacturer. In this case the husband was accused of killing his mate, cutting up her body, placing it in the vats of his plant and boiling it in a potash solution.

While Hearst was engaging in his peculiar brand of vigilantism, one of his men was exhibiting an enlightened view of crime and punishment. In an editorial for the Hearst newspapers, Arthur Brisbane wrote:

> Do criminals viciously and voluntarily arise among us, eager to lead hunted lives, eager to be jailed at intervals, eager to crawl in the dark, dodge policemen, work in stripes and die in shame? Hardly. . . .
>
> The boy . . . plays on the tenement staircase—cuffed off the staircase.
>
> He plays ball in the street—cuffed, if caught by the policeman. . . .
>
> He tries for work.
>
> "What do you know?"
>
> "I don't know anything; nobody ever taught me."
>
> . . .
>
> *"What's the charge, officer?"*
>
> "Attempted burglary; pleads guilty."
>
> "Three years in prison, since it is his first offence."
>
> In prison he gets an education. They teach him how to be a

good burglar and not get caught. Patiently the State boards him, and educates him to be a first-rate criminal.[20]

Opening of the Twentieth Century

The enlightened Brisbane editorial might be taken as a symbolic beginning of the modern era in journalism. But in actuality it did not mark a change in press treatment of crime. If there was an abstract expression of understanding in the Hearst editorial columns of the conditions that produced criminals, the news columns did little to promote calm deliberation and fair play when the investigation of crimes was under way.

YELLOW JOURNALISM

In 1896, Hearst's New York *Journal* and Pulitzer's *World* launched the style that became known as yellow journalism. Employing the familiar formula of crime news, scandal, and gossip, the yellow journalists topped their stories with scare heads in large black or red type, spiced them with faked pictures and interviews, and added superficial articles and other trivia. Papers in Boston, Cincinnati, St. Louis, Denver, and San Francisco followed the yellow style.

After Governor William Goebel of Kentucky was assassinated in 1900, the New York *Journal* carried the following quatrain:

> The bullet that pierced Goebel's breast
> Can not be found in all the West;
> Good reason, it is speeding here
> To stretch McKinley on his bier.

A little later another editorial barb was aimed at McKinley, a frequent Hearst target: "If bad institutions and bad men can be got rid of only by killing, then killing must be done." After President McKinley was shot, his assassin was reported to have had in his possession a copy of the *Journal* containing an attack on the President. Public outrage flared against Hearst.

Two other publishers who came close to outdoing Hearst in yellow journalism were Fred G. Bonfils and Harry H. Tammen of the Denver *Post.* Having bought the *Post* shortly after Hearst took over the New York *Journal,* Bonfils and Tammen tried in the Denver paper their own variations of the garish tricks employed by Hearst. A *Post* sob-sister called Polly Pry reported a story about a man accused of killing and eating his companion on a gold-hunting expedition. An attorney engaged to get a parole for the prisoner invaded the publishers' red-painted office (known in Denver as "The Bucket of Blood") and shot both of the partners. They lived to continue their red headline crusades.[21]

HEADLINE CASES—1906–1926

The Harry Thaw Case

In 1904–1905 the murder trial of Nan Patterson in New York received extensive attention. But in 1906 it was a slaying growing out of a lovers' triangle that gave the press the most sensational murder story up to that point in the new century. Harry K. Thaw, young heir to Pittsburgh steel millions, shot and killed famous New York architect Stanford White, because of White's alleged seduction of actress Evelyn Nesbit. As the case progressed through the trial of Thaw in 1907, it became one of the biggest crime stories in the history of American journalism.[22] A newspaper poll indicated that the public thought Thaw was justified, with a tally of the results showing 5,119 respondents voting "not guilty" and 2,054 voting "guilty."

Even the New York *Times,* which ordinarily devoted a minimum of space to run-of-the-mill crime news, gave extensive coverage to the shooting, which had occurred on the roof of Madison Square Garden, and to the subsequent trial. Adolph Ochs of the *Times* was chided by his friend, W. Moberly Bell of *The Times* of London, who pointed out that conservative British papers did not print so much crime detail that the crown would have difficulty in finding unbiased jurors when cases came to trial. Ochs' reply was that in this case broad coverage was justified on the ground that White was a noted architect and Thaw a representative of one of Pittsburgh's leading families. Therefore, he said, they were both unusual subjects for "sociological documents." This observation, of course, evaded Bell's point on prejudice.

The Charles Becker Case

A few years later (in 1912) the New York press had the chance to report a case of indisputable social significance when Herman Rosenthal, a West Side gambling house owner, was shot to death by four gunmen in front of a Times Square hotel. The murder brought into headlines a story of grafting politicians and policemen and their ties to the underworld. Two hours before he was cut down, Rosenthal had given the district attorney a statement about his dealing with Police Lieutenant Charles Becker, the head of the vice squad and a man who was close to Tammany Hall leaders. With ramifications of the case extending from City Hall to the state capitol, the story filled the front pages of New York dailies. Becker was brought to trial for complicity in the murder and convicted largely on the testimony of gamblers and ex-convicts who were identified as his accomplices. Four hoodlums were also convicted, and the five died in the electric chair for the crime.[23] To the end Becker proclaimed his innocence in connection with Rosenthal's death. While acknowledging that "a very strong argument" could be made in favor of the defendant because of the character of his accusers, the state Court of Appeals said the jury's verdict was conclusive. At least one lawyer-critic has blamed newspapers for what he considered to be the wrongful conviction of Becker.[24] Whether he was right or not, the point remains that the imposition of the death penalty (in the Becker case, as in others) eliminates a source of evidence, destroys all chance of correcting an injustice that may have been caused by the courts or the press, and implies a confidence in the infallibility of human institutions which experience does not warrant.

The Leo Frank Case

One of the most notorious cases in the annals of justice and of journalism grew out of the murder in Atlanta in 1913 of a 14-year-old girl named Mary Phagan. Leo M. Frank, twenty-nine, a pencil factory manager and a new resident of Atlanta, was charged with the crime. Before the case came to trial, local newspapers had fanned community prejudice against Frank. Tom Watson's magazine, the *Jeffersonian,* exclaimed: ". . . our little girl—ours by the Eternal God! has been pursued to a hideous death and bloody grave by this filthy, perverted Jew of New York." As the month-long trial progressed, public passions mounted higher. Courtroom crowds jeered, laughed, and applauded. Spectators jostled against jurors. The Atlanta *Journal* said a verdict of acquittal would cause a riot "such as would shock the country and cause Atlanta's streets to run with innocent blood." Frank was found guilty by a jury and sentenced to be hanged. Despite the evidence of mob pressure, appeals to higher courts, including the U.S. Supreme Court, proved fruitless. And Georgia Governor John H. Slaton was driven out of office after he commuted Frank's sentence to life imprisonment.[25]

On the night of August 16, 1915, a band of men dragged Frank from a prison hospital in Milledgeville, Georgia, drove him 125 miles to the scene of the crime and hanged him from a tree. The New York *Times* sent Charles Willis Thompson, one of its ablest reporters, to investigate the lynching. In a series of penetrating articles, he reported the facts, delved into the lynchers' motives, and explored the regional viewpoint, treating the case as objectively as possible. Meanwhile, the *Times* editorially denounced the gross miscarriage of justice brought about by the action of the mob. Thompson's series was a precursor to later journalistic exposés that were to portray the prejudice of Southern justice and help set the stage for reform in the next generation.

The Mooney-Billings Case

The year 1916 was one of rising public tension over possible United States involvement in World War I and on the West Coast an air of intense hostility between industry and labor prevailed. The West was then largely nonunion and most of the big utilities were militantly antiunion. Labor exhibited an equal militancy in behalf of its cause. During the summer of 1916, two union men, Thomas J. Mooney and Warren K. Billings, were trying to organize a strike of streetcar workers in San Francisco.

With the summer temperature high and human tempers soaring on more than one issue, the San Francisco Chamber of Commerce made plans for a Preparedness Day parade on July 16. Civic and business organizations supported the idea. Unions passed resolutions condemning it. But the parade was staged. As crowds watched at the corner of Market and Stewart Streets, there was an explosion of a crude homemade bomb that had been left in a suitcase on the pavement. Ten persons were killed and forty injured.

Five days later, Mooney and Billings were arrested. Numerous witnesses identified them as having been at the scene. Some said they had seen the two men place the suitcase where it exploded. The prisoners stoutly maintained they were somewhere else. The two were nevertheless put on trial a few months later, and both were convicted. Mooney was sentenced to death and Billings to life imprisonment.

The press was actively involved in the case on both sides. One of the first newspapermen to join a crusade for fair treatment of Mooney and Billings was Fremont Older, editor of the San Francisco *Bulletin*. On April 12, 1917, Older launched the fight in an article under a giant *Bulletin* headline declaring: "Fickert Framed the Mooney Case!" Fickert had been the prosecutor. The *Bulletin* published letters discrediting the veracity of Frank C. Oxnam, a major prosecution witness, and reporting the procurement of perjured testimony and the coaching of witnesses. Older's campaign set off a furious backlash from those who felt they had a stake in the conviction. The editor was cursed as a dangerous "red" and a defender of murderers. Ordered by his publishing superiors to stop the fight, Older resigned from the *Bulletin* and was invited by Hearst to come to the San Francisco *Call* and bring the Mooney case with him.[26]

But at the time when press exposure of injustice was most needed, the San Francisco newspapers were baying for blood along with the prosecution. A Mediation Commission, which was appointed by President Wilson in 1918 to inquire into the circumstances attending Mooney's conviction, reported that an "attitude of passion was stimulated by all the arts of modern journalism. It is not surprising then that Billings and Mooney were tried in an impregnating atmosphere of guilt." As a result of the Wilson intercession, the Governor of California commuted Mooney's sentence to life imprisonment.

Later the national Wickersham Commission on Law Observance and Enforcement presented detailed documentation of the prejudiced performance of the San Francisco press in alliance with the prosecution. In its conclusions on the case, the Wickersham report said:

> Immediately after the arrests of the defendants there commenced a deliberate attempt to arouse public prejudice against them, by a series of almost daily interviews given to the press by prosecuting officials. . . .
>
> The prejudice against the defendants, stimulated by newspaper publicity, was further appealed to at the trials by unfair and intemperate arguments to the jury in the opening and closing statements of the prosecuting attorneys.
>
> After the trials, the disclosures casting doubt on the justice of the convictions were minimized, and every attempt made to defeat the liberation of the defendants, by a campaign of misrepresentation and propaganda carried on by the officials who had prosecuted them.[27]

Meanwhile, newspapers across the country and some in other countries had taken up the campaign of justice for Mooney and Billings. The Baltimore *Evening Sun* chided the California Supreme Court for not granting relief for the defendants. William Allen White declared Mooney innocent and said his conviction was "a disgrace to American justice." The Scripps-Howard papers criticized the handling of the case. The Toronto *Star* and the Manchester *Guardian* attacked California justice. The New York *Evening World* said: "It is . . . American justice that is in prison."[28]

Despite the journalistic assaults, the defendants remained behind bars. When the *New Republic* showed sympathy for Mooney and Billings, the editor of a Colfax, California, newspaper responded:

> We may as well be candid and kindergartenish with you. . . . It is quite beside the point whether Mooney and Billings are guilty

> of the particular crime with which they were charged and convicted. The question is rather: Are Mooney and Billings the sort of people we want to run at large? We have decided this in the negative and have locked them up. We intend to keep them there.[29]

This editorial judgment turned out to be a literal reflection of the attitude of California officials. For twenty-three years Mooney and Billings remained in prison. In 1939 Governor Culbert L. Olson pardoned Mooney and commuted Billings' life sentence to the time served. Mooney died in 1942. In 1961 Billings, then sixty-eight, was given a pardon by Governor Edmund G. Brown. The press at that time reported the old story of a miscarriage of justice, but the irresponsible role of the papers of an earlier day was all but forgotten.

The Debs Case

The year after Tom Mooney and Warren Billings went to prison, another case with radical political overtones was to create a national sensation. As in the Mooney-Billings case, the press at the time when its influence counted most was on the side of the prosecution. On June 16, 1918, Eugene V. Debs, well-known Socialist and labor leader, was in Canton, Ohio, to address a state Socialist convention. Before going to the meeting he stopped at the Stark County Workhouse to visit three Cleveland Socialists who had been convicted and imprisoned under the Espionage Act for their antiwar stand. The Socialist Party in 1917 had issued a manifesto denouncing United States participation in the war. When Debs mounted the platform in Canton he reiterated the party's historic stand in opposition to all capitalistic wars. He praised the Russian Bolsheviki. He criticized what he considered to be the unfair treatment of Socialists under the Espionage Act, referring to the three jailed comrades he had visited, and adding: "I would rather a thousand times be a free soul in jail than a sycophant or coward on the streets."

Debs attacked what he conceived to be a double standard in the enforcement of the Espionage Act, a standard under which Socialists were penalized for saying things which politically powerful individuals could say and get away with. Alluding to the ten-year penitentiary sentence for Rose Pastor Stokes, he asked what it was she had said to invite such punishment. He continued:

> . . . She said that a government could not at the same time, serve profiteers and the victims of profiteers. Is it not true? Certainly it is and no one can successfully dispute it. Roosevelt said a thousand times more in the very same paper, the *Kansas City Star*.

In the same speech Debs also condemned Prussian militarism and declared that Socialists had consistently opposed the Kaiser. He said nothing about enlistment. But he had said enough to set off a storm of journalistic lightning.[30] The Chicago *Tribune* headline on the speech blazed:

DEBS WAKES UP
HOWLING AT WAR:
U.S. MAY GET HIM

On June 19 the Cleveland *Press* exclaimed:

> Debs is doing more to aid the Hun Kaiser than all the pro-German Germans in America. He is of greater assistance to the Boches in France than are the Turks, Bulgarians and the Austrians. His Canton speech, even now being spread broadcast through all Germany and all German trenches, will kill more American soldiers than all German submarines that hunt the American transport ships.

The *Press* didn't explain how Debs's words could have such killing power. In Debs's home town, the Terre Haute *Tribune* reported after the speech that "Terre Haute's noted radical is suspected by the United States government of being in a plan with the Trotsky group in Russia to spread Bolshevism in this country." [31]

Debs was indicted under the Espionage Act and charged, in connection with the Canton speech, with willfully obstructing the enlistment service. The New York *World*, showing no sympathy, declared that the Bill of Rights did not protect what Debs had done and added that "Justice belligerent and in peril" is "always sterner than Justice tranquil and secure." [32] But there were publications which recognized Debs for his humanity, sincerity, and courage, and in a few quarters his right to free speech was defended.

After the U.S. Supreme Court had upheld Debs's conviction, and the accompanying ten-year prison sentence, the Cleveland *Plain Dealer* observed:

> Debs's voice is now stilled as it should have been stilled long ago. Doctrines such as he has been pleased to preach are not to be tolerated. The question of free speech is in no wise involved. It is a question of national safety.[33]

The New York *Times* was more charitable. It commented: "Unlike nearly all the rest of his fellow-believers, who are lions on the platform and mice in the court, he did not . . . seek loopholes. He had the courage of his convictions. He challenged the law and the challenge has been met."

The Case of the "Wobblies"

By 1919 the war was over and Americans became concerned with the problems of a peacetime economy. Anxiety over reputed radicals was mounting. Among these groups, the Industrial Workers of the World was labeled one of the most extreme. As early as 1912 an editorial in the San Diego *Tribune* had suggested the wrath stirred by the IWW. "Hanging is too good for them," the *Tribune* exclaimed. ". . . they are the waste material of creation and should be drained off into the sewer of oblivion, there to rot in cold obstruction like any other excrement."

During 1917–1919 members of the IWW—or the "Wobblies," as they were called—were involved in a series of lumber strikes in the Pacific Northwest. As a result, there was bad blood between the IWW and the lumber manufacturers, some of whom were prominent in the American Legion. In 1918 an IWW hall in Centralia, Washington, had been demolished. On Armistice Day, 1919, the American Legion staged a parade in Centralia. As the Legionnaires halted in front of the IWW headquarters, three of them were killed by gunfire from the building and a fourth was killed in the ensuing melee.

The facts of the event were never established with certainty. The Legionnaires claimed the attack was unprovoked. The IWW members asserted that the firing started only when several of the Legionnaires stormed the hall with the intent of wrecking it. In any event, eleven of the Wobblies and an attorney for the Centralia IWW were accused of complicity in the murder of the paraders. On the same day as the shooting, one of the accused, an IWW member, was taken from jail by a mob and lynched. The subsequent trial of the remaining accused was one of the most publicized of the century up to that time. Most newspapers were hostile to the defendants, seven of whom were convicted of second-degree murder in a seven-week proceeding. Sentenced to twenty-five to forty years in the Washington State Penitentiary, six of the prisoners were released by executive action by 1939. The seventh died behind bars.[34] Journalistic treatment of the Wobblies' cases (like the Mooney-Billings case and the later Sacco-Vanzetti case) exemplified the role of much of the press in implicitly backing justice according to class, with members of a less-favored class being entitled to less lenient treatment.

The Sacco-Vanzetti Case

Many of the most publicized criminal cases of the war period and its immediate aftermath seem to have had political ramifications. Still another such case arose out of the holdup and murder of a shoe factory paymaster and his guard at South Braintree, Massachusetts, on April 15, 1920. Nicola Sacco and Bartolomeo Vanzetti, immigrant Italian anarchists, were arrested and charged with the crime. At their trial in Dedham, Massachusetts, in 1921, the atmosphere of prejudice and the acceptance of highly questionable evidence suggested that the two men were being prosecuted more for their political and economic beliefs than for the robbery and murder in South Braintree. Judge Webster Thayer clearly showed his bias against the defendants. Most of the press was hostile to the accused.

When the jury's guilty verdict came, however, it set off a determined six-year effort to correct what many believed to be a gross miscarriage of American justice. The case attracted world-wide attention and protest. Communists exploited it for their own purposes. In an editorial in 1921, the New York *Times* condemned

Communist agitation in connection with the case and spoke of two justly convicted criminals. Two months later the *Times* praised the denial of a motion for a new trial. The *Times* had a great deal of journalistic company in its antagonistic attitude, including the Boston *Transcript,* the Boston *Herald* and most other Massachusetts papers.

But there were important papers which condemned the unfair handling of the case, among them the St. Louis *Post-Dispatch,* the New York *World,* and in Massachusetts, the Springfield *Republican*. In 1926 the Boston *Herald*—until then a defender of the guilty verdict—reversed its own judgment and urged, in an editorial that later won a Pulitzer Prize, a new trial and an impartial review of the whole case. After the publication in 1927 of the defensive report of the Lowell Committee, appointed by the Massachusetts governor to make an inquiry, a number of newspapers took issue with the findings. Besides the New York *World,* the *Post-Dispatch,* and the Springfield *Republican,* the critics included the Baltimore *Sun,* the New York *Telegram,* and the Norfolk *Virginian-Pilot*. At that point, however, a great number of newspapers took the view that all that could be done to satisfy the processes of justice had been done. The New York *Times,* the Philadelphia *Inquirer,* and others, including the Boston *Herald,* were prepared to accept the Lowell report as a vindication of the conscience of the nation.[35] Sacco and Vanzetti went to the electric chair at Charlestown prison on August 22, 1927.

The Ward Case

While the Sacco-Vanzetti case was working its way through the courts, the press had been puffing several other cases into sensationally headlined stories. New York newspapers had a field day in 1923 with the trial of well-to-do Walter S. Ward for the shooting of Clarence Peters. Among the headlines designed to tempt the reader were:

GREAT WARD KILLING MYSTERY
THE TANNED SPHINX
WARD CALMLY CONFRONTS KIN OF HIS VICTIM
TO HEAR OF "LOVE NEST" [36]

The Leopold-Loeb Case

In 1924 Chicago was the scene of one of the most bizarre crime stories of the century because it involved such seemingly unlikely characters and such an improbable plot. After 14-year-old Bobby Franks disappeared, there was nothing improbable in his wealthy family's receipt of a letter saying the boy had been kidnapped and demanding a $10,000 ransom. But when Nathan F. Leopold, Jr., nineteen, and Richard A. Loeb, eighteen, youths from two other wealthy families were arrested in connection with Bobby's kidnapping and subsequent murder, the case seemed odd indeed. It became still more strange when the two brilliant youths confessed that they had committed the crime purely for the thrill and adventure to be derived from their acts.

The case was given instantaneous newspaper attention and was examined from every conceivable angle to satisfy worldwide public curiosity as to what fate would be meted out to the young murderers. When the two defendants pleaded guilty, the task of Judge John R. Caverly was to hear evidence as to the aggravation and mitigation of the offense and thus to determine the extent of the punishment. Clarence Darrow was engaged as one of the defense lawyers.

Newspapers not only jumped into the preliminary investigation but also prepared to give the case saturation coverage when the trial opened on July 21. A few days before the scheduled opening, the Chicago *Tribune* offered to broadcast the proceedings over its radio station and asked for the opinion of the public through a poll. In a satirical response the Chicago *Evening American* suggested that the White Sox baseball park be used as an open air courtroom. When the public voted 6,569 to 4,169 against the proposed broadcast, the *Tribune* dropped the idea.[37]

Before the appointed day the judge had received requests for special passes for more than twice as many people as the 300-seat courtroom could accommodate. Deciding that everybody had to be seated, Judge Caverly issued 200 cards of admission to official participants and to reporters. With crowds outside clamoring for admission, the remaining 100 seats became available on a first-come-first-served basis. There being no jury, the box normally used for that purpose was occupied by special correspondents from big newspapers across the country. Other out-of-town reporters were wedged into what space they could find close to the bench. Rows of bench seats on the right of the judge's bench were set aside for local press representatives, and on the other side of the rail were still other zones for correspondents.

Newspapers published pictures showing the defendants smiling in court and stories giving their responses to interviews in their cells. Pressed by a reporter to say whether he was sorry for what he had done, Leopold replied:

> As far as being remorseful, I can't see it. Life is what we make it, and I appear to have made mine what it is today. That's my look-out and nobody's else.

Coming upon Loeb reading newspapers, the same reporter asked him why he appeared to be having a good time in court. His answer was:

> I sit in the courtroom and watch the play as it progresses. When the crowd laughs, I laugh. When it is time to be serious, I am that way. I am a spectator, you know, and like to feel myself as one.

The Leopold-Loeb trial went on for thirty days, with extensive testimony as to the abnormal mental condition of the defendants being introduced and with Clarence Darrow making a long and eloquent plea for mercy and against capital punishment—an address during which he complained of the wild stories that had been published. When it was all over, the judge sentenced the young men to life in the penitentiary. Loeb was killed in a prison fight in 1936. Leopold was paroled in 1958 after commendable work in prison in such roles as a volunteer subject for medical experiments. In 1961 a Chicago crime reporter, looking back on fifty-two years in his job, called the Leopold-Loeb case the most thrilling crime story of his career. In more ways than one the press, like the defendants, had been looking only for thrills.

The Scopes Case

During the summer of 1925 national attention focused on the little town of Dayton, Tennessee. On July 10 John Thomas Scopes, a young high school teacher, was to be brought to trial in a test case for violating Tennessee's law forbidding the teaching of biological evolution. Some time before the opening day the town was crowded with newspapermen. H. L. Mencken was on hand to represent the Baltimore *Sun*. Public interest in the case was accentuated not only by the controversial issue but also by the presence on the prosecution side of the famed orator and religious fundamentalist, William Jennings Bryan; the defense side had Clarence Darrow, agnostic and political liberal.

As the so-called monkey trial began, more than 100 reporters representing big newspapers and the press associations were among those crowded into the hot little courtroom. The case went on the front pages of newspapers throughout the country. And, in addition, radio reports from Dayton gave home listeners a chance to absorb something of the event via this new medium of communication. On July 21 the Louisville *Courier-Journal* conveyed the atmosphere of the occasion with a headline announcing:

3,000 AT
APE TRIAL
GET THRILL

In the twelve days of the big show in Dayton, some two million words were filed for telegraphic transmission. Despite the obvious sympathy of the press for the defendant and the ridiculing of the prosecution, Scopes was convicted. Few expected any other outcome, since Scopes had indeed ignored the law. When his bail pending appeal was set at $500, the Baltimore *Sun* acted as bondsman. Scopes's fine was soon set aside by the Tennessee Supreme Court on a technicality,[38] but Tennessee was stuck with its evolution law, despite the campaigning of the press.

The Hall-Mills Case

For sheer manufactured sensationalism, few cases in the chronicles of American crime can equal a 1926 trial which resulted from a newspaper circulation war. Hearst's New York tabloid, the *Daily Mirror*—striving to overtake Joe Patterson's *Daily News*—headlined what it claimed to be important new evidence in the four-year-old murder of a little-known clergyman and one of his choir singers. In 1922 the body of an Episcopal minister, the Rev. Edward Wheeler Hall, had been found lying under a crab apple tree on a farm outside New Brunswick, New Jersey. Beside it lay the body of Mrs. Eleanor Mills, a soprano in his church choir. Both had been shot; the singer's throat was slashed, and love letters between Mrs. Mills and the married minister were strewn around. No indictments had been brought in at the time.

But in the spring of 1926 managing editor Philip Payne of the *Mirror* sent newshounds to sniff over the Hall-Mills murder trail. In July the *Mirror* broke a story under a headline which screamed: "Hall-Mills Murder Mystery Bared." As a result of pressure brought by the Hearst paper, New Jersey authorities indicted Mrs. Hall and her two brothers, Henry Stevens and Willie Stevens.

The trial which followed in Somerville, New Jersey, became a journalistic circus. On hand to cover it were some 200 reporters, including Mrs. Henry Stevens, wife of one of the defendants; James Mills, husband of one victim (signing stories but not writing them); Billy Sunday, the revivalist; Rita Weiman, playwright; Dorothy Dix, adviser of the lovelorn; Louella Parsons, movie reviewer; and Damon Runyon, sports writer. The Chicago *Tribune* had nineteen on the job and the Hearst papers, seventeen. A giant telegraph switchboard with 120 positions was set up in the basement of the courthouse to transmit wire reports. The telephone company put on eight additional operators to help in transmitting oral reports.

In the first eleven days of the trial an estimated five million words were put on the wires. During twenty days three New York dailies devoted 12,541 column-inches to news of the proceedings and an additional 4,332 column-inches to pictures. In this period even the New York *Times* gave 4,893 column-inches to news and 290 column-inches to pictures. As the trial progressed, the *Daily Mirror* openly championed the side of the prosecution and the New York *Evening Graphic* took the side of the defendants.[39] The prosecution's case rested chiefly on the claims of an avowed eye witness, a woman hog farmer named Jane Gibson. She was brought from a Jersey City hospital to the trial and was photographed testifying from a bed in the courtroom. After the "Pig

Woman's" own mother called her an incorrigible liar in court, it was not surprising that the case collapsed and the defendants were acquitted. The defendants later sued the *Mirror* for $1,500,000 damages and reputedly settled for $50,000.[40]

WAR OF THE TABLOIDS

The unseemly reportorial scramble over the Hall-Mills case represented one of numerous battles in the war of the tabloids then going on. Among the combatants were Patterson's *Daily News,* Hearst's *Daily Mirror,* and Bernard MacFadden's *Daily Graphic.* Presenting crime and sex in short, snappy style, liberally illustrated with pictures, the tabloids vied for the attention of bored subway riders. When an art editor named Albert Snyder was done to death by his wife, Ruth, and her lover, Judd Gray, the tabloids' hunt for horrors was on again. The New York *Daily News* brought this case to a shocking climax with a full-page photograph of Ruth Snyder dying in the electric chair in January 1928. It had been surreptitiously taken with a camera attached to the ankle of a *Daily News* man on the scene. One sordid sensation followed another, with the contestants sinking lower and lower into what Oswald Garrison Villard called "gutter journalism." After the *Daily Graphic* published what it called a "composograph"—in this instance, a faked picture of a bedroom scene—even the *Daily News* protested that, if this sort of thing went much further, readers would be "drenched in obscenity." The *Graphic* was commonly referred to as the "Daily Porno-Graphic." [41]

GANGSTERS AND THE PRESS

The gangster era of the 1920's and 1930's represented a law enforcement crisis in which the press met its responsibilities for the most part with tub thumping or indifference. The latter part of the 1920's saw the infamous conflict between rival gangsters for the control of Chicago's bootlegging and vice rackets. The worst phase of the gangster era began in 1924 with the murder of Dion O'Banion, leader of the North Side gang. Gang wars continued for nearly five years, bringing about more than 215 unsolved murders and reaching a climax in 1929 with the so-called St. Valentine's

Day Massacre, in which one group of thugs machine gunned to death seven hoodlums of a rival gang as they stood disarmed in a North Side garage. The masterminding of the Massacre was laid to Al Capone by George (Bugs) Moran, the leader of the murdered mobsters who had himself escaped the trap by mere chance. But no one was ever brought to trial for the crime. Some thirty gang murders occurred the next year.

Despite the failure of law enforcement authorities in bringing the St. Valentine's Day killers to justice, the Massacre nevertheless marked the beginning of the end of the Chicago gangsters' unbridled power. The machine gun killing shocked voters into demanding action against what the Chicago *Tribune* called "the universal threat to society." The New York *Times* referred to "the unholy alliance between politics and crime" in Chicago. In 1931 Al Capone was convicted for evasion of $215,000 in federal income taxes due on his profits from an empire which, according to government investigators, grossed $105,000,000 a year.

HEADLINE CRIMES IN THE THIRTIES

The Scottsboro Boys Case

In the same year that the Chicago trial of Al Capone was hitting the headlines, a far different kind of case was opening in northern Alabama. It was there in 1931 that nine Negro youths were arrested and charged with the rape of two white women. The treatment of the case of the Scottsboro boys by the Jackson County (Alabama) *Sentinel* was in keeping with the temper of the white community. The paper's headline proclaimed: "Splendid Capture by Deputy and Posse." A *Sentinel* news story reported that all of the Negroes were "positively identified" by the girls and one white boy who was held prisoner "while nine black fiends committed the revolting crime." Reaching a quick judgment of its own, the *Sentinel* said "that the evidence against the negroes is so conclusive as to be almost perfect." Therefore, the paper advised, "that the ends of justice could best be served by legal process."

Following the course favored by the *Sentinel,* an Alabama court found the nine defendants guilty and sentenced them to death.

By this time, however, the case of the Scottsboro boys had attracted nationwide publicity and interest. Many outsiders were convinced that the evidence did not support the conclusions of Alabama justice. The case was appealed to the United States Supreme Court and, in 1932 and again in 1935, the high tribunal reversed Alabama convictions of the rape defendants, first, because they were denied adequate counsel and, second, because Negroes were systematically excluded from the jury lists.

The second trial of the Scottsboro boys in 1933 was given blanket coverage by the New York *Times*. That paper's correspondent, Ray Daniell, was threatened with lynching, but he continued day after day for weeks with his reporting of the story, giving both sides impartially. Eventually four of the defendants were acquitted. Coverage of the national press may well have had an impact on provincial Southern justice. The convicted men were finally free by 1947.[42]

Dillinger Case and Others

In the early 1930's a number of specialists in kidnapping and robbery received national notoriety through the press, with top billing perhaps going to John Dillinger during the climactic fourteen months of his career in bank holdups and murders. Dillinger's days of renown ended on July 22, 1934, when he was shot down by FBI agents outside a Chicago theater. But there were others of almost equal fame during this period—such colorfully named performers as "Baby Face" Nelson, "Pretty Boy" Floyd, and "Machine Gun" Kelly—to say nothing of such big city racketeers as "Legs" Diamond, Dutch Shultz, Lepke Buchalter, and Arnold Rothstein, whose misdeeds provided editors with the stuff for dramatic headlines.

The Lindbergh Case

March 1, 1932, marked the occurrence of one of the most tragic and, in a sense, the most mercilessly publicized crimes of the century. On that date the 19-month-old son of Colonel and Mrs. Charles A. Lindbergh was kidnapped from his bedroom in the home of the world-famous flyer near Hopewell, New Jersey. As word got out, reporters began converging on the Lindbergh estate in the Sourland mountains in order to write a shocking new chapter in the life of a man America idolized. Associated Press and United Press representatives were soon on the scene, as well as reporters for the New York *Times* and other individual papers. The final edition of the *Times* on March 2 had thirteen columns on the kidnapping, including photographs and a description of the missing child.

The Lindbergh kidnapping story stayed on front pages for weeks, with many reports of expected discoveries but no baby. Reporters scurried over the countryside tracking down leads which turned out to be false. The New York *Times* alone assigned a large staff to cover developments.[43] Finally, on May 12, 1932, the baby's body was found in a shallow grave not far from the flyer's home. The Associated Press scored something of a triumph by being first to spread across the country the news of the finding of the body. At this turn of events, the outpouring of curiosity seekers was such that peanut and popcorn venders flocked to the scene.

The next dramatic chapter in the Lindbergh kidnapping story didn't begin until September 19, 1934, when Bruno Richard Hauptmann was arrested. At the opening of his trial at Flemington, New Jersey, on January 2, 1935, 150 reporters were squeezed into the area set aside for the press, a gallery at the rear of the courtroom. As soon as the questioning of veniremen (members of a group from which prospective jurors are picked) began, the role of the press became evident. Charles Walton, a prospective juror, was asked: "Have you read the Winchell column in the *Daily Mirror*?" Winchell, in newspaper columns and radio broadcasts, had flatly stated his opinion that Hauptmann was guilty of kidnapping and murder. Walton said he had not read the column but had heard an occasional broadcast. He added that he had not necessarily formed an opinion. The defense did not challenge him. So the questioning went, resulting in a relatively speedy selection of jurors, though one reporter had expressed the view that it might be necessary to draft all of the citizens of the county in order to find twelve persons who hadn't discussed the Hauptmann case or formed an opinion concerning it.

During its course, the Hauptmann trial at times drew from 700 representatives of the press to Flemington. Some 200 newspapers sent their own correspondents, and each of the major press services maintained a full staff at the scene. More than eleven million words were sent over the wires during the trial, about a million of them the first day.[44]

Since the judge had ordered the courtroom doors locked at the time the verdict was due and had barred all mechanical contrivances from the room, competing reporters had set up various signaling systems, including hidden transmitters, in order to get the news of the jury's decision out quickly. There was a mad scramble among press representatives to be first with the words of guilt or innocence, life or death. The Associated Press, in a confusion of signals, sent out a wrong bulletin before the verdict was really announced. Some papers printed it in extra editions. Wire service offices were flooded with demands from impatient editors across the country.[45]

The verdict—when it finally came at 10:45 P.M. on February 13, 1935—was the big story of the day, even in the New York *Times,* which had kept a wire open to Flemington in order to get the news for the early morning edition. Hauptmann was found guilty of murder in the first degree and sentenced to die in the electric chair some time during the week of March 18.[46]

World War II

The Lindbergh kidnapping produced so many excesses in journalistic treatment that for several years afterward any other criminal cases would seem anticlimactic. With the opening of World War II, the front pages of American newspapers were given over far less to the drama of the police station and the courtroom. During the war there was the mass sedition trial in Washington. While this 7½-month courtroom battle attracted a good deal of press attention at first, a declining interest was signified by a decrease in press representatives from fifteen to two or three by the end of the third month.[47]

The Postwar Period

CRIME MAKES HEADLINES AGAIN

After the war, crime was soon to come to the fore again as a source of news sensations. But so many studies have been devoted to press treatment of criminal cases in the past two decades that a summary of the 1945–1965 period should be sufficient for the last part of this historical survey of crime in the United States press. A brief reference to some of the major cases should suggest the nature of front page crime fare.

In Chicago in 1946 the trial of 17-year-old William Heirens for several murders produced in the papers of that city stories that eclipsed news of national events (see Chapter 6).

That same year national headlines were devoted to the trial in Lawrenceburg, Tennessee, of twenty-five Negroes charged with attempted murder as a result of their efforts to defend themselves against white mob action growing out of a racial incident in nearby Columbia, Tennessee. The performance of some papers in covering the affair reflected no credit on their service to justice, but there were also cases of exemplary coverage of the events.

Another case involving interracial friction occurred in 1947 with the trial and acquittal in Greenville, South Carolina, of a group of white taxi drivers for the lynch murder of a Negro named Willie Earle. Again national attention was directed to the matter of justice for the Negro in Southern courts. Again the performance of the press was uneven. After the event, however, *The New Yorker* published an account of the case by Rebecca West which portrayed truly remarkable insights into the various facets of criminal justice.

The Hiss Case

It was in 1948 that the dramatic case of Alger Hiss preempted the front pages of the nation's press. In the year that passed before the case finally reached the courtroom, every conceivable facet was examined in the news media. Looking at the case from different angles, observers found news treatment that prejudiced the position of one side or the other long before Hiss was tried for perjury in 1949 for denying that he had passed secret State Department documents to Whittaker Chambers (see Chapter 5). Despite the earlier virtual conviction of Hiss by the House Committee on Un-American Activities and news media partial to its position, the trial ended in a hung jury. But in the interim before the second trial, as A. J. Liebling put it, "the section of the press that had failed to obtain the political result it wanted took its case outside the courtroom." Hiss was convicted in a second trial. While some segments of the press emphasized only the sensational aspects and the political implications of the Hiss case, a few reporters won respect for their dependable coverage—among them, John Chabot Smith of the New York *Herald Tribune,* Thomas O'Neill of the Baltimore *Sun,* and Alistair Cook of the Manchester *Guardian.*[48]

A MISCELLANY OF CRIME STORIES

With the arrest in 1948 of Caryl Chessman as the Los Angeles "red light bandit," the press got its first scent of a case that was to be in and out of the headlines for twelve years until it ended with Chessman's death in the gas chamber in 1960.

In the same period a considerable variety of cases were claiming more than ordinary attention from the news media. A case of extraordinary political significance came in 1949 with the conspiracy trial in New York of eleven leaders of the American Communist Party. Testimony in the trial ran to about five million words and filled 15,000 pages of transcript. Covering the trial for the New York *Times,* Russell Porter spent 158 days in the courtroom and wrote a total of 175,000 words.

A marathon case of a far different kind began its course the next year with the $2,700,000 holdup of Brinks, Inc., in Boston. Not until six years after that were the accused robbers brought to trial.

Still another case with national political ramifications opened in 1951 with the espionage trial of Julius and Ethel Rosenberg, Morton Sobell, and David Greenglass. The next year the government began its much publicized but vain effort to try Owen Lattimore for perjury.

The Sheppard Case

In 1954 *Time* magazine called the Sheppard case in Cleveland "the biggest murder story in the U.S. press since the trial of Bruno

Hauptmann." Speaking of the prosecution of Dr. Samuel Sheppard for the murder of his wife, the managing editor of the Los Angeles *Herald-Express* said, with apparent relish, "It's been a long time since there's been a murder trial this good." As the trial opened, sixty-five out-of-town newsmen were on hand. Both the Hearst and Scripps-Howard chains sent in teams of reporters to cover the event. Three-quarters of the nation's leading newspapers, including papers in New York, Boston, Chicago, and Los Angeles, gave the story front page play. In Los Angeles, 2,500 miles away, it got a position equal to or just below the smog issue, then a matter of great local concern. The saturation coverage continued even though many newsmen raised the question of whether the case was worth it.[49]

LYNCHERS, SPIES, RACKETEERS, AND LOVERS

The nation's eyes were focused on Mississippi in 1955 for the trial of the accused white lynchers of a 14-year-old Negro boy named Emmett Till. After a five-day proceeding, widely and intensively reported, the two defendants were acquitted by an all-white, all-male jury. Though the Mississippi press for the most part reflected local white bias, other news media performed creditably on the whole.[50]

A case with international implications opened in 1957 in Brooklyn with the arrest on spy charges of Colonel Rudolf Abel, alleged Soviet secret agent. His trial and conviction came in October of 1957. When the United States Supreme Court in 1960 came within one vote of reversing Abel's conviction, newspaper editorials across the country denounced the four dissenting justices for being willing to give the defendant the benefit of the Fourth Amendment's protection against evidence seized without a warrant. The case wound up in a dramatic and unexpected denouement in 1962 with the exchange of Abel for Francis Gary Powers, an American pilot convicted of spying in the Soviet Union.

Reputed leaders of the nation's underworld came into the headlines in 1959 as twenty alleged racketeers were tried in New York for conspiracy to conceal the purpose of a so-called underworld convention near Apalachin, New York.

The Finch-Tregoff Case

The crime sensation of 1960 was the first trial of Dr. Bernard Finch and Carole Tregoff, his mistress, for the murder of Dr. Finch's wife, Barbara. This event in Los Angeles evoked another frenzy of press activity. Daily attendance in the press section of the courtroom ran to about fifty, with the number running as high as seventy-five on days when the testimony was expected to be particularly interesting. The United Press International staffed the trial with two and sometimes three men daily, and in addition hired a crew of court reporters to take down and transcribe the witness stand questions and answers. On what were considered better days, UPI transmitted up to 2,000 words of question and answer testimony on both the A.M. and P.M. cycles of its wire. The Associated Press staffed the trial with two reporters and a crew of five stenographers and transcribers to take down questions and answers. It sent out as much as a thousand words of transcript daily.[51]

HEADLINE CRIMES OF THE EARLY SIXTIES

One of the major crime dramas of 1961 was the New York trial on espionage charges of Dr. Robert Soblen, with his brother as the chief prosecution witness. After being convicted and losing an appeal, the defendant fled the country and finally, to avoid return to the United States, took an overdose of barbiturates and died a lingering death.

Another front page attraction in 1961 was the murder trial in Fort Pierce, Florida, of Joseph A. Peel, Jr., a former city judge. This highly publicized case, with its ironic twist for justice, ended with the conviction of the defendant jurist for plotting the killing of Circuit Judge C. E. Chillingworth.

Prominent play was given to the federal indictment in 1963 of Roy M. Cohn, businessman and former aide to U.S. Senator Joseph R. McCarthy. At his subsequent trial in New York on charges of perjury and conspiracy to obstruct justice, Cohn was acquitted.

THE KENNEDY ASSASSINATION

The crime of the century, eclipsing all others in the intensity, the prejudice, and the extent of the coverage it evoked was, of course, the assassination of President John F. Kennedy on November 22, 1963. Press disregard for the rights of the accused prompted many well-documented complaints, including that of the Warren Commission—though in the Kennedy case, it must be noted, that the press itself was operating under far greater pressure than it is in ordinary circumstances. The American public—in its anguish, shock, and uncertainty—was demanding information. It would have been justified in asking for more than long-delayed and fragmentary reports on what was going on.[52]

The reporting of the multitudinous aspects of the case went on for many months and included the trial of Jack Ruby in 1964 for the murder of Lee Harvey Oswald, the President's accused assassin.[53]

ANTICLIMAX IN CRIME

In view of the records set in the assassination coverage, anything that came afterwards was bound to be anticlimactic. With the Ruby trial already occupying the front pages, the press nevertheless shifted its attention to the trial in Los Angeles of three defendants for the kidnapping of Frank Sinatra, Jr. They were convicted after a much publicized courtroom drama in which the inflated journalistic attention stemmed from the popularity of the kidnap victim's father.

After a seven-year pursuit by the government and the press, Teamster Union President James R. Hoffa was found guilty in a Chattanooga courtroom in March 1964. The conviction of Hoffa for tampering with a jury in an earlier case came after four previous prosecutions on various charges had failed. A few months later the Teamster Union President was convicted again, this time after a trial in Chicago on charges of fraud and conspiracy in the handling of union pension funds. In contrast to the many trials that have won unusual attention from the press, the proceedings against James R. Hoffa involved matters that directly concerned millions of people.

In the early months of 1965 the criminal cases that made top headlines were the murder of Malcolm X, the former Black Muslim leader, and the arrest of a group of conspirators alleged to be plotting the destruction of such national shrines as the Statue of

Liberty, the Liberty Bell, and the Washington Monument. Meanwhile the press was still concentrating its attention from time to time on developments in crimes connected with the Negro's long struggle for racial justice—the murder of three civil rights workers in Mississippi in 1964 and the murder of others in Alabama in 1965.

This chapter's brief review of newspaper treatment of criminal cases in the United States since the eighteenth century indicates that the conflict of justice and the press is not a new development. It should also suggest to any disinterested student that—despite the opinions of many editors to the contrary—the prejudicing of defendants' rights is not just a matter of an occasional slip on the part of the press. The historical record shows that, as the lure of headlined crime sensations arose, editors often threw the rights of the accused to the winds.

CHAPTER FOUR

THE PRESS AS THE ACCUSED

Historic Quest for a Curb

THOSE WHO HAVE ACCUSED THE PRESS of prejudicing justice have long sought effective ways to deal with offending publications. More than 200 years ago English judges were concerned about out-of-court comment that might hamper the impartiality of the trial. As they searched for methods to curb biased outside statements, one promising approach seemed to be to take advantage of the judicial authority to punish such statements (or other conduct which threatened the fair administration of justice) as contempt of court.

In 1742, relying on a previously established judicial power to punish contemptuous conduct, Lord Chancellor Hardwicke applied the concept to remarks threatening to prejudice a pending case. He declared: "Nothing is more incumbent upon the courts of justice, than to preserve their proceedings from being misrepresented; nor is there anything of more pernicious consequence, than to prejudice the minds of the public against persons concerned as parties, before the case is finally heard."[1] In his decision, Lord Hardwicke initiated and justified the chancery practice of punishment of criminal contempt by summary proceeding, and in so doing incorporated the process in the common law. However, summary punishment for criminal contempt had formerly been used by the Star Chamber up to the time of that court's abolition in 1641. In England, contempt of court action, as a means of preserving discipline necessary for the administration of justice, has actually been traced to the twelfth century.

The case which most influenced the development of the law of contempt in both England and the United States was *The King v. Almon* in 1765. Because of a technicality no judgment in the case was ever rendered. However, Justice John Eardley Wilmot, in his opinion in the matter, expressed a doctrine which was accepted by Sir William Blackstone and, which, through his famous *Commentaries* (published in 1769), found its way into English and American law. Blackstone wrote:

> Some . . . contempts may arise in the face of the court; as by rude and contumelious behavior; by obstinacy, perverseness, or prevarication; by breach of the peace; or any wilful disturbance whatever; others, in the absence of the party; as by disobeying or treating with disrespect the king's writ, or the rules of process of the court; by perverting such writ or process to the purposes of private malice, extortion, or injustice; by speaking or writing contemptuously of the court or judges, acting in their judicial capacity; by printing false accounts (or even true ones, without proper permission) of causes then depending in judgment; and by any thing, in short, that demonstrates a gross want of that regard and respect, which, when once courts of justice are deprived of, their authority (so necessary for the good order of the kingdom) is entirely lost among the people. . . . A power therefore in the supreme courts of justice to suppress such contempts by an immediate attachment of the offender results from the first principles of judicial establishments and must be an inseparable attendant upon every superior tribunal.[2]

Because of the accepted dubious legality in England of publicizing preliminary proceedings before magistrates, not many contempt cases arose there prior to the passage of the 1888 Law of Libel Act. That act provided that "a fair and accurate report in any newspaper of proceedings publicly heard before any court exercising judicial authority shall, if published contemporaneously with such proceedings, be privileged . . ." Once it had permission to publish preliminary reports, the English press was encouraged to broaden its search for dramatic news. In 1902, however, the press ran squarely into a contempt decision for disseminating pretrial news in a criminal case. An enterprising editor had published news items containing matter highly prejudicial to the defendants in a pending case. After the defendants were convicted, both the editor and his reporter were found guilty of obstructing the course of justice and sentenced to six weeks in prison. This decision made clear that even a tendency to pervert justice was subject to contempt action.

Despite this adverse King's Bench ruling, British newspapers by this time decided that they had enough of a stake in criminal news reporting that they were willing to incur risks. For some years every sensational murder case was accompanied by a contempt proceeding, which often ended inconclusively. Finally, in "the Crumbles Murder Case" in 1924, a newspaper went so far as to send "investigators" to the scene and to publish their reports along with interviews with several witnesses who had been warned by the police not to make outside statements. The editor responsible for this performance was fined 1,000 pounds and warned that any similar conduct in the future would bring imprisonment. After this case, English newspapers began to exercise more restraint in the matter of investigation of crimes and the pretrial publication of evidence.

Under English law, there are two classes of contempt: civil and criminal. Civil contempt consists of disobedience of the orders of a court and is a wrong of a private nature. Criminal contempt is any act which hinders the administration of justice. It may take the form of direct contempt, which is an act committed in the presence of the court, or constructive contempt, which consists of acts impeding the administration of justice but committed out of court. In Britain the use of the contempt power by the courts has fairly well eliminated advance prejudicial effects on juries through adverse publicity in the press. When trials are held, they are, of course, public and may be fully reported. (For a further comment on the English contempt rule, see Chapter 8.)

Contempt Power in American Courts

In America, Congress provided in the Judiciary Act of 1789 that the federal courts should have the "power to punish by fine or imprisonment, at . . . [their] discretion . . . all contempts of authority in any cause or hearing before . . . [them]." State judges already had such power. Judges in a number of early American cases handed out contempt convictions for publications that attacked courts or litigants while proceedings were pending, the ground being that the items might prejudice the public mind and possibly jurors who would sit in the trials.

But judges in this period did not always find that the exercise of the contempt power encouraged respect for the courts. In 1828 John P. Shelton, editor of the *Gazette* in the frontier town of Detroit, criticized a court for waste of time. Jailed for contempt, the offending editor became a local hero. His fine was met from contributions by a great number of sympathizers, no one of whom was allowed to pay more than twelve and a half cents. Upon his release, his admirers honored him with a big banquet in the jail courtyard.[3]

In 1830, two convictions for contempt in Pennsylvania and others in New York led to the enactment of state statutes sharply limiting the scope of state judges' disciplinary power over out-of-court conduct.

Meanwhile, a case which was to have an important impact on the contempt power of the federal judiciary was moving toward a climax. In 1826 a lawyer named L. E. Lawless had written an item for a newspaper in which he criticized in detail an opinion by Federal Judge James H. Peck while an appeal from the decision was pending. The judge brought both editor and attorney into court. He then dismissed the editor with a reprimand but sentenced the lawyer to twenty-four hours' imprisonment and a fine, and suspended him from practice for eighteen months on the ground that he had caused a libel against the judge to be published. Lawless complained to his congressman, John Scott, who initiated an impeachment proceeding against Peck. In the 1831 impeachment trial, Peck was defended by William Wirt, who took the position that the judge was following in good faith the firm precedents of the common law as embodied in Wilmot and Blackstone. Peck was acquitted in the Senate by one vote. The very next day the House began work on a bill which, when it became law that year, strictly limited the contempt power of federal judges, providing that it should only extend to misbehavior of persons in the presence of the courts or "so near thereto as to obstruct the administration of justice."

Having observed how the new statute came to be enacted, federal judges were careful to observe its strictures. Many states copied the new federal law. This was an era when more than one judge found himself unpopular after a clash with a newspaper.

During the thirty years after the Peck trial there were very few convictions for indirect or "constructive" contempt of court arising from publications concerning judicial proceedings. Judges relied on other methods to curb press behavior deemed prejudicial.

Postponement of Publication

One means of curbing potentially prejudicial press coverage was tried in Massachusetts as early as 1830. While sitting as a trial judge in the case of John Francis Knapp and several others charged with the murder of Joseph White of Salem, Chief Justice Isaac Parker of the Supreme Judicial Court of Massachusetts simply announced that there was no objection to the publication of the state of the case as it advanced, but that there must be no publication of "the evidence" before the conclusion of the proceedings.[4] Two of the defendants were convicted and hanged; one was acquitted.

Employing a similar method to restrain the press during a sensational case in Pennsylvania, a federal judge in 1842 avoided interference from the 1831 statutory curb on the contempt power. One Alexander Holmes, a sailor, was on trial as a result of his action during a harrowing experience at sea after his ship had struck an iceberg and sunk. In striving to keep the ship's long-boat afloat, Holmes had thrown Frank Askin, one of its shipwrecked occupants, overboard. Praised by some of the survivors and condemned by others, Holmes was eventually charged with manslaughter and brought to trial in the United States Circuit Court for the eastern district of Pennsylvania. Presiding Judge Henry Baldwin ordered the press excluded from the courtroom unless it agreed to suspend publication of a report of the trial until after it was over. Newspaper representatives acceded to the order and the trial proceeded. Holmes was found guilty and sentenced to six months in prison and a $20 fine. The penalty was later remitted.

A similar curb on the press was imposed in 1854 at Elizabethtown, Kentucky, in another case that attracted a great deal of public curiosity. Matthews F. Ward, a member of a prominent family, was being tried for the murder of William H. G. Butler. As the trial opened in the circuit court of Hardin County, reporters were assigned seats inside the bar. But the judge issued an order, to which reporters yielded, forbidding the publication of testimony during the progress of the case on the ground that it would be likely to interfere with a fair and impartial trial. When Defense Attorney Nathaniel Wolfe, a leading member of the bar, called attention to the fact that the Louisville *Courier* had carried an account of several days' testimony despite the court order, there was a flurry of excitement. The *Courier* reporter told the judge that he had informed his paper of the rule. Embarrassed by the breach, he resigned his privileged place behind the bar. On inquiring, the judge discovered that the proprietors of the *Courier* had withheld the regular bundle of papers usually delivered in the town of the trial and that only stray copies had reached there. He therefore decided to take no further action. The trial continued. When it ended with a verdict of not guilty, a public meeting was held to protest the result.

In enforcing a postponement in the publication of trial news, these judges were overlooking the immediate corrective effect on justice that concurrent trial coverage might have. The prompt reporting of trial testimony might, for example, cause a reader with contradictory information to come forward and tell the court about it. If news of the questionable testimony became public only when the trial was over, the knowledgeable reader might reasonably conclude that his volunteering of information might be too late. And he could well be right. Once a proceeding is supposedly closed, the officials responsible for it acquire a kind of vested interest in the result. Any attempt to reopen it may seem like an attack on their conduct and would have to overcome considerable inertia, if not outright opposition. A forced delay in the trial news, therefore, could reduce the value of press coverage at a time when it might be the most significant.

Revival of Contempt Power in the States

Breasting the trend against control of the press by contempt action, the Arkansas Supreme Court in an unusual decision in 1855 upheld the contempt conviction of a newspaper for suggesting that the state high court itself had accepted bribery in a murder case. Despite an Arkansas statute limiting the authority of courts to cite for out-of-court contempt, the high court of the state reasoned that the act did not do away with the inherent power of the court to maintain respect for its judgments.[5]

More than forty years after the Peck case, the United States Supreme Court sustained the federal act which grew out of it. Speaking for the court, Justice Stephen J. Field recognized the power of Congress to restrict the reach of United States judges.[6] In state courts meanwhile, a trend toward the adoption of the Arkansas doctrine had begun, with many tribunals holding that, regardless of legislative enactments, courts had an inherent power to punish for contempt those publications having a "reasonable tendency" to interfere with the orderly administration of justice.

In a 1907 decision in a case originating in Colorado, the United States Supreme Court lent its support to the power of state courts to cite as contemptuous publications which "would tend to obstruct the administration of justice" while a case was pending. Pendency was the essential criterion, according to Justice Holmes, who observed that once the case was closed, courts were subject to the same criticism as other people, but until then they should not be denied the power to prevent interference with the course of justice by "premature statement, argument or intimidation." [7]

Lawyers Show Concern

While the courts during this period were sharpening the contempt power as a weapon to be used against offending publications, lawyers revealed the depths of their feelings by the caustic terms in which they chastised the press. In a book published in 1908, Arthur

Train denounced what he called "the most crying of all present abuses—the domination of the court-room by the press." He continued:

> It is no fiction to say that in many cases the actual trial is conducted in the columns of yellow journals and the defendants acquitted or convicted purely in accordance with an editorial policy. Judges, jurors, and attorneys are caricatured and flouted. There is no evidence, however incompetent, improper, or prejudiced to either side, excluded by the judge in a court of criminal justice, that is not deliberately thrust under the noses of the jury in flaring letters of red or purple the moment they leave the court-room. The judge may charge one way in accordance with the law of the land, while the editor charges the same jury in double-leaded paragraphs with what "unwritten" law may best suit the owner of his conscience or his pen.[8]

Recognizing, however, that lawyers sometimes misbehaved too, the American Bar Association about this same time showed its concern that attorneys should live up to their obligation to support the fair administration of justice. The organization in 1908 adopted its Canons of Professional Ethics, including one which implicitly recognized that lawyers were sometimes accomplices in the transgressions of the press.

Canon 20 declared:

> Newspaper publications by a lawyer as to pending or anticipated litigation may interfere with a fair trial in the Courts and otherwise prejudice the due administration of justice. Generally they are to be condemned. If the extreme circumstances of a particular case justify a statement to the public, it is unprofessional to make it anonymously. An *ex parte* reference to the facts should not go beyond quotation from the records and papers on file in the court; but even in extreme cases it is better to avoid any *ex parte* statement.

Despite the seeming strictness of this rule, it has often been disregarded with impunity. In the case of prosecuting attorneys, it is more honored by the breach than the observance.

Expansion of Federal Contempt Power

As the years went by, protests against the press in United States courts were such as to make the Supreme Court more receptive to an expansive view of the federal contempt power despite the supposedly restrictive legislation of 1831. In 1900 a federal district court in Pennsylvania declared:

> It is greatly to be deplored that a practice of which we see too many examples, should exist, and that persons accused of crime should be put on trial in the columns of the newspapers, and should be declared to be guilty and denounced as criminals before there has been a careful and impartial trial in the proper and lawful tribunal.[9]

By 1918 the reversal of the contempt doctrine supposedly embodied in the 1831 federal statute became complete. After the Toledo, Ohio, city council regulated the fares and restricted the franchise of a streetcar company, the firm sought relief in court. This brought a reaction from the *News-Bee,* which took the popular side of the dispute and opposed the transit company, suggesting in a series of articles that there could be but one decision by the federal judge before whom the case was pending, and that any other would evoke suspicion of the judge's integrity and fairness and would prompt public resistance. The judge cited the paper for contempt, and the resulting conviction was appealed to the United States Supreme Court. That tribunal upheld the lower court and, in interpreting the 1831 act, construed in a causal rather than a geographical sense its authorization of punishment of contemptuous behavior "so near" to the court "as to obstruct the administration of justice."

Speaking for a majority of five, Chief Justice Edward D. White said the act of 1831 "conferred no power not already granted and imposed no limitations not already existing." On the constitutional issue, he declared:

> . . . however complete is the right of the press to state public things and discuss them, that right, as every other right enjoyed in human society, is subject to the restraints which separate right from wrong-doing. . . . Not the influence upon the mind of the

particular judge is the criterion but the reasonable tendency of the acts done to influence or bring about the baleful result is the test.

Under the "reasonable tendency" test, the court left contempt proceedings against the press, regardless of where its offense occurred, largely to the discretion of the trial judge, with the implication that his discretion would not be questioned unless greatly misused. Holmes and Brandeis dissented; two other justices took no part.[10]

Newsmen Show Concern

A few years after this decision editors themselves exhibited an awareness of accusations against the press because of its coverage of crime news. At its first annual meeting in 1923, the American Society of Newspaper Editors approved certain rules of ethics, which were incorporated in what were called Canons of Journalism. Two of the canons—impliedly acknowledging that reforms were needed—applied to news of criminal cases:

6. *Fair Play*—A newspaper should not publish unofficial charges affecting reputation or moral character, without opportunity given to the accused to be heard; right practice demands the giving of such opportunity in all cases of serious accusation outside judicial proceedings.

a. A newspaper should not invade rights of private feelings without sure warrant of public right as distinguished from public curiosity.
b. It is the privilege, as it is the duty, of a newspaper to make prompt and complete correction of its own serious mistakes of fact or opinion, whatever their origin.

7. *Decency*—A newspaper cannot escape conviction of insincerity if, while professing high moral purpose, it supplies incentives to base conduct, such as are to be found in details of crime and vice, publication of which is not demonstrably for the general good. Lacking authority to enforce its canons, the journalism here represented can but express the hope that deliberate pandering to vicious instincts will encounter effective public disapproval or yield to the influence of a preponderant professional condemnation.

The canons also proclaimed the responsibility of the press to the public and exhorted the journalist against using his power "for any selfish or otherwise unworthy purpose" or for the "promotion of any private interest contrary to the general welfare." These provisions were soon put to a test in the case of F. G. Bonfils of the Denver *Post,* who used his position to blackmail Harry Sinclair, the oil tycoon. Bonfils got information that Teapot Dome oil leases were being obtained through government corruption, but he refrained from publishing news of the matter until he saw a chance to reach the wealthy oil lessees, whereupon the *Post* attacked. The lessees were compelled to make a contract by which the *Post* stood to gain $500,000. The attacks suddenly stopped. The episode led to an inquiry by the ASNE's Committee on Ethics, which as a result recommended that Bonfils be expelled from the society. After a fight over the disciplinary power of the organization, Bonfils was allowed to resign.[11]

A PRESS PLEA FOR A LEGAL CURB

Meanwhile, the Canons of Journalism had little noticeable impact on the presentation of crime news. In 1924 the Chicago *Tribune* became so concerned about the excesses of the press in the case of Leopold and Loeb, the two youths charged with the murder of Bobby Franks, that the paper urged a legal remedy. Seeing itself trapped by a necessity to pander to public curiosity about the case, the paper on July 23, 1924, called for a law to restrain itself and its competitors. The *Tribune's* editorial declared:

> Criminal justice in America is now a Roman holiday. The courts are in the Colosseum. The state's attorney's office is an open torture room of human souls. Exposure of the processes of justice, originally a public safeguard has been perverted into a public danger. . . .
>
> The Franks case has been a three months' moral pestilence imposed upon our people before the trial. It is an aggravated instance of what has happened with increasing frequency for two decades since the Thaw trial and before. There is reason for the statement by the chief justice of the United States that the product of our judicial machine is a national disgrace.
>
> The injury to justice is in *publicity before* the trial. Newspaper trials before the case is called have become an abomination. . . . It is mob murder or mob acquittal in all but the overt act. It is mob appeal. Prosecuting attorneys now hasten to the papers with their

> theories and confessions. Defense attorneys do the same. Neither dare do otherwise. Half-wit juries or prejudiced juries are the inevitable result.
>
> The *Tribune* has its share of blame in this. No newspaper can escape it. They have met demand, and in meeting it stimulated public appetite for more. . . .
>
> Papers that refuse to accept this harsh discipline of public demand will die. Many have died. . . .
>
> The slide downhill is inevitable. . . . General reform must be undertaken or none at all. The nation's press must act together.
>
> There is one remedy. Drastic restriction of publicity before the trial must be imposed by law. . . .

The editorial went on, however, to urge the fullest possible reporting of the actual trial, including radio broadcasting of the proceedings in important cases.[12]

THE GUILD'S CODE OF ETHICS

Newspapers did not act together on the *Tribune's* call to action and no general reform was undertaken. A decade later there was a manifestation of high-minded concern over the impact of the press on justice from some of the men who actually reported crime stories. In 1933 the American Newspaper Guild was organized. One evidence of the members' determination to raise the status of their craft was the adoption of a Code of Ethics which included the following provisions:

> 2. That the equality of all men before the law should be observed by the men of the press; that they should not be swayed in news reporting by political, economic, social, racial or religious prejudices, but should be guided only by facts and fairness.
>
> 3. That newspapermen should presume persons accused of crime of being innocent until they are convicted, as is the case under the law, and that news accounts dealing with accused persons should be in such form as not to mislead or prejudice the reading public.

THE CASE THAT SHAMED BOTH BAR AND PRESS

While the Guild was being organized, police were still looking for clues that might provide the solution of the mysterious 1932 kidnapping of the baby son of Charles A. Lindbergh. In the fall of 1934 the break came that was to lead to the nationally publicized trial the next year of Bruno Hauptmann in Flemington, New Jersey. As the case developed, both newsmen and lawyers stooped to the kind of shockingly unseemly behavior which suggested that none of them had ever heard of a code of ethics. The entire Hauptmann proceeding showed that, whatever misconduct the press may be accused of, there are often officers of the law aiding and abetting it. Within a week after Hauptmann's arrest, a New York newspaper carried a headline saying: "Clues Build Iron-Clad Case Against Bruno, Police Claim."

As the trial began in a courtroom with a seating capacity of 260 persons, the constables on duty admitted 275 spectators without passes to the already overcrowded room. Later attorneys for both sides issued subpoenas for favored friends in order to insure the admission of sympathetic spectators. While the serious business of deciding a man's fate was being conducted, some spectators leaned against the walls; others sat on the windows sills, looked over the balcony rails, or peeked through doorways. At times they whooped and guffawed at the most serious testimony, and the jury of eight men and four women on occasion joined in.[13] The judge was obviously not exercising control.

Although photography during the trial had been forbidden, pictures were taken and nothing was done about it. The authorities permitted telegraph lines to be installed in the courthouse itself. This operation necessitated the presence of 100 telegraph men on the premises.

The prosecutor, Attorney General David T. Wilentz, and the chief defense attorney, Edward J. Reilly, conducted their cases before a nationwide "jury" through both newspaper interviews and radio broadcasts. Wilentz at one point told a reporter that he would "wrap the kidnap ladder around Hauptmann's neck." On another occasion he declared in the courtroom: "I am not concerned about what the mob is clamoring for . . . but you can bet your life that if there is a clamor from the people of this country for this man's conviction I have sufficient faith in the American people to know that it is their honest belief . . . that he is a murderer." In making such an appeal to prejudice outside the courtroom as well as inside, Wilentz was obviously using the press to hurt the accused. And yet in failing to report such courtroom remarks, the press would have neglected to convey to the public vital information about the prosecutor and about his method of handling the case. This particular episode illustrates the point that the press may sometimes be unjustifiably accused for reporting the unjustifiable words of subjects in the news. In the Hauptmann case, however, the press and the bar were usually partners in offenses against justice, with the misdeeds of one hardly separable from those of the other.

Defense Counsel Reilly announced to the press that he would name the kidnappers and that they were connected with the Lindbergh household. He ordered stationery for Hauptmann to use in answering his "fan mail," as he put it. The letterhead was printed in red ink and carried a facsimile of the kidnap ladder.

During the course of the trial the press charged Hauptmann, among other things, with having "made senseless denials," and with being "a thing lacking in human characteristics." Even the conservative New York *Times* published much material that, if it were read by jurors, would have made impartial judging of the case difficult.

After the whole sorry performance was over, lawyers, editors, and publishers felt impelled to do something to prevent a repetition. In January 1936 through the initiative of the American Bar Association, an 18-member Special Committee Between the Press, Radio, and Bar was formed. Consisting of six representatives of the Bar Association, seven representatives of the American Newspaper Publishers Association, and five representatives of the American Society of Newspaper Editors, the Special Committee's purpose was to seek agreement upon "standards of publicity of judicial proceedings and methods of obtaining an observance of them, acceptable to the three interests represented." After personal consultation and study, and correspondence among themselves and with members of their respective organizations, the committee members in January 1937 approved a report to be submitted to the American Bar Association. This document observed that "the trial of Bruno Richard Hauptmann . . . exhibited, perhaps, the most spectacular and depressing example of improper publicity and professional misconduct ever presented to the people of the United States in a criminal trial."

Although the committee was unable to arrive at complete unanimity on all phases of its study, its members did agree:

1. that neither prosecuting attorneys nor defense counsel should, during the course of the trial, give newspaper interviews or make radio broadcasts "forecasting the effect of evidence yet to be produced or commenting upon evidence already introduced,"

2. that if local bar associations would "resolutely enforce" the requirements of the code of professional ethics upon lawyers, the "most glaring evils of improper publicity would be overcome,"

3. that "the surreptitious procurement of pictures or sound records is wholly indefensible,"

4. that "no popular referendum ought to be taken during the pendency of the trial,"

5. that "jurors, witnesses, or court officers should not take part in vaudeville performances, or give interviews, or write articles for publication during the progress of the trial."

Finally, the committee recommended that local bar associations appoint continuing committees to work with corresponding committees of the news media to regulate the relations under discussion.[14] (Fifteen years later a survey group of jurists was unable to find a case in which any bar association, following the advice of the 1937 Special Committee report, had ever taken action to discipline a lawyer for indulging in the practices denounced in the aftermath of the Hauptmann trial.)

BAN ON PHOTOGRAPHS—CANON 35

One outgrowth of the inquiry into the Hauptmann trial was the adoption by the American Bar Association in 1937 of Canon 35 of its Canons of Professional Ethics. It said:

> Proceedings in court should be conducted with fitting dignity. The taking of photographs in the court room, during sessions of the court or recesses between sessions, and the broadcasting of court proceedings are calculated to detract from the essential dignity of the proceedings, degrade the court and create misconceptions with respect thereto in the mind of the public and should not be permitted.

Adopted by order of the highest courts of twenty states and generally observed in all of the other states except Colorado and Texas, this rule was to have a wide effect in curbing courtroom photography and broadcasting. (In 1963, after almost ten years of committee studies and conferences devoted to a reexamination of the rule, the American Bar Association House of Delegates voted overwhelmingly to retain Canon 35.)

New Curb on Contempt

During the 1924 Leopold-Loeb trial, the 1935 Hauptmann trial, and others of that period in which there was an attendant furor over trial by newspaper, the courts made little attempt to assert any authority over the press—though for more than two decades after the United States Supreme Court's decision in the 1918 Toledo case, the doctrine of contempt by publication seemed to be firmly rooted in American law. Then in 1941 came the Supreme Court's ruling in *Nye v. United States,* in which the high tribunal effectively overruled the Toledo holding, rejected the "reasonable tendency" test, and once more construed the words "so near thereto" in a geographical sense so that misbehavior must occur in the vicinity of the court for the 1831 act to apply. By its decision, the Supreme Court reversed the petitioners contempt conviction for wrongfully inducing an administrator to dismiss a suit in a federal district court. Though the misconduct which brought on the contempt action in this case involved persuasion or coercion of a litigant rather than a prejudicial publication, the fact that it occurred more than 100 miles from the district court gave the Supreme Court a basis for returning to the geographical rule, which in turn had a bearing on the law respecting contemptuous publications.[15]

Having discarded the "reasonable tendency" test in the Nye decision, the Supreme Court had left the lower federal courts without a criterion for deciding when conduct, found to be within the required physical proximity to the court, constituted contempt. In *Bridges v. California,* decided the same year as the Nye case, the court supplied a standard, though it was not interpreting the federal statute. In that case the high court had before it two contempt actions in a California state court: (1) the conviction of labor leader

Harry Bridges for his publication of a telegram to the Secretary of Labor criticizing the decision of a judge in a case involving a labor dispute and threatening a strike if the decision was enforced, and (2) the conviction of the publisher and editor of the Los Angeles *Times* for the publication of editorials commenting on a pending case in a state court. Both convictions were reversed.

The Supreme Court indicated that "neither 'inherent tendency' nor 'reasonable tendency' [to interfere with justice] is enough to justify a restriction of free expression." Instead, the court prescribed as a test the concept that there must be a "clear and present danger," that "the substantive evil must be extremely serious and the degree of imminence extremely high before utterances can be punished."[16]

Following the Bridges ruling, the Supreme Court, in *Pennekamp v. Florida* (1946), reversed a state court contempt conviction of an editor,[17] and, in *Craig v. Harney* (1947), upset a similar conviction in Texas. In both the Bridges and Craig cases, however, Justice Frankfurter wrote strong dissents opposing the checks imposed on state courts' exercise of the contempt power.[18] Nevertheless, the contempt power has been rendered largely ineffectual as a means of protecting defendants from the effects of prejudicial publicity. Trial courts have in effect been told to turn to other remedies, such as granting motions for change of venue or for postponement of the trial.

Signs of Supreme Court Concern

Guidance for trial courts since the Bridges and Los Angeles *Times* rulings has come in a series of decisions in which the Supreme Court has shown its continuing concern over the prejudicial impact of the press by reversing convictions which appeared to have resulted in part from unfair publicity. In the 1951 Shepherd case the high court upset a Florida rape conviction which followed a great deal of inflammatory news coverage. Though the main ground for reversal was not prejudicial publicity, two of the justices protested against a flagrant form of trial by newspaper. Even before the four suspects had been indicted, an Orlando paper had published a front page three-color cartoon showing four empty electric chairs and demanding, "No Compromise—Supreme Penalty."[19]

In reversing the federal court conviction of Howard R. Marshall for the illegal sale of drugs, the Supreme Court in 1959 put the blame for an unfair trial squarely on Denver newspapers which had published articles reporting prior convictions of the defendant and other prejudicial information which the trial judge would not admit as evidence.[20]

Two years later in the Illinois case of *Irvin v. Dowd,* the Supreme Court set aside a murder conviction which followed a barrage of newspaper headlines, articles, cartoons, and pictures all tending to create a "pattern of deep and bitter prejudice" against the accused.[21] The inflammatory publicity was said to have resulted in 370 out of 430 prospective jurors having an opinion that the defendant was guilty.

In 1963 the Supreme Court upset a Louisiana conviction which came after thousands of people in the community where the trial occurred had seen a televised jail interview in which the defendant, Wilbert Rideau, had admitted to the sheriff a bank robbery and murder for which he had been arrested. Calling the telecast scene a "kangaroo court," the high tribunal ordered a new trial. One of the justices commented that the television "spectacle" had made the subsequent judicial proceeding but "a hollow formality." [22]

Again addressing itself to the effect of news media on justice, the highest court, in a 5-to-4 decision in 1965, threw out the swindling conviction of financier Billie Sol Estes, because his trial had been televised over his objection. The Supreme Court majority ruled that Texas, in permitting the televising of the preliminary hearing and subsequent trial, had failed to grant the defendant due process as guaranteed by the Fourteenth Amendment. Speaking for the court, Justice Tom Clark said that the presence of cameras might have a prejudicial effect on jurors, would affect witnesses' testimony because of their knowledge that they were on camera, might influence the judge's decisions, would subject the defendant to a form of mental, if not physical, harassment. But the court left to the future the question of whether the Constitution bars television from every criminal trial or only from those receiving such notoriety as the Estes case.[23]

The decision which climaxed a quarter of a century of Supreme

Court concern over the troublesome clash between freedom of the press and the rights of due process came in the case of Dr. Samuel Sheppard in June 1966 (as this book went to press). In any history of prejudiced justice, the case of Dr. Sheppard will stand as one of the most flagrant examples of irresponsible behavior by the news media, as well as by the judiciary and law enforcement officials.

By reversing the 1954 conviction of Dr. Sheppard, the high court left little doubt as to its attitude toward the misconduct on all sides in the handling of the case. Writing for an 8-to-1 majority in *Sheppard v. Maxwell* (34 U.S. Law Week 4451), Justice Clark criticized the pervasive pretrial and trial publicity which implied Sheppard's guilt; condemned law enforcement officials for making prejudicial statements to the press and for relaying purported incriminating evidence which was, however, never introduced at the trial; blamed the trial judge for permitting newsmen to create in the courtroom a carnival atmosphere that interfered with an orderly and fair trial and for failing to curb prejudicial comments by persons who could have been disciplined by the court. Besides advising judges to take steps to insure a judicial atmosphere in the courtroom, Justice Clark also urged them to postpone trials or to transfer them to other localities when justice is threatened by one-sided press coverage. The Clark opinion (see Appendix C) contains the most explicit high court guidance to date on how lower courts should seek to preserve due process from interference by the press. The remedies advanced by the Supreme Court in the Sheppard case parallel in many respects the recommendations in this book (see Chapter 9).

Action by the Press and Bar

Meanwhile further discussion and action was generated by the Supreme Court's indication of increasing concern over the press threat to due process. In Oregon, after considerable debate, a joint statement of principles on the handling of news of criminal prosecutions was signed by members of the bar and the press during the latter part of 1962.[24] In Massachusetts in 1963 members of the bench and bar cooperated with the press in drawing up a code of conduct for the guidance of members of their respective professions on the release of information in criminal cases. Twenty-six of the state's forty daily newspapers adopted the statement at the time. In the spring of 1965 members of the Kentucky Press Association approved a statement of principles on Free Press and Fair Trial. About the same time CBS news on its own initiative put out a set of guidelines for its reporting of pretrial and trial procedures.

But the performance of the press after the assassination of President John F. Kennedy in 1963 did more than anything else since the Hauptmann trial to prompt new efforts to find a remedy for publicity prejudicial to justice. Not long after the momentous events in Dallas, the American Civil Liberties Union issued a statement in which it said that:

> From the moment of his arrest until his murder two days later, [Lee Harvey] Oswald was tried and convicted many times over in the newspapers, on the radio, and over television by the public statements of the Dallas law enforcement officials. Time and again high-ranking police and prosecution officials stated their complete satisfaction that Oswald was the assassin. As their investigation uncovered one piece of evidence after another, the results were broadcast to the public.

Considering the cumulative effect of these public pronouncements, the ACLU asked whether in the state or nation twelve citizens could be found who had not formed a fixed opinion that Oswald was guilty.

Executive and Judicial Actions

Much the same conclusion was announced by the Warren Commission when its report was published at the end of September 1964. After criticizing both District Attorney Henry Wade and Dallas Police Chief Jesse E. Curry for their statements to the press on the evidence against Oswald, the commission expressed the opinion that the news policy pursued by the authorities would have harmed both the prosecution and the defense—the prosecution, because the defense would have made use of the misinformation released to cast doubt on the reliability of the state's case; the defense, because of the intense public feeling aroused against the accused. The commission saw a serious interference with Oswald's "constitutional right to a trial by an impartial jury." Although the group placed primary blame on law enforcement officials for failing to check the flow of undigested evidence to the public, it said part of the responsibility for "the unfortunate circumstances following the President's death" should be borne by the news media. Chiding newsmen for their lack of self-discipline and their role in creating the general disorder in the Police and Courts Building, the commission observed that the "promulgation of a code of professional conduct governing representatives of all news media would be welcome evidence that the press had profited by the lesson of Dallas." The experience in Dallas during November 22–24, it went on, "is a dramatic affirmation of the need for steps to bring about a proper balance between the right of the public to be kept informed and the right of the individual to a fair and impartial trial." [25]

Following the report by the Warren Commission, the evidence of widespread reaction to its comments was obvious.

In November 1964 the New Jersey Supreme Court—invoking its disciplinary powers over the bar under the Canons of Professional Ethics (Canon 20 in particular)—ordered a ban on potentially prejudicial statements by prosecutors and defense lawyers. The court also said that similar statements by policemen should be dealt with by superior officers as conduct unbecoming a policeman.[26] The next month the Philadelphia Bar Association proposed a set of guidelines for the release of news in criminal cases, but its recommendations were immediately condemned not only by most of the press in Pennsylvania but also by the chief justice and an associate justice of the state Supreme Court.

After carefully considering the problem, the United States Justice Department in April 1965 announced a set of guidelines governing the information which its personnel would and would not supply in federal criminal proceedings. While ordinary facts about an arrested person would be given out, the new policy would discourage the release of an accused's prior record and would bar the release of confessions and other evidence such as polygraph and fingerprint information.

In the months following the Warren Commission report, inquiries on how best to deal with the issues of a free press and fair trial were launched by the American Bar Association, the American Newspaper Publishers Association, the American Society of Newspaper Editors, and various other organizations and institutions.

PART TWO

Justice as a Product of Public Communication

CHAPTER FIVE

THE RANGE OF PRESS INFLUENCE

Breadth and Variety of Press Effects

The potentially prejudicial impact of the press on due process is usually presented as a peculiar problem occurring during the pretrial processing of a case. But the administration of justice cannot be so neatly compartmentalized. Nor is the role of the press in the pretrial stage so extraordinarily different that this phase of its relationship to justice requires exceptionally concentrated attention. The points at which prejudice may be brought to bear and at which injustice may occur still run through the gamut of the law enforcement process even though rules and procedures to insure fairness have been incorporated into every stage.

The law strives to reduce the chances for error by prescribing certain procedures for the handling of criminal cases. A citizen may not be forced to answer questions in connection with a crime. Before making an arrest, the police must have probable cause to believe their suspect committed the offense and, under some conditions, they must have an arrest warrant and a search warrant, if they intend to make a search. The arrested person must be given an opportunity to communicate with family or friends and an attorney. After the arrest, the suspect must be taken without undue delay before a committing magistrate, charged with a specific offense, and given a preliminary hearing. The accused must then be indicted, but only if the grand jury—or in some states, the prosecuting attorney—has found probable cause to believe him guilty. After being charged, the accused must be brought to trial within a reasonable time. These various preliminary procedures are intended to insure that only those persons against whom there is convincing proof are brought into court.

To make the trial itself a reliable mechanism for arriving at the truth, complex rules have been devised as to who may testify, what questions may be asked by attorneys, and what evidence is admissible as relevant. The defendant may not be forced to testify against himself, nor may testimony be required of persons having a confidential relationship to the defendant. To give effect to the law's presumption of innocence, the state must prove its case "beyond a reasonable doubt."

To correct errors in the trial, the convicted defendant may ask the judge for a new trial or may take his case to the appellate courts. Or—following another avenue—he may seek probation, a pardon, or a commutation of his sentence or, in time, a parole. These proceedings may provide a means to expose mistakes or to offset the harshness of the law.

Despite all the rules, the precautions, and the procedures prescribed to promote fairness, injustices still occur. They occur as a result of excessive zeal, errors, or outright dishonesty on the part of law enforcement officials. Despite notions to the contrary entertained by some lawyers, legal processes do not represent something akin to a laboratory search for truth. Neither the investigation of the crime, nor the preliminary procedures, nor even the trial itself, can be walled off from extraneous influences.

When a crime occurs, the people who first arrive at the scene do not customarily behave like careful scientists following the trail of truth by the precise methods of the laboratory. They are more often like hunters trampling the ground in the wake of baying hounds. The quarry may be escaping. The public wants somebody in custody, or at least it wants information. As the case is processed, the public by one means or another exerts an impact at every stage of the proceedings. The behavior of all of the responsible officials is shaped by the pressures of their respective constituencies as well as by their own emotional reactions. Thus the search for the truth about a crime is hardly one that is conducted under controlled conditions anywhere along the way.

The press is simply one of the channels through which the influence of the public is brought to bear on the law enforcement process. The influence of the public is also exerted through the presence of onlookers at various stages, through letters and communications to officials, and, indirectly, through the vote. Of all the various means of communication at work, none has a more legitimate place than the press. The press is actually intended as one of the many checks against injustice. It is not an intruder in the process of justice, as is sometimes suggested. Its effect, however, is good or bad, depending on the quality of its performance. By its participation in the search for truth, the press may either check error or dishonesty at some point along the way or it may compound it. Newspapers concern themselves with every stage of the law enforcement process—from investigation to the final court decision or the final administrative action. Newspaper reporting and comment can have an effect on the various preliminary steps, on the trial itself, and on posttrial proceedings. The press may deter or prompt arrest. It may influence the magistrate to hold or release the suspect. It may prod the grand jury to indict or not indict. It may have a bearing on whether there is a conviction or an acquittal in the trial. It may even sway the decisions of appellate judges or of governors or administrative boards. From the beginning, the press exerts its influence not simply by relaying to the public facts and opinions provided by law enforcement officials but by communicating its own findings and opinions on the case. Apart from its overt activity, the press exerts a considerable influence merely by existing, since officials are conscious of the possibility that at some point a reporter may be asking for an explanation of their conduct.

In gauging the breadth of press effect on criminal justice, consideration must be given the fact that newspapers devote comprehensive attention to only a fraction of the cases that arise. Clifton Daniel, managing editor of the New York *Times,* pointed out that 11,724 felonies were committed in New York City in January 1965, and that, of this number, only forty-one were mentioned in the

New York *Daily News,* a paper which gives more attention to crime than any other daily in the city. But while the impact of the press is most direct on specific cases covered, there is good reason to believe that the sway of the newspaper extends considerably beyond the cases actually appearing in its columns. From the cases that are covered, officials become conditioned to expect demands for stern treatment from the press, and in the unpublicized cases they probably act accordingly.

Studies of the effects of mass communication indicate that the tendency of much crime reporting would be to stimulate a public attitude of hostility toward criminal suspects (see Chapter 6). It therefore becomes important to consider how community attitudes created by crime reporting may be brought to bear on law enforcement officials, judges, and attorneys, and thus have a bearing on the outcome of a case as it goes through the various stages.

A clue to the effect on individual functionaries of a highly charged public attitude was suggested by a psychology experiment conducted at Harvard University some years ago. Participants in the experiment, which concerned the effect of social pressures on opinions, were shown lines of varying lengths drawn on cardboard and were asked to say which lines were longer. Most of the subjects, however, were instructed beforehand to lie deliberately as to what they observed. Thus a minority of the members were put in the position of being contradicted by the majority on matters in which they were at first sure they were right. After the experiment was repeated a number of times, those participants who were outvoted began to swing to the majority position. The author of the experiment observed that, whereas in ordinary circumstances individuals matching lines will make mistakes less than one per cent of the time, the minority observers in this case swung under group pressure to acceptance of the misleading majority's wrong judgments in 36.8 per cent of the selections.[1]

If we may transfer inferences from this experiment to the field of criminal justice, do they not suggest that officials—who must retain public approbation to remain in office—may yield to the often harsh popular judgments in cases they are processing? Undoubtedly there are instances in which the character of the official and the circumstances of the case will lead the agent of justice to stick by his convictions regardless of public clamor. If, however, the facts seem to lend themselves to a decision either way, the choice is likely to be one which does not invite ostracism or loss of job.

The police and prosecutor can exercise a great deal of undefined and unreviewable discretion in invoking or not invoking the criminal process. A keen student of crime news observed years ago that most of the decisions in criminal cases are made by the exercise of administrative discretion on the part of the prosecutor or the judge, or both, and that their decisions are quite likely to be colored by what they think the public has been led to believe through newspaper accounts.[2] Since only about 8 per cent of criminal cases are ultimately disposed of by jury trials, the impact of the press on those involved in the non-jury law enforcement process is extremely important.

From all this it should be apparent that an examination of justice and the press cannot be confined to what happens in the courtroom, or to what newspapermen alone do, or to what law enforcement officials alone do. Social pressure is an unavoidable and intangible factor. The press and law enforcement machinery interact on each other, and justice depends on how well both sides perform under pressure. In the law enforcement process the press theoretically serves as the eyes and ears and the conscience of the public. If it serves well, it can promote justice. It also has the capacity to cause injustice.

The Pretrial Stage

THE PRESS AND GENERAL COMMUNITY ATTITUDES

A newspaper may on occasion be the first agent of the community to enter a case. It may fan community hostility against a potential defendant even before there is any case against him. This is particularly true of politically unpopular figures. Certainly the press has stirred public animosity against alleged Communists and Communist sympathizers, regardless of whether they were known to have engaged in illegal activity. All of those reputed Communists or Communist helpers who were tried in the late 1940's and early

1950's stood half condemned before any specific charges were brought against them. The conviction of such defendants as the eleven leaders of the American Communist Party, and of Alger Hiss, William Remington, Judith Coplon, and Julius and Ethel Rosenberg was no doubt aided by the hostile climate toward Communists created by newspapers. By the standards of some readers, this is good, just as by the standards of others the press contribution to public condemnation of the Ku Klux Klan has had a salutary effect when alleged Klansmen were brought to trial. In the 1920's the New York *World,* the St. Louis *Post-Dispatch,* and other papers publicized Klan machinations in the same way that the press in the 1960's has thrown the light of condemnatory publicity upon new manifestations of Klan activity.

In a Detroit case in 1925 the press managed to rouse community hostility against both the Klan and the Klan's intended victims, with justice for a time being held in a balance of conflicting public emotions and the final verdict being shaped by the compelling performance of Clarence Darrow. On July 12, 1925, the Detroit *Free Press* carried a story telling about recent race riots in that city and of a gathering in which some 10,000 people were addressed by a man who—while standing "on a platform illuminated with the red glare of fiery crosses"—advocated a law to compel Negroes to live only in certain quarters of the city. This same story also announced a meeting to be held in a school diagonally across the street from a home recently purchased in a white neighborhood by Dr. Ossian Sweet, a Negro physician. All of the people of the neighborhood were being urged to attend the meeting in "self-defense." [3]

Some weeks later, after Dr. Sweet had moved his family into their new home, a mob surrounded the house. As it surged toward the dwelling, there was gunfire from the besieged building and a white man outside was killed. Feeling ran high. Detroit newspapers carried stories of alleged Negro crimes of the past year. Many unsolved crimes were attributed to Negroes. A spirit of revenge was in the air.

At a subsequent trial of Henry Sweet, a brother of the home-owner, the *Free Press* story of July 12 was read into the record and, according to one observer, had a noticeable effect on the jury. Henry Sweet, with Darrow as defense counsel, was acquitted.[4]

PRESS INVESTIGATION OF WRONGDOING

A newspaper may enter a case by taking the initiative in exposing wrongdoing and in uncovering evidence which brings about the arrest of a suspect. Managing editor Fremont Older of the San Francisco *Bulletin* made that paper an organ in the fight against municipal corruption. He not only gathered evidence but pressed cases in court. Largely as a result of his efforts the mayor of San Francisco was convicted and sentenced to the penitentiary in the early 1900's.

Klan Grand Dragon D. C. Stephenson of Indiana was convicted and sentenced to life imprisonment for murder and rape partly as a result of an exposé by editor Thomas H. Adams of Vincennes, Indiana.[5]

A more modern example of newspaper investigative activity which produced results is that of the Chicago *Daily News* in 1956. In that year the *Daily News* and its Pulitzer Prize-winning reporter, George Thiem, launched an inquiry which eventually brought about the conviction of Illinois State Auditor Orville E. Hodge and others for the theft of more than $2,500,000 in state funds.[6]

When a newspaper conducts its own investigation simultaneously with that of law enforcement officials, the same advantages and disadvantages to justice are present as in the situation in which it launches the inquiry. It may be helpful, as was the St. Louis *Post-Dispatch* in 1922 when its crime reporter, John Rogers, stepped in after local police had failed. Rogers produced evidence of a Ku Klux Klan murder in Louisiana—evidence which led to the conviction of several Klansmen.

During this same era the *Post-Dispatch* played a significant role in a prearrest investigation that was to involve far more powerful figures than Klansmen. For weeks the *Post-Dispatch* was the only paper that assigned a reporter to cover Senator Thomas Walsh's inquiry into suspected fraudulent leasing of Teapot Dome and other naval oil reserves. After the Senate committee thought it had finished its job, Paul Y. Anderson of the *Post-Dispatch* dug up enough additional evidence to keep the group going for three more years. Meanwhile, other papers, including the New York *Times* and the *Tribune* sought to smother the Senate inquiry, claiming Walsh was a character assassin. The Denver *Post,* which first revealed the Teapot Dome scandal, had dropped the campaign suddenly after its publisher, Fred G. Bonfils, received a payoff (see Chapter 4).[7]

Newspaper eagerness to outdo official investigators can, however, have questionable results. In a 1957 San Francisco rape case, a newspaper in that city searched for and found evidence which it thought linked a certain suspect to the crime. This man was later proved to be innocent before there was any move to indict him. But had the purported evidence been believed, it could have had tragic consequences for the suspect (see the Rexinger case in Chapter 6). By uncovering clues which are believed to be pertinent and then, as a result of excessive zeal, urging a follow-up, a newspaper can force an unwarranted prosecution.

Newspaper hounding of law enforcement officials in the Sheppard case in Cleveland in 1954 is an egregious modern example. Largely as a result of press pressure, authorities arrested, tried, and convicted Dr. Sheppard in a proceeding that, upon later close examination, showed many marks of a miscarriage of justice. Vigilantism is as dangerous, if not more dangerous, when practiced by the press as it is when engaged in by others.

GENERAL NEWS OF A CRIME

Apart from their investigative activity, newspapers can be both a help and a hindrance in the solution of crimes through the news they print about the subject. They may help by publishing descriptions of suspects, of material witnesses, of automobiles, and of instruments. Someone in the paper's wide readership may be able to furnish useful leads to the police on the basis of the published information. On the other hand, news stories may sometimes thwart police work. By disseminating detailed accounts of certain clues that have been discovered and the time and place when they will be investigated, newspapers may bring about the destruction of evidence or enable wanted persons to avoid capture. For example, the suspects in a criminal case a number of years ago probably would (if they had had the opportunity) have thanked the newspaper that published a story saying that the police were watching a motor launch with the expectation that the suspects would return to get it.

Conceivably a single news story might have in it items which could both aid and hamper law enforcement. The same publication which might induce a knowing person to communicate a tip to police might also provide offenders with information that is useful in effecting their escape or in avoiding conviction. Hence, the publication of some kinds of crime news is not simply (as some law enforcement officials would have it) an interference with police work, or (as some newspapermen would have it) a means of apprehending criminals. Often the decision to publish or not to publish —or to report all or only part of what is known—is a matter of acute editorial judgment as to what the net effect will be.

NEWS OF THE ARREST

Newspapers can influence justice in one direction or another merely by publishing the facts of arrest. If the arrest turns out to have been without justification, the press may stigmatize the name of the arrested person by publishing the fact of arrest and not following it up with a report on the disposition. Eleasar Lipsky, a onetime assistant district attorney in New York, has told of a hearing at which he accused an arrested suspect of fleeing from the scene of a hit-and-run accident. Lipsky later found he was wrong; the suspect was freed and the assistant district attorney publicly admitted his error. His original statement was widely publicized but not the retraction.[8]

Despite the occurrence of such injustices, newspapers may advance compelling reasons for publishing the facts of arrest. Public knowledge of such facts can help to protect the citizen against arrest without just cause. The true magnitude of the illegal arrest problem is obscured by the vagueness, lack of uniformity or total absence of statistics. As Justice William O. Douglas has observed, there is no crime known as "suspicion."[9] Yet in 1964 a total of 102,106 persons were reported arrested on grounds of "suspicion" by 3,977 agencies.[10] Other arrest grounds which camouflage the inability of the police to present any specific charges are the following: "investigation," "en route," "loitering," "vagrancy," and "disorderly conduct." In some cities the very low conviction rate for such offenses as "disorderly conduct" and "loitering" leads to the inference that these labels are used to record arrests on suspicion or for investigation. Except in the few cases in which police have seen the crime committed, or in which they have probable cause (probable cause, according to the Supreme Court, being more than mere suspicion) to believe that a suspect has been involved in a felony, the proper procedure for officers is to investigate first and then make the arrest. They are not supposed to make arrests on suspicion and for questioning. But arrest followed by interrogation continues to be the favored sequence despite the questionable legality of the procedure.

Diligent editors and police reporters have at times shed light on the extent of illegal arrests. In 1958 the York (Pennsylvania) *Gazette and Daily,* after frequently complaining about the police technique of jailing persons up to forty-eight hours "on suspicion" or "for investigation," finally got a ruling from the state attorney general that the practice was illegal.

Newspaper watchfulness may, on the other hand, goad police into making justifiable arrests which they might otherwise be inclined to neglect. In 1960 a Bethlehem, Pennsylvania, city councilman was arrested and later convicted in connection with a shooting fracas which was exposed only because the Bethlehem *Globe-Times* got wind of the incident and published a story based on its own investigation. There had been no police record of the affair, although officers had been summoned to the scene after the shooting.[11]

In cases in which arrest seems warranted, close press observation of the police is nonetheless desirable in order to protect the citizen against illegal detention. Nearly all states have laws requiring a prompt preliminary hearing for arrested persons—that is, the police are called upon to take such persons without unnecessary delay before a magistrate, where they are informed, probably for the first time, of the charges against them, of their right to counsel, and of their right to remain silent. It is at the preliminary hearing or "booking" that the fact of arrest ordinarily becomes public knowledge. But even though the very purpose of arrest is to bring the accused before a magistrate, the police often evade the prompt preliminary hearing requirement—in which case vigilance by the press in disclosing the fact of arrest can perform a valuable service to justice. Extended secret detention by the police before the preliminary hearing allows abusive and unfair practices to flourish. It is during such delay between arrest and hearing that police may be tempted to employ the third degree or other means of coercive interrogation. By such practices, the police not only violate the rights of real offenders but also run the risk of implicating the innocent.

In recent years the problem of illegal detention has come into public discussion as a result of the 1957 United States Supreme Court decision in the Mallory case. The Court in that case, following closely a similar ruling in the 1943 McNabb case, held that in the trial of a criminal defendant, admissions elicited from him by interrogation during an unnecessary delay before a preliminary hearing could not be offered as evidence. But this rule is applicable only to federal cases and, strictly speaking, only to the relatively few cases that reach the trial stage. While the prompt hearing rule (incorporated in the federal rules of criminal procedure and given effect by the Supreme Court) probably has a restraining effect on federal agents, it apparently has little effect in the states, which process many more criminal cases than the federal government. Though they have statutes against undue delay in the booking of suspects, the states, through their courts, have shown little interest in enforcing them by following the Mallory rule in their own prosecutions.

There are indeed indications of the widespread prevalence of illegal detention. The Illinois Division of the American Civil Liberties Union, after a study of arrests in Chicago in 1956, concluded that each year more than 20,000 persons are secretly held in Chicago police stations for lengthy periods before being booked. There is no reason to think that Chicago is or was unique in this respect.

Arbitrary arrest and secret detention are the marks of a police state. Even though these methods are sometimes defended by critics of the Mallory rule as essential to law enforcement, they are not justifiable. Police are generally conceded the right to seek information by interviewing suspects under noncoercive circumstances (as in the home) before making an arrest.[12] Holding suspects incommunicado and subjecting them to marathon questioning can be upheld only under an end-justifies-the-means test. The higher standards of investigation set by the police in Britain have shown that local police if they are well trained, patient, and diligent, can accomplish their mission without such means—that is, without violating the law. Illegal methods, however, are likely to multiply in direct proportion to the absence of public information about them.

Exposure of questionable police techniques requires initiative on the part of the press. But it can produce results. The Boston *Traveler* in 1961 won the Sevellon Brown Memorial Public Service Award for its four-month investigation of and report on the death of a derelict alcoholic of multiple fractures while he was in police custody. A series of stories and editorials in the *Traveler* led to a grand jury inquiry which in turn resulted in action to correct police, hospital, and jail practices.

NEWS OF THE PRELIMINARY HEARING

As has already been noted, it is at the preliminary hearing that police charges are made public. It is here too that the decision is reached as to whether to release the suspect for lack of evidence or to hold him for further action. In Pittsburgh several years ago, the *Post-Gazette's* publicizing of a magistrate's failure to hold gambling suspects for court—ostensibly for lack of evidence—resulted later in the holding of suspects on similar evidence by the same magistrate. If a magistrate decides to bind a suspect over for prosecution, he also determines whether the accused is eligible for bail and, if so, the amount of the bond.

News of evidence introduced and the decisions taken at preliminary hearings is regularly published in the press. Publication of the facts of the hearing is ordinarily considered a service not only to the public, because it may elicit additional evidence, but also to the accused. Especially if the decision is to hold the suspect, publication of this fact can help to safeguard his rights. It may help him to get counsel or prompt others to reveal exonerating or mitigating circumstances. Or the newspaper may be the direct instrument of justice, as was the Cleveland *News* some years ago, when it helped free a suspect from a murder charge by investigating and showing that a revolver—which had been linked to the murder by a ballistics expert—had actually not been sold until a month after the commission of the crime.

POLICE AND PROSECUTION NEWS

In the United States, newspapers usually do not limit themselves to the simple facts elicited by the preliminary hearing but make a special effort to get *ex parte* statements from the police and little or no effort to get corresponding statements from the accused.[13] There is a ready justification for constant press pursuit of the police and the resulting widespread publicizing of successive police statements, each purporting to provide additional explanations of the crime or to point to new evidence. According to the press argument, pressure on the agencies of law enforcement and publicity for what they are doing prevents them from relaxing their efforts to combat crime, and counteracts any inclination on the part of the police to make deals with their quarry.

Press pursuit of pretrial information and comment usually does not end with the police. There is customarily a close tie between the prosecuting attorney's office and the press. And where the police leave off the prosecutor takes up. The extent to which the press and prosecuting attorneys make use of each other hardly needs documentation. It is apparent in news stories every day. The relationship is advantageous to both sides. For the press, the prosecutor provides a source of highly dramatic and readable news. For the prosecutor, the press provides a means of publicizing his office and obtaining the popular approbation necessary to his political advancement.

One example should be sufficient to illustrate how prosecutors step up along with police to make a joint claim on crime investigation publicity. The following passage, concerning the murder of a

15-year-old girl, is taken from the Boston *Herald* of November 6, 1954:

> District Attorney Myron Lane and state police detectives swiftly joined Norwood police, who have been keeping a series of thwarted attacks suppressed from the public over a period of two months. Lane declared he was optimistic that the killer would be found.

Lane revealed, in a late afternoon press conference following a preliminary autopsy, that the girl suffered a massive brain hemorrhage, that she was strangled as well, and that there was no doubt a sex attack had at least been attempted.

The same paper the next day reported the detention of a 15-year-old boy, Peter Makarewicz, Jr., and gave what purported to be a detailed explanation of how he committed the crime. The source was Norwood Police Chief Mark Folan. The story told of how the boy was questioned by investigators "throughout the night" and how he finally broke when police placed the victim's clothing on a desk in front of him. The account continued:

> Then the boy launched into a confession most of the details of which are being kept secret [It seems to be characteristic of investigators to release selected portions of evidence.] by Dist. Atty. Myron Lane, who with Folan headed the investigation.
>
> Why? Dist. Atty. Lane says "We have evidence that he had reason, although he didn't say." . . .
>
> Tonight Lane said that despite Peter's youth he can go to the electric chair if convicted of first degree murder without a jury recommendation of mercy.

Makarewicz was convicted of murder with a jury recommendation that the death sentence not be imposed. The judge sentenced the defendant to life imprisonment, and the Supreme Judicial Court of Massachusetts affirmed the judgment.

Actually police and prosecution statements made outside of official proceedings are not generally recognized as the kind of conditionally privileged matter which newspapers may print without incurring libel suits. Yet newspapers usually disregard the rule, trusting that most of the people who become subjects of police news will not sue. Out-of-court police and prosecution statements and speculation may or may not turn out to be admissible in evidence. If they should be inadmissible at the trial, their publication makes them nevertheless unofficially a part of the evidence that is likely to be considered. It is practically impossible to seal off a community from contact with pretrial publicity. On the affirmative side, the justification for such publicity (as in the case of the preliminary hearing publicity) is that it may bring forth more evidence helpful to the prosecution or may, on the other hand, pry out information that is useful to the accused.

Most police investigation publicity is hardly the type that breaks favorably for the individual suspect. It is not unusual for newspaper headlines and stories to indirectly pronounce guilt solely on the basis of police assertions. Such is the net effect of the following headline:

> $200,000 KIDNAP CASE SOLVED
> FBI NABS RING LEADER
> IN DRAMATIC ARREST

The word "solved" here surely implies that there is no doubt as to the arrested persons' responsibility for the crime, although this is a question which a trial is supposed to decide unless the accused pleads guilty. (There had been no such plea in this case at this time.) The same implication of certainty attaches to the words "ring leader," used without qualification in the same headline. Another damaging kind of pretrial publicity is the frequent use of derogatory terms which fix suspects in the public mind as disreputable characters before the aptness of the characterization is established by evidence: When a headline says: "Thugs nabbed after beating, robbing 15," it goes part way toward convicting the arrested suspects by planting in readers' minds an unsavory impression of them as "thugs."

Sometimes the unreliable character of pretrial evidence, generated by law enforcement officials and publicized in the press, becomes apparent in the news itself. On December 8, 1960, an Associated Press dispatch from Ukiah, California, reported that Sheriff Reno Bartolomie of Mendocino County, California, had issued a murder warrant against an 18-year-old girl named Mary Catherine Hampton in connection with the 1959 hitch-hiker killing of Perry Ten Eyck, a University of California athlete. Sheriff Bartolomie was quoted as saying: "I think this solves the Ten Eyck case." Six days later a second Associated Press dispatch reported from Gooding, Idaho, where Miss Hampton was a witness in another case, that she had been released from jail "after Mendocino County, Calif. authorities said they would not attempt to extradite her [in connection with the Ten Eyck case] because of insufficient evidence." Both stories were carried in the Palo Alto (California) *Daily Times*. Not often, however, does a law enforcement officer's mistake become so evident in print.

NEWS OF CONFESSIONS

In the welter of pretrial evidence commonly aired by the police, prosecutors, and the press, there are two kinds which deserve special discussion: confessions and prior police records of suspects. Pretrial publication of confessions is often defended by the press not only on the usual ground that it insures prosecution (that is, prevents behind-the-scenes deals) but also on the grounds that (1) it is a means of exposing police resort to duress and, (2) it may lead to more accurate information, if the confession contains inconsistencies. Undoubtedly newspapers perform a laudable service in those cases in which, by their own investigative efforts, they expose the use of coercion to extract confessions. They serve the same end if their factual accounts of confessions lead to inferences that force has been used and prompt others to investigate. In an entirely different way, press interest in confessions may promote justice, as did the St. Louis *Post-Dispatch* when one of its crime reporters induced a man to admit a murder after police were ready to pin the crime on an itinerant gangster. As a result the mistakenly suspected man was freed.[14]

Seldom, however, do newspapers exhibit a cautionary attitude stemming from a recognition that many of the confessions they report may not have been voluntarily given.

The case which may go down in the annals of police investigation as a classic in publicized false confessions is that of George Whitmore, Jr., a 20-year-old, semi-literate, itinerant Negro laborer arrested by New York City police on April 24, 1964, after he was identified by Mrs. Elba Borrero, a 21-year-old Puerto Rican woman, as the youth who attempted to rape her on a Brooklyn street the previous midnight.

After twenty-two hours of interrogation by the police, Whitmore was held not only for the attempted rape of Mrs. Borrero but also for the murder on April 14 of 46-year-old Mrs. Minnie Edmonds and for the stab slaying in August 1963 of Manhattan career girls Janice Wylie and Emily Hoffert, a crime that had received enormous publicity and that had shocked the city. Whitmore, whose arrest was hailed in the press as a triumph for the police, was said to have confessed to the three murders and to have revealed details of the Wylie-Hoffert stabbing which, curiously enough, coincided precisely with the earlier police reconstruction of the crime. In confirming the confessions to the news media, Chief of Detectives Lawrence J. McKearney declared: "We got the right guy, there's no doubt about it." [15]

On consulting with a lawyer, whose advice he had not had prior to the police announcement, Whitmore said he was withdrawing his confession and asserted he had been beaten into making it. In time the prosecutor's office began to have doubts. Later Whitmore's attorneys produced evidence that he was somewhere else at the time of the Wylie-Hoffert murders. In January 1965 an assistant district attorney in the office of District Attorney Frank S. Hogan admitted that the police, by "brain-washing, hypnosis, fright . . . made him [Whitmore] give an untrue confession." In May 1965 a state Supreme Court fully cleared Whitmore of the murders of Janice Wylie and Emily Hoffert. By this time another suspect, who was arrested with considerable attendant publicity, was being held.

After a 1964 conviction in the Borrero case was reversed, Whitmore was tried again and convicted in 1966. A 1965 trial of Whitmore for the Edmonds murder ended with a hung jury, and in June 1966 the prosecutor reluctantly had the murder indictment dismissed because Whitmore had not been properly informed by the police of his right to counsel.

As the Whitmore case progressed, each stage received substantial coverage by the New York press as well as intermittent attention from newspapers across the country. The failings and the misconduct of the New York police were duly reported. After experienced defense attorneys became involved in the case, they were given much help in demolishing the tainted confession by reporters for the New York *Post,* the *World-Telegram,* and the *Herald Tribune.*

Though only one case has been described here, there are enough verified examples of various kinds of untrue confessions to warrant an attitude of wariness on the part of the press when the police report a confession.

It is such examples as these that have made the courts extremely leary about admitting confessions in evidence. In a 1959 case the United States Supreme Court reversed a conviction based on the confession of a mentally incompetent defendant.[16] The late Professor Edwin M. Borchard, in his book, *Convicting the Innocent,* observed: "While confessions may often seem conclusive, they must be carefully examined. Persons charged with crime are not infrequently of defective or inferior intelligence, and, even without the use of formal third-degree methods, the influence of a stronger mind upon a weaker often produces, by persuasion or suggestion, the desired result." [17] In a 1961 case the nation's highest court again upset a conviction based on a confession. The police had questioned the suspect for six hours without results. Then they pretended to issue an order that his wife be brought in for questioning, whereupon the harassed man agreed to confess. Justice Frankfurter implied that this was psychological pressure of the type that made the confession involuntary. For twenty-five years the high court has held that the Constitution prohibits the use of "involuntary" confessions in criminal prosecutions. And it has defined "involuntary" broadly.[18]

It is because of the strict rules as to the admissibility of confessions in evidence that pretrial publication of confessions is questionable. The confession may be repudiated by its author, but there is no guarantee that the repudiation will be reported or, if it is, that it will be read or believed by all who read the original publication. If prospective jurors read such publications, they may be influenced in the direction of guilt even though nothing is introduced in the courtroom that would have the same effect.

NEWS OF PRIOR POLICE RECORDS

The second category of questionable pretrial evidence which the press frequently disseminates is the prior police record of the suspect. It is worth noting that a police record may even include arrests for which there was no follow-up or no conviction.

Despite a demonstrated need for caution in drawing inferences from police records, the existence of such "evidence" often induces police to believe that suspects are guilty and to try to pin crimes on them. The press and the general public are no doubt swayed in the same manner. Evidence of prior convictions, says Borchard, is often fatal to accused persons, and he notes that such evidence was a factor in twenty-two of the wrongful convictions which he reports.[19] U.S. Court of Appeals Judge Jerome Frank, in *Not Guilty,* another work on miscarriages of justice, also speaks of the unfair effect of disclosing previous convictions.[20] The undue emphasis on prior convictions by both police and reporters may stem from cynicism, an occupational disease they share. The same callousness may cause them to be uncritical of their suspicions and stubborn about surrendering them.

In actual trials, courts limit to some extent the possible unjust influence from evidence of prior convictions by barring such evidence unless the defendant chooses to testify. If the defendant takes the stand, the prosecution in most jurisdictions is allowed to introduce his record to cast doubt on his credibility, the theory being that the word of an ex-convict is untrustworthy. As a result of this rule, defendants often decline to take the stand, recognizing the devastating effect which the introduction of a prior record might have. In court they at least have a chance to prevent the presentation of such evidence. No such choice is available with regard to what the press does. Yet out-of-court reports of defendants' past criminal histories may be even more harmful to them than what may be offered in trials, for press accounts may be more detailed than material admissible under rules of evidence and may have with the jurors the character of forbidden fruit.[21]

PRESS INTERVIEWS WITH TRIAL PARITICIPANTS AND THE PUBLIC

Besides seeking factual information and opinions from police and prosecution officials, newspapers sometimes interview defense attorneys, witnesses, and potential jurors in connection with pending criminal proceedings. In this manner the whole range of potential evidence, admissible and inadmissible, may get a pretrial test run in the court of public opinion.

The prosecution lays out its case for the press; the defense answers. Usually the defense does not get the kinds of breaks in the press that the prosecution enjoys, but skilled defense lawyers have learned how to handle the press. They strive to find and communicate to the press dramatic facts which cast doubt on the prosecution's side or human interest angles which build sympathy for their clients. Federal Judge Leon R. Yankwich has written that a criminal proceeding "often becomes a battle of communiques between the prosecution and the defense." [22]

If the press goes out and solicits the "testimony" of witnesses, another element of the trial is introduced at the pretrial stage. In a 1955 murder case the San Francisco *Examiner* quoted the father of the victim as saying, before there was any indictment, that he had no doubt as to the guilt of the chief suspect, but that he doubted the man would ever get the gas chamber. The newspaper further quoted the father as wishing he could get his hands on the suspect.[23] (The suspect, incidentally, was later convicted and executed in the gas chamber.)

To the testimony of prospective witnesses, the press may add the opinions of potential jurors expressed through interviews or letters to the editor. Within less than two weeks after the arrest of Bruno Hauptmann in the Lindbergh kidnapping case in 1934, a New York newspaper announced that "twelve men and women selected at random" by a reporter had convicted the suspect. The headline declared: "Bruno guilty but had aids, verdict of man in street." [24] If pretrial views such as this become known in any trial, their authors presumably would be disqualified for jury service. But publication of such opinions is nevertheless grist for the out-of-court "trial" of the case.

PRESS AS PROSECUTOR OR JURY

Sometimes the press itself reacts to a case as though it were a prosecutor or a jury sitting in judgment, except that its opinions are not hidden as the jurors' would be during their deliberation. A case in Houston, Texas, in 1960 provides a detailed illustration of how a newspaper undertook to substitute its own judgment for the prosecutor's. Mrs. Wilma Selby was murdered, supposedly by a slayer procured by her husband, Joseph. Mrs. Selby had been killed by a .22 bullet. A tip led police to investigate Mrs. Maggie Morgan as the person who might have done the hiring of the murderer for Selby. A German-made .22 revolver was found in the possession of Mrs. Morgan's husband. But a hardware merchant said he had sold Mrs. Morgan bullets for an American-made .22, and ballistic tests did not prove conclusively that the bullets which came from the dead woman's body had been fired from the German-made revolver. Faced with a critical lack of evidence, the police seemed defeated and the district attorney quoted the law and said he wouldn't lay the case before the grand jury.

At this point the Houston *Press* launched a campaign keyed to the words: "Somebody is getting away with murder—and little is being done about it." Declaring editorially that the Selby murder was "perhaps the most horrible crime in Houston's history," the newspaper added that there had been "far too much complacency about it." The district attorney and his staff were told that it was high time for them to "get aroused about this terrible crime and . . . to stop talking about what they CAN'T do and start thinking about what they CAN do." In a concluding barb, the paper exclaimed that it did not believe such a "diabolical plot can go wholly unpunished."

Soon the mayor and the sheriff were calling the paper about the case and the police were expressing a welcome for aid from the sheriff in searching for the triggerman. But the prosecuting attorney was still uncertain. In a few days the *Press* loosed another editorial blast saying: "Stop all those gobbledegook statements and face-saving . . . and get on with solving it and some indictments." The next move by the *Press* was to offer a reward for clues. Public excitement over the case mounted. Tips began pouring in and, on the basis of one of these, officers arrested Clarence Collins, a suspect who had already been taken into custody once in connection with the case and had been released after being questioned and given a lie detector test. This time police questioned him for hours and he finally confessed that he had shot Mrs. Selby.

At this point the prosecutor promised to take the case to the grand jury. Indictments and a trial followed, with Selby, Mrs. Morgan, and Collins all being found guilty.[25] Perhaps justice was done in the Selby case. If so, it was accomplished despite press-generated public pressure of a kind that could weaken the procedural safeguards designed to protect the rights of citizens ("stop talking about what they CAN'T do . . . stop all those gobbledegook statements . . . get on with . . . some indictments").

In few cases does a defendant enjoy such a position in the community that he may become the beneficiary of a favorable pretrial judgment by the press. Yet this is what Whittaker Chambers believed happened in the case of Alger Hiss, against whom he was to be the principal witness when the latter was tried for perjury in 1949. Chambers wrote:

> In effect, not Hiss, but I, henceforth [after August 25, 1948] became the defendant in a great public trial, in which, in a manner startlingly reminiscent of the mechanics of the great Soviet public trials, press, radio, public personages, organizations of all kinds and a section of the Government itself were mobilized against the chosen victim while public opinion was enveloped in a smog of smearing whispers that rolled across the nation and far beyond its frontiers. Through almost every medium of communication, the personal assault upon me was kept at a peak of uproar.[26]

The accused in a majority of cases is a member of a submerged class which confers on him no benefits of publicity.

PHOTOGRAPHS

Persuasive pretrial newspaper evidence is not necessarily limited to the printed word. The publication of gruesome pictures of the victim may stir popular prejudice. Or photographic evidence may be influential in other ways before the case goes into the courtroom. During the popular furor leading up to the notorious Scottsboro rape trial in Alabama in 1931 a local newspaper printed photographs of the Negro suspects and of the girls who were their alleged victims, and captioned the pictures: "These girls identified all of the negroes above as attacking them."[27] This was only one of many prejudicial items which appeared before the trial in which the defendants were convicted.

The publication, at the request of police, of photographs of wanted suspects can have a damning effect, especially if the press, as it does on occasion, treats the information on police interest as though it were conclusive evidence of guilt. The use of such pictures, of course, can be helpful to police investigations. But the police should not be regarded as clairvoyant. Sometimes, for example, photographs of bank holdups by hidden cameras do not provide clearly identifiable likenesses of the robbers. Yet newspapers print without question pictures from police files of wanted suspects without making clear that the police search for these particular suspects is based on little more than a hunch that they are the same as the persons whose fuzzy images appeared in the bank photographs.

Under different circumstances, however, the pretrial publication of photographs may help a defendant, as in cases in which he or she is young, attractive, or naive looking. George T. Davis, the San Francisco criminal lawyer, was once called on to defend an 11-year-old boy who had fatally shot a middle-aged teacher and whom the district attorney was seeking to have tried as an adult would be for first-degree murder. The child's mother told Davis that her son did not even realize he had committed murder. Davis interviewed the boy in jail and arranged to have a photographer take pictures of the session. After the photographs and accounts of the interview were published in the papers, the case was transferred to juvenile authorities.[28]

Whenever photographs are being considered by editors, they should be acutely conscious of the need for responsible judgment and for the careful choice of words in captions and accompanying stories, for obviously pictures can be prejudicial to the rights of the accused.

PRESS COMMENTS ON THE LAW

In addition to carrying pretrial reports of and comments on the evidence in criminal cases, the press may also print comments on the law in advance of trial and in this manner play a significant role in the outcome of the proceeding. This is an aspect of press influence that is not often recognized.

According to a theory of neatly compartmentalized justice, the judge interprets the law and the jury simply finds the facts and applies them to the law as the judge directs. By a further extension of the distinction between judge and jury, the occupant of the bench is deemed to be more immune to outside influence than the twelve so-called triers of fact. Thus advance out-of-court arguments on the law are often assumed to have little bearing on the result of a trial. Judges are considered somehow to be impervious to them. A recent law review note summed it up this way: "A judge is typically exposed to a wide variety of statements and offers of proof that would constitute prejudicial error if presented to the jury."[29] Judge Jerome Frank spoke of the tendency to believe that "judges are super-human or that the humanness of judges has virtually no effect on how courts decide cases."

Judges, by the nature of their offices, of course, must be exposed to more prejudicial material than juries. Someone has to decide, according to rules of evidence, what should or should not be submitted to the jury as relevant to the decision in the case. And judges are assigned the function of ruling on what is too prejudicial to put before the jury. Nevertheless it is foolish to pretend that judges (both trial and appellate) are not swayed by the same prejudicial facts and arguments which might sway a jury and that such persuasion is not reflected in their rulings. Justice Frankfurter once observed that judges strive not to be "influenced *consciously*" [Italics added] by what is judicially inappropriate, and then continued: "However, judges are also human, and we know better than did our forebears how powerful is the pull of the unconscious and how treacherous the rational process." A Maryland Court of Appeals judge made the same point when he said in a case involving prejudicial publicity that "judges are not so 'angelic' as to render them immune to human influences calculated to affect the rest of mankind." A New York psychiatrist asserted recently that, while judges' weaknesses are concealed from the public by an aura of respect, they (the judges) are nevertheless affected by the same human motivations as everybody else.

There are a number of ways in which comment can be directed to a crucial interpretation of the law at the pretrial stage. The Miami

Herald gave a pointed illustration of one way when in 1944 it chastised a judge who had quashed a rape indictment because it was improperly drawn. Referring to the "seeming ease and pat facility with which the criminally charged have been given technical safeguard," the paper went on to suggest that the courts were being "subverted into refuges for lawbreakers." The judges who were the targets of this and another editorial revealed their sensitivity to the criticism by citing the publisher and associate editor of the *Herald* for contempt. By their successful appeal to the United States Supreme Court, the cited *Herald* officials brought about a landmark decision that was to be known as the Pennekamp case.

Unlike its stance in the Miami case, the press may be on the defense side when a similar issue is presented. In the Lattimore case a few years ago newspapers debated whether an indictment for perjury was warranted. The defendant was charged with lying when he said before a Senate subcommittee that "he had never been a sympathizer or any other kind of promotor of communism or Communist interests." Some newspapers challenged the legality of the indictment, and it was later thrown out of court. Similarly the indictment of a group of so-called underworld leaders in the Apalachin case was discussed in the press and questioned by some editors. The conviction of the Apalachin defendants was later reversed. In other situations the question of whether a court has jurisdiction to hear a case may arise and be subject to press comment. It is highly unlikely that judges are completely oblivious to such public discussion.

The Trial Stage

Once the preliminary proceedings are over and the trial has begun, the general assumption of the law, as was noted earlier, is that the courtroom is a world unto itself, and that the rules of evidence and admonitions by the judge can exclude the world outside. The law supposes that, if communication from outside is curbed, participants in the trial can arrive at the truth by the kind of controlled communication among themselves that the court permits. Such control is more theoretical than real.

PRESS INFLUENCE ON JUDGES, LAWYERS, WITNESSES, AND OTHERS

The possible influence of the press on others than jurors—already noted with respect to the pretrial stage—is also applicable during the period of the trial. During the trial the press may be the agency for exerting social pressure in a concentrated form, not only on jurors but also on judges, attorneys, witnesses, and others. At this time all of the actors in the drama of justice are on a single stage, and by this time community opinion may have polarized around an expected result. If there is evident pressure for one kind of decision, trial participants may find it difficult to play roles which lead to a decision of the opposite kind. Like the participants in the previously described Harvard psychology experiment who changed their minds under social pressure, courtroom performers may change their minds under the glare of community opinion reflected through publicity on the trial. Witnesses may change their minds about what they thought they saw at the scene of the crime. Prosecutors and judges may change their handling of the trial to conform to what they think the community wants. In most states these officials are elected. To retain popularity and thus be reelected or to achieve some other political ambition, they may yield to subtle influence without even being aware of what they are doing.

PRESS INFLUENCE ON THE JURY

The trial participants deemed to be most in need of protection against prejudice are the jurors. Yet an indication that the law attributes a kind of disinfecting quality to the courtroom may be seen in the general rule that a prospective juror will not be disqualified if he has formed or expressed an opinion (based on pretrial publicity) that the defendant is guilty, so long as the court is convinced that he will be able to lay aside his prejudice or preconception in reaching his verdict.[30]

After a process of trying to weed out veniremen with fixed pretrial prejudices comes the problem of protecting the jury against prejudicial influence from outside the courtroom during the course of the trial. Even the sealing off of outside prejudice is not easy. Jurors are not supposed to have access to press material touching on the case they are hearing. In murder cases they are sometimes quartered in a hotel for the duration of the trial and their reading material is screened. Yet even when the jurors are locked up and obey the judge's instructions as to what they may read, there is no assurance that they will be completely unaffected by prejudicial publicity. They may sense the atmosphere of the courtroom which, in turn, may be charged by sensational accounts in the press. Justice Holmes once observed that "any judge who has sat with jurors knows that in spite of forms they are extremely likely to be impregnated by the environing atmosphere." The mood of the courtroom may be communicated to the jurors by the responses of spectators—sighs, laughs, groans, gasps, or verbal expressions of approval or disapproval, which, however much they may be enjoined by the judge, cannot be removed from the consciousness of the panel.

This possible indirect communication of newspaper prejudice is not, however, the main problem of justice and the press in the courtroom. The subject for major concern is the direct effect of criminal trial reporting and comment by the press. In most cases jurors are not sequestered but are simply directed by the judge not to read, look at, or listen to anything bearing on the case. Yet a Washington, D.C., attorney has observed that: "All jurors read newspapers and listen to radio and television, or at least talk to others who have done so. No amount of warning by the trial judge will change that." U.S. Circuit Judge William Hastie indicated that he entertained a similar view in an opinion in a 1960 case in which jurors had looked at newspapers despite explicit instructions against it.

If jurors admittedly ignore instructions and read or listen to prejudicial news and comment, what impact may it have? Objective studies on the subject are limited. Florence Kelley, one-time attorney in charge of the criminal division of the Legal Aid Society of New York, once said that many jurors had told her that they were influenced by something they read in the paper. A study of jury deliberations conducted by the University of Chicago Law School produced a record of a personal injury case in which the plaintiff in fact was suing for $35,000 but in which the papers had carried a story saying he was suing for $50,000; the jury proceeded to deliberate on the assumption that he had asked for $50,000.

More than thirty years ago the New York Crime Commission interviewed readers of several newspapers which were selected as biased or neutral in their reporting of a sensational trial in progress at the time. The study concluded that a higher percentage of the readers of the biased reports had made up their minds in advance of the verdict than had the readers of the neutral accounts. If the same conclusion may be drawn with regard to juror readers specifically, newspapers clearly have the potential for producing a result that would not be reached if the law were left to its own devices of searching for truth.

REPORTING OF INADMISSIBLE EVIDENCE

The various specific ways in which newspaper reporting may exert an extraneous influence on the trial itself are obvious. As in the pretrial stage, press articles are not limited to what the law considers to be admissible as evidence. Legal rules of evidence limit what may be introduced in court to that which is deemed to have probative value, and screen from the jury that which may be misleading such as hearsay (gossip). Yet the press may freely air hearsay or other forms of unreliable "evidence." News stories may include references to the prior record of the defendant. In the 1959 Marshall case, mentioned in Chapter 3, the United States Supreme Court ordered a new trial for the defendant because his conviction came after jurors during the trial had seen news articles telling about his previous convictions. While the trial was in progress, the judge had refused to allow the prosecution to offer evidence as to Marshall's prior convictions on the ground that it would be "prejudicial" to him. Yet the evidence was in effect introduced anyway through the medium of Denver newspapers.

Otherwise inadmissible evidence of confessions may also be "introduced" by the press. In 1954 the Illinois Supreme Court approved a new trial for a prisoner who had been convicted of rape in a trial in which the jurors were not locked up and during which two Chicago newspapers printed stories saying the defendant had, in addition to the crime with which he was charged, confessed to two murders and had assaulted some fifty women.

Often evidence that is not admissible directly in the courtroom is nevertheless indirectly admitted through the readiness of the press to publish out-of-court statements originating with the prosecution. In Baltimore in 1957 Mrs. Thelma Sarah Burgess was being tried as a conspirator and accessory in the murder of her husband, Leonard H. Burgess. While the trial was under way the Baltimore *News-Post* carried an eight-column banner reading: "Say Widow Planned Burial Prior to Burgess Slaying." To illustrate the headline and story references to the burial, there was also a photograph taken at the grave of Burgess during his funeral and an accompanying caption. The headline was based on the prosecutor's statement of what he hoped to prove in the case. During the trial, however, the prosecutor was unable to produce actual evidence supporting what he had said he expected to prove about the widow's premurder plans for a burial. No photograph was offered in evidence. The judge granted a defense motion for a mistrial and observed that "the headline and photograph were clearly improper."

Sometimes the press has access to other sources on the prosecution side. During the trial of Alger Hiss in 1949 the New York *World-Telegram* obtained and printed the secret and as yet unpublished testimony against Hiss that Whittaker Chambers had given the previous December before the House Committee on Un-American Activities.

The prosecution side, however, is not always the one to seek an advantage through the agency of the press. During the famous Scopes "monkey trial" in Tennessee in 1925 the defense planned to put a number of scientists on the stand to testify as expert witnesses in support of the theory of evolution. The issue, of course, was whether the defendant had violated Tennessee's law barring the teaching of evolution in the schools. Since Defense Attorney Clarence Darrow expected Judge John T. Raulston to rule against the seating of the witnesses, he asked each of them to prepare statements for the press saying what they would have said if allowed to testify in court. As the experts were writing their statements in the stenographer's room Judge Raulston looked in and asked what they were doing. When told, the judge went to Darrow and said to the attorney that he must not release the testimony, adding: "It might reach the jury." Darrow responded: "Your Honor, you can do what you please with that jury. You can lock it up, but you cannot lock up the American people. The testimony will be released." (The witnesses *were* barred from testifying in court.)

Such outside evidence as is described in these cases clearly can have a bearing on the outcome of trials if it is seen by the jury.

POOR REPORTING OF COURTROOM EVIDENCE

The introduction of evidence that would not otherwise enter into consideration is not, however, the only way in which the press may convey a different impression of the case than that gained by an observer in the courtroom. Such courtroom evidence as is reported may be presented in a lopsided fashion, stressing the sensational aspects of the case and thus conveying to the public and perhaps to the jury a persuasively different version of the case from that offered at the bar. In the trials of Dr. Samuel Sheppard at Cleveland in 1954, and of Dr. Bernard Finch and Carole Tregoff at Los Angeles in 1960, the press, as in so many cases, looked for salacious angles to emphasize. The trial of Alger Hiss was for the most part poorly reported and was milked for its sensational values and its political implications. A detailed study of how two San Francisco papers reported the Hauptmann trial in 1935 showed that the reporting was accurate as far as it went. Yet it fell far short of being adequate, not because of a lack of space (the tremendous amount published indicated no significant space limitations) but because of stress on unimportant aspects. Sensationalism was the criterion of emphasis.

Another form of extraneous influence may be exerted through the coloring of the courtroom evidence by the writer's opinion. Reporters and editors are largely free to draw their own conclusions as to the witnesses and the evidence. Hauptmann's guilt was suggested by many reporters in advance of the verdict. Alexander Woollcott wrote:

> Yet if there is one thing clear as crystal in this curious and intricate case, it is that the young man [Hauptmann] to whom the

designated go-between handed over the $50,000 was either the kidnapper himself or one so privy to the crime at its very inception as to be black with guilt from head to toe.

Jack Lait of the Hearst press commented, "I doubt anything could send a shudder through Bruno Richard Hauptmann except an electric current of high voltage."

An Ohio editor who observed the coverage of the Sheppard trial declared afterwards:

> Once the trial began all three Cleveland newspapers offered extensive daily summaries of testimony from which they repeatedly drew their own conclusions, either directly or by adroit manipulation of headlines. The press never left any doubt of the verdict it expected, not surprisingly in view of having plunged so deep into the processes of administering justice by its own rules.

One pertinent illustration of how a reporter, like a judge, can make a ruling on the evidence should be appropriate. It is taken from a news story in the Pittsburgh *Post-Gazette*.

> Although Assistant District Attorney Samuel Strauss indicated he would seek a second degree verdict because of the youth of the defendant, the testimony of two witnesses yesterday indicated that elements of first degree murder were present in the crime.

DESCRIPTION OF DEFENDANT

Sometimes reporters may slant the impression of the case which the public receives merely by the way in which they describe the defendant. Ruth Snyder, one of the defendants in the lurid Snyder-Gray murder trial in 1927–1928, was pictured as "a chilly looking blonde with frosty eyes."

When Al Capone was on trial in Chicago in 1931 Damon Runyon wrote that Capone was a "terrific disappointment" to the sight-seeing Chicago tourist who felt that "Al should have been vested at least in some of the panoply of his reputed office as Maharajah of the Hoods. Perhaps a cartridge belt." Obviously Capone in a cartridge belt would have presented a more threatening image to the public.

Hauptmann was described during his trial by various writers as being "distinguished looking," having the "face of a corpse," being the "cold, silent, morose type of old world criminal," having an "ice water disposition." Few of the characterizations reflected a disposition on the reporters' part to reserve judgment as to the defendant's guilt.

Dr. Sheppard was referred to by reporters as the "Romeo of the rubbing table," an implication that there was another woman in the case and that therefore Sheppard had a motive for killing his wife.

The word pictures of the defendant do not invariably convey an unpleasant or guilty implication. Carole Tregoff was frequently described as pretty and her sobs were shown in photographs. The press image of a defendant is more likely to be favorable if he or she is young or attractive.

From all that has been said, it should be apparent that the picture of the courtroom which the public gets can be colored and varied in a thousand different ways by the manner in which the press reports the proceedings. While evidence in court is affected by judicial rulings and by the idiosyncrasies of the trial participants, the case as presented in trial news and comment is affected by such added filtering factors as the competence or incompetence, the industriousness or laziness, the objectivity or bias of reporters and editors, and finally by the amount of attention the press chooses to give the event.

CAMERAS AND MICROPHONES

At this point it seems pertinent to ask whether a truer picture of the courtroom proceedings would be conveyed by direct images provided by modern instruments of communication that in most places have not been admitted to the courtroom. Up to now visual portrayals of trials in progress have been—with the exception of the few jurisdictions where cameras are admitted—provided only by artists assigned to sensational cases.

Though this book was conceived as a study of the impact of newspapers on criminal justice, its theme would be incomplete without recognizing that justice is also affected by such newer media of communication as the camera and the microphone, and without at least briefly analyzing the role of these modern communications media as compared to that of the older print medium. This seems an appropriate point to consider the question of whether news photographers and television cameramen should be admitted to the courtroom. They are already ubiquitously present at other stages in the processes of law enforcement, exerting an influence for justice or injustice similar to that which they might exert on a wider scale if their area of operation were to be broadened.

Though television coverage and even still photography are now permitted in only a few jurisdictions, the question of their effect is still important. Broadcasters and news photographers have not given up their effort to gain access to the courtrooms of America.

Would the camera's entry into the courtroom serve the cause of justice? To answer this question, a distinction first has to be made between the still camera and the television camera. Pictures taken with a still camera would add to the reporting of a trial a dimension that might be of value. If taken unobtrusively or even without the awareness of the participants, they would not be likely to disturb the proceedings—though it must be acknowledged that pictures, like words, can be edited and used in a way that gives a distorted image of an event. Permission for still photographs, however, would not represent a radical change from the present methods of reporting trials. Their impact on justice would be conditioned by the same kinds of use or misuse to which printed words are subject.

Television reporting, however, would represent a radical change. The TV camera, unlike the still camera, produces a transformation both in the character of the trial participants and in the nature of the audience. In a sensational trial the audience might include the whole community or even the whole nation. The defendant, the judge, the attorneys, the witnesses would be transformed into actors or actresses whose dramatic performance might have a greater bearing on the outcome of the trial than the integrity of their words.

It cannot be denied that trials, as they are now conducted, are often a form of dramatic contest, with lawyers and other participants vying with each other to impress the jury audience. But a vast enlargement of the live public audience by means of television could bring a reverberating impact on the courtroom from the outside world that would be far more influential than the delayed feedback that now comes from readers.

Members of the TV audience would identify themselves with the *dramatis personae* of the screen and would seek to shape the plot even as they do with broadcast soap operas. Courtrooms are not now—and, especially with the admission of television, could not be —sealed off from public emotion, despite the elaborate pretense by many judges and lawyers that a rule against receiving sets and newspapers in the jury room somehow insures an unprejudiced trial atmosphere. (This is not intended to imply that newspapers, radios, and TV sets should be allowed in the jury room.) Television would greatly intensify and magnify the public participation that already exists.

There is no denying that the entrance of television into this new field would give the American public new insights into, and additional general information on, law enforcement and their legal institutions. The process would undoubtedly have educational value. There is no denying either that television on occasion might even sway a trial in the direction of surer justice. But so far the record of television, particularly of local stations, in public affairs offers little reason to hope that it would conduct itself in the best interests of justice even if it could. If performance in other areas means anything, television would select events and tailor its coverage of them in order to produce the cheapest and most magnetic shows and not in order to promote the best law enforcement.

Like newspapers, which by habit seek to satisfy the public taste for blood, the television medium would more often than not lend itself to the cause of the prosecution rather than strive to be an objective instrument for the discovery of truth.

Some newspapers, mindful of their duty to the Bill of Rights, try to carry out their role responsibly. Some television executives and editors would try to be worthy of their new responsibility if cameras could cover trials. Most of them, however, have given little sign of a commitment to public service. To introduce television to the judicial process would not only amplify the flaws in trial news coverage that already exist but would create an entirely new and powerful potential for adversely influencing justice. Though the abstract principle of freedom of the press may call for the admission of the television camera to the courtroom, the practice of most stations has not demonstrated a maturity that shows them worthy of such a freedom.

COMMENT ON LAW AND OTHER FACTORS

The public's (and the participants') impression of a case may also be shaped by general press comment on the law and on aspects of the trial not dealt with in the courtroom. During the Scopes trial H. L. Mencken, in his dispatches to the Baltimore *Sun,* daily referred to the people of Rhea County (where the trial was being held) as "morons," "hillbillies," and "peasants." He wrote about "degraded nonsense which country preachers are ramming and hammering into yokel skulls."[31] Editorializing about the same trial, the Chattanooga *Times* deplored the "crusade against intelligence" in Dayton and the timorous "skulking up alleys" of Tennessee's educated citizens. "Had they had the courage and boldness to speak out when this thing began," the *Times* declared, "they might have saved themselves and their state from the humiliation that has come upon them."

The Scopes trial was covered by representatives of the press from across the nation and illustrates how, when the issue being tested attracts wide interest, newspaper coverage can have a bearing on the public judgment of it. Evolution lost in the Tennessee courtroom but, largely as a result of extensive press coverage, it won in the eyes of the nation. While the Tennessee anti-evolution statute was upheld, prohibitive bills which were pending in other states were dropped or killed.

In 1944 the mass sedition trial in the nation's capital of a group of allegedly pro-Hitler defendants was another nationally publicized courtroom drama on which general press comment seemed to have an impact. During the event the Washington *Post,* which had originally urged prosecution, denounced the lumping together of twenty-six cases in a single trial and said this approach made the proceeding too complicated and lengthy. Such procedure, said the *Post,* might make the outcome "a black mark against American justice for many years to come." As the trial dragged along in its fifteenth week, the *Post* referred to it as a "courtroom farce," a "sorry spectacle," and a "travesty." Only after the affair had run for seven and a half months did it finally end in a mistrial because of the death of the judge from a heart attack. While the effect of press comment in this case cannot be documented, it is significant that the prosecution was never resumed. As in the case of so much of the communication inside and outside the courtroom, it is difficult, if not impossible, to tell which words from what source are having or have had the greatest effect.

POSTVERDICT PRESS INFLUENCE

Once the jury has heard all the evidence and has retired, the outcome might appear to be immune from press influence. But at this point there are still many moves that may be made before the trial stage is closed. There may be a motion with the trial judge for a directed verdict (in which the jury is ordered what to decide on the basis of a judicial interpretation of the law), a motion for a mistrial or a new trial. If a guilty verdict is brought in, the judge must decide the nature of the sentence. He may be asked to put the defendant on probation. Any one of these judicial decisions may be swayed one way or the other by the press. Yet once the case is in the hands of the judge, American newspapers generally consider that practically all restrictions are off and that whatever they want to say is permissible. This attitude is grounded not only in Supreme Court decisions allowing great latitude to free expression during the judicial phase of the proceedings[32] but also in the generally accepted idea that judges ought to be subject to criticism and ought to be able to take it.[33] Press pressure after the jury has done its work is so common and so uninhibited that its prevalence and range hardly need to be demonstrated. A description of cases exemplifying several facets of press activity at this stage should be sufficient.

Judges are the persons who are subjected to the most severe kind of postverdict pressure. An editorial in the Los Angeles *Times* which gave rise to one of the leading Supreme Court decisions on the press and the courts is a trenchant illustration of this point. Two Teamster unionists had been convicted in Superior Court in Los Angeles in 1938 of assaulting two non-union truck drivers. After their conviction they asked for probation. Calling the defendants "gorillas" and "sluggers for pay" and charging them with hiring out their muscles "in aid of a racket," the *Times* declared that the judge would be making "a serious mistake" if he granted them probation, adding that the community needed "the example of their assignment to the jute mill." [34]

Besides exerting posttrial pressure on the judge, the press at times engages in a particularly irresponsible practice with a potential for indirectly influencing justice through the jurors in a later new trial. What if the jurors are interviewed, as they were in 1949 after the first Hiss trial in which the panel deadlocked? In that case New York papers—particularly the *Journal-American,* the *World-Telegram,* and the *Herald Tribune*—conducted a campaign of intimidation (using comments of Congressmen and material supplied by pro-conviction jurors) by the device of damning the judge and some of the jurors as prejudiced in favor of Hiss. Jurors who voted for acquittal were soon being threatened by cranks. At the next trial of Hiss another judge was on the bench and another jury in the box. This time the defendant was found guilty. When the issue, as in this instance, was an acutely controversial matter of loyalty to the nation, judge and jury were in a peculiarly sensitive position.

When jurors, as frequently happens, are asked how they voted in a sensational case, the publication of their answers may tend to intimidate those who held out for a minority position. Perhaps jurors during the course of the trial would not ordinarily be apprehensive about the prospect of such interviews and thus would not be deterred from voting their convictions. But after the interviews have been held and the results published, the effect might well be to keep jurors in any new trial from holding out for a minority position for which they would be subject later to criticism and ostracism.

The Posttrial Stage

After the trial stage is concluded, appeals may be filed with higher state courts or in federal courts. Following a decision on appeal, there may be a motion for a rehearing. Appellate judges also read newspapers. And after the final appellate ruling, there may be moves to obtain a pardon for the prisoner, a commutation of the sentence, or a parole. During all of these phases the litigation, according to a loose interpretation of the word, can still be "pending"[35] and thus subject to influence by the press. Yet few restraints, voluntary or otherwise, are imposed on prejudicial publicity in the posttrial stage.

INFLUENCE ON APPELLATE COURTS

Appellate judges often are the targets of press barbs and advice. And while they may be less vulnerable the higher they are in the judicial hierarchy, even the Supreme Court of the United States has been said, not inaccurately, to follow the election returns—which it no doubt does, in part through the medium of the press. Supreme Court Justice Robert H. Jackson once expressed doubt that the occupants of that high bench could remain indifferent to a nationwide attack from the press.

After the conviction of American Communist Party leaders in the historic conspiracy trial in 1949, the Supreme Court got columns of editorial argument both for and against the constitutionality of the statute under which the defendants were found guilty.[36] The sheer volume of editorial comment supporting the validity of the act probably exceeded that on the other side. The Supreme Court in 1951 upheld the statute. No one can really say whether the press swayed the high court in this case.

Though newspaper comment intended for the high court justices may be reasoned and temperate most of the time, it is not always so. After the United States Supreme Court in 1935 reversed the conviction of the Negro defendants in the much publicized Scottsboro case, the Montgomery *Advertiser* editorialized:

> Mr. Hughes's pontifical deliverance of the opinion is a lot of baloney. The *Advertiser* may be dumb, but to save itself it cannot see what the political rights and privileges of Negroes in Alabama have to do with the guilt or innocence of the gorillas who are charged with criminal assault upon two women.[37]

Southern editorial opinion in the wake of the Supreme Court school desegregation decision was equally intemperate. If the nation's highest tribunal usually seems calm and unaffected by the storm of publicity that sometimes rages around its rulings, the reason probably is that the justices are appointed to their exalted positions for life and are practically immune to pressure.

PRESS INFLUENCE ON ADMINISTRATIVE OFFICIALS

Even after the final appellate decision has been handed down, the press still exerts its sway on justice by influencing the decisions of executive and administrative officials. When the Pennsylvania State Board of Pardons met in Pittsburgh in 1960, the Pittsburgh *Post-Gazette* proclaimed the event with a headline saying: "Pardon Our Murderers' Season Opens in County." Members of the board have complained that they find it difficult to recommend clemency in deserving cases because of the vengeful heat of newspaper publicity. The hot breath of the press also bears down on and restricts the dispassionate functioning of parole boards. Criminologist Donald R. Taft has noted this effect and has attributed it to the tendency of the press to reflect the public demand for revenge. Harry Elmer Barnes and Negley K. Teeters have written: "It is no exaggeration to state that no single force does more to prevent and frustrate the rehabilitation process than our newspapers and other agencies of publicity." [38]

Sometimes, however, the role of the press has a favorable bearing on a public official's life-and-death decisions with regard to a prisoner. Charles F. Stielow had been convicted and sentenced to death for the murder on March 22, 1915, of Charles B. Phelps in Orleans County, New York. The case excited a good deal of public interest, with considerable sympathy being shown for Stielow, whose guilt was doubted by some. After the defendant's court remedies had been exhausted, Governor Charles S. Whitman scheduled a public hearing. Sensing something fishy about the conviction, the New York *World* published some letters of one Ervin King, who showed he had an incriminating knowledge of the case. The governor had King brought to Albany for interrogation. As a result, Stielow was eventually pardoned by the governor. So was Nelson Green, another man who had been wrongfully convicted.[39]

Another instance of press aid to the exoneration of an innocent man occurred in Chicago in 1945. As a direct result of a series of articles in the Chicago *Times,* Joe Majczek that year was released from prison, fully pardoned, and remunerated by the state after serving twelve years for a murder he did not commit. The articles in the *Times* showed that he had been convicted on the basis of false testimony given by a witness who had been threatened by the police with prosecution for violating the prohibition law unless she identified Majczek as the killer in the case of a slain policeman.[40]

During the same year that Majczek was cleared, Willie Calloway, a young inarticulate Negro, was sentenced in Michigan to life imprisonment for murder. After he had served eight years behind bars, his case was called to the attention of Ken McCormick of the Detroit *Free Press*. McCormick's articles helped to exonerate Calloway and to secure his release.[41]

In a relatively recent case in which the press was outspokenly involved in posttrial decisions of life and death, the final order was in favor of death. As the Chessman case was grinding to its ineluctable conclusion in 1960, the consideration of the death penalty in the governor's office and in the California legislature promoted a worldwide press discussion of the subject, with various publications taking sides as to whether or not Chessman should be executed. But California publications, particularly those published in the Los Angeles area where the trial had taken place, were out for blood. They referred to the prisoner variously as "a stealthy, vicious animal," "a psychopathic degenerate," "a depraved fiend," "a loathsome criminal." The Santa Monica *Outlook* had conducted a poll among its readers and announced that, by three to one, they favored death for Chessman. Chessman later was put to death in the gas chamber. While many newspapers had opposed the imposition of the death penalty, one critic of the Los Angeles press was of the opinion that it had dictated Chessman's end.[42] Since these papers were closest to the officials involved, their influence may well have been paramount. Whatever their impact was, Los Angeles newspapers showed little appreciation of the meaning of enlightened justice.

And as has already been shown, the performance of the Los Angeles press in the Chessman case is not an isolated example. The press is often a vehicle for exerting pressure for the death penalty. Not only does it in some cases specifically demand the execution of the offender but in many cases it contributes in a capricious manner to the pressure for execution simply by the way in which it singles out certain cases for special attention. The headlines in the case may be blown up for no other reason than the dullness of the news on the other fronts—a condition which is compensated for by an emphasis on crime. So goes the constant search for bait to attract readers.

INDIRECT PRESS INFLUENCE

Besides exerting an influence on justice in obvious direct ways by reporting and commenting on cases from arrest to release, the press also affects the criminal process in countless indirect ways: by reporting and commenting on the appointment or election of prosecuting attorneys, judges, and others with law enforcement responsibilities, by reporting and commenting on proposed or existing criminal rules and statutes, by reporting and commenting on the manner in which penal institutions are organized and administered.

Not only does the press help to shape justice for the individuals directly involved in criminal cases but it also subtly extends the unofficial range of the criminal process to those whose lives are touched by the suspect or defendant. The law usually exerts its force only on the individual believed to be guilty of the crime in question. But the press often exerts its own kind of pressure on family and friends of the defendant, subjecting them to questioning, reporting on their lives, exposing them to the extra-legal "punishment" of public scorn and ridicule. The reach of the press sometimes extends far beyond the reach of the law in time and effect. By recalling the criminal record of a convicted offender long after he has supposedly paid his debt to society, by linking the offender with members of his innocent family whenever he or they are in the news, the press may cause prolonged and unnecessary suffering in excess of that prescribed by law. When public curiosity and the right to privacy conflict, editors usually give priority to the former.

SUMMATION

In summary, newspaper influence may be brought to bear at every stage of the law enforcement process—from the initial investigation of the crime to the final administrative action in the case of the convicted offender. It may also affect the nature and reach of the criminal process outside of cases prosecuted. But the performance of the press is not governed entirely by the whim and initiative of editors and reporters. Police, lawyers, judges, politicians, and the public have a stake in press treatment of crime. And they seek to aid and abet the kind of treatment that serves their ends. Even if they are not themselves agents in the creation of news, they are very likely to be influenced by it. Thus criminal justice is swayed by the constant and continuing interaction of press and public officials on each other. Since the initiative in the production of prejudicial news comes from one side in one case and from the other side in another case, neither side can be proven to be a major source of injustice, though the press has the ultimate responsibility for what is printed. Since prejudicial news sometimes serves both sides, neither side can claim to be pure-minded.

Ideally, of course, the press should—and on occasion does—contribute to the search for truth outside the courtroom. When it does, it complements and aids the search for truth inside the courtroom. When it does not—as so often happens—it magnifies the degree of error in justice, because its audience is so much wider than that of the courtroom.

CHAPTER SIX

INJUSTICE IN THE PRESS

THE QUESTION OF PRESS TREATMENT OF CRIME NEWS should not be examined simply in terms of the coverage of individual cases and the way such coverage affects their outcome. To gain any meaningful understanding of the impact of the press on justice, we must not only analyze individual cases but also study the kinds of crime news presented in the press, the extent and nature of the news treatment, the motivation of the press in presenting the news as it does, and the public's interest in and reaction to crime news.

POPULAR TASTE FOR CRIME

The modern public's appetite for concentrated doses of crime is reflected in every medium of communication. Among American newspaper readers, stories dealing with major crimes have been found to rank ninth in a preference listing of forty categories of news.[1] A study some years ago showed that the murder mystery accounted for one out of four books of fiction published or reprinted annually in the United States.[2] Periodicals find that it pays to allocate a substantial segment of their space to crime articles and stories, and about twenty magazines devoted solely to crime are being published, to say nothing of the flood of so-called comic books which treat the same subject.

In the motion picture field the popularity of the crime theme is signified by the prevalence of such thriller titles as "How to Murder Your Wife" and "Signpost to Murder." And on the home screen the ratings of the numerous crime shows leave little doubt as to the inclination of television viewers. Commenting wryly on television's affinity for homicide, Morris Ernst noted that there were 8,000 murders in the nation in 1964, while one network alone showed 10,000 murders, not all of which were "in the Macbeth or Hamlet social set." [3]

The Need for Scapegoats

Observers from many fields have sought to explain the hold that crime has on the public mind. Literary critics have attributed the popularity of crime fiction to a revolt against frustration or to a search for escape from impending disaster in a world in which it seems impossible to pin down responsibility. As Edmund Wilson has put it—speaking of such a world in which nobody seems guiltless and nobody safe—there is "relief" when the murderer is finally spotted; "he is not, after all, a person like you or me. He is a villain—known to the trade as George Gruesome—and he has been caught by an infallible Power, the supercilious and omniscient detective, who knows exactly where to fix the guilt." To critic Charles J. Rolo, the detective story is modern man's Passion Play, a production in which even Mickey Spillane's Mike Hammer can emerge as a flaming sword, a messenger of Jehovah.[4]

Specialists in criminology, though they phrase the matter in more prosaic terms, offer similar explanations for the public's obsession with crime. They observe that in the case of some types of offenses the ordinary citizen, through a kind of paradoxical romanticism, may seek to escape from daily dullness by identifying himself with the law violator. Accounts of crimes of bravado, such as piracy and bank robbery, provide a vicarious thrill which he may secretly enjoy.[5] In the current literature of crime there are endless portrayals of the daring acts of tough bad men and the smooth talk of suave underworld figures. The viewer or reader in search of adventure can choose his hero or his villain.

Like the offender who is a secret popular hero, the one who is a villain also serves a purpose. The average man has, and has always had, a need for a scapegoat, someone to blame for his misfortunes. If he lacks a convenient scapegoat, he creates one. Often this is not necessary because he has society's delinquents as ready targets, persons on whom he can give vent to his aggressions by having them punished. The ordinary man is filled with resentments and pent-up hostilities which, under stress, may be transformed into antisocial actions. But usually, instead of committing criminal acts, he lets off steam in other directions, often against the latest offender about whom he has read. He mentally penalizes the accused offender for the evil he himself subconsciously feels and thinks.[6] The psychiatrist, Karl Menninger, has observed that "taking it out on criminals is by all odds the most satisfactory method [of finding scapegoats]. It is perfectly proper and ethical and legal and highly moral to do so." [7]

The rationalization for this point of view is that crime is the willful act of a free moral agent—or, put less philosophically, a sin—for which outraged society must exact payment in the form of punishment. This concept serves more readily to provide targets for the community's frustrated aggressiveness than does the modern idea that crime is often the product of factors beyond the control of the offender. Thus, despite the findings of modern psychology which contradict the notion of voluntary perversity,[8] the old idea, with some modifications, continues to dominate the public mind and contemporary criminal jurisprudence.[9]

News Space for Crime

Both the public's extraordinary interest in crime and its harsh view of criminal justice are reflected in the editing of newspapers. Besides the play and slant of the news, which are the major indicators of press catering to public taste for crime, the amount of space devoted to crime and violence is itself a sign of the effort to satisfy the public preference. Crime occupies from 2 to 7 per cent of the total news space in the press, the percentage depending on the type of newspaper.[10] Though detailed studies for limited regions point up expected variations between papers, the percentage range is much the same as that found for larger areas. A press content analysis of Michigan's four largest and four smallest dailies several years ago revealed that the space allocated to crime ranged from 3.6 per cent for the Detroit *News* to 6.5 per cent for the Flint *Journal*. The same study (based on an examination of issues for the week of October 16–21, 1961) showed that, among the small Michigan dailies, the amount of space given to crime ranged from 2.5 per cent for the South Haven *Tribune* to 5.9 per cent for the Dowagiac *News*.[11]

If even the maximum space figures do not seem large, they should be considered in comparison to the amount of attention given by the press to all of the other socially important issues competing for space. More important still, the newspaper space given to crime should be judged in terms of the peculiar facet of the problem of criminality to which the space is allocated. Most of the space is devoted to the dramatic confrontations between law breakers and society and not to constructive examinations of causes and cures for crime.

Violence is the key ingredient. A survey in 1962 of ten leading United States newspapers—geographically representative and with the largest circulations in their areas—showed that the daily news space given to descriptions of violence ranged from 2.1 per cent in the St. Louis *Post-Dispatch* to a high 33.5 per cent in the New York *Daily News*.[12] Among those papers devoting the highest portion of their news columns to crimes of violence, this type of law breaking is certainly accorded exaggerated significance; and the resulting demands of their reading public for a violent crackdown may be expected to rise correspondingly. This kind of pressure on authorities is not necessarily conducive to justice.

Play and Slant of the News

In weighing the effect of the press upon justice, the play and the slant of crime news are even more important than the amount of space allocated to the subject. The influence of crime news is obviously affected by headlines, placement, pictures, and other means of emphasis. The large and dramatic headline on the front page gets more attention from readers than a small unprovocative line buried in the back pages.

In big city newspapers sensational crimes are often emphasized over news of national and international events. In Chicago in 1946 a 17-year-old youth named William Heirens was charged with several murders. After the trial and sentencing an exhaustive study of how the case was handled by the (then) five Chicago newspapers disclosed some striking facts about the treatment of the Heirens story in contrast to that given other important news of the time. During the period that the Heirens case was moving from arrest to sentencing there were several top national news events: the atomic bomb tests at Bikini; the operations of the Office of Price Administration, then being heatedly attacked; and a sharp debate in Congress over the authorization of an American loan to Britain. The study of eighty-five issues of Chicago newspapers of the period revealed that sixty-two banner headlines were given to the Heirens case, eleven to the OPA, four to the atomic bomb tests, and two to the British loan. The Heirens case got a higher percentage of the combined space of the five Chicago dailies than any of the major national issues.[13] The performance of the Chicago press in the Heirens case is not an uncommon kind of occurrence among competing metropolitan papers.

While the sensational play of crime news is probably most prevalent in competing metropolitan dailies, press preoccupation with crime is by no means limited to those areas where there is rivalry for the attention of the masses of the big cities. Consider the performance during an arbitrary period of the Palo Alto (California) *Daily Times,* an unsensational paper with a circulation of 36,000 in a university community. In a 52-day period in 1961 that paper ran forty-seven crime stories and eighteen crime pictures on its front page. Twenty-one of the forty-seven stories were printed above the fold and thirty-two of them ran to more than ten column-inches. The length of individual stories ran as high as forty-six column-inches. Crime was missing from the front page of only fifteen of the fifty-two issues published during the period in question.[14]

Though crime occupies less than 7 per cent of the total news space in the press, the prominent play given to crime news suggests that the impact of this kind of news is markedly greater than the space percentage would indicate. By giving front page play to crime, the press adds weight to the scales in behalf of its often questionable brand of justice.

The effect of the press on the administration of justice is keyed not only to the space and the prominence given to crime news but also to the kinds of crimes chosen for headline treatment. Though some types of cases are ignored or played down, the run of each day's events usually produces a supply of the kind of cases that fit the editor's peculiar formula for sensational display. There are sexually titillating aspects or other circumstances that are thought likely to stir the emotions; children are affected; the victim attracts extraordinary sympathy; the crime is peculiarly revolting. All one need do to realize the character of crime fare in the news media is to think for a moment about the front page of his regular newspaper or concentrate briefly on the content of the ordinary local news broadcast. Shootings, rapes, holdups, and burglaries are regularly featured in headlines and on the home screen. By focusing the vengeful fury of the public on some defendants and on limited categories of cases, the press helps to bring about a capricious kind of justice.

The formula which motivates editors in the choice of cases to be headlined was probably well expressed by Ed Murray, managing editor of the Los Angeles *Mirror,* when he said of the Marilyn Sheppard murder: "The case has mystery, society, sex and glamour." One or more of these criteria would apply to almost every case that has been voraciously covered by the press—cases that, as far as the problems of criminal justice are concerned, are often less important than dozens which are slighted. Certain types of offenses—slum knifings, homicides among Negroes, white collar crimes, and cases involving violations of the law by business—are often played down or completely ignored,[15] while the "glamorous" cases get exaggerated attention.

Prominent play is understandable for cases revealing deficiencies in law enforcement—as in the Whitmore case, described in the last chapter—or having national political ramifications—for example, the Ruby, Hiss, and Rosenberg trials, or, in an earlier day, the trial of Aaron Burr or the prosecution of those implicated in the assassination of Lincoln. These cases raised questions that affected the destiny of the nation. But most sensationally played cases have no political angles nor any special relevance to the effectiveness of the agencies of justice.

The kinds of cases usually selected for emphasis by the press refute the argument often given by editors to justify copious coverage of every detail of some police investigations and of the minutiae of certain criminal trials. The time-worn press argument was forcefully stated many years ago by the late Grove Patterson, editor of the Toledo *Blade,* when he said:

> I will say, simply and frankly, at the very start that in my judgment the newspapers will go on printing all the crime news that is available, in the future as in the past, and that furthermore they should continue to do so as a matter of good newspaper making and sound public policy. Only publicity will arouse public opinion. Publicity, more than anything else, will stir laggard public officials to courageous action. This publicity, copious and unpleasant, frequently hated by every conservative element in the community, disliked and deplored by the newspapers themselves, offers the surest and most sweeping approach to the clean-up.[16]

This rationale may have guided the respected Toledo editor in the treatment of crime in his own paper. But the applicability of the rationale to newspapers in general is highly doubtful. If the Patterson thesis were really applicable, the cases selected by the American press for the most detailed attention would reflect greater variety and would be characterized by their legal or sociological significance rather than by juicy tidbits of tangled love affairs as presented in such sensationally covered stories as the trials of Dr. Samuel Sheppard and Dr. Bernard Finch.

Crime Factor in Circulation

The editorial fixation on crime apparently calls for a basic explanation other than the altruistic one of concern for law enforcement or a desire to report the day's most significant events to the community. The true explanation, however defensible it may sometimes be in the interest of journalistic self-preservation, seems to be a mercenary one. Harry Overstreet has written that "the newspaper has found its vested interest in catastrophe." The 1947 report of the privately endowed Commission on Freedom of the Press expressed the matter succinctly when it observed: "To attract the maximum audience, the press emphasizes the exceptional rather than the representative, the sensational rather than the significant"—and added that in most news media activities with important social consequences "are crowded out by stories of night-club murders, race riots, strike violence, and quarrels among public officials."

According to the commission, the journalist means by news something that has happened within the last few hours "which will attract the interest of the customers," the criteria of interest being recency, proximity, combat, novelty, and human interest.[17] When events are judged by such criteria, those with the greatest degree of violence naturally come to the fore.

In view of the evident human curiosity concerning crime, there is an obvious economic reason why newspapers devote such attention to the subject. Newspapers are inclined to respond to popular interest and taste. Like their competitors, the electronics media, newspapers seek to supply what the market demands. Circulation is the gauge to which newspaper publishers are especially sensitive. The history of circulation battles, with crime news being used as ammunition, goes back at least to the days of the early nineteenth-century penny press. But this sort of press competition is not merely a phenomenon of the distant past.

In 1926 the Hall-Mills case was first exploited by the New York *Daily Mirror* to gain a circulation advantage over its competitors. Showing no reluctance to accept the challenge, other New York dailies were soon in full cry on a trail that led to the secret love affair between the murdered Episcopal clergyman and one of his choir singers.[18]

Thirty years later the Grimes case was exploited by Chicago newspapers in a similar manner. On December 28, 1956, two teen-age sisters, Patricia and Barbara Grimes, left home to go to a movie and were not seen again until their murdered bodies were discovered. With sexual assault suspected as one element in the case, the Chicago papers outdid each other in priming reader curiosity. The *Tribune* and *Sun-Times* published pictures of models dressed in clothing like that of the girls. Claiming a beat on the arrest of a skid-row character named Bennie Bedwell, the *Tribune* carried the first report that he had made a confession to authorities. A digest of the confession was published in an eight-page supplement in the Sunday *Tribune*. The confession was later found to be full of discrepancies and was repudiated. The *Tribune* day city editor later admitted that if the editors had "had more time," they would not have printed Bedwell's unsubstantiated statement that he had gone to bed twice with one of the girls.

To show its enterprise, the Chicago *American* had one of its reporters track down a Bedwell companion named in the purported confession. Later an *American* editor also had second thoughts on his paper's performance. He said the *American* should have hesitated and checked further before bannering a story that a slip belonging to one of the teenagers had been found in Hammond, Indiana, a story that later turned out to be false.

At the time of excitement, however, circulation seemed to be uppermost in the minds of editors. Headlined stories on the murdered sisters lasted two months and were said to have increased circulation of individual papers by as much as 50,000 on some days.[19]

In San Francisco in 1957 the city's four dailies had a similar field day with a rape case in which the victim was manacled and tortured.[20] The *Chronicle* labeled the attacker the "Torture Kit Rapist," because he had used a knife, adhesive tape, manacles, and scissors in the course of committing the crime. The *Examiner* called him the "mad rapist." And the *News,* not to be outdone, dubbed him the "Fang Fiend"—since he was described by the victim as having "canine teeth, which protruded fang-like over his lower lip." As the police pressed a hunt among those formerly involved in sex offenses, the papers built up the case with headlines and with details of the attack. The case blossomed into banner headline proportions when a 23-year-old warehouse clerk named John A. Rexinger was arrested.

For more than a week after Rexinger's arrest the case was seldom off the front pages. Columns of news space were given to the printing of stories and features on various aspects of the case, including Rexinger's literary strivings, taken by police from a tape recording he had in his room and intended by them to furnish clues to his guilt. Only when the investigation was ended by the confession of another man did the press let up in its sensationalizing.

Meanwhile the San Francisco newspapers, during each day of the nearly two-week play of the torture rape case, sold an average combined total of probably 15,000 copies more than normal. The

Rexinger case had enabled the papers to almost equal their performance earlier in the year when a young man named Burton W. Abbott had been executed for the murder of a 14-year-old schoolgirl. On the day that Abbott was put to death, street sales of the San Francisco *News* alone were some 20,000 copies higher than usual.[21] Albert Colegrove, *News* editor, called it the second biggest circulation day in San Francisco newspaper history, a day that was exceeded only by the day of a San Francisco earthquake the same year (1957). He defended the handling of news in a way that would attract such readership, observing that in the absence of crime news there would be many fewer readers and thus many would be denied the opportunity to read about such worthy activities as the United Crusade.[22]

Some publishers minimize the drive for circulation as a factor in the treatment of crime news.[23] And they may be right with respect to the more responsible and more secure papers and with respect to communities where competitive infighting has been reduced through conquest of the local newspaper market by a monopoly publisher. But the tendency to play news in a fashion calculated to boost sales is obviously widespread and a matter of long habit. It is especially noticeable in big cities with competing newspapers.

Press Pressure for Harsh Treatment

By shaping its content to what it deems to be the public "demand" and the public taste for crime news, the press brings to bear a generally severe attitude toward law enforcement. Criminologists, sociologists, and other authorities frequently complain that a punitive and uncompromising public outlook is more often than not aided, abetted, and echoed by the press and that this tends to hamper deliberative justice administered on the basis of modern techniques.[24]

James V. Bennett, former director of the Federal Bureau of Prisons, has noted the prevalence of newspaper editorials complaining about "coddling" criminals.[25] And criminologist Donald R. Taft has observed:

> Newspaper advocacy of penal methods has generally reflected dominant public opinion rather than pioneered for a new penology.

. . . A great many newspapers have apparently been suspicious of efforts to test the sanity of criminals; have inclined towards the determinate rather than the indeterminate sentence; have thought of probation as "giving another chance"; and have violently attacked parole as unwarranted softness.[26]

The existence of such attitudes has not only been asserted by sociological and legal authorities[27] but is evident in frequent headlines:

'CODDLING' SCORED
AT BOY'S FUNERAL

PRIEST'S SERMON SAYS SLAYING
CAME FROM CITY'S POLICY:
'THERE IS NO BAD BOY'[28]

PASTOR SAYS ACTS
CALLED DELINQUENT
ARE REALLY CRIMES[29]

Kindness Wrong
CLERIC URGES
PUNISHMENT FOR CRIMES[30]

The Worry Clinic
WHY PAMPER YOUNG
CRIMINAL OFFENDERS?[31]

Though events themselves exert some influence on the shape of the news and though the foregoing exhibits of editors' preferences are admittedly selected examples, they nevertheless are illustrative of the public and journalistic view of crime about which criminologists and others testify.

If the public mood in most headlined cases is given a channel for expressing itself, the result is not likely to be an enlightened kind of justice. In newspaper treatment of crime it is far easier to observe manifestations of savage public emotions than it is to find the civilized qualities of reason and mercy. Press pressure for the execution of those convicted of murder and rape is common. In its most virulent form, such pressure does not even wait for conviction. When lynching was more prevalent than it is today in the southern United States, there were many instances in which the crime was condoned or even encouraged by the county dailies and weeklies of the affected communities.[32] While daily papers of the larger Southern cities denounced lynching, their denunciations tended to decrease in vigor as mob lawlessness came within proximity of their own operations. As late as 1955, the year of the lynching of Emmett Till in Mississippi, the press of that state swung from an initial condemnatory attitude to one of defensiveness concerning the atrocity.[33] It was apparently mirroring the attitude of its readers.

Except for a few papers with courageous editors, the Southern press tends to reflect the prejudices of a majority of its white readers and to excuse injustice toward Negroes, if not actually promoting it. When Negroes have been the victims of bombing, burning, and shooting and white perpetrators are suspected, the whites are the beneficiaries of prejudice. The crimes are often blamed by officials on outside agitators or on inside put-up jobs, and the press often goes along with this sham. But if Negroes are suspects, the Southern newspaper reverts to vengeful style. An intensive campaign for retributive justice is mounted as in a 1949 Florida rape case involving a 17-year-old white girl and four Negro suspects. The local press was eager to rush the accused to the electric chair as soon as possible.[34]

The South, however, is not the only region where the press reflects the grosser feelings of its constituency. Negroes are the victims of prejudiced justice in the South; in all regions the members of ostracized classes—pro-Germans, during the war against Germany, and pro-Communists, during the cold war—may be the victims. Across the country day in and day out newspaper headlines, stories, and comment reflect hate, anger, cruelty, the urge to punish, the spirit of revenge, the search for scapegoats.

After the disastrous Cocoanut Grove night club fire in which 500 people lost their lives in Boston in 1942, there was mad public and press clamor for scapegoats, someone to blame and possibly to prosecute. The spotlight fell first on a busboy, then on an "unknown prankster," and later on political officials and the owner. Often when there is a prison break, an escape of an inmate deemed dangerous or an exposure of graft in municipal government, the event is greeted with outraged and aimless cries for a scapegoat. Anger must have a victim.[35]

One need not look far to find many examples of how the hot wrath of the public has shaped the newspaper image of the accused and, vice versa, how the newspapers have shaped the public's image through ugly word pictures. The process is cyclical.

If the public seems to take a harsh view toward a certain type of offense, newspaper reports concerning this offense are likely to reflect the same outlook. (Conversely, an indulgent public attitude toward illegal conduct is also likely to be mirrored in news stories.) The mass media are more effective in reinforcing people's basic attitudes than in converting them to new attitudes.[36] Evidence of the tendency of the press to channel and reinforce severe public attitudes is visible in the vocabulary of crime stories. Consider the extent to which crime news is flavored with the following words: gangster, gunman, mobster, bandit, public enemy, thug, hoodlum, trigger-man, fiend, pervert, psychopath, sadist, dope-fiend, firebug. These are all words which, according to a recent study of American villain-types, tend to put the person so identified in an evil category, to set him off from society as an individual of "inherent depravity and malice toward mankind." [37] The frequent use of such words in initial newspaper accounts of crime suggests that the press is verbalizing the condemnatory view which the public commonly assumes toward suspects. There are, of course, some kinds of offenses and some cases in which circumstances or the appearance and character of the accused induce public and press to be more lenient or at least more nearly neutral. White collar crimes and offenses by popular figures apparently fall into this category.[38] These types seem to get less hostile emphasis in the news.[39] But the most publicized crimes and the most publicized alleged offenders provide ready targets toward which public and press may vent suppressed aggressiveness.[40]

If most crime news is sprinkled with descriptive words, many of them with villainous connotations, the community's view of criminal cases is not likely to be unaffected. The late Dr. Samuel A. Stouffer observed that people's attitudes are more easily reached through their emotions than through their intellects. Applying this observation to crime news, which is often highly charged with emotional signals, it seems fairly clear that the press can be very influential in swaying its readers. All of us, according to Professor Clyde Miller, are "creatures of conditional reflex," and these reflexes may be prodded by flashing trigger words. In crime news villain tags for suspected offenders would seem to serve as trigger words. They set off latent hostility which can hardly fail to be visited upon the person involved in the news. Because few if any persons actually fit a villain-type except in a role that represents only one aspect of personality,[41] there is bound to be an unjustified generalization in the vilifying description.

It seems safe to assume that the press, in taking a hostile view of criminal suspects, either accentuates an already existing outlook or nudges the public in that direction. For the occasion in which communication can best shape attitudes and behavior arises when it conveys something that satisfies the wants or needs of the recipient.[42] In the case of crime news, need is satisfied by providing a vicarious outlet for suppressed antagonism. The means of expression is the vocabulary of vilification which is still widely utilized orally and in print despite the findings of social science indicating the inappropriateness of popular tags. Indeed, mass communication seems to have created new opportunities for vilification by making the outlets more readily available.

Alarm over Statistics

Another manifestation of the generally severe public and press attitude is evident in the reaction to statistics on crime. Each year the issuance of the FBI's uniform crime reports is followed by a rash of news stories about the alarming increase in criminal activity and a spate of editorials calling for a law enforcement crackdown. These superficial evaluations usually fail to take cognizance of any positive trends.[43] James V. Bennett called attention in 1964 to the false impression created by the press portrayal of crime statistics. Though the average newspaper reader is likely to feel that crime is increasing ominously, Bennett pointed out, the national homicide rate actually dropped by nearly 50 per cent between 1930 and 1962; bank robberies—a crime much advertised in the press—accounted for an aggregate loss of $3,400,000 to 609 banks in 1932 as compared to only $1,800,000 in 461 holdups in 1962 (a year when there were some 5,000 more banks); the general prison population of the country is declining, with the ratio of prisoners per 100,000 people being considerably lower in 1963 than it was in 1939, the year the federal government started publishing prison statistics.[44]

Dr. Thorsten Sellin of the University of Pennsylvania, president of the International Society of Criminology, has observed that, while crimes against property have gone up, crimes against persons have gone down in the last 150 years. Our society has improved much since the Civil War, according to Dr. Norton Long of Brandeis University's Institute on Violence.

Despite the signs of some changes for the better indicated by close analysis, the raw crime statistics are often disseminated by the press (with the help of the FBI) to suggest a great rise in lawlessness unrelieved by any signs of improvement. At times the repetition of stories about certain types of offenses, first in one city and then nationally (if the offense makes good copy), creates the erroneous impression that the crime is being committed with more than average frequency. Lincoln Steffens told of creating a "crime wave" in New York City by writing a story about an unusual burglary, which prompted editors of other papers to send their reporters after similar news.[45] The same kind of self-generative process is observable in reports of crime waves today. Actually there is no evidence that such a phenomenon as a "crime wave" exists, although statistics might reflect a slight rise in specific crimes for certain periods of time.[46]

But as a result of police and journalistic talk of crime waves and the presentation of sensational statistics without reference to the population rise and other qualifying factors, the public demands stern action by the police and courts, with no delays or detours for legal technicalities. With popular alarm ringing in his ears, a local editor may interpret his own headlines as requiring urgent action. It happens with noticeable regularity.

Response to a "Crime Wave"

Consider the effect of one such editorial crusade:

A New Jersey paper in 1948 launched a campaign for capital punishment because of what it called "an intolerable crime wave," which had been climaxed by the killing of an old man named William Horner. In an editorial entitled "The Idle Electric Chair," the Trenton *Times* noted the presumably deplorable fact that there had not been an electrocution in the state in more than two years.

The events that followed the Trenton *Times* editorial are instructive. The next day police officials in that city organized a special squad armed with Tommy guns and given orders to shoot to kill and to arrest any "suspicious-looking" person found on the streets after dark. The city's director of public safety declared, "Well-meaning people may accuse us of acting like a Gestapo, but if we can bring in the Horner killers, or save one life, I'm willing to take all their criticisms." Three days later, in another editorial, the *Times* demanded that the police solve the Horner murder "through one means or another." Within the next few days six suspects, all Negroes, were arrested without warrants. Though there had been no witnesses to the crime and all six of the accused had alibis corroborated by witnesses, they were all convicted by an all-white jury and sentenced to death. The verdict, said the Trenton *Times,* "seems to have stunned the entire city." But the local press had not helped to forestall the outcome.[47] Under the relentless pressure of newspaper publicity—such as that in the Trenton case—both the police and public are likely to forget the Bill of Rights.

The case of "The Trenton Six" became a *cause célèbre* and for a time was caught in the toils of a Communist propaganda drive. Eventually—through the efforts of a distinguished Princeton committee, the American Civil Liberties Union, and the National Association for the Advancement of Colored People—four of the defendants won acquittal in a second trial and a fifth won his freedom after commutation of his sentence. The sixth died in prison.[48] But there is little reason to doubt that in this case several innocent men were subjected to a cruel experience as a result of public hysteria which the press helped to whip up. As is so often the case, the kind of newspaper publicity likely to help the defendants did not begin until well after the original miscarriage of justice.

Press Aid for Prosecution

Though no comprehensive study of the nation's newspapers has proved that there is greater favoritism for the state than for defendants, it would seem reasonable to conclude on the basis of general observation that the severe attitude taken by the public, and reflected in countless cases by the press, usually gives an advantage to the prosecution and militates against the law's traditional presumption that an accused is innocent until proven guilty.

Until cases actually get into court, the police and the prosecutor are the sources of most of the news concerning them—even the news of what the accused has to say. The police do not customarily make suspects available for interviews. And the majority of them, under long-prevailing conditions, cannot afford and have not had a lawyer to speak for them in the initial stages of the case when so much of the damning publicity occurs. Even when a defense attorney represents the accused, reporters are not in the habit of seeking him out.

Studies of individual cases tend to support the thesis that the press is generally biased against defendants before the jury has rendered its verdict. In 1950 Robert E. Bednasek was tried in Iowa for the murder of his college girlfriend, Margaret Jackson. Bednasek claimed that her death was accidental and at the trial pleaded not guilty. There were no witnesses who saw Miss Jackson die, so that the case involved Bednasek's word against such circumstantial evidence as the prosecution could assemble and present in court. A study of how the case was treated by nine newspapers showed that during the period of police investigation and before the presentation of any evidence in court, the newspapers used a varying number of times some fifteen different descriptive words (such as strangled, murdered) that implied guilt on the part of the suspect. Five Iowa papers used the highest percentage of prejudicial words during the initial stage, when such publicity has the greatest potential for damaging a suspect.[49] The press treatment of the Bednasek case is fairly typical of that in similar cases depending on circumstantial evidence. Luckily for Bednasek, his attorney was able to overcome whatever prejudicial effect the publicity had, and the defendant was acquitted.

An analysis of the Heirens case (which had a different outcome) in Chicago in 1946 revealed that the Chicago papers printed initially, and then repeated, a far higher percentage of statements issuing from the police and prosecution than from Heirens, his parents, his attorneys, and friends.[50] Whether or not this treatment of Heirens could be defended from the standpoint of the good of society, the conclusion seems inescapable that the defendant's case was weakened in the process.

Sevellon Brown, a conscientious editor, affirmed the common practice of the press in a 1955 speech deploring the way in which crime reporting sacrifices the rights of the individual. He observed, "Almost any editor in almost any city on almost any week could go over his routine police file and pick out example after example of reporting that was clearly prejudicial."

By its handling of news of criminal cases, the press naturally and without any special effort aids the side of the prosecution. As has already been noted, the two sides profit from a cooperative relationship in which the police and prosecutor, on the one hand, supply readable news, and the press, on the other, publicizes the accomplishments of the law enforcement authorities and aids in promoting their professional and political fortunes. On the surface, at least, the friendly press-prosecution liaison is difficult to quarrel with. The prosecution represents the protector of society and the accused is its presumed enemy. By its very acceptance of such a presumption, however, the press abdicates its proper role as impartial observer of government and, when the need arises, as champion of the individual against overweening state power.

News of "Confessions"

The most common forms of questionable prosecution information to be published by the press are prior records of suspects and reported confessions. Despite the possible occasional value (referred to in Chapter 5) of publicizing confessions and prior records, the press handling of these kinds of news is usually so careless and the result can be so harmful that news of confessions and prior records should be regarded as a special category of injustice in the press.

Press reports of confessions are so commonplace that the raising of any question as to their propriety would seem comparable to an attempt to turn off the rain. Newspapers often take pride in getting stories about confessions. The Chicago *Tribune* in 1960 scored a beat in publishing the confession of a man who was said to have admitted murdering three Riverside, Illinois, matrons at

Starved Rock State Park the previous March. To capitalize on this feat, the *Tribune* in record time distributed nearly 100,000 copies of the issue containing the exclusive news. They went not only to the Chicago area but to downstate residents of Ottawa, LaSalle, and Streater, near the murder scene.[51]

Seldom do news stories about confessions give a clue to the possible dubious aspects of the reported occurrence. A confession may even be voluntary and yet false. A half century ago the Harvard psychologist, Hugo Münsterberg, described cases in which mental aberrations led to untrue confessions. There are situations, he said, "in which a neurotic mind develops an illusory memory as to its doings in the past."[52] Münsterberg himself was excoriated by the press when he made a vain attempt to save from execution a man he believed to have confessed a crime he didn't commit. Dr. Theodore Reik, in his work *The Compulsion to Confess,* explains such cases by observing that one who confesses falsely has an "emotional claim to the deed" prompted by an unconscious feeling of guilt which is based on suppressed tendencies.[53]

In some cases innocent men who are quite rational may be influenced to confess in order to exculpate others, or in the hope of gaining lenient treatment when they are caught in a chance net of damaging evidence, which is seemingly inescapable even though it doesn't represent the true facts. In the famous Boorn case in Vermont in 1820 two brothers confessed falsely to the killing of their brother-in-law because the circumstantial case against them was so overwhelming that they saw an untrue confession as the only way to change the degree of the expected guilty verdict from murder to manslaughter and thus save their lives. They were nevertheless sentenced to die and were saved from execution only because a newspaper published a description of the alleged victim, on the hunch that he was still alive, and asked him to return to his home village. He did and the condemned brothers were exonerated.[54]

The ingenuity used by unscrupulous investigators to force admissions of guilt is endlessly varied. Detectives in a homicide case once dragged a suspect to a mortuary and forced him to look at the corpse and stroke it. After having previously denied responsibility for the crime, he made a full confession. A jury, when later informed of the circumstances of the confession, acquitted him.[55] Professor Borchard, in his book *Convicting the Innocent,* tells of an instance in which a private detective induced a weak-minded suspect to confess by making him believe that a mob would get him if he didn't. He was later exonerated.[56] A more typical case was that of the murder suspect who in 1954 was beaten by the Springfield, Massachusetts, police until he signed a confession. After serving three years of a life sentence, he was found to be innocent.[57]

Though there are ways—as indicated in the previous chapter—in which the publication of purported confessions can aid the defense, the press too often is not skeptical enough about admissions of guilt reported by the police. It reports them as a matter of course, seldom bothering to dig beneath the surface to find out whether there are any questionable angles. Some years ago a Florida editor said that if a story about a confession was not denied within two or three days he assumed it to be true—as if a poor, ignorant, and friendless suspect confined to a jail cell has any effective means to communicate a denial. In a review of the proceeding which followed the confession referred to by the Florida editor, Justice Jackson of the United States Supreme Court said the "trial was but a legal gesture to register a verdict already dictated by the press and the public opinion which it generated." [58]

Typically, the press is inclined to reflect the apathetic attitude of the public as to police methods and the assumption that the third degree is used only in "extreme cases," whereas there is good reason to believe that physical and psychological force are still widely used in American police stations to extract admissions of criminal offenses over which investigators feel frustrated.[59]

Publicity of Prior Records

Newspaper stories relating arrested persons' previous encounters with the law are, if anything, more commonplace than reports of confessions. While this information usually comes from investigating authorities, the press sometimes takes the initiative in delving into the life history of the accused. In many, if not most, cases the past record of a suspect has nothing to do with whether he is guilty of the particular charge for which at the moment he is being held.

The most plausible rationale for reviewing suspects' criminal histories in news accounts is that in some cases the suspect's record—by indicating a peculiar way of behaving or offenses of a similar nature—may suggest his connection with the new crime. Such evidence, however, is at best only circumstantial.

On the other hand, publication of the prior record of an accused is very likely to have an adverse effect on his case with potential jurors even if he is innocent. They may easily conclude that, since he was a proved criminal in the past, he is still a bad man with a criminal propensity, who probably committed the offense with which he is now being charged. Despite the injustice that may result from publishing such records, the press often opposes any effort to discourage the practice.

Press Disdain for Rights

The press, with some notable exceptions, is prone editorially to overlook the fact that procedural rights, including the rights to have prior police records and coerced confessions excluded from evidence, were established to protect the innocent and to prevent mistreatment of the guilty. When Lewis F. Powell, Jr., as president of the American Bar Association, questioned the trend of court decisions strengthening the rights of the accused, his address was widely acclaimed on editorial pages. The Pittsburgh *Press* approvingly quoted his remark that "There are valid reasons for criminals to think that crime does pay, and that slow and fumbling justice can be evaded." [60] The *Press,* one of the Scripps-Howard chain (with eighteen newspapers and three million circulation), went on to say that "some requirements have been ground so fine that arresting officers are almost afraid to pass the time of day with suspects on the way to the station for fear their talk will be interpreted as coercion and result in a criminal's being freed." Making its point obvious, the *Press* was in favor of reexamining the whole theory of criminal justice and passing congressional legislation and amending the Constitution if necessary. Many other Scripps-Howard editorials have been phrased in the same vein. A similar editorial attitude is observable in the Hearst chain and in many individual papers whose insensitivity to procedural rights is revealed in their news columns. Their harsh attitude reflects none of the wisdom in the observation by David C. Acheson, when he was U.S. Attorney for the District of Columbia, to the effect that "court decisions on how to treat a criminal after arrest have about as much effect [on crime] as an aspirin on a tumor of the brain."

Editors and Their Critics

When all of the various potentially unjust effects of the press are considered, they add up to a good reason for concern over the subject of a free press and fair trials. But the concern must be directed to a much broader question than the mere prejudicing of the minds of jurors. As shown in this chapter and in the previous chapter, the manner in which the press customarily operates is conducive to undue pressure for conviction at many stages of the law enforcement process.

Though more conclusive scientific findings as to the impact of press coverage of criminal cases would be desirable, the current widespread acceptance of the possible adverse impact of the press on justice is not so completely unsubstantiated as the Press-Bar Committee of the American Society of Newspaper Editors suggested in its report to the society in the spring of 1965.

The ASNE report deserves to be analyzed, since its expressions of doubt about the unjust effect of crime news reflect the attitude of a large segment of the press. While acknowledging a responsibility on the part of the press to take corrective action to avoid even minor injuries, the report advanced the view that no proof exists to support the theory of widespread infringement of the right of fair trial as a result of press coverage of criminal proceedings. The report observed that: (1) the authors knew of "no competent demonstration of the effect of pre-trial and trial publication on the minds of jurors," that (2) judges differ widely on the question, and that (3) the statistics as to reversals on grounds of prejudicial publication—with only three such reversals by the Supreme Court in ten years—do not indicate a serious problem. Moreover, said the ASNE committee, only a small fraction of criminal cases go to jury trials and, of these, a still smaller fraction are reported in the press.[61]

Echoing the ASNE report, Newspaper Association Managers,

Inc., put out a statement minimizing the ill effects of inflammatory press publicity by observing that, after an estimated 40,000 jury trials for major crimes in the United States in 1963 and 1964, only three convictions were reversed because of prejudicial pretrial coverage.[62]

When all of the factors mentioned by the ASNE committee are considered, they do not necessarily add up to a showing that there is no reason for concern. In the first place, the focus of concern should be much broader than the impact of the press on jurors, since the prejudicial influence of newspapers on justice obviously makes itself felt at all stages of the law enforcement process and undoubtedly affects policemen, witnesses, lawyers, and judges as well as jurors.

In the second place, since the jury deliberative process is not readily subject to scientific testing, a conclusive demonstration of the effect of pretrial and trial publication on the minds of jurors would be almost impossible to arrange. And since juries traditionally have not been interviewed and required to say categorically whether they were unjustly influenced by the press, no one can offer a file of cases containing incontrovertible "proof" that the press has caused justice to go astray. Even when juries are polled on such a question, they may not actually know what persuaded them. And if they thought the press did, they would not be likely to admit that they shirked their duty by allowing themselves to be improperly influenced.

Conclusions on the issue, therefore, must be based in large part on historical and circumstantial evidence and on inferential reasoning. Considered in the light of this kind of approach, press coverage of criminal cases is a matter for serious concern. In innumerable cases since the 1700's both English and American judges have inveighed against the press for sabotaging the machinery of impartial justice. This fact is more significant than that some judges do not think juries are prejudiced by the press. There are always some occupants of the bench who are insensitive to the rights of defendants and others who are unwilling to say anything that might alienate the press.

As for the significance of reversals on grounds of prejudicial publication, the weight of statistics in this area is hardly a reliable measure of the problem. If some judges, because of insensitivity or fear, are disinclined to speak out against the press, there are many more judges who for other reasons hesitate to grant motions for mistrials or to upset convictions based on biased news. Such judicial actions mean that the state would have to invest extra time, effort, and expense in new trials. The reluctance of judges to respond to pleas for relief from the effects of prejudicial publicity is nowhere better illustrated than in the case of Dr. Sheppard, whose arrest and trial for the murder of his wife were widely acknowledged by lawyers and newspapermen alike to have been virulently infected by prejudiced news coverage. Paul Holmes, who covered the case for the Chicago *Tribune,* was convinced that Sheppard was innocent and got a raw deal from the press.[63] And yet lawyers for Sheppard, after protesting to many courts, up to and including the United States Supreme Court, were finally able during eleven years to get only one judge to act, though several commented on the misbehavior of the press. In July 1964 U.S. District Judge Carl A. Weinman, acting on a habeas corpus petition, ordered Sheppard released from prison on the grounds that he had been denied a fair trial, in part because of the prejudiced performance of Cleveland newspapers. Judge Weinman in May 1965 was overruled by the United States Court of Appeals for the Sixth Circuit in a decision in which the judges conceded that the defendant had received unfair treatment by the press.[64] In the various briefs and opinions in the Sheppard case, extreme examples of trial by newspaper were fully documented. Finally the United States Supreme Court, after a second appeal, agreed to consider the issue of press interference with the defendant's rights. In June 1966, twelve years after the jury's guilty verdict, the high court reversed Sheppard's conviction and ordered him released unless Ohio gave him a second trial within a reasonable time. The district attorney decided to hold another trial.

Because the Supreme Court can hear only a comparatively few cases—those in which its guidance on some point of law is necessary—its failure to hear and rule on various appeals based on alleged press interference with due process does not mean that such appeals lack merit. Hence there is little significance in the statistic that the Supreme Court ordered only three reversals on this ground in a decade. Actually the trend of Supreme Court decisions indicates a greater concern with the problem than ever before. And lower courts, following the lead of the Supreme Court, have begun setting aside convictions which they feel resulted in whole or in part from unfair news treatment.[65]

However editors may try to minimize the significance of the court decisions, recent rulings nevertheless reflect a growing uneasiness over the impact of the press on justice.

Press Role in Accusations of the Innocent

The newspaper's adverse influence on justice—if it has been present—should be most clearly observable in cases in which, by official acknowledgment, innocent persons have been wrongfully accused. There have been at least four book-length studies dealing with more than 100 actual convictions of innocent persons in American courts.[66] In the book, *Convicting the Innocent,* by Professor Borchard and another, *Not Guilty,* by Judge Jerome Frank (see Chapter 5), the authors note the effect of public clamor egged on by the press in producing wrongful convictions.[67]

Manifestly the press is not the sole cause of injustice to the wrongfully accused. Furthermore, its baleful effect can seldom be segregated and verified with absolute certainty. Yet the contributing role of newspapers in making the innocent suffer is obvious not only from a check of some of Professor Borchard's and Judge Frank's cases but also from a study of other criminal proceedings in which innocent persons were either convicted or subjected to a severe ordeal before being cleared.

The Preston Case

Take as a first example a case involving the careless reporting of a piece of evidence that turned out to be false. James W. Preston was arrested in Los Angeles in 1924, and became a suspect in the robbery and shooting of Mrs. Dick R. Parsons that had taken place a few days earlier. The police had found that the robber, whoever he was, had left fingerprints on the window screen of Mrs. Parsons' home. After Preston's arrest Los Angeles newspapers carried stories saying Preston had been identified as Mrs. Parsons' assailant through the fingerprints. Mrs. Parsons read these accounts and when Preston was brought to her hospital bedside she identified him as the man who had entered her home and shot her. As the only witness to offer direct evidence against Preston at his later trial, Mrs. Parsons again identified him as her assailant. No fingerprint evidence was offered by the prosecution. But the judge, obviously having read the newspapers, referred after the verdict to incriminating fingerprints.

Through it all Preston maintained his innocence, but he was convicted and sentenced to eleven years to life. Eighteen months later he was released from prison when another man, after asserting that Preston was innocent, was himself positively identified as the real culprit through the window screen fingerprints and was convicted.

Surely Mrs. Parsons' inclination to identify Preston as the robber was reinforced, if not created, by the Los Angeles newspaper stories linking him with the crime by fingerprint evidence—the kind often regarded as infallible. The attitude of the judge, who was required to preside impartially at the trial, may also have been swayed by the press "evidence." The papers' published reports obviously came from an unreliable source. Yet the damning "evidence," which could have such a crucial effect on the outcome, was in effect introduced at the pretrial stage where it could not be challenged.[68]

The Wentzel Case

In a second case involving an unjust conviction, the press contributed to the result by placing undue credence in the statements of investigating officials. When a young divorcee named Miriam Green was murdered in Pottstown, Pennsylvania, in 1946, her friend, Gerald C. Wentzel, was caught in an incriminating web of circumstances. When first picked up for questioning, he said he had been on a hunting party 200 miles away on the weekend she was killed; he did not let police know that he had been aware of the murder. Then he admitted that he had found the body when he went to Mrs. Green's apartment late Sunday night. At first he told investigators he had found her door open; then he admitted he had a key. The reason for Wentzel's evasions was that he was badly frightened and thought a straight story would implicate him in the crime. Moreover, though he was a married man with a child, he had been keeping company with Mrs. Green.

In the light of these circumstances, Wentzel's case was hardly strengthened when the press publicized his contradictory statements. His case was weakened still further when the Philadelphia *Inquirer* quoted the following statement by the district attorney handling the case: "Miriam Green was strangled by someone she thought her friend and the killer was driven to his crime either by a desperate vengeance or a frantic fear the woman would betray his guilty secret."

A few days later the *Inquirer* ran the following headline on page one:

POLICE KNOW
MURDERER OF DIVORCEE

SLAYER IS CALLED
'CENTRAL FIGURE' IN
POTTSTOWN PROBE

The story below said investigating authorities had "definitely identified the murderer" and that evidence on hand supplied the "clincher." Despite these indications of certainty, there was no arrest. Apparently the authorities were not as sure of their evidence as they indicated to the press (they said they were simply awaiting further FBI laboratory reports). Soon a Pottstown borough official publicly criticized the police and demanded proof that they were not shielding possible suspects because of their lodge connections (Wentzel was a member of a hunting lodge). The official's demand for a "showdown" was headlined in the *Inquirer,* as were the investigators' denials. Then the headlines began promising an arrest.[69]

After this buildup of expectations, an arrest *was* made. Wentzel was taken into custody, tried, and convicted for the murder of Miriam Green—all of this despite clear evidence from the condition of her body that she must have died while Wentzel was on the hunting trip about which he told and which was corroborated by alibi witnesses. Two and one-half years after Wentzel began serving a ten- to twenty-year sentence, another man confessed to the crime. Though this occurrence did not bring about Wentzel's immediate release, it started a train of further investigation which finally brought him freedom through action by the Pennsylvania Board of Pardons.[70] (To its credit, the Pottstown *Mercury,* after some initial prejudicial reporting of the case, took a key role in the inquiry which eventually freed Wentzel.)

Actually, despite newspaper stories to the contrary, the investigators did not know the murderer of Mrs. Green at the time they were saying they did. But their confident talk, well publicized at the time, led the community to think that they did. It led, moreover, to a challenge to produce the guilty culprit. Next there were promises of an arrest. Even though they were unsure of their evidence, investigators would have found it hard to back down at this point. They took the case to trial. And a jury, which could scarcely have been shielded from all the damning publicity about Wentzel's connections with Mrs. Green, brought in a verdict of guilty.

The Blair Case

In a third example of the detention of an innocent party, the press contributed to the injustice by placing extraordinary confidence in the reliability of a child witness and overemphasizing investigators' theories of the guilt of the accused. The case involved a grocer named Guard Young who in 1952 was driving to his store in Chester, California, from the nearby town of Westport where he had just withdrawn $7,328 from a bank. He was accompanied by four children, three of his own and one of their playmates. The Young car was believed to have been intercepted by two men who took the money, bludgeoned Young and the children, and left them at the roadside. Young and three of the children were found dead. But 3½-year-old Sondra Gay Young, though beaten, was alive. She was the sole living witness of the tragedy.

As officials began investigating the case, Sondra's account of the crime was liberally quoted and played on the front page of the San Francisco *Examiner*. The words attributed to her were simple but the narrative was remarkably straightforward, precise, and uncontradictory for a tot of three and a half. She said, according to the account, that one of the men was big, wore a mask, didn't have any hair in front and his hair in back was black. The two men, she was quoted as saying, drove a big blue car. The paper said the child's description seemed to explain the arrest of Louis Blair, who drove a blue car and owned a movie theater in Chester next to Young's supermarket. Blair's arrest led to a series of front page *Examiner* stories. As so often happens with suspects, the headlines gave greatest prominence to official efforts to counteract Blair's alibis and declarations of innocence. At one point the sheriff was quoted as saying that investigators were only "trying to make a bigger liar out of him [Blair] than he already is." Blair's penchant for wearing women's clothes was repeatedly publicized, though this evidence of transvestitism had no connection whatever with the alleged offense other than that hinted by the *Examiner*'s later vague reference to "a strange woman in white" having been seen the day after the murders in the vicinity of the crime. Blair was reported in the *Examiner* as having been quoted by an unnamed person to the effect that some day he (Blair) was going to kill Young.

Finally, Mrs. Young came to Blair's defense by saying she couldn't conceive of his participation in such a crime. Later she reported that the child had said Blair did not do it. Not until the widow interceded did the headlines begin to go Blair's way. Her statements seemed to have a cooling effect on officials. After being held in jail a week, questioned repeatedly, and finally given lie detector tests, Blair was released.[71] A criminal gang was later implicated in the murders. Blair meanwhile, as a result of the merciless publicity and its inevitable effect on his reputation, felt obliged to move away from Chester.

The Foster Case

A fourth illustration of a miscarriage of justice involved newspaper reports of the past criminal record of a suspect and the bearing this may have had on a wrongful conviction. On the night of June 19, 1956, Charles Drake was shot dead in his home on the outskirts of Jefferson, Georgia, by an invading robber. A few days later the police picked up James Foster in connection with another charge, but became more intensely interested in him when he seemed to fit a description of the robber given by Mrs. Drake. Foster was taken to Mrs. Drake's home where she identified him as the killer. Jackson County, where Drake was highly regarded, had meanwhile become highly incensed over the murder; the populace and the press were up in arms. The Jackson County *Herald* and other papers carried stories about Foster's prison record; he had been convicted and sentenced to eighteen months in Florida as an accessory to a robbery and had only recently been released. Newspapers also reported a statement by Foster's cellmate to the effect that Foster had admitted murdering a man in the area.[72]

When the trial was held at Jefferson a few weeks after Foster's arrest, his lawyer moved for a change of venue on the ground that the publication of his past record had prejudiced every potential juror. The motion was denied and Foster was convicted and sentenced to die. The execution was forestalled while Foster's lawyer fought on, exhausting his appeal remedies. After Foster had been in jail for two years, another man was implicated in the Drake murder by his former associates and he then confessed. Foster was set free.[73] No one knows, of course, to what extent the minds of the jurors and of Mrs. Drake, the most important witness, had been poisoned against Foster by the knowledge of his unrelated offense in Florida. But the publicizing of Foster's past misdeeds certainly didn't help him in his fight to exonerate himself.

The Rexinger Case

As a fifth and final example of sustained press unfairness to an innocent suspect, consider the 1957 Rexinger case (already mentioned) in which a San Francisco warehouse clerk was arrested and held in connection with the rape and torture of a 19-year-old student nurse in Golden Gate Park. The case merits detailed examination because it is an object lesson in how the press and police should not treat a criminal investigation. Rexinger, a parolee from San Quentin, first came under suspicion because police said, according to the *Chronicle,* "he had a record of sex crimes," and because he resembled a police sketch of the assailant. It was the resemblance to the sketch that led police to take Rexinger to the nurse's hospital room where she identified him as her tormenter.

Stories published in the *Examiner* immediately after the crime should have flashed warning signals to the press not to form any hasty judgments. The first account said that the girl and her escort were both "so dazed and shocked they were unable to give police a coherent account of the attack, nor describe the sadist." The next day the *Examiner* reported that the assailant had worn a stocking cap which partially obscured his features.[74] Yet the *Chronicle* reported on the same day that the police were working with a detailed description of the rapist. And the next day the *Chronicle* said that the police, after talking again with the girl and her escort, had broadcast a new and even more detailed description of the assailant —including the information that he was "either bald or with a receding hairline" (no explanation of how this could be seen through a stocking cap) and had a "long nose and prominent buck teeth." The word descriptions were supplemented by a police sketch of the attacker which was dutifully and unquestioningly published by the papers. While the drawing did bear a resemblance to Rexinger, no editor apparently bothered to ask how—considering the initial uncertainty of the victims—such a likeness could be produced.

In addition to Rexinger's similarity to the police sketch, the part of his background that brought him under suspicion was his "record of sex crimes" (note plural), which was emphasized by the *News,* the *Chronicle,* and the *Examiner*. For good measure, the *Examiner* headlined that Rexinger had served time in San Quentin "for assault." [75] Had the reporters and editors taken the trouble to examine the record and their own reports more carefully, they would have conveyed a different impression in their presentation of the news. The only offense for which Rexinger had ever served time was forgery, a crime with no element of violence. The only sex offense for which Rexinger had ever been convicted, and for which he was never imprisoned, was statutory rape. Statutory rape, under California law, is an act of intercourse with a girl under eighteen *with* her consent. The crime by definition does not imply violence. And in Rexinger's case, the offender was put on probation, a procedure that is ordinarily followed when authorities feel that the offense is technical in nature and involves no aggravating circumstances.

Rexinger's alleged violent proclivities in sex matters were headlined by the *Examiner* as follows:

REXINGER'S POETIC RAMBLING
INDICATES HE'S SEXUAL PSYCHOPATH
INSPECTOR SAYS

The story underneath told about a tape recording which Rexinger had made of one of his literary compositions and explained that, while Inspector Frank Gibeau conceded that he was no literary critic, he was of the opinion that the tape "clearly indicates he [Rexinger] is a sexual psychopath and sadist." The inspector was pitting his expert opinion against that of Walter Stone, chief of the State Division of Adult Parolees, who had told the *Chronicle* earlier that he was reserving judgment as to Rexinger's guilt because the suspect had undergone "frequent and intensive psychiatric examination" and there was "no evidence whatsoever of any sadistic drive." The *Examiner* never bothered to contrast Stone's opinion with Gibeau's. The *Chronicle* had buried Stone's remarks in the page-four continuation of a front page story that was headlined "Cops Find Holes in Torture Alibi."

The papers went out of their way to compare Rexinger with Burton W. Abbott, the young man who had been executed in California earlier the same year for the murder (and suspected rape) of a 14-year-old high school girl. Under the headline stating that Rexinger denied guilt, the *News* ran a deck saying: "Rexinger Tale Recalls That of Abbott." Drawing attention to a physical resemblance between the two men, the same paper printed pictures of both taken in identical poses. The *Chronicle* said "Rexinger's appearance and mien have been compared to that of Abbott." Referring to the Abbott case in a way that would cast doubt on Rexinger's veracity, the *Examiner* said: ". . . Rexinger, in a manner reminiscent of Burton W. Abbott, the executed kidnap-slayer of 14 year old Stephanie Bryan, steadfastly denied any role in the shocking torture rape." (The *Examiner* had played an influential role in the pre-indictment "trial" of Abbott.)

So the press "crusade" went for eight days after Rexinger's arrest. Every move in the police campaign to prepare the case for court was headlined. There were interviews with the suspect in which he protested his innocence, but many more interviews with the police in which they sought to crack Rexinger's alibis. Pictures of the suspect were published alongside reproductions of the police sketch. Rexinger was described on various occasions, either in the reporters' own words or in police or neighbors' words, as "testy," "suspicious," "con-wise," "insular," "withdrawn," "evasive," and "querulous." (Who wouldn't have seemed so under the circumstances?)

In its zeal the *Examiner* went out and dug up purported evidence. One of its reporters found a length of Venetian blind cord (the girl had been bound with cord) in a flower bed near Rexinger's apartment. He observed that "the hair clinging to the cord was similar to that of the girl." He did, however, add the caution that the cord was considered of secondary importance because the suspect's landlord was in the Venetian blind business. Another *Examiner* reporter made a tour of army surplus stores which sold manacles, until he found one in which two clerks identified Rexinger from a police line-up picture as a customer who had visited the store. A picture of a girl clerk holding Rexinger's picture was published on the front page. The *Chronicle* reported on page one that a clerk had identified Rexinger as a man who had actually purchased manacles. The next day it reported on page four that the clerk had really not remembered what Rexinger purchased.

On one occasion, after he had been in jail for nearly a week, Rexinger got a break in the headlines. It came when an attorney from the public defender's office talked to him and then expressed the opinion that the police were holding the wrong suspect. The *Chronicle* on another occasion headlined the district attorney's assertion that the case against the suspect was "weak," an admission that the *Examiner* saw fit to mention only in small type on page twenty-four. At one point a Rexinger alibi claim got banner headline treatment in the *Chronicle*. That was when he recalled receiving a telephone call from a wrong-number dialer and sought to have this fact confirmed by the caller so that he could establish his presence in his room during the evening of the crime. (The caller never did verify the event.) Except for a few lapses such as these, the papers bore down with their stories about the police forging "new links in their chain of evidence."

The *Examiner* even saw something suspicious in Rexinger's failure to seek legal counsel, an oversight which has been noted in many mature and supposedly well-informed persons. It remarked that the suspect's "long apparent disinterest in obtaining the counsel of an attorney has been regarded as extraordinary for a person held on such a serious felony."

Not until August 2, 1957, more than a week after the arrest, did the police and the press relax their pressure on Rexinger. On that day it was announced that another man, picked up for another offense, had confessed to the rape. The real rapist, Melvin Bakkerud, 21-year-old drug addict, had been arrested, not for the Golden Gate Park offense but on charges of peddling narcotics. He was linked to the rape only when a watch found in his room turned out to be that stolen from the girl's escort. He then led police to the tape, cord, scissors, and knife used in the attack. Microscopic examination of his belongings revealed fibers which matched those of the victim's clothing.

Bakkerud turned out to have neither the receding hairline, the buck teeth, nor the long nose that the rapist, according to the papers, was supposed to have. He was barely five feet tall; the assailant had been reported to be five feet, nine inches.

With the exception of the *News,* the San Francisco papers had the good grace not to hold up the case as exemplary for justice. Editorially, the *News* remarked on the "spotlight of public interest which said in effect, 'you must be certain; you must prove your case.' . . . Our kind of society demands facts. Spurred on by public interest, police produced the facts—and cleared him [Rexinger]."

They did, but they did it almost by accident. And the newspapers had done nothing to make the police more observant of the requirements of fair procedure. They had not a word of protest when the police violated an elementary rule of investigative practice by having the victim identify the suspect as he stood alone in front of her instead of in a line-up with others. (The *News* chided the police for this procedure only after the case was solved and Rexinger had been cleared.) They had not a word of recognition that Rexinger's rights might have been infringed by his being subjected to a week of incessant questioning without advice from an attorney to guide him. Rexinger in one sense was lucky. Miraculously in his case the right man was caught less than two weeks after the commission of the crime. But during the interval that he was in custody the press did little to promote the ends of justice and much to intensify the imprisoned man's harrowing experience.

If unprovable but probable cases of press publicity which wronged the innocent were to be cited, the list would be endless. In the absence of proof as to where the overall weight of publicity comes to rest on the scales of justice, we can only observe that—given the usual conditions: the unattractiveness of the suspect, the outrage of the community over a wrong, the demands for action, the avenging nature of the public, the customary police-press alliance, and the imitative character of the press—publicity tends to fall on the side of the prosecution.

And in the light of the voluminous record of press unfairness to accused persons, it should be fair for critics to ask whether the obligation of newspapers is limited simply to giving the public what it seems to want or whether there is a higher duty to provide coverage that is as balanced and objective as possible. In so far as the fictional crime dramas of book and screen are concerned, the portrayal of "heavy" characters has no direct bearing on justice. They are creatures of imagination. But the characters in newspaper crime stories are very much alive. If, through the agency of the press, they are made to serve the baser public passions, justice is thoroughly perverted.

The emphasis in this chapter on all of the various ways in which the press contributes to injustice may give the impression that newspapers are always at fault. Of course they are not. As shown in other chapters in this book, there are times when the press in general is the defender of justice and there are outstanding individual papers which consistently battle for the Bill of Rights. But in general the performance of the press in the reporting of crime news does not inspire confidence. And its resistance to criticism suggests a far from adequate recognition of its obligation to due process. The foregoing summary of injustice in the press is deliberately designed to offset the all too typical self-satisfaction and complacency implicit in the remark of Alexander F. Jones, past president of the American Society of Newspaper Editors, when he challenged a press critic "to produce one case where newspapers have so hounded any individual or influenced any court or jury that a man was sent to prison in a miscarriage of justice." [76]

CHAPTER SEVEN

INJUSTICE UNDER LAW

SINCE LAW IS NOT AN EXACT SCIENCE with predictable outcomes for given inputs, no study can presume to separate, measure, and describe the effects of the press on law enforcement without reference to other deleterious influences that may have an unknown bearing on the same cases affected by the press. Besides the injustices that seem most directly attributable to the press, there are other causes of injustice which the law allows or has as yet no effective means to counteract. One such source of injustice is the harsh impact of public pressure.

INJUSTICE UNDER POPULAR PRESSURE

The public, as has already been shown in previous chapters, is an intimate participant in the law enforcement process from the opening of a criminal case until its final disposition. As has also been suggested, the press—acting as the eyes and ears and, ideally, as the conscience of the public—is likewise a participant in the entire process. The press, at its best, when guided by responsible owners and editors, can and does promote the cause of justice. At its worst, the press can do and does grave harm to the cause of justice. Yet even when it is doing an injury to justice, the press is not acting as a detached institution, independent of and unrelated to the society which it serves. Its words and its outlook are dictated to a greater or lesser degree by that society.

If the newspapers and the men who run them are shaped by their public, so are the law enforcement agencies and men who run them. They are in fact creatures of the public, and the press is simply a means of communication between them and the public. It is not, as some imply, an interloper which corrupts a relationship that would otherwise be pure. Nor is it merely a means of one-way communication—from public to the agents of the law; it is also a means of communication from officials to the public. And these officials, without any encouragement from newsmen, often use the press to prejudice the cause of justice.

When the law enforcement process seems to go awry, it may in a restricted sense be responding to the pressures of the press. But in a larger sense it is simply responding to the cruder pressures of the democratic society it serves. In a democratic society the agencies and agents of law enforcement naturally tend to reflect the popular mood or what they take to be the popular mood. In the relationship between public and the agents of justice, the press may exert a modifying influence in particular cases. But the law enforcement machinery, whatever the role of the press, can hardly be divorced from the public or fail to reflect the imperfections of all human institutions. The aim of this chapter is to show that there are many causes of injustice that are more basic than the influence of the press and that the offenses of the press, however reprehensible they are on occasion, must be viewed in a context which includes the other defects of our democratic institutions.

Edward Radin, in *The Innocents,* a book on wrongful convictions, has estimated that the nation's law enforcement machinery, viewed in the most favorable light, still brings about the conviction each year of 14,000 people who may be innocent. This figure was arrived at by calculations based on a respected judge's opinion that the judicial machinery errs in 5 per cent of the cases tried. The 14,000 total represents 5 per cent of 280,000 felony convictions a year. The author himself had gathered information on 300 unjust convictions.[1] Professor Borchard and Judge Frank, in their books in the same field (mentioned in earlier chapters), described more than one hundred cases of convictions of the innocent in American courts. The verified and publicized cases of wrongful convictions undoubtedly represent only a fraction of the unrevealed instances in which justice has gone amiss.

On the other hand, law enforcement agencies may fail to apprehend and convict some persons who ought to be penalized. The agents of justice are not automatons, nor are the institutions through which they work equivalent to a laboratory in which conditions may be imposed as in a controlled experiment. Agents and institutions tend to project the morals and mores of the community in which they operate. The results they produce must be acceptable to the community. As Roscoe Pound once wrote, "the end of law is the adjustment or harmonizing of conflicting or overlapping desires and claims, so as to give effect to as much as possible with the least sacrifice."

The tendency of law enforcement to mirror public moralty is readily observable. Gambling is widely indulged in by the public from coast to coast, and enforcement of antigambling laws is notoriously lenient. Widespread public apathy toward, or resistance against, prohibition brought lax prosecution of bootlegging and speakeasies and eventual abandonment of the Noble Experiment. Nor is the breakdown of law enforcement, when the public is lethargic, a passing modern phenomenon. There is historical evidence of similar behavior in other times. In the colonial period a mob spirit, exemplified by lynchings and night riding, was exhibited in Massachusetts. After the Revolution, widespread resistance to law was registered by Shays' Rebellion and the Whisky Insurrection. The breakdown of law was common in the settling of the West. Defiance of the law by big business was rampant in the late nineteenth century and was matched by lawlessness on the part of workers who organized such terrorist groups as the Molly Maguires.

These historic examples are but a few illustrations of the capacity of a total community or powerful segments of it to pervert the law enforcement process or shape it to its own ends when there is no countervailing pressure from a broader source of sovereignty. Justice, in other words, is what the public says it should be.

More specifically, justice is what the most potent and articulate elements in the community say it should be. The old saying that "laws grind the poor and rich men rule the law" may not be as true as it once was, but it is still true in essence. Vagrants and floaters get the most summary kind of treatment from police and municipal courts. Some 60 per cent of indicted persons cannot afford their own counsel. And defendants with unpaid lawyers or no lawyers are most likely to get the harshest treatment from judges. Poor defendants are the ones least likely to get their cases reviewed and corrected on appeal. Negroes, because they are usually poor and occupy a minority or subservient political status, are victims of unequal justice.

Because courts are staffed by people from the middle or upper classes, they are prone to regard middle- and upper-class defendants as more vulnerable to suffering and therefore more entitled to sympathetic treatment. In 1961 a special sessions justice in New York heard a woman lawyer plead guilty to lying before a grand jury which had investigated rigged television shows. He immediately suspended sentence on her, saying: "I think the defendant has suffered enough. There is no punishment I can impose that will make her suffer more."[2] Such a merciful attitude, while it may be admirable, is seldom shown to more ordinary defendants. For some reason the punishment of humiliation is not considered sufficient for those offenders who plead guilty to theft or some other crime which may ensnare less privileged people. They are evidently considered incapable of being humiliated.

Officials, from beat policemen up through to the highest echelon of law enforcement, tend to react as their social backgrounds dictate and as their various constituencies demand. They are, in a measure, prodded by the press. But the press, too, has its constituency, which is similar to but not necessarily identical with that of the officers of the law. The complex relationship of law enforcement agencies and press to the public seems to boil down to the point that the behavior of each has an effect on the other. Law enforcement agencies are guided by the representatives from the public which they take to be their "clients." Newspapers are guided by those elements which they take to be their "clients." Law enforcement agencies and press influence each other, with the press playing the more vocal role. But neither institution is completely independent of the public.

Such independence as they exhibit—and some degree of independence is certainly desirable—must be fortified not only by an extra measure of individual integrity in newsmen and law enforcement officers but also by deliberate steps on the part of the public. (These will be discussed in a later chapter.)

POLICE AND THE PUBLIC

Police performance clearly reveals the pressures of the constituency it serves. Sheriffs, constables, and other county law enforcement agents are usually elected by direct popular vote. City policemen are appointed by municipal officeholders who are themselves elected. In communities where labor is organized and politically powerful, the policing of industrial disputes is handled with greater consideration for strikers than in cities where workers are unorganized. Police are inclined to overlook certain kinds of extremist picketing activity—for example, vandalism and strong-arm tactics—such as would be dealt with as crimes in nonunion areas. On the other hand, the police in nonunion towns may themselves engage in strong-arm tactics against activity which elsewhere would be regarded as peaceful picketing.

In the South and in the ghettos of Northern cities, Negroes are often the victims of night-stick "justice" simply because they are members of a group which exerts less influence in municipal affairs. In Southern states, with Alabama and Mississippi the worst examples, sheriffs and city police have brought trumped-up charges against Negro victims of violence and have exhibited a consistent inability to determine who is responsible for bombings, church-burnings, shootings, and other crimes against Negroes and civil rights workers.[3] Southern peace officers have been known to connive with lynch mobs, or at least to look the other way. They were reflecting the most vocal sentiment of their communities.

In some of these situations the press, motivated either by conscience or by its conception of its own interests, may raise a restraining hand. But in any event, the press is only an instrumentality for registering a greater or lesser segment of community sentiment. In the context of an industrial dispute it may reflect the antiunion position of large advertisers. In a setting of racial controversy it may reflect the moral pangs of the more favored elements of the community. Whatever its role, the press is not inclined to get too far out of line with majority sentiment. And whatever the press's role, the close liaison between press and police is usually observable. Stories about crime originate with the police, not with offenders. Moreover, police are known to grant favors to reporters in return for good mention. Press and police, therefore, have a stake in each other's activities. In 1964 the Lorain (Ohio) *Journal* carried its favoritism for police to an extreme when it solicited funds for the defense of two policemen who were under federal indictment for beating a prisoner into making a confession and thus denying him his civil rights.[4] An exception to the normal press-police alliance must be noted in the restraining surveillance of Southern police maintained by national press coverage of civil rights activities in the 1960's.

Justice is affected not only by police response to public pressure but also by simple human weakness and deficiencies on the part of the police and a corresponding public indifference toward police misconduct. Carelessness and lawlessness in law enforcement is a constant and recurring problem. In 1961 the United States Civil Rights Commission said: "Police brutality—the unnecessary use of violence to enforce the mores of segregation, to punish, and to coerce confessions—is a serious problem in the United States." After 1961 the continuing nature of the problem was attested by mounting demands in many cities for civilian review boards to check on abuses by police.

Negligence or corruption on the part of the police occurred in nine of thirty-four cases of unjust convictions related by Judge Frank.[5] Professor Borchard showed that overzealousness of police or private detectives helped to convict the innocent in seventeen cases. And in nine such cases Borchard found that the police exhibited gross negligence; in two others they actually suppressed evidence of innocence.[6] Radin, in *The Innocents,* blames the police for a tendency to rely on the infallibility of a single witness.

Policemen not only misbehave in enforcing the law but some of them also commit crimes. After Denver's police scandal broke in 1961, fifty men were stripped of their uniforms and dropped from the force, and thirty of them were sent to prison following their conviction in connection with a series of burglaries in which law enforcement officers participated. That same year eight Chicago policemen were convicted in one 24-hour period of having conspired with a thief to commit burglaries and to conceal stolen property while in uniform and on duty. In the early 1960's cases of burglaries by police also occurred in Detroit, Cleveland, Kansas City, Mo., Bristol, Connecticut, and Burlington, Vermont. Investigations of police corruption were launched in Syracuse, New York, in 1962, in Milwaukee in 1963, and in New York City in 1964. In Baltimore in 1966 the police commissioner resigned after the release of a report condemning misconduct and corruption in his department. These cases represent but a sampling of reported instances of police misconduct or crime in recent years. Offenses by law enforcement officers signify that they are subject to the same delinquencies that they are supposed to police. But beyond that they suggest that in the complex relationship of public, police, and press, there are many imperfections that detract from the attainment of perfect justice.

LAWYERS AND THE PUBLIC

Like newsmen and policemen, lawyers too conduct themselves in a manner that they think will meet with popular approval. Lawyers are conscious of the fact that their practices are affected by the reputations they have for abiding by the conventions of their communities. Recently a former high government official told an audience of attorneys in Los Angeles: "This is the age of the image. It is a telling word and one we lawyers cannot afford to discount or ignore."

The image varies from one community to another. But wherever they are, lawyers dare not depart too far from the acceptable standards of speech and behavior. This means that attorneys are often reluctant to defend unpopular clients or to voice unpopular views. A Columbia University law professor, after examining issues of the *Alabama Lawyer* from 1954 to 1964, reported that he found it "a single-toned organ of orthodoxy" based on "the constant premise of white supremacy," and added that he looked in vain for "the nonconformist reaction of some disputatious lawyer." [7]

Attorneys are licensed by the state. To acquire a license, they must not only pass an examination on law administered by a board representing the public but they must also embody certain traits of character which the board deems suitable for attorneys. Furthermore, would-be lawyers must, practically speaking, avoid appearing to be unorthodox in their beliefs. No one has enunciated a categorical rule to this effect. But decisions of the United States Supreme Court have the same result. The high court has upheld states in denying admission to the bar to applicants who, on grounds of freedom of conscience and speech, have refused to answer questions about their views or associations. Orthodoxy is also enforced by contempt proceedings against lawyers with left-wing sympathies and by disbarment or threats to disbar such lawyers. In 1956 Harry Sacher, a lawyer who defended top-ranking American Communists charged with violating the Smith Act, was convicted of contempt of Congress for refusing to answer questions of the Senate Internal Security Subcommittee. In several states bar associations have moved to disbar attorneys who have been identified with Communist views or defendants.

The pressure which the public exerts on lawyers is hardly the kind that is helpful to the cause of justice. In the South, the fear (often well founded) of public revenge has frequently kept lawyers from taking the cases of Negroes and civil rights workers. And in all parts of the country suspected Communists and other unpopular defendants have on many occasions lacked adequate defense counsel because lawyers recoil from the prospect of public disfavor.[8]

Not only do individual lawyers seek to remain in public favor, but the legal profession itself exerts little effort to invoke the canons of ethics against violators whose publicized misconduct might then tarnish the bar's image. Bar associations have committees whose mission is to investigate alleged unprofessional conduct and to initiate disciplinary action. But the power, or at least the inclination, of the disciplinary groups seems hardly equal to the task. A casual reading of the Canons of Professional Ethics will make even the ordinary observer aware that lawyers are seldom called to account for common practices that the canons are supposed to curb. In 1962, the most recent year for which statistics were available, only seventy-four lawyers were disbarred in the United States; ninety were suspended and forty-five quit under pressure. This means that only .08 per cent of the members of the profession were found to have transgressed its high standards of ethics. In 1965 Lewis F. Powell, the outgoing president of the American Bar Association, remarked on the "unwillingness by lawyers to discipline their fellow lawyers." [9]

Canon 27 contains the following admonition to lawyers:

> Indirect advertisements for professional employment such as furnishing or inspiring newspaper comments, or procuring his photograph to be published in connection with causes with which the lawyer has been or is engaged or concerning the manner of their conduct, the magnitude of the interest involved, the importance of the lawyer's position, and all other like self-laudation, offend the traditions and lower the tone of our profession and are reprehensible.

Yet lawyers realize that publicity produces clients and they often indicate that they would appreciate being mentioned in news stories.

Among attorneys, public prosecutors are most addicted to publicity-seeking. As Roscoe Pound once wrote: "When a sensational crime has been committed, coroner, police, and district attorney may each go out for glory or publicity. Politics require taking advantage of possibilities of publicity." [10] A prosecutor's election or reelection depends largely on the reputation he has with the public. And the press is one means of building a reputation. If he is running for the first time, a district attorney candidate may be able to cite his experience as a special prosecutor. If he is running to succeed himself in office, a frequent tactic is to appeal for votes on the basis of his record of convictions. Criminal defense attorney George Davis has observed that at prosecutors' conventions there is often talk that successful prosecutions of a sensational nature can send a district attorney to new heights, as shown by the career of Thomas Dewey. Yet there is grave danger to justice in such an attitude. The late Judge Jerome Frank made it clear when he said:

> The menace to the guiltless becomes singularly great when a politically ambitious prosecutor seeks to advance himself through newspaper renown for the large number of convictions he obtains.

> Such a prosecutor, eager to prove a suspect guilty, will carelessly, or even sometimes deliberately, neglect painstaking investigation, before indictment or trial, of leads that might well show the suspect's innocence. Such a prosecutor will all too easily develop what Sam Hobbs (a lawyer with much experience in prosecution) calls an "occupational disease," a "habit of drifting into a chronic spirit of hostility toward each new suspect." [11]

Newspaper examples of prosecutor boasting on convictions are not hard to find. A few years ago a prosecutor in New York put out a statement noting that during the preceding year his office had obtained convictions in 97.9 per cent of the cases closed.

Prosecuting attorneys, like other law enforcement officials, are attuned to what the public wants and tend to reflect popular demands. In the South this may mean the excusing of lynching or failure to prosecute. Or in any region it may mean harsh treatment of defendants in cases in which public passion is excited. Sometimes the zeal to convict becomes so intense that the prosecutor casts aside caution and even honesty. Judge Frank showed how prosecutor negligence was involved in at least five convictions of innocent defendants[12] and outright prosecutor dishonesty was a factor in two wrongful convictions.[13] In thirteen cases related by Borchard the prosecution's overzealousness was the operative factor in causing the erroneous conviction.[14]

Not only do prosecutors use the press to promote their personal reputations, but they also use it to help them secure convictions. The prosecution practice of trying cases in the newspapers is so universal that any district attorney's reluctance to do so becomes a matter for comment. Thus District Attorney Frank S. Hogan of New York County prompted widespread discussion among newsmen and attorneys by announcing a number of years ago that members of his staff were "not to make public disclosures of the evidentiary contents, or the substance, of statements that have been given to them by defendants, or by persons who may become defendants . . . because as lawyers we have an obligation to protect the rights of persons who may be accused of the commission of crime." [15]

Prosecutor appeal to public prejudice through the press is rampant despite Rule 20 of the Canons of Professional Ethics which in its revised form says:

> It is unprofessional for a lawyer to make, or to sanction the issuance or use by another of, any press release, statement or other disclosure of information, whether of alleged facts or of opinion, for release to the public by newspaper, radio, television or other means of public information, relating to any pending or anticipated civil action or proceeding or criminal prosecution, the purpose or effect of which may be to prejudice or interfere with a fair trial in the courts or with due administration of justice. The foregoing shall not be applicable to publications of statements made in Court, or from depositions, or filed or served pleadings, or affidavits filed or submitted to the Court. . . .

Courts are more inclined to reprimand prosecutors for their press activities than to take affirmative action to counteract the effect of their statements. In the Stroble case in 1952 the Supreme Court of the United States condemned a district attorney for releasing to the press the details of an alleged confession and for expressing his belief that the accused was sane and guilty. But the court upheld the subsequent conviction and left it to Justice Frankfurter to observe in dissent that there had been a denial of due process because of the prosecutor's action. Justice Frankfurter went on:

> To have the prosecutor himself feed the press with evidence that no self-restrained press ought to publish in anticipation of a trial is to make the State itself through the prosecutor, who wields its power, a conscious participant in trial by newspaper, instead of by those methods which centuries of experience have shown to be indispensable to the fair administration of justice.[16]

In the Leviton case in 1952 the United States Court of Appeals for the Second Circuit affirmed the conviction of a defendant during whose trial the prosecutor had called a press conference and released damaging "evidence" which was never adduced in court. In dissent Judge Jerome Frank remarked that "had the prosecutor written letters to the jurors retelling this story, of course we would reverse. He did the equivalent."[17]

During the trial of Julius and Ethel Rosenberg in 1952 the prosecutor arranged to release news of the perjury indictment of a purported government witness in such a way as to damage the defense. The implication of the prosecutor's press statement was that the witness had been indicted for backing out of an arrangement whereby he was to corroborate the government's case. In its opinion in the case the Court of Appeals later declared: "Such a statement to the press in the course of a trial we regard as wholly reprehensible." But, on a technical ground, the court refused to reverse the conviction.[18]

The Illinois Supreme Court in a 1954 case affirmed the granting of a new trial to a defendant who was found guilty in a proceeding in which the prosecutor gave to the press a statement describing what he said was a confession by the accused to various crimes in addition to the one he was being prosecuted for.[19]

If there were any doubt about the value prosecutors place on their relations with the press, it should be dispelled by the attitude which many of them take toward proposals to change the relationship. In 1964–1965 prosecuting attorneys in New Jersey, New York, and Pennsylvania sided with the police and the press in condemning recommendations to limit the release of potentially prejudicial publicity. During a 1957 meeting of the New York State Bar Association members were discussing a proposed revision of Canon 20 designed to curb the prejudicial effect of lawyers' statements on criminal justice. Edward Silver, Brooklyn district attorney, rose and announced that it was "the unanimous feeling" of members of the New York State District Attorneys Association that the suggested amendment was "too restrictive to public prosecutors and endangers the proper exercise of their functions." Among several questionable arguments which Silver advanced, was one to the effect that the district attorney would be prevented from issuing a statement denying a news item reporting falsely that a certain person was being investigated for a crime. Actually the proposed canon would have had no such effect, since it would specifically discourage only those statements which would "prejudice or interfere with a fair trial." The speaker probably came closer to revealing the real reason for the district attorneys' opposition when he said:

It puts the prosecutor in an embarrassing situation when facts that have actually occurred, that did not emanate from him, are put to him, and it becomes most difficult for him to say "No comment."

The press can bring a great deal of embarrassment to a prosecutor when they deal with the District Attorney and say he is repressing news, and he is charged with unwillingness to inform the public of what is happening or, indeed, is covering up an evil or whitewashing crime or corruption.

Another example of a prosecutor attitude toward the press and criminal justice was provided by Bronx County District Attorney George B. DeLuca at an earlier meeting of the New York State Bar Association. DeLuca declared that there was not "the slightest indication" that in his county prior press coverage had "adversely affected the defendant in any given case." In support of this strong generalization, he cited the presumably germane fact that most criminal cases receive little press attention. But then he proceeded to offer the totally irrelevant *a priori* contentions that, in his experience, the court had never seen fit to lock up a jury during the progress of a trial and never, as a matter of law, barred the admission in evidence of a confession—as though these attitudes on the part of judges *proved* that the press had not had a prejudicial influence. DeLuca concluded by opposing any restrictions on the press.[20]

The weight of prosecution publicity is so overwhelming that some defense attorneys frankly say they will not refrain from putting their own cases before the reading public.

So common are attorneys' prejudicial statements to the press that only the most flagrant examples give occasion for comment and even fewer cases result in mistrials or in appellate reversals. In a 1961 argument before the Supreme Court of the United States, opposing counsel traded blows over each side's alleged use of the press to try its case. Three persons had been convicted in California for the killing of Olga Duncan, a Santa Barbara nurse. Defense Counsel A. L. Wirin told the Supreme Court that public statements released to the press by Ventura County District Attorney Roy Gustafson had prejudiced the jury and had resulted in an unfair trial for his clients. He described what happened as "trial by the prosecutor in the newspapers," and added: "There were really two trials. The first was in the public press in which the District Attorney acted as prosecutor. The second was before a judge and jury, but was a trial only in form, since the verdict had already been rendered." The defense named seven newspapers, including four in Los Angeles, in which it said the "prosecution" was conducted.

Assistant Attorney General William E. James of California argued for the prosecution that the case had received "a fair and full news disclosure" and that "the news media were not perverted or slanted by anyone, certainly not the District Attorney." In a comment from the bench, Chief Justice Earl Warren noted that the defense itself had released sixty-nine different statements to the press—to which Mr. Wirin replied that these were issued "in self-defense" as a retaliation for the statements released by Mr. Gustafson.[21] After hearing these claims and counterclaims, the Supreme Court later refused to grant the defense's request for a new trial in a different county.

With disciplinary action by bar associations at a minimum and remedial action by the courts limited, the verbal dueling between opposing counsel goes on outside as well as inside the courtroom, but usually with defense lawyers at a decided disadvantage in their relations with the press. Like prosecutors, defense attorneys too can profit from a reputation built in the newspapers. But unlike prosecutors, they do not have a public platform from which to command attention. Only when they get sensational cases or after they are established as wizards in the courtroom are they likely to be sought out by reporters. In his autobiography Clarence Darrow tells how, during his early career, he was disappointed at not being mentioned in the papers, and how in later years he was anxious to keep out of the press but couldn't avoid it.

Some established defense attorneys have learned how to use the press to help their causes. Thus George T. Davis of San Francisco could say that he welcomed a liaison with newspaper reporters and photographers. Davis sums up his credo on lawyers and the press this way:

> When I am representing a defendant who has been the target of an attack by police and prosecutors in the press, and thus had

> his defense prejudiced, I think it is my duty to set forth my contentions on the case to any newspaper reporter who interviews me on the subject. If I refused to do so, I would, in my opinion, be violating professional ethics in the most flagrant manner. Lawyers are governed by a rule which transcends all other rules. Regardless of the compensation involved, he must fight for the legal rights of his client, use all fair and legitimate means in doing so and disregard any personal danger and inconvenience to himself.[22]

Years ago Samuel Leibowitz, then a highly effective defense lawyer, was defending a woman who was charged in a much publicized trial with murdering her lover. When Leibowitz emerged from a long session with his client he was stopped by reporters who wanted to know whether he had anything to say. He replied, "You bet I'll say something. I have heard Laura Parr's [the defendant's] story and I can say that legally, morally and from every other human standpoint, Dr. Gebhardt [the victim] got what was coming to him. She'll tell her story in court." The defendant was later acquitted.[23]

When they discuss the issue, after reflection, many defense lawyers are inclined to deplore the usual role of the press in criminal cases. George T. Davis believes newspapers are usually biased against defendants. Edward Bennett Williams has spoken of press prejudice against defense attorneys. Clarence Darrow saw grievous harm from "savage stories carried by newspapers" and lamented over press campaigns that reeked "with venom."[24] However censurable such press campaigns may be, lawyers frequently provide material for them, and courts seldom take disciplinary action.

JUDGES AND THE PUBLIC

With most trial judges having to gain their seats by approval of the voters, judicial candidates are acutely conscious of the importance of the image they present to the public and the press. When they run for judicial office—as they must in some thirty-five of the states—lawyers are careful to present themselves as family men, as church participants, as civic promoters, and as John Q. Citizens who are conscious of and responsive to the public will. In order to remain on the bench or to aspire to higher office, judges must be careful not to offend their constituencies or the press. Supreme Court Justice Robert H. Jackson once observed,

> From our sheltered position, fortified by life tenure and other defenses to judicial independence, it is easy to say that this local judge ought to have shown more fortitude in the face of criticism. But he had no such protection. He was an elective judge, who held office for a short term. I do not take it that an ambition of a judge to remain a judge is either unusual or dishonorable. . . . Of course, the blasts of these little papers in this small community do not jolt us, but I am not so confident that we would be indifferent if a news monopoly in our entire jurisdiction should perpetrate this kind of attack on us. . .[25]

Judges are not too Olympian to use attention-getting devices to attract public favor. A Pittsburgh judge posed as the epitome of juristic virtue when he advised fathers and mothers to adopt what he proclaimed to be the "Ten Commandments of Parenthood." Appropriately phrased in biblical style, the judge's commandments consisted of a series of tedious injunctions of which the following is illustrative: "Thou shalt teach thy children respect for the law and keep them from companionship of children who indicate disrespect for the law."

While such sententious advice is harmless enough, it is suggestive of the lack of imagination which the elective jurist so often represents. He is bound by the mores of his constituency and instead of displaying the independence which the judiciary should exhibit, his decisions are dictated by the common denominator of public morality. In a strongly unionized community, the judge is acutely mindful of the voting power of labor. In labor-conscious Pittsburgh several years ago a judge refused a supermarket's request for a temporary restraining order against Teamster union violence which was being used to prevent trucks from loading equipment at the firm's warehouse. In another Pittsburgh case a few years earlier a judge dismissed criminal charges against two Teamster union members who were indicted for allegedly attempting, during a department store strike, to run down two store supervisors with an automobile. If the judge was right in saying that the charge was brought under an unsuitable statute, it was nevertheless significant that the assistant district attorney who handled the case neglected to employ a commonly used charge (assault and battery with an automobile), that the case did not come up for a hearing until twenty months after the alleged incident, that it was heard only after five postponements of the proceedings, and that the indictment was never redrawn after the dismissal. One should be justified in wondering, under the circumstances, whether political pressure, express or implied, was involved.

In a 1965 Chicago case a Negro judge's decision showed signs of having been influenced by his particular public. Judge George Leighton, a former president of the Chicago chapter of the National Association for the Advancement of Colored People, acquitted two Puerto Ricans charged with aggravated assault against a policeman who had tried to arrest them. The ground for acquittal was that the defendants were defending themselves against an unlawful arrest in which the policeman was using a gun. But the Chicago *Tribune* —with a different constituency from Judge Leighton's—did not share his concern over the use of "excessive force" by the police. It castigated the judge for extending an "invitation to anarchy."

In Southern communities judges have been blatantly responsive to popular passion. In 1964 nine white men were arrested in connection with the bombings of three Negro homes in McComb, Mississippi. After they pleaded guilty or no contest to charges that could have brought the death penalty, Circuit Judge W. H. Watkins assessed fines or suspended prison sentences against the defendants and then freed them, observing that they were "unduly provoked" by civil rights workers, were from good families, and deserved a second chance.[26]

A generation ago a Negro was being held in jail in Cartersville, Georgia, after he had been in a scuffle with a police chief during which the officer was killed. When the prisoner's lawyers sought a change of venue because of public excitement in Cartersville, the judge denied their motion and went on to say from the bench that the people of Cartersville would demonstrate that the accused would be looked after. That night the jailed man was taken from his cell by a mob and hanged to a utility pole. The judge later expressed satisfaction that there had been no mutilations and suggested that this indicated the "orderly" way in which the lynching was carried out and the "high class" of people who conducted it.[27]

A few years later another Southern judge learned a bitter lesson from having failed to yield to popular wrath. After the second trial of the Scottsboro boys in Alabama, Judge James E. Horton set aside the jury's verdict of guilty. It was the climax of a proceeding (in 1933) in which he had tried to rule fairly throughout and had dealt firmly with would-be demonstrators. When Judge Horton came up for reelection two years later he was reviled as a "nigger lover" and was defeated. Five years afterward he died a heartbroken and disillusioned man.

The concern most judges show for the figure they present to the public is often demonstrated from the bench. While presiding over the case of a rape defendant in 1961, a general sessions judge in New York City said to the accused who was standing in front of him:

> In all my 23 years on the bench, I have never had a man before me as vicious, as degenerate, as depraved and as criminal as you are.
>
> I would not dignify calling you a man. You are the lowest type of animal who has ever appeared before me.[28]

Since it is highly doubtful that this lecture would have any therapeutic effect on the accused, it could only have been useful as a purgative for the judge and as a way of showing the public that its elected representative shared its outrage over the offender's dastardly doings. In a Pittsburgh case a rape defendant who was berated from the bench actually told the judge that nothing he (the defendant) could say would make any difference to the court.

In view of the public's customary retributive view of justice, it is a rare judge who dares to display a sympathetic feeling for the defendant. He must in the ordinary case be as stern as the electorate in his demand of an eye for an eye. Justice Curtis Bok of the Pennsylvania Supreme Court said it bluntly in his book, *Star Wormwood:*

> Old Judge Parkinsen was assigned to preside at the trial. He declared, and was quoted, that he would sit day and night to bring

> the young miscreant to book. He hastily had to issue a rider in the next edition that of course the defendant's legal rights would be scrupulously protected. What it meant was that Judge Parkinsen intended to murder him.
>
> There is a Judge Parkinsen in every legal community, a man of outward judicial demeanor but with a head full of sawdust and the soul of a man-eating shark. The community gets him because it deserves him.[29]

Judges are not only mindful of the image of themselves which they must convey to the public through the press but, because of their dependence on the newspapers for this task, they may be blind to what the papers are doing to justice. In 1961, after a nationally headlined Florida trial in which prejudiced press coverage was an issue, the presiding judge and the twenty-seven attending reporters and photographers congratulated each other on their sterling performance. Speaking for the press, Jim Bishop of King Features Syndicate, presented Judge D. C. Smith with a citation on the last day of the month-long trial. On the same day Judge Smith (taking care to note that he had jotted down his remarks two nights earlier) extolled the press in general and praised the particular reporters and photographers who had covered the trial, saying that he gave them all "an A plus," and telling them that their profession had "occasion to be proud" of them. *Editor and Publisher,* in the same issue in which it reported the exchange of pats on the back, joined the chorus with an editorial panegyric for the press.[30]

The event from which the court and the press were drawing so much self-satisfaction was the trial of Joseph A. Peel, Jr., a former West Palm Beach municipal judge, in connection with the 1955 murder of Palm Beach County Circuit Court Judge C. E. Chillingworth. Before the March 1961 trial occurred there had already been a change of venue to Fort Pierce, Florida, because of previous press prejudicing of the defendant's case. Yet just before the Fort Pierce proceedings began Jim Bishop wrote a series of five articles detailing the prosecution's entire case, its claim that Peel was covertly working for racketeers, that he had hired two killers to get rid of Judge Chillingworth because he was afraid Chillingworth was about to disbar him for some professional misconduct, and that this would end his usefulness to the rackets. Bishop's big pretrial buildup for the prosecution was presented with few qualifying phrases and with no indication that he had sought out the defense side of the story.

Across the country the San Francisco *Examiner* gave Bishop's stories front page play under headlines which told readers that "Murder in Palm Beach" was "Stranger Than Fiction," and which informed them, among other things, that an "Ugly Trio Joined Up in Racket Protection." The long account of the murder of Judge Chillingworth and his wife was accompanied by drawings purporting to show exactly how the crime was committed.

Peel protested in vain that public opinion was inflamed by the press.[31] He was convicted of being an accessory to murder and sentenced to life imprisonment. Though the result may have been just, all of the press representatives on the scene were hardly entitled to an "A plus" from the judge for objective reporting.

Another aspect of the reciprocal relationship between judges, the press, and the public is illustrated by the fame a Pennsylvania judge won by setting herself the goal of jailing a thousand young delinquents. If in the Peel trial in Florida, it was the press which won a judicial accolade, in Philadelphia the situation was reversed when Judge Juanita Kidd Stout in 1965 became the beneficiary of widespread press plaudits for sentencing great numbers of children to indefinite terms. She was applauded despite a lack of evidence to support her conviction of the young defendants.

By advocating a system which is perennially popular with a considerable segment of the press, Judge Lester H. Loble of Helena, Montana, made something of a national reputation in the early 1960's. This judge's simplistic cure was to turn the spotlight of publicity on children charged with delinquent acts and to lecture them and their parents in open court. Newspaper articles and editorials began to promote the idea that the Loble procedure was stamping out delinquency in all of Montana, and proposals for Loble laws—allowing public hearings in Juvenile Court—swept across the country. When the National Council on Crime and Delinquency sought statistics from Judge Loble to substantiate the claims made for his method, he refused to make court figures available. Such figures as the NCCD was able to obtain from an "informed source" did not support the claims of a drop in crime.

Because of the privileged position they occupy, judges are peculiarly immune from public and press scrutinizing of their off-the-bench conduct. Yet even judges at times yield to the kinds of temptation that cause other men to be brought before them as defendants. Several cases of dishonest judges have made headlines in recent years. In 1962 former New York Supreme Court Justice J. Vincent Keogh was convicted and sentenced to two years in prison for attempting to fix a federal court sentence in Brooklyn while he had been on the bench. The next year in the same state Supreme Court Justices Louis L. Friedman and Melvin H. Osterman were removed from office—Friedman, for obstructing a court-ordered investigation of "ambulance chasing" in King's County; Osterman, for obstructing an inquiry into the State Liquor Authority. Osterman later pleaded guilty to three counts of conspiracy to fix liquor license cases.

In 1964 Connecticut Circuit Court Judge J. Allen O'Connor, Jr., was convicted of indecent assault and given a six-month suspended sentence. The Oklahoma Supreme Court was rocked by scandal in 1964 when a former justice, Nelson S. Corn, and a sitting justice, Earl Welch, were convicted in federal court and sentenced to fines and prison terms for evading federal income taxes on money they allegedly received as a bribe for a favorable ruling in a corporation case. In 1965 another justice of the Oklahoma Supreme Court, Napoleon Bonaparte Johnson, was convicted and removed from the bench after an impeachment trial in the state Senate growing out of the same bribery charges. Though cases such as these are unusual, they nevertheless suggest that the image of righteousness that is sometimes conveyed from the bench is not always justified even for the judiciary.[32]

JURIES AND THE PUBLIC

Of all the various participants in the law enforcement process, juries are perhaps most representative of the public, reflecting both the strengths and weaknesses of collective popular judgment of cases. Despite the prevailing legal dogma to the contrary, the jury operates as more than a simple instrument for deciding what the facts of the case are. It is actually a device for projecting the mores and standards of the community into the courtroom.[33] As the late Judge Jerome Frank put it, men want the law to be "father-like, aloof, stern, coldly impartial," but they also want it to be "flexible, understanding, humanized." Through the judge and jury they can have it both ways.

> The judge, wearing a false-face, which makes him seem like the child's stern father, gravely recites the impersonal and artificial rules which command respect; but the juries decide the actual legal controversies.[34]

Judge Frank's theory of the jury as a humanizing influence on the law, though it was expressed with some reservations, is borne out in a University of Chicago study comparing judges' attitudes to those of juries in 1,500 criminal cases. In a questionnaire sent to 500 judges in regard to jury trials over which they presided, the judges were asked to say, prior to the rendition of the jury's verdict, how they (the judges) would have decided the case. The judges, their responses showed, were considerably more prone to convict. If all of the defendants in the 1,500 cases had been tried by a judge, the number of acquittals would have been cut about in half—from about 500 to about 250. The greatest percentage of disagreement between judges and jurors came in cases of statutory rape, an offense in which the prime determinant of guilt is the youth of the female rather than any violence on the part of the male. In first offense drunken driving cases, juries frequently acquitted when judges would have convicted, though judges in these cases sometimes said they were pleased with the juries' conclusions but felt that they themselves were bound to uphold the law.[35] Actually, however, judges influence far more cases than juries, since 75 to 90 per cent of criminal cases are processed in nonjury trials in which defendants plead guilty—often after bargaining with the prosecutor.[36]

In a vast literature on the jury system, many reasons have been advanced to show why the jury is a popular institution—among them, that it keeps the administration of justice in accord with the wishes and feelings of the community, that it gives the people a feeling that they are a part of the judicial process and enables them to prevent its arbitrary use or abuse, that it is an excellent form of public entertainment which, at the same time, interests the people in the administration of justice and in the crime problem.[37]

Stories in the press frequently suggest the ways in which juries reflect the public's idiosyncrasies and unpredictability. In Pittsburgh, within a period of a few years, juries were chastised by judges for ignoring the evidence and acquitting alleged drunken drivers and numbers writers, for finding a college student not guilty after he admitted knowingly driving a stolen car into another state, and for acquitting a young man charged with assaulting a policeman. In this last case, a woman juror on her way out told the defendant: "You'd better straighten yourself out."

The fact that juries project popular mores and personal prejudices is especially evident in cases involving racial conflict. In San Francisco in 1964 a Negro juror in a civil rights case caused a municipal court judge to declare a mistrial when she stood up as the jury foreman was about to announce the jury's decision and exclaimed: "I was assassinated and crucified in the jury room because I am a Negro." White members of the jury, on the other hand, said she disregarded the evidence and the judge's instructions and wanted to decide the case on a racial basis.

In another part of the country, however, the question at issue is a different kind of juror bias. Never in the history of Mississippi has a white man in that state been found guilty of murder in the first degree when the slain person was black. Juries dominated by whites have conveyed in their verdicts the prevailing white attitude that the taking of a Negro's life by a white assailant is not comparable in heinousness to the killing of a white person.[38] A similar point of view has, of course, been reflected by juries in other Southern states. In recent years juries in Alabama and Georgia, as well as in Mississippi, have refused to convict white defendants who were linked by strong evidence to the killing of Negroes or of white sympathizers with Negroes. Near the end of 1965 two all-white Alabama juries broke the established pattern of justice in that state by convicting defendants connected with the murder of a Negro and of a white civil rights worker.

In Mississippi in 1962 a LaFayette County grand jury accused Chief U.S. Marshal James J. P. McShane of deliberately inciting a riot at the University of Mississippi when McShane and other federal marshals were protecting Negro student James H. Meredith from a white mob. Later a federal jury in Mississippi cleared two white men charged with attacking federal officers with pistols and gasoline bombs during the riot.

Another example of jury reflection of popular prejudice occurred some years ago in the unionized community of Herrin, Illinois, when about 200 members of the local mine union were indicted following the killing of a score of strike-breakers and guards who attempted to operate a coal strip mine. Two groups of defendants were tried and all were acquitted by local juries made up of workers and farmers. The remaining indictments were finally quashed.[39]

The quirks and prejudices in the outlook of jurors are endlessly varied. A few years ago researchers for Fairleigh Dickinson University tested and interviewed nearly 500 men and women from all parts of the United States and gave them a chance to act out their conscious and unconscious prejudices in a jury situation. Though the study pertained especially to civil cases, its findings undoubtedly would have implications for criminal cases too. The researchers discovered that, of eleven characteristics which influenced jurors' opinions of litigants, those on which bias was most often based were sex, income, religion, education, and occupation. Among the miscellaneous findings were that salesmen have an unconscious bias against lower income groups, that housewives have a hidden bias against the rich, that religious bias is most pronounced against Seventh Day Adventists, Jehovah's Witnesses, and fundamentalists.[40] It should not be necessary to point out that, however valid these findings are under some circumstances, they would not apply to every community. Yet the study calls attention to still more of the countless imponderables that go into the making of court decisions. Since the jury in a sense is the public, the law cannot do much to rid it of common public prejudices that might be present without press misconduct.

WITNESSES AND THE PUBLIC

Like policemen, lawyers, judges, and jurors, witnesses also may be swayed by the public. Witnesses are not immune to social pressure. And if the popular judgment seems to demand a certain outcome, they may tailor their testimony, even unconsciously, to help bring about that outcome. More than one legal observer has said that witnesses are prone to see what they want to see, that they may have a strong bias in favor of what they believe to be the justice of the case so that with entire innocence they may recall things that never occurred. In view of this possibility, the reliability of evidence in the courtroom obviously may be affected by a contaminating source more integral to the judicial process than the press.

HOSTILITY TO RIGHTS OF THE ACCUSED

Because of recognized flaws in our system of justice, certain procedural safeguards were written into the Constitution and entrusted to the guardianship of the courts. But the Supreme Court's current concern for the Bill of Rights has not been wholeheartedly shared by the public, by the legal profession, or by officers of the law. In the past ten years its decisions upholding the rights of the accused have made the court the target of repeated attacks. Bills have been introduced in Congress to override its decisions. In 1958 the Conference of State Chief Justices adopted a resolution chiding the high tribunal for not showing "proper judicial restraint" in the interest of preserving "local self-government." The next year the governors of the American Bar Association gave their support to a series of broad recommendations by a special ABA committee urging congressional revision of the Supreme Court decisions relating to the prosecution of alleged Communists and subversives. In 1962 John C. Satterfield, president of the American Bar Association, denounced the Supreme Court for giving "inordinate weight" to individual rights and not enough to the needs of law enforcement and national security. During the 1964 presidential campaign Senator Barry Goldwater attacked the court's decisions on procedural rights in criminal cases. The next year President Lewis F. Powell, Jr., of the

American Bar Association was thunderously applauded by 3,000 lawyers when he said that the rights of citizens to be free from criminal attack must be placed ahead of the constitutional rights of persons accused of crime.[41]

The most vehement reaction to Supreme Court decisions on fair procedures for the accused has come, however, from spokesmen for police organizations. Addressing the annual convention of the International Association of Chiefs of Police in 1964, Police Chief William H. Parker of Los Angeles said police work in the United States had been "tragically weakened" through a progressive "judicial take-over." A few months later Police Commissioner Michael Murphy of New York declared that the Supreme Court's decisions on confessions and searches and seizures had "unduly hampered" law enforcement. He said: "What the Court is doing is akin to requiring one boxer to fight by Marquis of Queensberry rules while permitting the other to butt, gouge and bite." These comments are fairly typical of criticism by police across the country.

Even lawyers have joined in the anti-Supreme Court chorus. In an article in 1964 objecting to various high court rulings, Dean Daniel Gutman of the New York Law School derided the "practice of being oversolicitous of the criminal and indifferent to the rights of the citizenry at large."[42]

In 1965 Congressman Robert J. Corbett of Pennsylvania sent a questionnaire to his constituents in which he asked: "Do you believe that the courts are over-protecting the rights of the accused in criminal actions?" Eighty-two per cent of the respondents answered *Yes*.

The Supreme Court, of course, has had staunch and able defenders in the bar and the press whenever it has been assaulted from high positions. But the variety and frequency of the criticism of the court in recent years suggests the intensity of public feeling against implementation of the Bill of Rights provisions on due process and a lack of recognition that constitutional safeguards for the accused are intended to protect society from arbitrary and oppressive law enforcement. Obviously the frequent disdain or indifference of the press toward due process is shared by a considerable part of its constituency.

VIEWS OF CRIME AND PUNISHMENT

Public attitudes on crime and punishment are as much out of focus as the popular outlook on criminal procedure. These attitudes too must be considered among the many factors that are conducive of inequities in the treatment of accused or convicted law violators. When they are confronted with questions about the causes of crime, well meaning people are inclined to oversimplify the problem and to explain it in terms that show little awareness of modern findings about the sources of delinquency. Civic leaders make speeches saying that crime is a sign that the nation has forgotten God, that American society lacks moral discipline and has strayed from the spiritual ideals of our forefathers. J. Edgar Hoover, reflecting the views of many law enforcement officials and echoed by an admiring press, attributes crime to a deterioration of the nation's moral standards. Judges, with monotonous frequency, link the growth of crime to the neglect of old-fashioned virtues, pampering by parents, and the mollycoddling of criminals.

These simplistic explanations seldom show any recognition of modern discoveries by social scientists which suggest that crime sprouts from roots having little relation to popular maxims. Delinquency may be related to an adrenalin deficiency which deprives children of a feeling of anxiety. Biological and physical factors may be as important as environmental factors in explaining behavior disorders in children. Violence may be triggered by social stress which presses the wrong button in certain personalities.[43]

A study by William and Joan McCord of several hundred young men, whose life histories from early childhood had been carefully recorded and many of whom turned to crime, showed the error of a number of popular notions. While home discipline had an effect on the beginning of criminality, the influence of discipline was dependent on other factors; and some other factors had a greater impact. Boys who were disciplined in a consistent manner tended to avoid criminality, while those who were disciplined in a punitive, erratic fashion were actually more likely to commit every type of crime except traffic violations. Broken homes precipitated many men into criminality, but a quarrelsome and neglecting home was even more conducive to criminal activity. Of all the influences which played a part in the genesis of crime, the mother's personality appeared to be most fundamental. Maternal cruelty, absence, and neglect led to a high proportion of sons who committed a wide variety of crimes.[44]

Even a cursory examination of the conclusions of criminologists reveals that the causes of crime are complex and multiple, not simple and unitary, as the popular moralizers of podium and press suggest. Many different explanations must be sought for a wide variety of offenses, ranging from white collar crime to murder committed in jealous rage.[45] But whatever the explanations, public opinion usually does not look with favor on a milder form of justice tailored to fit the individual.

In the face of overwhelming evidence that punitive, retributive methods have failed, this form of justice still dominates the American scene. In 1964 James V. Bennett, then director of the Federal Bureau of Prisons wrote:

> Our criminal laws are the most severe in the world, and our legislative bodies are still at work making them more severe. Except possibly for "enemies of the state" in countries where people are sent to prison for political reasons, the American criminal on the average serves several times as long a sentence in prison as his counterpart anywhere else in the world.[46]

Writing in much the same vein, Judge David L. Bazelon of the United States Court of Appeals for the District of Columbia, has called attention to the "imperative to punish." Judge Bazelon sees a persistent adherence to a system of harsh punishment because of a need on the part of the public and judges for scapegoats (criminal offenders) on whom to bestow repressed but forbidden impulses and thus be rid of them. While the real aim of making the sinner suffer is sometimes candidly acknowledged, more often the rationale is that punishment deters criminals. Yet, as Judge Bazelon pointed out, the excessive emphasis on punishment with a consequent neglect of genuine rehabilitation has been accompanied by "a disastrously high level of recidivism." Between 1949 and 1958 the number of serious offenders in federal prisons who had had two or more previous commitments grew from 39 per cent to 46 per cent. What this meant was that punishment neither reformed nor deterred.[47]

Judge Bazelon's position on punishment represents a minority view in the judiciary. A harsh, punitive attitude is far more common among judges, as indicated by their frequent tributes to tough justice. Though Judge Samuel Leibowitz is perhaps more extreme than most, his stern outlook is widely shared on the bench. Several years ago he was quoted as saying he would put every professional criminal on a Devil's Island. In 1964 a woman took great pains to help New York police apprehend a man who had made obscene telephone calls. She was distraught when a judge, after the man's conviction, sentenced him to ninety days in jail instead of committing him for psychiatric help.[48]

In a speech before 200 Pennsylvania judges in 1964, Chief Justice John C. Bell, Jr., of the state Supreme Court attributed a crime wave of "epidemic proportions" to the failure of parents and public officials to take stern disciplinary measures. Deploring the "mollycoddling" of criminals, Justice Bell castigated visionary psychiatrists, lenient parole board members, and unrealistic judges. He called for sterner punishment, for reducing the age for juvenile offenders to fourteen, and for an end to treating juveniles as fragile flowers "just in need of rehabilitation."[49]

The continuation of the death penalty in the laws of most of the states is one more sign of the harsh popular and official attitude toward punishment. Though the use of execution chambers is declining, the retention of the extreme penalty is still a source of acute injustice more basic than the most common forms of prejudicial publicity. Capital punishment subjects the condemned prisoner to a prolonged form of mental torture that is incompatible with the humane standards of a civilized society. The execution of convicted defendants eliminates all possibility of correcting tragic miscarriages of justice in the case of those wrongfully convicted. The number of authenticated cases of innocent defendants put to death is great enough to undermine any naive certainty as to the infallibility of the machinery of justice.[50] The death penalty is usually levied against the poor, the ignorant, and the disadvantaged—those without the mental resources to put up a good defense themselves or the financial resources to get the ablest legal counsel to speak in their behalf. Negroes, because of their deprived and depressed status, have suffered disproportionately through the discriminatory application of the death penalty. A study in the Northern state of Ohio showed that 78 per cent of all Negroes convicted of a capital crime were executed, whereas only 51 per cent of whites convicted in the same period were put to death.

In trials in which the death penalty is an issue, the procedural law actually contains a built-in element of unfairness: It insures the state of a jury willing to impose capital punishment and, by the same token, denies the defendant the protection of jurors who are against the legal taking of life.

After two years of study, the American Civil Liberties Union in 1965 issued a new statement of position on the death penalty which cogently summarized all of the reasons why this form of punishment is unjust. It constitutes cruel and unusual punishment, denies equal protection of the law, and removes guarantees of due process of law.[51]

Criminologists and psychiatrists generally oppose the death penalty, pointing out, among other things, that the long history of this form of punishment shows no indication of a decline in offenses for which it was imposed.[52] Most murders, for example, are committed in the heat of emotion as a result of arguments between relatives and friends, with the murderer taking no thought of future punishment. The homicide rate in states which have abolished the death penalty is approximately the same as in those which maintain it.[53]

Yet public and official backing for capital punishment persists. Though a few newspapers, such as the Washington *Post,* have editorially crusaded against capital punishment, most of the press has been content to accept the status quo. Though a few lawyers like defense attorney George T. Davis of San Francisco have long fought against executions by the state, most members of the bar seem indifferent at best.

Prosecuting attorneys tend to support the death penalty. When George M. Scott, president of the National District Attorneys Association, took the unusual position at a 1965 meeting of the organization of urging abolition of capital punishment, his proposal (the first such public recommendation by an NDAA president in the 15-year history of the association) found little support among the 300 delegates.[54] The usual attitude of district attorneys has been reflected in recent years by public stands in favor of the death penalty on the part of prosecutors in Dade County, Florida, in San Mateo County, California, and in Allegheny County, Pennsylvania, as well as by the organized district attorneys of Pennsylvania. In Allegheny County, Pennsylvania, eleven of the sixteen Common Pleas judges indicated in 1961 that they were for retention of the death penalty in the state. Four of the others, however, simply could not be reached during the canvass and one had not made up his mind.

Despite increasing activity in behalf of abolishing the death penalty and accumulating revelations of injustice, the shift by popular opinion and state legislatures away from support of this most extreme form of punishment has been slow.

Forty states, in early 1965, still held on to their electric chairs and gas chambers. In 1961 a California legislator, who favored abolishing capital punishment, indicated that he was opposed to submitting the issue to a referendum because he feared the voters would defeat the abolition move. In 1965 Governor Roger D. Branigin of Indiana vetoed a bill to abolish capital punishment in that state, saying that in his heart he was against taking the life of another but that he didn't think the death penalty should be eliminated unless there were a mandate of the people in an election in which the matter was an issue. He added, however, that until "the issue is decided, no man's life should be taken." That same year (1965) *The Christian Herald,* a Protestant interdenominational monthly magazine, reported that, in a poll in which it asked: "Is the death penalty ever morally justifiable?" 64 per cent of the 13,500 readers who responded said *yes*.

The late Justice Curtis Bok of the Pennsylvania Supreme Court, a jurist with rare insight, said capital punishment should not be regarded "as a solitary evil but only the most dramatic form of a more general evil, that of punishment." His view that "punitive penology has failed utterly"[55] is shared by many specialists in the field. Karl Menninger has pointed out that the popular notion that punishment deters further crime is a myth.[56] Criminologists have referred repeatedly to the evidence that punishment by incarceration does not prevent crime, as indicated by the high proportion (from 50 to 70 per cent) of prison inmates who are serving second, third, or fourth sentences.[57] Yet the urge to punish still prevails.

Injustice Under Custom and Precedent

Besides the imperfections in the law enforcement process that are incidentally produced by popular involvement, other obvious hindrances to justice have been built into the trial mechanism by law, custom, and precedent. When these adverse factors merge with the pressure of public and press, there are so many subtle influences combining to produce the ultimate unjust result that no one can precisely measure and define the chief causes of injustice. Yet any survey of justice and the press must take cognizance of the existence of all of the factors that are conducive to injustice in an attempt to evaluate the role of the press and its relative impact. Moreover, the press, as an observer of public affairs, ultimately has a responsibility for at least calling attention to all sources of injustice, including those that are built into the trial system.

Trial by Trick

Governed by what Dean John H. Wigmore called "the sporting theory of justice," the trial, instead of being treated as an instrument for the discovery of truth, is often looked upon as merely a game between lawyers, with certain ground rules enforced by the trial judge as referee, and with the jury awarding the decision to the most effective legal player. Under this theory, the law, as Dean Roscoe Pound once noted, asks only whether all the rules of the game have been carried out strictly and, if any material infraction is discovered, awards new trials or reversed judgments just as the football rules put back an offending team five, ten, or fifteen yards.[58]

Under such circumstances, the criminal trial is hardly the kind of inquiry which assures a logical and fair outcome after the fashion of the scientist who gets predetermined results by mixing the right ingredients in test tubes. (Jurors' minds have been compared to test tubes by some lawyers.) There are too many extralogical and inexact considerations entering into the shaping of the judgment. But instead of minimizing the occurrence of extraneous influences on the courtroom inquiry, the tactics used under the game or fight theory of justice actually increase the possibilities for obscuring the truth.

The late Professor Edmund Morgan, an able student of trial techniques, once commented sorrowfully on the reliance of the legal profession on "the manipulation of courtroom procedures for the obfuscation of issues and the confusion of juries." [59] To aid lawyers in creating a muddle to the detriment of the other side, dozens of manuals on trial tactics have been written—designed, of course, to be read only by members of the profession. These books advise attorneys on how and when to abuse and confuse honest witnesses so as to destroy the effect of their testimony. The various wiles and stratagems include: rapid cross-examination of a truthful but overcautious witness so as to make it appear that he is concealing important facts; goading an irritable witness so that he will lose his temper and seem spiteful; catching a witness in a minor inconsistency and blowing it up to huge proportions so as to make him appear unreliable.

Besides trying to bamboozle and trap witnesses, trial lawyers use various other tricks to prevent juries from looking at the facts alone. Histrionics and appeals to prejudice are regularly employed. In a 1957 trial of Teamsters' president James R. Hoffa for bribery, Defense Attorney Edward Bennett Williams suddenly asked a prosecution witness in front of the jury, which included eight Negroes, whether the witness had once been engaged to investigate the National Association for the Advancement of Colored People in a labor dispute. The question was irrelevant to the subject at issue and the judge sustained the prosecutor's objection and told the jury to disregard it. But a subtle message was conveyed. In cases in which lawyers get forbidden information before a jury, a judicial admonition, according to prevailing legal fiction, is supposed to enable the jurors to erase the objectionable statement from their minds.

A favorite trial tactic is to spring a surprise in the courtroom so that the other side is unprepared to answer. At the first trial of Dr. Bernard Finch for the murder of his wife, the prosecutor suddenly introduced tape recordings of an interview between the police and the defendant shortly after his arrest. Neither the accused nor his counsel knew that the exchange had been recorded.

Wily courtroom methods are not only condoned by the legal profession but are actually regarded as the emulative marks of skillful advocacy. It is no wonder that Judge Jerome Frank once referred to the average criminal trial as a "sublimated brawl" rather than a painstaking, orderly pursuit of truth.

When lawyers discuss crime news, they often stress the desirability of having impartial jurors who haven't been prejudiced by the press. But when they go to pick jurors, they want people who are biased in favor of their side. Attorneys often try to line up juries whose racial and religious ties would make them sympathetic to their clients. At the same time, of course, they are on guard against factors that suggest prejudice against the client. Clarence Darrow said he was more concerned with the religious, political, economic, and moral beliefs of the jury and the defendant than with the actual circumstances of the crime.

Speaking of the selection and use of the jury, Benton S. Oppenheimer observed,

> We commonly strive to assemble twelve persons colossally ignorant of all practical matters, fill their vacuous heads with law which they cannot comprehend, obfuscate their seldom intellects with testimony which they are incompetent to analyze or unable to remember, permit partisan lawyers to bewilder them with their meaningless sophistry, then lock them up until the most obstinate of their number coerce the others into submission or drive them into open revolt.[60]

Many commentators have observed, of course, that there can be no such person as an ideally impartial juror who has no knowledge or predispositions that would affect his perception in the courtroom or color the inferences that he may have to make during the course of a trial. The significant fact, however, is that lawyers frequently seek to win not by making an objective, reasoned presentation to an impartial panel but by appealing to the emotions of the jury and by trying to persuade it with facts or opinions not in evidence.

Sometimes the court allows outside influences to be brought to bear on the jury. A defense lawyer in the trial of Bruno Richard Hauptmann charged that the jury was not properly sequestered and that, while its members were walking back and forth between the courthouse and their hotel, a street crowd shouted such phrases as "Burn that Dutchman." [61] During the 1961 Colorado trial of Joseph Corbett, Jr., for the slaying of wealthy brewer, Adolph Coors III, the defense moved for a mistrial when coffee was taken to the jury room in a Coors brewery box. The motion was denied.

JURY WEAKNESSES

In addition to the unintentional outside messages or the deliberate manipulative influences directed toward it, the jury is subject to its own intrinsic weaknesses. In their role as witnesses of what goes on at the trial, they may make mistakes; they may misunderstand or forget some of the testimony. Inattention may mean that a significant fact is missed or not comprehended, and that fact may be essential in proving the defendant's innocence. Jurors have been known to fall asleep on the job, a practice which is not usually condoned by judges. But when jurors, on the other hand, have exhibited more than ordinary alertness by taking notes, courts have frowned on such a show of diligence.[62]

Like any human institution, the jury, of course, is subject to the frailties of its individual members and it may, therefore, make capricious decisions. In a case reported in 1956 a mother admitted that she was so anxious to get through with a trial and get back to her children that she voted for the conviction of a defendant accused of rape, although she did not believe there was enough evidence to prove his guilt. Juries have been known to reach a decision by flipping a coin or by drawing slips with alternative verdicts from a hat and deciding the outcome in accordance with that alternative drawn by a majority of the jurors.[63]

Since the total sealing off of the jury is almost impossible, the group may be subject to various kinds of unknown and immeasurable influences. A juror in the second trial of Dr. Bernard Finch admitted afterward that she had discussed the case with many people in spite of a judicial admonition against such communication.[64] Even when juries are sequestered, surveillance over them is not likely to be so strict as to prevent members from listening to television or radio news concerning the case (newspapers may be more easily screened) or from discussing it in phone conversations. While jurors were deliberating in the trial of Dr. Samuel Sheppard, some of them made unauthorized outside phone calls.

In 1964 a New Jersey court granted a new trial to a convicted defendant after his lawyer protested that the jury's deliberating room had been the scene of card playing, deciding the details of a baseball pool, and watching the World Series. Such conduct is not often brought to the attention of the judge, if for no other reason than that the defense does not know of it.

WITNESS WEAKNESSES

Like jurors, witnesses too are less than perfect instruments of justice. There are few eye witnesses to most crimes. And even under the best of conditions, the observations of such witnesses cannot be completely dependable. In recreating an event, human beings are subject to numberless errors of perception due to such miscellaneous factors as faulty senses, inattention, the mood of the moment, personal involvement in the action, failure of memory, poor lighting of the scene, or some other barrier to accurate observance.[65] Many experiments with staged events have shown that the descriptions of the scene by surprised witnesses vary widely, some of them omitting vital facts and others adding action which did not occur.[66] Witnesses' views and recollections of events are affected by their temperaments and experiences and many other nonrational factors. Judge Jerome Frank mentioned an analysis of the testimony of 20,000 persons who were asked to describe the physical characteristics of a person they saw commit a crime. The study revealed that, on average, they overestimated the height by five inches, the age by eight years, and gave the wrong hair color in 82 per cent of the cases. In his book narrating thirty-six cases of wrongful conviction, Judge Frank told of at least twenty-three tragic errors by witnesses.[67]

More than thirty years ago Roscoe Pound observed ruefully that the progress of psychology had revealed the inherent imperfections of human testimony but that it was likely to be a long time before the law of evidence permitted practical use in court of better methods for discovering truth. He called attention to an English case in which an innocent man was twice convicted and served a long prison term for the crimes of another because, under the elaborate rules of evidence developed in connection with trial by jury, the crucial evidence which, if gone into, would have established the defendant's innocence, was excluded as irrelevant.[68]

Besides the witnesses who make honest mistakes, there are others who are coached by lawyers or police or who, for other reasons, misrepresent or deliberately lie about the event in question. A white woman whose husband was stabbed at her side in Times Square in 1964 later admitted that she had lied in saying the assailant was a Negro. Her purpose was to shield the attacker, a former boy friend, who was white. Judge Frank describes seven instances of dishonesty by witnesses in the cases of wrongfully convicted defendants.[69]

Despite all of the evidence of witness fallibility, courts continue to entertain detailed testimony about every facet and focus of happenings observed by witnesses many months or years earlier. And juries continue naively to accept such accounts as proof of guilt.

MISCONDUCT BY PROSECUTORS AND POLICE

Miscarriages of justice may also be caused by the misconduct of prosecutors or the police in the gathering or presentation of evidence. Courts, of course, will grant relief upon satisfactory proof of such misconduct. In 1962 a New York court granted a new trial to a man convicted of murder sixteen years earlier in a trial in which the key witness against him had been induced to testify through the district attorney's promise that charges against the witness' wife would be dropped. In another New York case a year earlier (1961) a judge upset a 1942 murder conviction after the prisoner's attorney brought out that the prosecutor at the time had covered up perjurious testimony by the chief witness. A Maryland judge in 1964 granted a new trial to two men convicted of rape in 1961. The decision was based on the prosecutor's suppression of evidence as to the emotional instability of the victim and her allegations of rape by other persons while the defendants were awaiting trial. After the Maryland Court of Appeals in 1965 reversed the new trial order, the United States Supreme Court agreed to review the case.[70]

The overwhelming majority of cases, however, are not subject to correction on appeal, simply because the defendant does not have the money, the intelligence, or sufficient proof to get a hearing in a higher court. Ninety-five per cent of all cases end in the trial courts. In most of the few cases that are appealed, the appellate judges accept the trial courts' findings of fact—which means, in effect, that in only about 2 per cent of convictions do higher tribunals look into the factual merits of the guilty verdicts.[71]

Examples of police misconduct in securing evidence, as shown in many places in this book, are far more common than those involving prosecutors. Disclosure of brutality, coerced confessions, and manufactured evidence have occurred with increasing frequency following Supreme Court decisions condemning such practices. In 1961 Supreme Court Justice William J. Brennan, Jr., wrote,

> Far too many cases come from the states to the Supreme Court presenting dismal pictures of official lawlessness, of illegal searches and seizures, illegal detentions attended by prolonged interrogation and coerced admissions of guilt, of the denial of counsel, and of downright brutality. Judicial self-restraint which defers too much to the sovereign powers of the states and reserves judicial intervention for only the most revolting cases will not serve to enhance Madison's priceless gift of "the great rights of mankind secured under this Constitution." For these secure the only climate in which the law of freedom can exist.[72]

THE LAG IN LAW

Despite the new insights on crime supplied by behavioral sciences, our legal system continues to reflect the traditional condemnatory popular view that crimes are committed by perverse and morally irresponsible people who have simply failed to switch on the mechanism of self-control which every free-willed individual has within him. Most lawyers, in their view of the law, are as much wedded to tradition as the public. In their book, *New Horizons in Criminology,* Harry Elmer Barnes and Negley K. Teeters observe that in no other profession is there so much "culture lag" as in law—a lag that is suggested by the fact that a surgeon of 1750 would be bewildered in a modern operating room, while a good lawyer of the eighteenth century would find much that is familiar in the atmosphere and jargon of our courtrooms.[73]

Legal thinking, Judge Jerome Frank wrote, is affected by a "belated scholasticism," a "blighting medieval prepossession." He criticized the rigidity of the criminal law and the popular tendency to regard it as the embodiment of paternal omnipotence, with the "father-judge" on hand to exert discipline.[74]

Illustrative of the traditional orientation of the law is the importance of the idea of *mens rea,* the guilty mind, which expresses the concept that degrees of culpability are to be judged by specified states of mind. Yet states of mind are difficult to determine. Most psychiatrists hold that man's behavior is largely subject to the influence of antecedent determining factors and that unconscious motivation influences a great many of his decisions in a major way and is probably involved to some extent in all of them. This does not mean that psychiatrists would not consider the "normal" individual to be morally responsible and therefore accountable for his acts under the law.

The difference between psychiatrists and lawyers is over the criteria to be used in determining who should be held responsible for his acts and who should not. The dispute is nowhere better illustrated than in the law's tenacious adherence to the antiquated standard for determining legal insanity as laid down in the M'Naghten Rule stemming from an English case in 1843. Under that rule, the essential criteria for determining insanity are as follows:

> . . . to establish a defense on the grounds of insanity, it must be clearly proved that at the time of committing the act the accused was laboring under such a defect of reason, from disease of the mind, as not to know the nature and quality of the act he was doing, or if he did know it, that he did not know he was doing what was wrong.

In an effort to bring the law more into line with the views of modern psychiatry, the United States Court of Appeals for the

District of Columbia in 1954 overthrew the M'Naghten Rule and adopted a rule to the effect that "an accused is not criminally responsible if his unlawful act was the product of mental disease or mental defect. . . ." Known as the Durham Rule (because the case in which it was enunciated was *Durham v. United States*), this new standard had the effect of changing the problem of insanity from a matter of law to matter of fact. Under it, the expert medical witness can testify about the mental condition of the accused without being forced to describe it in terms of mental states that have existence only in the conceptual schemes of lawyers.[75]

In order to clarify for the jury the meaning of the terms "mental disease" and "mental defect," the Court of Appeals in the 1962 McDonald case said that, in determining criminal responsibility, the jury should be told that "a mental disease or defect includes any abnormal condition of the mind which substantially affects mental or emotional processes and substantially impairs behavior controls."

Though the Durham Rule was adopted more than a decade ago in an attempt to make the criminal law more realistic, the M'Naghten Rule, with some modifications is still in use in most of the United States. The District of Columbia and New Hampshire, from which the District of Columbia appellate court took its new standard in 1954, apply the Durham Rule. And by mid-1965 Illinois, Vermont, New York, Maine, and Missouri had liberalized their laws on criminal insanity. In most of the other states, however, the law's resistance to change is still evident.

The lag in the law produces such perverse results as that which occurred in a 1961 California case involving an 18-year-old youth, Anson B. Stout, Jr., who stabbed and strangled to death Mrs. Helen Prendergast, 53, while she was baby-sitting in her son's home in San Bruno. Stout later turned himself in and, upon examination, was found psychotic by four psychiatrists. But because he was legally sane under California law, his attorney, after consultation with the prosecutor, advised him to plead guilty so that he might be sentenced to life imprisonment instead of the gas chamber. However, his term had to be served in a state prison rather than in a mental institution.

The same anachronistic treatment of mental illness by the law was evident in a 1965 federal trial in Lincoln, Nebraska, where a jury found 22-year-old Duane Pope guilty of murder and ordered that he die for the admitted killing of three persons in a bank robbery, even though psychiatrists from Lincoln and the Menninger Foundation had testified that he had had a mental breakdown and was not responsible for his actions. The government, after putting on its own expert witnesses who testified that they had found no conclusive evidence of schizophrenia, called the case one of premeditated murder with the motive of self-enrichment.

Though psychiatry knows no such word as "insanity," the law continues to use it and to adjudge guilt under the devil-possession idea which it connotes. And such outmoded concepts of the law—the effect of which is exacerbated by press misrepresentation of psychiatrists' views—continue to hamper the effort to modernize treatment methods for mentally ill offenders.

HAPHAZARD CHANGE IN LAW

Not only does the law fail to keep abreast of advances in other fields of knowledge, but in many states the provisions of criminal law, considered on their own merits, have become inconsistent, ineffective, and unjust because of the haphazard fashion in which they have been allowed to grow through hundreds of years of statutory additions and judicial decisions. In Pennsylvania there are some thirty provisions on stealing, a number of them inconsistent. The penalty for conspiring to commit murder is less than the penalty for conspiring to cause an arrest. Under the Pennsylvania Penal Code, the maximum penalty is five years for incest and larceny, six years for misprision of treason, seven years for perjury and assault with intent to kill, ten years for pandering and robbery. And so it goes in many states.

Distinctions in the penalizing of different offenses have been drawn without any reference to the relative harmfulness of the conduct involved and the corresponding importance of preventing it, without any allowance for the probable differences in danger from the individuals whose conduct is in question. As explained by Professor Herbert Wechsler of the Columbia University School of Law, the legislature typically makes its penal determinations not on any systematic basis but rather by according its *ad hoc* attention to some area of criminality in which there is a "current hue and cry." Under the political pressure of the occasion, legislation of this kind is dictated by the reelection demands of "voting against sin." [76]

The inconsistencies of the criminal law as written may be increased or modified in the application, depending on who the judge is. Sentences by different judges are notoriously unequal and the inequalities are not necessarily geared to the degree of the offense. The background characteristics of judges are related to the judgments they make in assigning punishments for various offenses. For example, persons from rural areas, research has shown, are inclined to assess harsher penalties for such crimes as arson and the cutting of utility lines, acts which are considered more serious in rural sections. Punishments are also likely to vary according to the social class of the offender.[77] Grossly unequal sentences by different judges often lead to acute feelings of resentment among prisoners when they compare notes. When the history of an unjust case is analyzed, it is sometimes impossible to say whether the perverse result may have been induced by a capricious judge, an outmoded law, or some other pernicious influence.

In recent years some progress has been made in bringing order out of the chaotic differences and inequities in the penal law of various states. Louisiana, Wisconsin, Illinois, Minnesota, and New York have enacted completely revised criminal codes. In California, Connecticut, Georgia, Kentucky, Maine, Montana, and Pennsylvania legal draftsmen in 1965 were working on recodificatons of penal law. The American Law Institute in 1962 gave final approval to a model penal code that had been in preparation for ten years.

The criminal law in three-fourths of the states, however, is still in confusing disarray, the product of irregular and unplanned accretion over many years. In those states where new codes have been adopted, the law has been improved, modernized in some respects, and pruned of many inconsistencies. New York's new penal code (the first major revision in that state since 1881) softens mandatory sentencing requirements, gives parole boards far greater discretion, narrows the definition of kidnapping, and simplifies the definition of murder so that it hinges only on intent to kill. These and other provisions have the effect of ameliorating the harsh, retributive character of the criminal law in New York.

Yet even in New York, one of the latest states to adapt to change, many vestiges of the primitive past remain. The legislature voted to retain adultery and homosexuality in the criminal law despite pleas from the Penal Law Commission that they should be treated instead as matters of private morality. The governor vetoed an amnesty bill that would have erased the criminal record of a first offender after he had served his sentence.[78] The National Council on Crime and Delinquency attacked the new code for maintaining unduly long term sentences and for failing to abolish minimum sentences. The New York Civil Liberties Union criticized the code for neglecting improvements in the areas of obscenity, abortion, and narcotics addiction and for perpetuating many vague definitions of crimes.

Neither the new codes of individual states nor the model code of the American Law Institute resolve the ideological dichotomy between (1) the traditional school of penology based on the concept of punishment as a deterrent and the related notion of making the penalty fit the crime and (2) the modern school based on the ideas that the sentence should fit the offender and that treatment of the offender is the most effective means of protecting society. Though neither school is made up exclusively of the members of any one profession, lawyers and judges tend to support the old view (grounded in the philosophy of Immanuel Kant) which sets great store by the rigor of the punishment and the enduring isolation of the culprit. Criminologists and psychiatrists adhere to the newer view that the offender is a disordered person who requires therapeutic measures, with his reformation and the prevention of crime being the only valid aims of the law. If the offender's treatment requires institutional commitment, it may be ordered for the length of time necessary to insure some kind of cure but not with the purpose of vindictive deprivation.

INJUSTICE IN PRISON

Our prison system, however, still reflects the rationale of vindictive deprivation.

Most prisons, though they are supposed to provide a cure for criminality, are merely schools for crime and make their inmates completely unfit for normal life outside. The reasons why have been explained by many, but none has done it more clearly than Dr. Ralph S. Banay, former director of the psychiatric clinic at Sing Sing:

> Prison populations are made up of the least conformable elements of society, thrown together under conditions that deepen destructive tendencies. An oppressive atmosphere, a relic of the time when punishment was designed to generate remorse . . . produces instead hopelessness and despair, intensifying bitter defiance and contempt for society. Even the best prisons are archaic in spite of expensive efforts to improve plants and administration. The regenerative spirit of man is ignored in the disrespect for human dignity.
>
> Not only separation from family and friends, but the denial of self-expression, a withdrawal of personal privacy, rigid regimentation, sexual deprivation and exposure to the crudest of vicious deviations and animalities are the pattern. Instead of invoking self-redemption, prison life accentuates the baser traits, magnifying the antiauthority element that sent the convict to prison in the first place.
>
> The dominant traits in prison are brutish habits, foulness of tongue, vulgarity, perversion of feeling, suspicion, distrust and malignancy. Nothing is sacred or esteemed. The watchword is dog eat dog. In the inmates' cynical philosophy, the only difference between them and the people outside is that they were caught. An atmosphere of human stagnation and decay is inhaled by the prisoners. It is the spoor of generations of prison inhabitants. The corruptive factors in convict life produce in the strongest-minded inmate a reckless disregard for traditional virtues and even contempt for life itself.[79]

In his book, *Break Down the Walls,* John Bartlow Martin wrote that the "American prison system makes no sense." He explained why in detail. But public indifference to this key element in our system of justice has kept progress in reform of the American penal system to a glacial pace.

Even this brief treatment of injustice under law should have made clear that in the United States many people suffer grievous injury from the actions of incompetent or misbehaving policemen, lawyers, and judges, from the errors of an anachronistic trial process, and from the dehumanizing rigors of an avenging prison system—all accepted by a public that is unaware or apathetic or coldly approving of stern methods for curbing supposed enemies of public safety and order. In any event, the inadequate performance of the agencies of justice is in part a projection of the public mood. Improvement would not occur automatically if the press, as one means of communicating the temper of the public, were to be suddenly muffled. On the contrary, a press that is aware of the various shortcomings in the administration of justice and alert to its responsibilities could be a vital stimulus for reducing injustice under law.

PART THREE

The Inseparable Forums of Justice

CHAPTER EIGHT

RESPONSIBILITY FOR THE PRESS

The Proposed Remedies

DESPITE THE BREADTH AND RAMIFICATIONS of press prejudice to justice as shown in previous chapters, many critics assume that the only real problem is pretrial news coverage and that the answer is simply to deal sternly with press methods of treating pretrial events. One remedy occasionally proposed by lawyers is the adoption of the English system under which judges summarily punish for contempt of court newsmen responsible for publicizing evidence or comment which is or may be inadmissible at trial—that is, such material as confessions of suspects, information as to prior convictions of the accused, comments or accusations relating to past misbehavior or immoral conduct, matter ridiculing the character of the accused, press exposés of purported evidence, or any expression of opinion concerning a pending case. One of the most ardent proponents of the English approach is Common Pleas Judge Chauncey M. Depuy of Pennsylvania, who has said: "It seems to me the British system is an acceptable adjustment of the two conflicting interests and ought to be adopted in the United States." Commenting on the widely publicized 1957 British trial of Dr. John Bodkin Adams in connection with the suspicious death of an elderly patient, Judge Depuy concluded:

> In short, the trial was being carried on in the court room and the people had to wait until that time in order to read the evi-

> dence; what was competent evidence according to the rules of law was heard at the trial and was printed in the newspapers; the side issues, spurious emotional jags and other legal tinsel were excluded from the public view. Nobody suffered but the washerwoman, gossipers and the idle curious in general, and possibly the newspaper circulation.[1]

Another kind of outright ban against potentially prejudicial pretrial publicity has been advanced in the form of suggestions of legislation that would prohibit public officials from giving out certain types of information. Dean Erwin N. Griswold of the Harvard Law School in 1964 recommended statutory curbs on the release by police or other law enforcement officials of any sort of information about a person charged with crime other than his identity and the nature of the charge. The prohibition would cover any evidence or any statements about the evidence, any information to the effect that the accused had confessed or that he had not confessed, any information that he had been charged with or convicted of any other crimes in the past, any characterization of the defendant as "a notorious hoodlum" or anything else.[2] A statutory curb similar to the Griswold proposal, and applicable to newsmen as well as to police and lawyers, was recommended in 1962 by Justice Bernard S. Meyer of the Supreme Court of Nassau County, New York.

On January 6, 1965, Senator Wayne Morse of Oregon—acting for himself and fourteen other sponsors and saying he was prompted by a growing concern over the threat to fair trials—introduced a bill (S. 290) saying it should constitute a contempt of court, punishable by a fine of up to $1,000, for any federal employee or any defendant or his attorney or the agent of either to "furnish or make available for publication information not already properly filed with the court which might affect the outcome of any pending criminal litigation, except evidence that has already been admitted at the trial." Morse noted that his bill was supported in principle by the United States Judicial Conference.

The foregoing proposals are representatives of many made in recent years as recommendations for offsetting the threat to due process from prejudicial pretrial publicity.[3] Some, such as the one favoring imposition of the English system, are aimed directly at the press. Others, such as the Morse bill, are aimed only at sources of information. But the common characteristic of all of these suggested mandatory curbs is that they would arbitrarily restrict the flow of information about criminal cases and would enforce the restriction by criminal penalties. Thus they would employ law to impede the operation of a free press, even though all of them would not apply sanctions to editors and reporters.

English System Unsuitable for United States

Analysis of each type of proposed legal curb shows why none of them is in keeping with the American concept of a free press as an observer and critic of government. As one of the most stringent methods of control, the English system should perhaps be considered first. An examination of the English experience suggests many reasons why it should not be assumed to provide a suitable model for American practice. Anthony Lewis of the New York *Times,* a man who has observed both American and British practice and who is sensitive to the issues involved, has noted some of the reasons why rules that are good for Britain may not necessarily be good for the United States. Britain is a small nation with relatively little organized serious crime. Politics does not intrude into the courtroom. With only 2,100 barristers in England, the trial bar is comparatively small. The members know each other. And since attorneys may be appearing for the prosecution one day and the defense the next, the competitive spirit is limited. Lawyers and judges do not gain political advancement by making a record in sensationally publicized criminal trials. The British system of criminal justice reflects a respect for the ideal of fairness. Suspects are accorded generally decent treatment and a genuine concern is shown for the objective of an impartial trial. Because of a strong tradition of integrity in the law enforcement process, police corruption is virtually unknown. Parliament is keenly sensitive to abuses by policemen, judges, or prosecutors.[4]

Even though curbs on the press seem on the whole to work well in safeguarding due process in Britain, satisfaction with the system is not universal among Britons themselves. The late Harold J. Laski expressed doubt about the British rule on contempt. In a report on the British press, published by a political and economic planning group of civic and government leaders in 1938, the following significant comment was made:

> One of the chief legal hindrances to the liberty of the Press is the uncertain nature of the offense of contempt of court, and the arbitrary judicial procedure in such cases. While it would evidently be undesirable to permit cases to be tried in the newspapers in advance of the trial, or to allow confidence in the quality of justice to be undermined by abuse or ridicule, there is no doubt that a great deal of reasonable criticism of the administration of justice is thereby discouraged.[5]

Rebecca West, one of Britain's most gifted journalists, complained in 1948 that she was forced by the English contempt rule to abandon a newspaper assignment on anti-Semitic riots in London because the disturbances were connected with a prospective election campaign for the seat of a member of Parliament who was scheduled to be tried for alleged black market offenses.

Anthony Lewis told of the conviction over a lengthy period in Britain of twenty-six innocent persons as a result of evidence planted against them by a detective sergeant who was found later to be mentally disturbed. Noting that many people wondered how the detective could have fooled his colleagues and the courts for so long, Lewis reported a widespread feeling that the situation might have been broken sooner if the press could have spoken out.

Whatever the doubts about the English contempt rule in Britain itself, there are a great many more doubts in the United States about the wisdom of applying a similar rule to newspapers in this country. The United States is an immense and diverse country where conditions warrant the watchfulness of the press more than in Britain. Not only is crime more prevalent and in greater variety but there is an organized underworld such as Britain does not have. To make matters worse, the law enforcement machinery in the United States is neither as competent nor as incorruptible as in Britain. On the one hand, policemen and even judges have been bought by criminal elements in the United States and have allowed the law to go unenforced. On the other hand, policemen, prosecutors, and judges with different kinds of motivations have enforced the law carelessly or dishonestly, thus causing unjust convictions. In a country as large and varied as the United States with no unified system of law enforcement and no central ministry of justice with authority to keep an eye on the performance of state and local agencies, the eyes of the press are needed to search out negligence and misconduct in the administration of justice.

If American newspapers have on many occasions been heedless of the requisites of impartial crime reporting, they have at times also demonstrated how aggressive news coverage and editorializing can compel lax officials to enforce the law impartially. In the early 1930's wealthy Llewellyn A. Banks of Medford, Oregon, sought to maintain his political power in that area by corrupt methods. In the aftermath of an election dispute he shot and killed a constable who tried to serve papers on him. Partly as a result of an editorial campaign by the Medford *Mail Tribune,* Banks was prosecuted, convicted of murder, and sentenced to life imprisonment and his principal lieutenant, a county judge, went to jail for a ballot theft conspiracy.[6]

During the same decade the St. Louis *Post-Dispatch* carried on a nation-wide exposé of racketeering in theatrical unions. Among other things, the paper revealed that John P. Nick, boss of the St. Louis theater unions, had collected $16,500 from movie owners while sitting on his members' requests for higher wages. Nick and an alleged accomplice, Edward Brady, were indicted for extortion. When Judge Thomas J. Rowe, Jr., of the Circuit Court in St. Louis released Nick on the ground that the evidence showed Brady had taken the money and then released Brady for "lack of evidence," the *Post-Dispatch* denounced the proceeding in editorials and cartoons as a "burlesque of justice." Judge Rowe sentenced Ralph Coghlan, editor of the editorial page, to twenty days in jail and a $200 fine; Fitzpatrick, the newspaper's cartoonist, was given a 10-day jail sentence and fined $100; the paper itself was fined $2,000. The Missouri Supreme Court unanimously reversed all of the contempt convictions. Nick was later convicted in federal court and sentenced to five years in prison on the basis of the same evidence that Judge Rowe had rejected.[7]

From 1950 to 1953 the Long Island newspaper, *Newsday,* hammered at William C. DeKoning as a racketeer and not a legitimate labor leader. There were protests about the paper's "scurrilous" treatment from DeKoning's attorney, David Holman, a former Nassau County assistant district attorney who held shares in two area race track organizations. But as a result of *Newsday's* continued prodding, District Attorney Frank Gulotta started an investigation which led to the indictment of DeKoning for extortion in connection with irregularities at the Roosevelt Raceway. He eventually pleaded guilty and went to prison.[8]

In the United States the application of the British rule on contempt by publication would probably hamper the public spirited impulses of the press and at the same time fail to prevent trial by newspaper. The judicial system in the United States is simply not constituted for the most efficacious use of the contempt power in this field. Most judges, being elected, would hesitate to use the power for fear of retaliation by the press at the time of the next campaign. (English judges are not elected.) Those judges with courage and integrity who honestly sought to protect defendants' rights by invoking the contempt power would, at election time, probably become the targets of those segments of the press who were the worst offenders against due process. The judges who perhaps would have the most to gain would be those dishonest ones who might employ contempt as an offensive weapon to divert attention away from their own or their accomplices' misconduct.

The performance of judges in various American jurisdictions in recent years supports an inference that, even with their present limited power, occupants of the bench are tempted to use contempt as a means of retaliation against critics.

When Margaret Davis, a Houston *Press* reporter, violated the order of Judge Billy Ragan forbidding her to sit inside the railing of his Harris County Criminal Court, he fined her $100 for contempt. Mrs. Davis had earlier written a front page story saying the judge spent half his time running an insurance business. The contempt order was set aside in 1962 by the Texas Court of Criminal Appeals.[9]

In 1963 the *Democrat,* a weekly newspaper in Morrilton, Arkansas, was put out of business with libel judgments totaling $275,000. The paper had had the temerity to criticize the political machine headed by the sheriff of Conway County, Arkansas, and to question the manner in which the machine won elections with absentee votes. In the course of his fight with the machine, the paper's publisher, Eugene Wirges, was summoned before the circuit judge of the county and put through an inquisition on articles he had written about politics and court decisions. The same judge later sentenced the publisher for contempt for refusing to divulge the name of the author of an unsigned article. In the libel suit, which led to Wirges' loss of his paper, several of the jurors were later shown to have close ties with the plaintiffs' attorneys.[10]

A case occurring in New Mexico in 1964 revealed a judge's readiness to use the contempt power as a weapon against criticism aimed at his own conduct in criminal proceedings. Will Harrison, a New Mexico columnist, was found guilty of criminal contempt and sentenced to ten days in jail and a $250 fine by District Court Judge Paul Tackett as a result of Harrison's sharp comment on two judges' unequal treatment of two similarly culpable drunken driving defendants—one an assistant district attorney who was handed by Judge Tackett a $500 fine (which was suspended) and a deferred sentence, and the other a Mexican-American (with no court connections), who was sentenced by another judge to a one to five year prison term. The New Mexico Supreme Court later set aside the contempt conviction.[11]

In another part of the country in 1964 the implications of the judicial contempt power were called to national attention. The court in question was that of Judge Durwood T. Pye of Atlanta, where pretrial as well as posttrial comment on the judge's conduct was very much in order. The most effective comment, however, came from the floor of Congress where Representative Charles L. Weltner (whose district includes Atlanta) took advantage of his congressional immunity to say things about Judge Pye that many Atlanta citizens felt but dared not voice.

Judge Pye—who once held Atlanta newspapers in contempt and fined them $20,000 for the way they reported a criminal case[12]—had been setting bail as high as $20,000 for arrested civil rights demonstrators and, after trials, had been handing out prison sentences up to eighteen months for defendants charged with nonviolent conduct. Congressman Weltner condemned Judge Pye for his harsh and unfair treatment and concluded:

> Courts are of especial dignity and should not be criticized for light or transient causes. Yet, here, the machinery of the law, designed as the servant of justice, has been manipulated so as to become its oppressor. And none can speak without jeopardy of contempt.[13]

The conflicting interests of judicial dignity and freedom of expression came into headlong confrontation in a 1965 Indiana case. Editor James T. Neal of the Noblesville *Daily Ledger,* a 7,500 circulation paper in central Indiana, wrote a front page column in which he criticized a newly announced policy of Hamilton Circuit Court Judge Edward F. New, Jr., requiring all persons charged with moving traffic violations to be brought into court and indicating that those convicted would be jailed. Neal referred to inconsistency in law enforcement, claimed that the New plan would tend to punish the innocent rather than the flagrant offenders and called the judge's policy "an excellent example of shotgun justice." The judge ordered the editor arrested and brought to court under $50,000 bail, but he was released on his own recognizance after being cited for criminal contempt. The citation described the column as "a disdainful, despicable, scurrilous and contemptuous article . . . intended to inflict ridicule and indignity on the image of the Hamilton Circuit Court and embarrass the judge thereof, and all law enforcement officers in the county." Mr. Neal faced the prospect of a 90-day jail term or a $500 fine or both if convicted. The clash over traffic law enforcement represented another in a series of differences between the editor and the judge which began to arise as soon as the judge took office on January 1, 1965. The judge had early in his term placed a ban against all legal advertising in the *Ledger*. He lifted the ban in a few weeks but reinstated it at the time of the criticism of his traffic policy.[14]

Though the foregoing examples are unusual, they nevertheless suggest that freedom of the press would be in danger from the use of an expanded judicial contempt power. However such freedom may be abused at times, it is too important to be left to the tender mercies of potentially censorious jurists.

Legal Curb on Release of Information Unwise

Despite the fact that some practices of the press are offensive to due process, the proper remedy is not to "try" the offender, to "convict" it, and restrict its liberty. Nor would it be wise to subject to criminal trials those who aid the press in publicizing forbidden material. No matter how plausible the rationale, the exercise of censoring authority which interferes with press coverage of the initial part of the law enforcement process is just as objectionable as that which impairs reporting of the trial process or of other phases of government operations.

To legally bar officials from giving out certain information during the pretrial stage or to prohibit the press from publishing such information would discourage press scrutiny and would be tantamount to acknowledging an extraordinary confidence in the integrity of law enforcement officers or at least an extraordinary faith in the ability of the courts to correct any wrong that might otherwise have been exposed by timely publicity. Though juvenile court proceedings in some jurisdictions have been closed to the press and public, no firm conclusions can yet be drawn as to the effect of the rule on justice. Whatever experience may show with respect to juvenile court judges whose performance is unreported in the press, the rationale (the protection of children) under which they escape scrutiny does not apply elsewhere. The record of police, prosecutors, and other judges does not suggest that they are entitled to such faith in their rectitude, competence, and wisdom.

The editor of a prison newspaper, whose readers presumably include the direct victims of prejudicial pretrial publicity, recently expressed opposition to a rule which would require officials to withhold information and forbid pretrial statements. Hugh Dillon, associate editor of the *Spectator,* the newspaper of Southern Michigan Prison, observed in a 1965 article:

> Somewhere along the line, some overzealous police official is going to take advantage of the opportunity to "stack the deck" if he feels that the press won't be watching the "game."

If the right of a free press is going to be subjected to "exceptions," where will the line be drawn?

The press has shown the value of its contribution to justice in the pretrial stage when it plays its role responsibly.

In 1953 the prosecutor's office in Phoenix, Arizona, was preparing to try 26-year-old Joseph Altheide for murder committed during a robbery. Sure that it had the evidence to secure a conviction, the prosecution expected to ask for the death penalty and get it. But reporter Gene McLain of the Arizona *Republic,* in a month-long investigation, dug up key information in support of Altheide's alibi claim that he was 500 miles away in Texas at the time of the crime. Though officials cooperated with McLain, and though it was a policeman (intending to disprove the alibi) who actually collected the exonerating evidence, the freeing of Altheide three days before his scheduled trial was largely the result of a policy which gave a newspaper reporter access to information and to the suspect.[15]

In the pretrial stage of a 1964 Florida case the Miami *Herald* played an important role in preventing what might well have been a gross miscarriage of justice. Lloyd Astley Cuff, a 25-year-old Jamaican seaman, was being held at the Miami airport for deportation when he shot and killed a deputy sheriff and a private investigator. Tagged as a cop-killer, Cuff was charged with first-degree murder, for which the penalty in Florida is death in the electric chair. On the basis of five hours of leg work by a staff writer, the *Herald* published an account of the double shooting as given by the only two witnesses of the event. The police had not found the witnesses. According to the eye-witness story, Cuff had grabbed the gun of one of the officers and begun to shoot while the two men were in the act of beating him. On the third day investigators took statements from the witnesses whom the *Herald* had located. A month after the shooting the Dade County grand jury refused to indict Cuff on either of two first-degree murder charges, reducing both to second degree. Because of his persistent manifestation of a persecution complex, Cuff, at the request of defense and prosecuting attorneys, was given a psychiatric examination. Eventually ruled insane, he was ordered committed to a state mental hospital for treatment. Stories in the *Herald* exposed police brutality as well as overzealous prosecution efforts by the police. The *Herald* also found out that Cuff's civil detention by a private investigator was in fact illegal.[16]

Besides helping to prevent the conviction of the innocent or unwarranted harsh treatment of the guilty, newspapers have also successfully pressed for the vigorous prosecution of defendants whose political connections had been affording them protection. In 1951 in Chicago a grand jury failed by one vote to indict Michael Moretti, a state's attorney's policeman who had shot and killed two youths and wounded a third, all of them unarmed. The Chicago *Sun-Times* began an investigation which disclosed that the Moretti family had helpful political ties, that Moretti had made false statements on becoming a policeman, that the assistant state's attorney in charge of the case before the grand jury had given Moretti a protective cover, that the shooting, instead of being in self-defense as he claimed, was an unprovoked assault in drunken anger. The *Sun-Times* disclosures and a vigorous editorial page campaign for reopening the case in the interests of justice led to a recommendation by a blue ribbon coroner's jury that Moretti be held for a second grand jury on a charge of manslaughter. He was indicted by that grand jury on charges of murder and was eventually convicted and sentenced to life imprisonment.[17]

These cases should indicate why maximum press accessibility to police records and other pretrial information is necessary to help protect citizens from illegal detention and from arrest or conviction without cause, to safeguard the community against the unjustifiable release of arrested persons through pressure or influence, and to insure the integrity of police records that might otherwise be tampered with. One answer to harmful pretrial publicity is the exercise of wiser judgment by editors and not censorship by officials.

Censorship is antithetical to the philosophy of the American system and its use almost always leads to excesses. Newsmen, with the support of others who recognize the value of full information, are constantly—and with good reason—inveighing against attempts to restrict access to news in various branches of government. In the executive arm of the federal government, some agencies, notably the Defense and State Departments, have been unduly secretive—with the Pentagon, for example, going for years to the extreme of classifying its telephone directory. The same yearning for secrecy is observable at times in the legislative arm of government, as congressional committees meet in executive session and state and municipal legislative bodies quarrel with the press over whether some of their proceedings should be covered.

Alfred Friendly, managing editor of the Washington *Post,* summed up some of the undesirable effects that could be produced by a flat legal curtailment (as in the Morse bill) of all information that might prejudice the outcome of criminal litigation. If police and court authorities in some city connive to railroad an innocent man or to put the fix in for a guilty man who has connections, how is the public to know of evidence never offered or of circumstances kept in the dark? Under a prohibition enforced by legal sanctions, an insider with knowledge of what is happening would have to risk disbarment, fine, or imprisonment (depending on the specified penalties) for telling the press that the full disclosure of the facts is not being made. An information curb could be used with especial effectiveness in the South where the power structures of closed communities could apply it to camouflage their double standard of justice—one for whites and another for blacks—with the outside world being kept in the dark when the Negro defendant is being framed and the white law violator is being let off.

Other unwanted results could flow from an absolute barrier against the release of details in the initial stage of a criminal case. An indicted party, whose conduct might be at least partly excused by extenuating circumstances, would be prevented from explaining his side. Under some circumstances, the publicizing of details might bring forth witnesses or information helpful to the defense (see Chapter 5). Certainly in cases involving complex financial transactions, such as embezzlement, fraud, misrepresentation, the public's understanding of what is at stake would be limited by a failure to elaborate on the meaning of charges and answers.

Finally an outright ban against references to the record of suspects could thwart the dissemination to the public of helpful information relating to fugitives from justice.

In addition to considering the undesirable direct impact on criminal cases that might be brought about by a tight restriction on information, we must also examine the effect that such a policy might have in general on proper press surveillance of public officials. Under the theory behind the First Amendment, the press should be the watchdog of the judicial as well as the executive and legislative arms of government. It should have maximum freedom to report on and to criticize government, including police departments and courts, which are quite as capable of error, dishonesty, and tyranny as are other official agencies. Like officious military censors, legally ensconced controllers of crime news would be tempted to misuse their powers. The power to control the release of information or to punish for its publication could be used as a carrot or a stick to secure immunity from criticism for the censor or his friends. If the power of censorship were conferred on police chiefs or on an attorney general (as was proposed in the Masschusetts legislature in 1964) or on judges (as in the English system), these officials might well use it to cover up mistakes or misconduct of law enforcement officers and the courts or to curb justifiable criticism.

The record of biased or lawless law enforcement in the United States (briefly alluded to in the last chapter) does not indicate that police departments, prosecutors' offices, and judges should be further removed from the prying eyes of the press.

Responsibility for Voluntary Reform

Yet if the press wants to be worthy of its trust and at the same time to forestall attempts to impose compulsory remedies, it should stop peevishly and irrationally berating its critics, should frankly recognize its faults, and take steps on its own to improve its treatment of crime news in the interests of justice. Under the emerging "social responsibility" concept of mass communication, described by Wilbur Schramm and others, the privileged position which the press enjoys under the Constitution obliges it to be responsible to society for carrying out certain essential functions. These functions, according to various critics cited by Schramm, include providing an intelligent account of the day's events in a context which gives them meaning, serving as a forum for the exchange of comment and criticism, maintaining free expression so as to raise social conflict from the plane of violence to the plane of discussion.[18]

To fulfill its obligations to justice under the social responsibility theory, the press obviously needs to upgrade its performance not just in the pretrial phase but in the whole range of the law enforcement process. As was shown in Chapter 5, prejudicial newspaper influence may be brought to bear at every stage, from the initial investigation of the crime to the final administrative act in the case of the convicted person. As shown in Chapter 6, the press often contributes to injustice by placing undue emphasis on sensational and violent crime, by giving the prosecution a ready vehicle for one-sided presentations of evidence, by serving as a voice for harsh treatment of suspects and vengeful punishment of convicted offenders, by exerting pressure against penal reform, and against enlightened practices in probation, pardon, and parole.

Long and arduous efforts, aided by expert advice and stimulated by outside pressure, may be needed to bring about a fresh and more dispassionate press approach to the whole field of criminal justice. But any conscientious editor can begin the process of reform by adopting for criminal cases the same standards of caution, fairness, and objectivity which most papers already apply, or try to apply, in the reporting of other news. Ordinarily when Mr. Big Business, for example, is charged by some government official with a public-be-damned attitude in allowing his plant to pollute a river, the press would make a scrupulous effort to balance the charge with a statement by the criticized industrialist. If the businessman or a spokesman for him could not be reached for comment, the responsible paper would carry in its story a notation to this effect, and it would try to reach him later. But when Mr. Down And Out is charged by the police with having held up a bank and taken $5,000, the average newspaper thinks nothing of publishing the charge with no answering statement from the accused. Derogatory terms, barred as editorializing in most news stories, are freely applied to suspects in crime stories.

An instructive case illustrating superficial and one-sided press coverage of a crime story occurred in New York City several years ago. It was Edward R. Murrow of CBS who called attention to the inadequacies of newspaper reporting of the case. An old man had been killed in Highland Park, Brooklyn. The police charged 15-year-old Peter Manceni with murder, even though they should have harbored doubts as a result of a statement by the victim before he died to the effect that two big boys had jumped him. All during the buildup of the case, the police made no public reference to the old man's statement. And as so often happens in such cases, the press simply accepted what the prosecuting officials said and took no pains to dig beneath the surface. The district attorney was quoted, but there was no sign of any effort by the papers to seek balancing comment from the defendant's side. No attempt was made to talk to the boy or his family, and no reference was made to the fact that the Manceni family was the target of a steady flow of crank letters and phone calls. In the majority of New York newspapers Peter Manceni was portrayed as a vicious killer. An old man had been slain, and vengeance required a scapegoat. During the trial facts favorable to the boy were noticeably absent in the news coverage. Finally the suppressed statement of the dead man came out. And Peter Manceni was found not guilty.[19] More thorough probing and less baying for blood on the part of the New York press might have spared the boy some of the ordeal he suffered.

In most cases the accused is not produced for the press. Even if reporters are given access to him, he is often unwilling to talk or unable to talk articulately. In such situations, the press should at least report as a matter of routine that the suspect was not made available or that he had nothing to say. It should seek from police and report information as to how long the accused was interrogated. Most important of all, it should report whether he had been given an opportunity to call a lawyer and, if so, when the call was made and whether a lawyer was obtained. If the arrested individual has a lawyer, the lawyer's comment should be sought to balance any statement made by police or prosecutor. The consistent practice of rules such as these would help to give effect to the law's presumption of innocence and would upgrade the objectivity of criminal case coverage, which many newspapers now seem to regard as fair enough if the term, "police said," is liberally spaced through crime stories. Such minimal steps as reporting the suspect's unavailability, or the absence of a defense lawyer or, on the other hand, the comment of a defense lawyer (if there is one) could be adopted as customary procedure even by those newspapers which are adamantly opposed to adherence to a code of fair practices as a matter of principle.

Guidelines for Crime Reporting

There is no reason, however, why newspapers should not publicly commit themselves to certain guidelines for the coverage of crime news as long as the step is voluntary and provided they make due exception for the circumstances under which they would not be bound. As the philosopher William Ernest Hocking once put it, "since in our system of liberty a free press must be legally free to distort, twist, omit, and lie up to a certain point, the cure [for bias] will have to depend on an element of press honor."

In recent years many national journalistic organizations and some of the media themselves have begun to respond to the challenge to their honor implicit in Supreme Court decisions and in the Warren Commission report (see Chapter 4). Discussions between editors and lawyers have already produced mutually agreed upon guidelines in some areas (see Appendix). And continuing studies are aimed at the formulation of a more generally responsible position on the part of the press. No self-policed policy is likely to be entirely satisfactory to all of those concerned with the handling of criminal cases. Even those who have accepted guidelines will on occasion find themselves wanting to sidestep some provision. But the promulgation of statements of principle should nevertheless encourage the press to live up to higher standards and should also give the public and professional observers a basis for judging the performance of the news media.

Though statements subscribed to by newsmen are less explicit than most bar statements and are not couched in binding terms, nearly all of them recognize the potentially prejudicial effect of publicizing reputed confessions, prior police records, and police and prosecutor comment elaborating on criminal charges not yet heard in court. Vague as these statements are, their general adoption would help to eliminate the most flagrantly prejudicial practices of the press.

Various kinds of opposition to proposed voluntary standards or codes of fair practice for the press always arise. There are the automatic protests of self-righteous defenders of freedom of the press who say that even self-imposed guidelines amount to a form of censorship. In 1964 the Philadelphia Bar Association proposed a set of guidelines for the bar and the press in connection with the release of news in criminal cases. The proposals were certainly not perfect and debate on them was needed, especially on those provisions relating to press access to police records. But the shrill reaction of some newspapers left the impression that the Philadelphia lawyers were recommending the repeal of the First Amendment.

Two months after the approval of the guidelines, the Public Relations Committee of the Pennsylvania Bar Association reported that of 135 Pennsylvania newspaper editorials on the subject only five were favorable or conciliatory. The Pittsburgh *Press* spoke of a "gag" on crime news. The *Evening Bulletin* of Philadelphia wondered how many in that city had been denied a fair trial for reasons of prejudicial publicity (the implication was that none had) and raised the question of whether members of the Philadelphia bar had decided that freedom of speech or of the press "should be chipped away. . . ." Referring to the Philadelphia Bar Association guidelines and to discussion of similar proposals in the American Bar Association, John S. Knight, president and editor of the Detroit *Free Press,* was so alarmed that he called attention to the "censorship of the press" in other countries and added:

> We want no such suppression in the United States, whether through "managed news" or codes of journalistic ethics drafted by lawyers and accepted by a supine press.
>
> There can be no "truth" in news if reporters are shackled by punitive restrictions and forced to accept a bar association's concept of what should and what should not be printed.[20]

This is hardly the sort of rational discussion that the various bar association proposals deserve. Most such suggested voluntary statements of policy would simply put into explicit form certain standards to aid newsmen in making judgments of the kind they already exercise. In writing almost every story reporters must decide what is important and what is not, what may reliably be relayed as factual and what must be qualified. In deciding what to publish each day, editors must of necessity leave out a great deal of the material available to them. In deciding how to play what they do print, they must decide on placement, headline emphasis, and length. Each decision of this kind involves the same kind of judgments which editors and reporters, with the guidance of codes of fair practice, would be called upon to make as to whether certain details of a criminal case should be reported or even whether the case itself should be ignored. Obviously newsmen do not and cannot print everything they hear about or even know about a criminal case or any other subject in the news.

Conforming in general with agreed-upon fair practices in reporting criminal cases would be equivalent to the voluntary self-restraint which newspapers observe in honoring future release dates on important announcements, in delaying in the public interest and publication of news of some event in which premature discussion might undermine a delicate negotiation, in refraining during wartime from reporting certain kinds of news that might endanger the national security. The success of such a system is dependent on the exercise of responsible news judgment, on a general recognition of its value, and on custom. Newsmen should find it possible to accustom themselves to new ways of handling crime news once they are persuaded that the rules are in the interest of fairness and are generally accepted, but with the understanding that individual editors may decide when overriding public considerations call for exceptions.

Newspapers have for many years shown that, when the circumstances seem to call for it, they can voluntarily refrain from publishing certain kinds of information in criminal cases. In 1937 Cleveland newspapers, for example, voluntarily refrained from publishing the names of witnesses who were testifying before a grand jury in a labor racketeer case. When the trial occurred the newspapers, at the request of the prosecutor, voluntarily refrained from taking pictures of witnesses. The purpose was to avoid the possibility that witnesses would be threatened or that they would neglect to testify fully because of a fear of being threatened.[21] In 1959 the New York press, in order to prevent a mistrial stemming from prejudicial publicity, observed a prosecutor's request to voluntarily restrict its comment on and coverage of the trial of twenty underworld figures charged with conspiring to conceal the real purpose of their 1957 meeting near Apalachin, New York.

Some critics might differ with the judgment of the editors who observed restraints in these cases. But the point is that in these instances and many others that could be cited, editors have already voluntarily imposed curbs on themselves. Thus there is nothing radically new in the suggestion that newspapers voluntarily refrain from pretrial publication of purported confessions, of prior criminal records, and of *ex parte* harangues by prosecutors. Commitment to a policy of voluntary restraint does not mean, of course, that newsmen should not seek and be given access to information in order that they may be prepared to publish it when and if they deem such publication to be in the public interest. Ceaseless inquisitiveness on the part of the press may, on the one hand, prevent the police from mistreating suspects and, on the other hand, from being lax in enforcing the law. If the press is vigilant, however, and the police know it, there may not be any occasion to report, for example, that police brutality has occurred or that tickets have been fixed.

In agreeing on and becoming habituated to certain standards for the presentation of crime news, editors would be acting in accordance with the best traditions of a free press. As Barry Bingham, editor and publisher of the Louisville (Kentucky) *Courier-Journal* and *Times,* told the International Press Institute in 1965:

> Every thoughtful journalist will admit that there is a line somewhere beyond which press freedom deteriorates into press license. The difficulty is to determine exactly where that line truly runs.
>
> We don't want government to draw it for us, heaven forbid. We must draw it ourselves, then. If we reject outside discipline, as we always must, then we have to accept self-discipline.

Speaking for the New York *Times,* a newspaper which has long observed high standards of self-discipline, Clifton Daniel, the paper's managing editor, revealed in 1965 how that publication has reacted to new pressures for voluntary changes in press methods in handling criminal news. Addressing a meeting of the Inland Daily Press Association, Daniel said the *Times* is more responsive now to advice, guidance, and admonition from the bench and from prosecuting attorneys, wherever the right of fair trial is involved. "We are more careful than we used to be," he said, "about using prejudicial terms such as 'confession,' 'the holdup man,' 'the killer,' and so on." For years the *Times* has worried editorially about the unjust effect of prejudicial reporting of crime news. Though the *Times* has traditionally been careful and unsensational in its reporting of crime, that paper, like other nationally respected papers, has regularly published confessions, criminal histories of suspects, and pretrial prosecutor comments. These papers exhibit a curious ambivalence—often standing firmly on their editorial pages for a strict observance of procedural rights in criminal cases but offering in their news pages dubious material which may undermine such rights.

The most promising possibility for reform is in the exercise of leadership by responsible newspapers which recognize the existence of a problem—papers like the New York *Times,* the Washington *Post,* the St. Louis *Post-Dispatch,* the Louisville *Courier-Journal,* and others. The wire services, such as the Associated Press and the United Press International—which have not been any more attentive to the rights of the accused than the average newspaper—could bring about great improvement by reassessing their practices and by establishing more careful criteria for the reporting of criminal cases. Whatever the behavior of the socially blind or conscienceless papers may be, the responsible media of communication could bring about appreciable change for the better by setting a different example and by taking upon themselves the duty to criticize bad practices. As newspaper awareness of the unjust impact of prejudicial news grows wider, the task of getting reforms accepted should become easier. The steady decrease in the number of competing newspapers, whatever its ill effects in lessened debate on public issues, should simplify the effort to inaugurate new standards with less fear that the competition will achieve some cheap victory by violating them.

Another kind of negative reaction to proposed voluntary guidelines on the reporting of crime news comes both from thoughtful doubters who say such self-imposed rules of conduct won't work and from cynics who would second the comment of H. L. Mencken that "journalistic codes of ethics are all moonshine." For such objections there is no wholly satisfactory response. The widespread maintenance of high standards in crime reporting will indeed be difficult. Yet the possible means for holding the press to a higher level of performance are not entirely lacking.

Specialists for Crime News

One of the first steps needed to improve the quality of crime reporting is to raise the caliber of crime reporters. Only a few years ago Norman E. Isaacs, then managing editor of the Louisville *Times,* stirred consternation in an audience of newsmen and others at Northwestern University when he bluntly asserted that the crime of crime reporting was that it was basically the same kind of job that was being done twenty-five or thirty years earlier "and it was a rotten job then." The "same hacks who were once unlettered cowboys," he continued, "are now unlettered police reporters," who wouldn't know what a good city editor meant by significant police reporting. Though there are some able crime reporters, a check on the staffs of many papers would probably substantiate the truth of Isaacs' contention that the competence of police reporters has not advanced in the same way as that of newsmen in other fields. The late Supreme Court Justice Wiley Rutledge observed in an opinion in the leading Pennekamp case that, with some notable exceptions, "there is perhaps no area of news more inaccurately reported factually, on the whole, . . . than legal news." [22]

As long ago as 1930 Raymond Moley suggested that newspapers "employ specialists to report all matters affecting the administration of justice." A group of nine Nieman fellows who in 1947 published a book on the ideal newspaper noted that they would have specialists to cover police headquarters, the district attorney's office, and the courts. Obviously real specialists could be afforded only by wealthier papers. The Nieman fellows said nearly two decades ago that they would expect to pay from $10,000 to $25,000 a year to get some of the writers they wanted.[23] A few newspapers have begun to realize the importance of special competence in the legal field. The New York *Times* assigned Anthony Lewis, a gifted layman, and then Fred P. Graham, a lawyer, to cover the Supreme Court. The same paper hired for its city staff Sidney E. Zion, a former assistant United States attorney in New Jersey, and assigned him to specialize in legal news. James Clayton of the Washington *Post* is another specialist on the Supreme Court. Newspapers generally, however, have not recognized the need for specialists in crime and law to the same extent that they have in such other fields as science, health, and education. In 1962 the Newhouse newspaper chain revealed that it was organizing a staff of "reporter-specialists" in such fields as politics, labor, business, education, and welfare. Crime was not mentioned.

At the same time that there is a general absence of competent specialists in the field of crime, there is a special need for good reporting in this area. With crime costing an estimated $27 billion or more a year and exacting an inestimable price in wrecked lives, with correctional methods on the whole failing dismally, with law enforcement techniques and attitudes in need of vast improvement—there are few subjects more deserving of knowledgeable and enlightened newspaper treatment. Yet many editors still cling to the notion that anybody can cover the police beat and that this is a good place to start cubs. Editors would be registering an advance over this provincial attitude if they at least provided special preparation for police reporters through some kind of in-service training program, perhaps under the joint sponsorship of a number of newspapers.

Not only should publishers and editors recognize the importance of hiring or training specialists to cover law enforcement activities, but reporters themselves should take an interest in upgrading the competence and skill of members of their craft. If they have no social conscience and look upon their occupation merely as a way of supplying shoes and stew meat for the family, then reporters can hardly be expected to take any notice of the general performance of fellow practitioners. But most reporters (at least when they are young) are not so misanthropic; they do take pride in skillful and discerning reporting.

When the American Newspaper Guild was organized in the early 1930's, some optimists hoped that it would establish itself as a professional society devoted to raising journalistic standards as well as improving the pay of its members. But the Guild has concentrated on salaries, hours, and working conditions. Important as these issues are, they should not be the only questions which engage the serious attention of an organization of working journalists. By registering an interest in the writing performance as well as the special competence of reporters in their respective fields, the Guild could help to raise the professional level of its members, including those engaged in crime reporting.

This show of interest need not take the doctrinaire stance of insisting on designated degrees for writers in specialized fields. Some of the most proficient and informed reporter-specialists do not have academic backgrounds that neatly fit their particular assignments. Anthony Lewis, who is not a lawyer, displayed extraordinary perception and knowledge in reporting the actions of the Supreme Court in meaningful terms for readers of the New York *Times*. The Guild—or at least that segment of it made up of writers—could urge publishers to pay more attention to the craftsmanship and expertise of their staffs and could communicate approval when certain minimum qualifications are met and disapproval when they are not. Though the ultimate responsibility for the capabilities of the staff would have to rest with the publisher, the Guild could lend its voice to improvement and in so doing could not only advance the standards of journalism but also foster *esprit de corps* among its members, enhancing their feeling about the social value of their craft.

Codes of Ethics

To further promote higher standards of performance, the Guild might also revive its long-neglected Code of Ethics, including that section on crime reporting. The same goes for the American Society of Newspaper Editors. Such codes, which have been adopted by more than 200 American professional and business groups, are enforceable only through voluntary self-policing and hence are not very effective. The experience with canons of ethics of the American Bar Association, the American Society of Newspaper Editors, and the American Medical Association[24] has shown that malpractices can flourish despite the lofty preachments of codes. And yet some disciplinary actions do occur. And some individual professional grievance committees are more sensitive and more active than the usual kind. Their influence can be salutary. Moreover, the mere publication and periodic invocation of precepts of conduct should have some educational value and should have some minimal appeal to conscience.

Newspapermen are no different from other mortals in having some bad actors in their ranks. Commitment to a code of ethics would at least help to imbue members of the group with some sense of responsibility for the behavior of the others. A case arising in Chicago many years ago was unusual but it suggests what can happen under unobserving eyes. John Rogers, a reporter for the St. Louis *Post-Dispatch,* paid a visit to the office of Colonel Robert R. McCormick of the Chicago *Tribune* to tell him that a *Tribune* reporter named Jack Lingle had been murdered because he was also a racketeer and had used his *Tribune* job to help other racketeers. McCormick said Rogers couldn't print that, but the *Post-Dispatch* did and, incidentally, scored a beat on Chicago newspapers, including the *Tribune.*[25] If the *Post-Dispatch* cared enough in a case of this kind to be the keeper of the *Tribune's* conscience, organizations of professional newsmen should also care about playing such a role. As operators of semipublic institutions, newspapermen should be more alert to improper behavior among their colleagues than automobile dealers, undertakers, and some of the others who have promulgated standards of professional conduct.

Agencies for Press Criticism

The unhappy record of codes of ethics and of internal disciplinary machinery to enforce them might not continue to be so discouraging if there were more vehicles of external criticism to help in delineating shortcomings of the press and in bringing misconduct to light. Such agencies to appraise and report on the performance of the press already exist in Great Britain and several other countries but not in the United States, though the idea has been repeatedly advanced.

In 1953, as a result of a recommendation by the first Royal Commission on the Press (1947–1949),[26] the British Press Council was organized. Ignoring the Royal Commission's proposal that the Council have a lay chairman and that one-fifth of its members be drawn from outside the journalistic profession, the organizers created a body of twenty-five members made up entirely of press representatives—fifteen editorial members and ten managerial members.[27] (After a second Royal Commission in 1962 reiterated the recommendation that the Council contain lay members and a lay chairman, the agency was reconstituted along these lines.)

Designed as a private voluntary agency, the Press Council was established, among other things, for the purposes of:

- preserving the established British freedom of the press.
- maintaining the highest professional and commercial standards for the press.
- promoting methods of recruitment, education, and training of journalists.
- promoting proper working relationships among segments of the profession.
- promoting technical and other research.
- studying developments tending toward monopolization.
- hearing complaints about newspapers and, when it was deemed necessary, rebuking them publicly.
- publishing periodic reports about its own work.

Costs of the council were to be paid by subscribers to the managerial and working journalists' associations, whose members make up the agency. Incidentally, the National Union of Journalists, representing a majority of the working newspapermen in Britain, had a key role in organizing the council.

The British Press Council is guided by a constitution, but it adopted no code of ethics. Its method was to consider disputes brought to it and to establish precedents (in the common law tradition) through a body of influential decisions based on its findings.

Though the agency was given no power to impose sanctions and its decisions would not be binding on anyone, its supporters hoped that its public reprimands would have a chastening effect.

In its first years of operation the Council showed that there was scant reason to justify the howls of outrage from the press that had greeted the proposal for its creation. It did not try to clamp down on the press with an iron hand. Though the Council's impact has not been as broad as had been hoped, and though some of its judgments have been questioned with good cause by responsible journalists, its findings have met with more praise than criticism. In 1961 Arthur Christiansen, for many years editor of the *Express,* wrote in the *New Statesman* that the Council's influence on press standards in recent years had been immense. The Council's censuring statements have received wide publicity, including space in publications being rebuked. It has been credited with cleaning up the gossip columns, notorious for their invasions of privacy, and with improving press coverage of day-to-day events. Doubt has been expressed, however, as to the Council's capacity to prevent press excesses in big stories such as the Kennedy assassination and the sexual improprieties of John Profumo, British minister of war.

Among the Press Council's actions have been criticisms of newspaper bad taste and unnecessary invasions of privacy, defenses of reporters against unethical demands of editors, condemnations of the identification of innocent relatives with persons found guilty of crimes. The group has not been slow to reprimand newspapers whose editors or managers were members.

In the United States organized publishers and editors have stubbornly rebuffed numerous suggestions from responsible quarters for the creation of a voluntary agency to evaluate the work being done by the press in this country, to receive complaints, and to advise on improvements. In 1947 the privately organized Commission on Freedom of the Press (financed by Time, Inc., and the Encyclopaedia Britannica, Inc., with no strings attached to the grants) recommended the establishment for a trial ten-year period of a privately endowed independent agency to appraise and report annually on the press in the United States. Among other things, the agency was to point out the "inadequacy of press service in certain areas," investigate "instances of press lying," define "workable standards of performance," and seek the "widest possible publicity and public discussion" of its activities.[28]

Subsequent discussion of the commission recommendation by press executives and others made clear that the American press was not receptive to an agency to pass upon its performance or to bring pressure of any kind on newspapers to change their practices. In 1950 a ten-man committee, which had been designated by the American Society of Newspaper Editors to study the issue raised by the commission, delivered a lengthy report in which it pointed out that a large degree of self-examination and criticism already existed within the industry and suggested that the society "take whatever action may be necessary from time to time to clarify understanding of American newspapers by the public, and to keep editors alert to their responsibilities. . . ."

In 1955 Robert M. Hutchins, who had been a member of the Commission on Freedom of the Press, told a meeting of the ASNE that its efforts to act as a critical agency had "come to nothing" and renewed the appeal for the establishment of an appraising agency. But his plea went unheeded.

Gordon Gray, principal owner of the Winston-Salem (North Carolina) *Journal and Sentinel,* observed in a 1960 address at the University of North Carolina that the American Newspaper Publishers Association and the American Society of Newspaper Editors were not providing adequately for criticism, and challenged "the press as a whole to take a clear and honest look at itself" by establishing a National Commission on the Press, "independent of government or other influence," whose function would be "to assure the most thorough and searching appraisal of the problems, deficiencies, limitations, opportunities and potentials of the press in America." This proposal also came to naught.

Similar recommendations for agencies to keep tabs on the press have been suggested in recent years by Harry Ashmore, former executive editor of the *Arkansas Gazette;* by J. Edward Gerald, professor of journalism at the University of Minnesota; by Dr. Edmund C. Arnold, professor of journalism at Syracuse University. None of these thoughtful suggestions met with any promising affirmative response from United States newspaper organizations up to mid-1965.

In rejecting the idea of an appraising organization, the American press, with some notable exceptions, has reacted in its characteristic hypersensitive fashion to criticism. When Sigma Delta Chi, the professional journalistic fraternity, proposed a survey to assess the fairness of press coverage of the 1952 presidential campaign, Roy A. Roberts, president of the Kansas City *Star,* snorted, "tommyrot."[29] The ASNE in 1953 voted down a mild resolution which simply called for a committee of its own members to study the 1952 campaign coverage and report its conclusions to the society. Sigma Delta Chi was again rebuffed when it attempted to implement a plan for a broad and disinterested survey of objectivity in news reporting in the 1956 presidential campaign. As with criticism of political news coverage, the press in many instances has responded with equal vehemence and irrationality to more recent criticism of crime news coverage.

Self-criticism by the Press

Since an effective outside vehicle for criticism is lacking, newspapers might reasonably be expected to fill the vacuum in part at least by criticizing each other. But one of the cardinal and most faithfully observed unwritten rules of the daily press is that papers should not speak ill of each other. Though they may differ on issues, newspapers regard it as somehow a violation of the unvoiced code of honor to vigorously debate other papers by name or to upbraid other publications for gross errors, unfair treatment of subjects in the news, or other misconduct.

In the fall of 1964 Mrs. Lucille Miller was being tried in California for the murder of her husband. While the jury selection in the nationally publicized case was in progres, the San Bernardino *Sun-Telegram* printed a story quoting Sheriff Frank Bland as saying he had information on Mrs. Miller's alleged involvement in the earlier suspicious death of a prominent San Bernardino attorney's wife. The story caused a mistrial to be declared. The Los Angeles papers reported the mistrial and the reason for it. But "not one word of editorial comment criticizing the *Sun-Telegram* was printed in the newspapers or broadcast over television or radio," according to Joe Nevins, managing editor of San Gabriel Valley Publications in testimony before a Senate subcommittee conducting hearings on the Morse bill.

The St. Louis *Post-Dispatch* and the Chicago *Daily News* performed in a highly unusual manner when in 1949 they exposed the fact that fifty-one Illinois newspapermen, including editors and publishers of more than thirty papers, were on the state payroll while holding their regular jobs and had collected nearly $500,000 in public salaries, which many of them had earned by printing canned editorials and news stories lauding accomplishments of the Republican administration of Governor Dwight H. Green.[30]

In the absence of a Press Institute or Press Council or Press Commission of the type so often suggested and as often scorned by the press, Americans have no institution comparable to the British Press Council, to which they can look for informed, dispassionate assessments of shortcomings of the press and to which they can take grievances when they feel they have been wronged in print. Even though the American press on the whole is probably better than Britain's (perhaps better than that of any other country) and even though newspapers of integrity will try to make amends for recognized misconduct, no human institution is so free of fault that it cannot benefit from responsible external criticism. Moreover, there are individual newspapers which are quite as capable of corrupt conduct as other businesses. The ordinary business customer who feels he has been defrauded by a deliberately sold $25 item of defective merchandise can at least go to the Better Business Bureau. But the man who feels that a newspaper has robbed him of his good name, far more valuable to him than merchandise, or that he has otherwise been victimized in the press, has nowhere to go if the paper itself won't give him satisfaction and if the dubious method of a libel suit seems to promise no relief. In no other area of news coverage have American citizens perhaps been more often wronged than in the reporting of criminal investigations. An appraising agency would be one means of inducing improved reporting and of correcting injustices.

All efforts to establish a national press commission having failed so far, some foundation could render a valuable service by financing such a project for an experimental period. If the financing of a national commission is not feasible, a privately endowed commission in a single city could serve as a pilot project for a national agency. Ably staffed and responsibly led by citizens of standing in the community, a city commission could set an example by observing the local press and taking it to task when it fails to measure up to its obligations.

A press commission would be in the best traditions of the American system. The tripartite federal government was founded on the concept that its separate branches would serve to check and balance each other—the legislative branch checking the executive and the judicial branch (appointed by the executive but with life tenure) checking both of the others. The press, which has sometimes been called the fourth branch of government, was given a privileged place under the Constitution in order to enhance its capacity to counteract the three official arms of government. Sometimes it has done its job well. But there is no reason why there shouldn't be an institution with sufficient resources and immunity from retribution to serve as a check and balance against the press. Indeed, such a watchdog agency would be a worthwhile modern extension of the founding fathers' check-and-balance innovation. It would be a private variation of the grievance machinery represented in government by the ombudsman's office, already in existence in Scandinavian countries, Great Britain, and New Zealand, and being proposed in some American states.

The role of press critic could also be assumed by voluntary *ad hoc* citizens' groups, though their work would of necessity be more limited and less effective than a full-time staffed organization. Law schools and bar associations should be especially suited to supply inspiration, talent, and leadership for such a volunteer effort aimed at examining and judging press performance in the area of criminal justice. Any serious, objective, and knowledgeable endeavor of this kind that is undertaken could add a useful dimension to the minimal press criticism that now emanates from schools of journalism through such organs as the *Columbia Journalism Review* and the Freedom of Information Center publications from the University of Missouri.

A New Outlook for the Press

No amount of outside criticism and pressure can be as effective in bringing about enlightened press treatment of the administration of justice as can the voluntary adoption by publishers and editors of a brand new outlook toward the role of the newspaper in this field. Increasing signs of more understanding and informed attitudes in newspapers are already evident. More editors are coming to realize, for example, that the treatment of juvenile delinquency is not just a matter of applying the rod, that narcotic peddlers can't be cured simply by sending them to jail, that alcoholism is a disease which won't be wiped out by treating chronic drunkenness as a crime. Examples of a more compassionate, positive attitude toward justice have been provided by newspapers which often take the lead toward new trends in journalism—by the Washington *Post,* in a series of articles on teen-age drinking and alcoholism;[31] by the St. Louis *Post-Dispatch,* in the sympathetic portrayal of a prison without bars;[32] by the New York *Times,* in the reporting of experimental methods of dealing with narcotics addiction.[33] The New York *Times,* more than any other paper perhaps, has for years recognized and reported on socially significant new trends in the field of justice as well as in other areas. The prospect for a similar trend on the part of a greater segment of the press is improving. American newspapers are getting better.[34] Their staffs are made up of more college-trained people. They indulge in fewer of the vulgarities common to the earlier cutthroat eras of journalism. If Babbitt values still are manifest in some editorial offices, they are not as prevalent as they once were.

With the development of television, newspapers are being given a chance to adapt themselves to a new role in the presentation of information and interpretation concerning public affairs. Obviously the electronics medium can completely outclass the print medium in the coverage of the kind of sensational spot news that papers once thrived on. The murder in the bedroom can be more quickly and vividly dramatized on the home screen than in 96-point type with photographs on the front page. Editors are beginning to recognize the communicative function in which television and radio are superior. Newspapers don't put out extras any more. There are fewer boxcar headlines on crime or other matters. Yet persistent use of old formulas is still apparent. In a time when street sales are far less important than they once were, banner heads are still employed to tell about the coming snow storm or the stabbing of a blond barmaid.

Newspapers cannot ignore spot news. Their readers still want to find out about important events through the printed word. But the competition between different papers and between newspapers and television is not such that there is any longer much justification for highly sensational front page play and for news stories that merely repeat what listeners have already heard on the air. By leaving more of the trivia to the electronics media, newspapers could report on matters of local public concern, including crime, in a different way—providing background information and perceptive interpretation patterned after the style set by magazines and syndicated writers on the national scene but rarely provided at the community level. Newspapers now have an opportunity to apply the more discursive approach that is acutely needed on local issues and that cannot readily be provided in spoken words, particularly not in the ten-minute newscast. Today newspapermen need not be as bound to the clock as they once were. Television and radio reporters are the new slaves of the minute hand.

Not only do members of the print medium have a new freedom but they also have a new obligation to use it wisely. As Walter Cronkite of CBS news said in a 1965 discussion with a group of newspapermen—if 55 per cent of the American people (as the polls show) get most of their news from television, then "55 per cent of the public is inadequately informed." Cronkite went on to observe that newspapers should fill the gap that television leaves; that, instead of trying to compete—as many of them do—they should complement the other medium.

In the area of criminal justice, the possibilities for new types of newspaper treatment are numerous. For example, local papers could examine the question of how crime and law enforcement in their communities compare with the national picture. In 1964 police counted more than 2,600,000 serious crimes in the United States. This represented fourteen serious offenses a year for each 1,000 persons in the nation. In 1964 some 2,132,220 persons were arrested in 1,751 United States cities for offenses ranging from vagrancy and drunkenness to criminal homicide. This figure represented about 3.6 per cent of the 58,915,000 people in these communities.[35] But in some states and cities the rates are considerably higher or lower than the national rates. Newspapers could go far beyond their usual simple reporting of the figures for their own areas and strive to interpret their meaning—why, for example, Nevada, California, and Arizona had the highest state crime rates in the nation in 1964 and Vermont, West Virginia, and the Dakotas, the lowest; why in the first six months of 1965 crime decreased in Houston, Rochester, and Atlanta but went up in New York City and Los Angeles. Certain answers would not be available, but sociologists, criminologists, and others have theories that might be helpful to the public.

Another area calling for more careful scrutiny and reporting by newspapers is the development of new techniques for investigating crime and apprehending suspects: the use of computers in processing data, the installation of closed circuit television for surveillance and hidden cameras and microphones for recording scenes and voices, the analysis of criminal evidence by means of radioactive trace elements. What potential do these methods hold for police efficiency, for individual rights? Newspaper readers in any big city would be interested in knowing why crime of every type has recently decreased in Chicago.

Other areas of criminal procedure in which perceptive press examination is needed are: the equality of justice (or lack of it) provided in the administration of bail, the rehabilitation of convicted offenders through work-release programs outside of prison and through the establishment of halfway houses for newly released prisoners, the granting of amnesty and a clean record to deserving first offenders. In the field of substantive criminal law, the press could help to educate the public by an enlightened exploration of new ways of looking at abortion, nonviolent sex improprieties, and other acts still defined as crimes but no longer generally regarded as subjects for harsh legal penalties.

In every community the standards of law enforcement, the quality of justice in the criminal courts, and the conditions in places of incarceration should be subject to periodic exploration in depth by the press. Newspaper coverage of these areas need not be dull and unrewarding. Even serious subjects can be made provocative and readable by lively style, the exploitation of human interest angles, the use of pictures, and other tried techniques.

In 1956 the Cleveland *News* published a series of articles by reporter Howard Beaufait on the topic, "So You're Arrested." The demand for them was such that the paper printed them in pamphlet form for distribution by itself and by the Cleveland Bar Association.

In 1962 the Panama City (Florida) *News-Herald* won a Pulitzer prize for a 1960–1961 series of stories and editorials which brought about federal and state investigations of gambling and bootlegging operations in its area. The series led ultimately to the removal of Panama City's police chief and Bay County's sheriff and to federal indictment of both of them on charges of conspiracy to violate state and federal liquor laws.[36]

One of the most telling and justifiably angry recent newspaper portrayals of judicial arrogance and callousness toward litigants was done by William F. Buckley, Jr., after visiting a minor court in New York City.

In 1963 John Hemphill, a reporter for the Nashville *Tennessean,* got himself arrested, after which he spent four days in the metropolitan jail and workhouse to investigate conditions. His subsequent series of articles on the harsh treatment of prisoners prompted measures to improve the food, the cramped quarters, the unclean facilities.

While they are studying new areas for interpretive reporting, editors might also reexamine some of their conventional attitudes about what cases and issues are most worthy of a newspaper's emphasis and crusading zeal. In the light of the customary pressure of an aroused public and the usual zeal of police and prosecutor in cases of violent crime, editors might well ask themselves whether there is any social justification for giving sensational play to most murders, rapes, bank holdups, and the like. The pressure of the press is needed far less to prod the prosecution of the ordinary defendants who are involved in assaults on people and property than to prod the investigation of corruption in government or to prod the prosecution of those rarer defendants with money and influence.

Normally a homicide or a rape case, once the event is publicly noted, is likely to be properly processed without any banner headline attention from the press. But the observant eyes of the press may be needed to alert the public to irregularities in government that call for prosecution. And the constant, prominent, and, hopefully, judicious notice of the press may be required to bring about even-handed justice in the case of an Aaron Burr, an Albert B. Fall, or an Alger Hiss. Highly placed defendants not only have the resources to put up a more effective defense but they also have friends who may intercede for them both with law enforcement agents and the press.

While the press unquestionably can cause injustice to be done to prominent people by adopting a persecutive and sensational approach, it is in such cases that editors must be most on their guard against playing the news in accordance with the personal interest of the accused rather than the public interest. When Walter Jenkins, a member of the White House staff, was arrested on a morals charge in the fall of 1964, friends of the accused pleaded with the Washington papers for secrecy, compassion, or delay in the handling of the case. Editor John T. O'Rourke of the Washington *Daily News* explained the delay in the publication of the news by saying that it "made it possible to get Mr. Jenkins into a hospital, made it possible for the White House to prepare for the announcement of his resignation and last, but far from least, made it possible for members of his family to brace themselves for a shattering disaster."[37] Admittedly the charge against Jenkins was a minor one which in the case of more ordinary arrested persons would have been ignored by the press; admittedly the story eventually was sensationally played because he was a highly placed public figure. But readers would be justified in asking why editors, in processing news of embarrassing charges against lesser defendants, shouldn't exhibit O'Rourke's commendable caution and concern for sensibilities in various quarters. Instead of playing most crime news largely according to its dramatic value, wouldn't the press be exercising its function more responsibly if it balanced the potential harm to the accused against the social usefulness of the story in the same way the Washington editors did in the initial phase of the Jenkins case?

Instead of worrying so much about "the right to know" from the police the criminal histories of suspects, editors might show more interest in "the right to know" about what goes on in secret marathon interrogations in police stations. Instead of concentrating on getting cameras into courtrooms, they might seek more often to get probing reporters into prisons and into interrogation rooms. Instead of devoting the front page to the accused as he goes into court or into jail, they might more often give extended coverage to what happens to an offender after he comes out of prison—virtually penniless, unwanted by employers, angry at the world, and infused with the lore of crime by fellow prisoners. Instead of giving excessive attention to crimes of violence (in which press prodding is hardly needed to arouse public concern), they might inquire into the extent and significance of white collar crimes such as fraud, the rate of which is higher than robbery, rape, or arson. Perceptive reporting on these subjects would do more to upgrade law enforcement, to reduce crime generally, and to promote justice than giving saturation publicity to the prior records and reputed confessions of those suspects whose cases are deemed dramatic enough to be accorded headline treatment.

The services which the press has performed for justice and which it can render in the future are many: the finding of missing suspects and witnesses, the exposure of crime and corruption in government, the revelation of misconduct by law enforcement officials, the vindication of the innocent, the education of the public on the law enforcement process. Indeed, one of the essential preconditions for upgrading the machinery of criminal justice is better reporting and comment by the press. But all of these contributions are devalued if the press unwittingly helps to bring about the conviction of the innocent.

To guard against such a possibility, the editor's philosophy in crime news coverage should be based on a constant awareness that the law regards an accused as innocent until he is found guilty in a court. If the editor is guided by this philosophy, he will always seek to make his paper an objective instrument for the discovery of truth about the process of law enforcement rather than simply a channel for the presentation of the prosecution's case.

Given the great resources of the state and the ordinarily minimal resources of the defendant, the trial is normally an unequal contest anyway. And if the prosecution should be overzealous, or in error, or vindictive, the aid of the press accentuates the injustice.

There are times, of course, when an apathetic or corrupt prosecutor must be prodded into action by crusading articles and editorials. But in most criminal cases the press can serve justice best by simply reporting events impartially, by striving to present the defense side as fully as that of the prosecution, by seeking to elicit missing facts, by asking questions when the score does not seem to add up properly.

By maintaining a skeptical attitude to the end, the press acts in accordance with the law's presumption of innocence and should be able to carry out more often an essential function, which at times it has performed well—that of preventing miscarriages of justice. The vital point for editors to remember is that under the American system, which guarantees both a fair trial and a free press, the press upholds the two constitutional interests best by serving as an independent observer of government rather than as its mouthpiece.

The responsibility of the press was succinctly summed up in 1964 by Arthur J. Goldberg, then an associate justice of the United States Supreme Court, when he said before the annual meeting of the American Society of Newspaper Editors:

> The entire Bill of Rights is in the press' charge—not only the Free Speech Clause of the First Amendment. A newspaper which fails to exercise its right of free expression in protest against the invasion of any branch of government—the executive, the legislative, or the judicial—of freedom of thought, of conscience, of assembly and of the person defaults in its most elementary duty and responsibility. The press must be the protector of all the Amendments not only against their invasion by government, but against their infringement by the press itself.

CHAPTER NINE

RESPONSIBILITY FOR THE BAR AND BENCH

The Bar's Blind Spots

Just as many newspapermen dismiss the need for any improvement in press practices in the interests of justice, so many lawyers pay little attention to the need for improvement on the part of the bar. If the press seems smugly satisfied that the sensationalizing of lurid cases fulfills its obligation to justice, the bar is no less smug in its attitude toward its obligation. In 1964 Chief Judge J. Edward Lumbard of the United States Court of Appeals for the Second Circuit observed that the bar in general looks down upon lawyers who practice in criminal courts, that most leading lawyers will not handle a criminal case, except antitrust or income tax cases against corporate executives, and that these lawyers are fearful that their business clients would not understand their appearance in the criminal arena.[1] The scarcity of lawyers in the criminal field is further accentuated by the fact that less money comparatively can be earned in this area. Thus lawyer shunning of criminal cases seems to be grounded in economic motives just as press preoccupation with certain kinds of crime coverage seems, on the other hand, to be based on the hope of economic gain through circulation increases.

Perhaps because they are unwilling to face their own broad responsibilities in the field of criminal justice, lawyers tend to concentrate on such an issue as Free Press v. Fair Trial. It supplies them with a vicarious adversary proceeding and—as in the case of the press offensive against its critics—minimizes the necessity for serious self-examination. The typical lawyer approach is to assume that, if newspapers restrained themselves or were restrained by law, the criminal process is already adequately designed to produce satisfactory justice. Thus the bar tends to focus on ways and means by which lawyers and judges can discipline the prejudiced press, while at the same time its members fail to recognize that jurists themselves might harbor prejudices that should be exposed.

In 1959 John and Sylvia Powell and Julian Schuman were being tried in a California federal court on charges of sedition for publishing in the *China Monthly Review* stories allegedly exaggerating American battle casualties in the Korean war and asserting that the United States used germ warfare. The prosecution charged that the stories were used in brainwashing American prisoners of war in Korean prison camps. At one point in the proceedings Judge Louis E. Goodman was discussing with the prosecutor, out of the presence of the jury, whether testimony that the *Review* was delivered to Korean POW camps was admissible. The judge told the prosecutor that such testimony could not be admitted because seditious acts, with which the defendants were charged, may be committed only in the United States or on the high seas under United States admiralty jurisdiction. In the course of ruling out the testimony, however, the judge also remarked to the prosecutor that treason can be committed anywhere and that he thought a *prima facie* (self-evident) case of treason had been established.

Because this unjudicial comment was publicized by the press, the judge granted a defense motion for a mistrial, meanwhile blaming the press for the unexpected termination of the trial.[2] The case suggests that the legal profession, like the press, has blind spots concerning its own shortcomings. (Incidentally, it also illustrates why it might not be wise to give judges greater power over the press. Would newspapers be as likely to expose judicial prejudices if judges could more easily subject them to punishment for contempt?)

While the bar has been perennially preoccupied with the problem of press prejudicing of fair trials, it has largely ignored some of the major hindrances to justice on its own side. Despite the fact that many of the guarantees of due process have long been recognized in principle, their full implementation in practice has not yet been realized. The organized bar has done little to change the situation in which the right to counsel, the right to a speedy trial, the protection against self-incrimination, the provision against excessive bail have all been less meaningful guarantees for the poorest defendants[3]—the bulk of those accused—than they have been for those with the means to employ effective legal talent. Only in the last generation has the United States Supreme Court begun to apply federal standards of due process to defaulting states. The translation of the Bill of Rights into an effective instrument for the protection of all accused persons is still a developing phenomenon in law, just as the creation of an objective press is still a developing phenomenon in journalism. Justice requires that the bar and press keep their sights set respectively on these broad objectives rather than allowing their concern to degenerate into a nit-picking argument over the narrow question of how much the press prejudices the minds of jurors.

Groundwork for Reform

As a result of the leadership of the Supreme Court, moves have been made on several fronts in recent years to upgrade the processes of criminal justice in the United States. In 1964 the American Bar Association launched a three-year project designed to promote the establishment of nationally recognized minimum standards for the administration of criminal justice. Directed by U.S. Court of Appeals Judge Lumbard and financed by $750,000 in foundation grants, the study was designed to deal with a broad range of subjects: police training, qualifications, and methods of interrogation, the right to counsel, bail, the role of prosecutors, publicity, uniform sentencing, probation, prisons, and the social welfare functions of courts. After they have been formulated, the new criteria of justice will be circulated by the American Bar Association in an effort to have them adopted in each state by statutes, codes, or court rules. The purpose would be to provide better protection for both the public and the accused.

Another sign of concern for justice came in 1964 when Attorney General Robert F. Kennedy, not long before leaving office, created within the Department of Justice an Office of Criminal Justice with the assignment of improving the handling of such matters as federal arrests, the provision of counsel for the poor, and psychiatric examination of prisoners. Conceived as an agency to "deal with the whole spectrum of the criminal process, from arrest to rehabilitation," the new office was held out as a way of making the Department of Justice more than just a "Department of Prosecution."

In 1965 President Johnson sent Congress a special message on Law Enforcement and the Administration of Justice. While making several proposals for federal legislation to deal with such problems as the interstate shipment of firearms and the sale of dangerous drugs, the President recognized that crime stems in some cases from inexplicable maladjusted personalities and, in other cases, from the frustrations of such broad social ills as poverty, ignorance, and disease. He also noted the failure of the nation's correctional system as evidenced by the "endless, self-defeating cycle of imprisonment, release, and reimprisonment." To conduct a comprehensive, penetrating analysis of the origins and nature of crime and to make long-range recommendations, the President later the same year appointed a 19-member Commission on Law Enforcement and Administration of Justice.

With all of these innovative studies under way, the groundwork is being laid for what could be an essential remodeling of the entire machinery of criminal justice, beginning with the barbarous interrogative methods still applied in many police stations in the name of the law, and extending through the scandalous practices still employed by unlettered or corrupt justices of the peace across the land, the callous or at best insensitive attitudes toward procedural rights still exhibited in many state trial courts, the wholly inadequate provisions for the correction of injustice by appeals and, finally, the dehumanizing and ineffectual form of punishment by long-term, cage-like incarceration and total ostracism. Without broad reform in these various areas, the total cessation of prejudicial publicity would still represent a minor palliative for the grievous conditions of injustice that should be engaging the efforts of the press and the bar.

There is danger that the bar, in concentrating its energies on the highly visible evils of trial by newspaper, and the press, in defending its supposed vested interest in crime news, will both neglect the more basic but less obvious problems of justice. We have already noted in Chapter 8 that editors seem to be wedded to pretelevision formulas of reporting and playing dabs of superficial spot news, ignoring an opportunity to probe more perceptively into social trends. Lawyers (as indicated in Chapter 7) seem even more preoccupied with the past, slavishly doing obeisance to rules and precedents after they have been proved valueless or when the purpose for which they were designed is no longer being served. This chapter will refer again to some of these outdated concepts and will suggest proposals for improvement in order to show that lawyers, like the press, should be amenable to change.

The change would represent little more than an illusion of reform if lawyers only committed themselves to avoid making prejudicial statements about defendants before trial. To make a really meaningful contribution to the administration of criminal justice, the bar must first take a more general professional interest, as distinguished from an individual lawyer-client interest, in what happens outside the courtroom or the attorney's office.

Police and Rights

LIMITS ON DRAGNET ARRESTS

One subject for professional concern should be the police practice of making dragnet arrests—a capricious method whereby all ill-kempt people in a neighborhood, all those known to have a certain kind of police record, or all those violating a curfew are willy-nilly taken into custody. Sometimes numerous innocent victims are repeatedly harassed or questioned about a particular crime merely because they happened to belong to the unlucky category. Several years ago in Odessa, Texas, the police, following the rape of a white girl, arrested every 17-to-20-year-old Negro male found on the streets.[4] This method of law enforcement smacks of the police state and should be forbidden by regulation.

CURB ON THE JAILING OF ALCOHOLICS

Another gross infringement of the rights of innocent parties is the incarceration of great numbers of drunks who have not created any threat to the personal security of others. Though the police are the instruments of this practice, they are acting only because most communities have failed to provide any better way of dealing with a troublesome problem. A few years ago Chief Justice John M. Murtagh of the New York Court of Special Sessions remarked that the arrest of millions of drunks annually in this country constituted a far more serious violation of civil liberties than the American Civil Liberties Union ever had concerned itself with. He said the use of criminal sanctions against common drunks as widely practiced in the United States was bringing the entire judicial system into disrepute and urged that the police should be restricted to those cases in which threats were posed to the security of other persons.

At a Senate hearing in 1965 Attorney General Nicholas deB. Katzenbach pointed out that approximately one third of the six million arrests in this country in 1964 were for drunkenness. He observed that the resulting crowding in courts and prisons affects the efficiency of the entire criminal process. The skid-row drunk is in and out of courts and jails so often that sociologists have come to call his kind "the revolving door population." Despite the fact that chronic inebriates are obviously ill and need help desperately, most American communities continue to ignore them or treat them as criminals. The appellate courts, however, may eventually force a change. The United States Court of Appeals for the Fourth Circuit ruled in early 1966 that a chronic alcoholic could not be prosecuted as a criminal, although he could be detained for medical treatment. The defendant in the case, Joe B. Driver, 59, of Durham, North Carolina, had been convicted more than 200 times of public intoxication and had spent some two thirds of his life in jail.

Philadelphia in 1965 reported good results from an experimental rehabilitation and relocation program for Skid Row "down-and-outers," including alcoholics. In the same year New York City took the initiative in building its first rehabilitation center for derelicts, a place containing experimental "detoxification" facilities, and providing vocational training and long-term treatment for alcoholics. In his discussion of alcoholism in relation to the criminal process, Attorney General Katzenbach said there must be better ways to handle drunks than tossing them into jail. Noting that other countries are using "sobering-up stations," he suggested that similar social agencies might be used to keep alcoholics separate from the criminal process. He also suggested, incidentally, that large numbers of assaults and other offenses arising out of family disputes or landlord-tenant differences be removed from the criminal process.

STRICTER REGULATIONS ON USE OF FIREARMS

An all too frequent practice by which police threaten or (in some cases) destroy the rights of suspected law violators or bystanders is in the use of firearms to stop suspects in relatively trivial offenses when the lives of neither the officers themselves nor of citizens under their protection are in danger from the fleeing person. In 1965 Pittsburgh police raided an open air dice game and when one of the scattering players, a Negro youth, failed to halt on command he was shot dead.[5] Such senseless use of guns occurs so commonly as to suggest a widespread need of better training and tighter regulations on the use of firearms.

SAFEGUARDS IN INTERROGATION

The time and place in which police are most likely to violate the rights of suspects are in the interrogation process in the precinct station. This is the stage at which abusive practices are least subject to observation and correction. Figures on the number of arrests based on "suspicion" (102,000 in 1964)[6] or "for investigation" hint at the possible extent of abuse; arrests are supposed to be made only when the police have probable cause to believe the suspect committed the offense in question. The courts are getting increasing complaints of forced confessions, but they seldom have an effective way to evaluate the validity of such claims; often they can only balance the complainant's assertion against the police denial.

General reform in the interrogative process is urgently needed.

Though the bar could be leading the way in this effort, a group of lawyers in the American Law Institute offered in 1965 a so-called model prearraignment code which left doubt as to their commitment to constitutional guarantees for the accused. The code proposed by the ALI reporters allowed extensive police station questioning of suspects without assuring them of the assistance of counsel.

A procedure better calculated to protect the rights of the accused was initiated in 1965 by District of Columbia Police Chief John B. Layton on the advice of United States Attorney David C. Acheson. It required an arrested person to be plainly informed that any statement that he made could be used against him, that he need make no statement at all, that he be given an opportunity to notify a relative or friend and to consult an attorney, if he had one; that the aggregate period of questioning not exceed three hours, exclusive of interruptions, between arrest and the completion of any confession, admission, or statement; and that the questioning, whenever reasonably possible, be witnessed by an impartial third party or be recorded or transcribed verbatim.[7]

During the 1965 New York mayoralty campaign, candidate William F. Ryan, who had served seven years as an assistant district attorney, proposed sweeping changes in police interrogation methods: a standardization of regulations and procedures, the advising of all suspects before questioning of their right to remain silent and their right to counsel, the assignment of an assistant district attorney to be present during the entire interrogation of homicide suspects, the conduct of interrogations of suspects for all major crimes in borough or central police headquarters whenever possible, the closed-circuit televising of the interrogation process.

Though the police tend to resist the broadening of protections for the suspect at the interrogation stage, a trend in that direction has already begun without the predicted adverse effects on law enforcement. Judge George Edwards of the United States Court of Appeals for the Sixth Circuit, who resigned from the Michigan Supreme Court to become police commissioner in Detroit in 1962–1963, told the Midwestern Regional Conference of Attorneys General in 1965 that he had run the Detroit police department under the same rules recently applied by the United States Supreme Court and that "murder and pillage did not run rampant." Edwards asserted that "it was not exactly easy" but that the police under his direction had sought to observe the rights of suspects in such areas as searches and seizures, confessions, legal counsel, and arraignments. He added, "We stopped 'alley court' and 'falling on the precinct steps' . . . . And we did take prisoners promptly before a judge."

In Essex County, New Jersey, prosecutor Brendan Byrne, shortly after the 1964 Escobedo decision, ordered police in his jurisdiction to warn suspects of their rights and to provide indigent ones with lawyers when they were requested after the warning. He reported a year and a half after the change that no confessions had been lost as a result of the warnings and offers of counsel. In Philadelphia, where the same system was instituted later, prosecutor Richard Sprague reported a similar experience. Contrary to police estimates that 75 to 85 per cent of convictions for major crimes are based on confessions, a study of 1,000 Brooklyn indictments in 1965 by state Supreme Court Justice Nathan R. Sobel showed that fewer than 10 per cent involved confessions. Justice Sobel commented that the usual police contention that confessions are the backbone of law enforcement was "carefully nurtured nonsense." [8] Immediately after the Sobel study was reported, Brooklyn District Attorney Aaron E. Koota said he thought that a person should have access to a lawyer "at the moment he comes into contact with the law." He remarked:

> If a man has a constitutional right to a lawyer the mere fact that it might impede law enforcement or make it more difficult to prosecute is not a reason to deny him those rights. I think that is fundamental to our judicial process and our form of government.[9]

It was in Brooklyn that police in 1963 extracted a false murder confession from George Whitmore, Jr., without advising him of his right to counsel. The New York Police Department had consistently refused to issue such advice and New York law did not require it. Both Sobel and Koota were soon being disputed by New York County District Attorney Frank S. Hogan, who said that in countless incidents "it is the defendant and only the defendant" who gives the evidence that results in his conviction. He said the whole purpose of a police investigation would be frustrated if a suspect were entitled to have a lawyer during preliminary questioning.

While many lower courts and attorneys were still arguing over the circumstances under which the Escobedo decision required counsel to be provided, the United States Supreme Court went a long way toward settling the argument by ruling in the Miranda case (in June 1966) that a suspect is entitled to have a lawyer during the period of questioning by the police and that, if he wants an attorney and cannot pay for one, the interrogation by police must cease unless court-appointed counsel is provided. The Court also held that the police, before questioning a suspect, must tell him of his right to remain silent and respect his decision not to speak.

ADMINISTRATIVE GUIDANCE FOR POLICE

The Supreme Court, however, should not be required to assume the primary responsibility for seeing that the police observe the law and respect the constitutional rights of citizens. As Professor Herbert L. Packer of the Stanford University School of Law has observed, the obligation is one for legislators and administrators. But because these officials on the federal, state, and local levels have generally defaulted on the job, the high court has sought to fill the vacuum and to influence police behavior in the only way it can—by dealing in its traditional way with specific cases. If the result has led to uncertainty, to differences in lower court rulings, and to complaints that the police cannot operate under rules being laid down by the judiciary, the fault is not the Supreme Court's. If lawmakers adopted and administrators applied detailed codes of permissible police practices, there would be less need for the Supreme Court to police the police.

Instead, legislators and administrators, many of whom are lawyers, have failed to recognize the values the court was protecting and have tended to blame the court for using the only sanction it has—the reversal of convictions when the police violated the Constitution in securing their evidence. Though the Wickersham Commission more than thirty years ago produced voluminous information on abusive police practices, little has been done to improve the codes under which the police operate. Though the Supreme Court has changed its view of the law in the last generation, far too many officials have clung to the outdated outlook that H. L. Mencken satirized in the 1920's:

> . . . once a policeman, he is protected by the legislative and judicial arms in the peculiar rights and prerogatives that go with his high office, including especially the right to jug the laity at his will, to sweat and mug them, to subject them to the third degree, and to subdue their resistance by beating out their brains. Those who are unaware of this are simply ignorant of the basic principles of American jurisprudence, as they have been exposed times without number by the courts of the first instance and ratified in lofty terms by the Supreme Court of the United States. The one aim of the controlling decisions, magnificently attained, is to safeguard public order and the public security, and to substitute a judicial process for the inchoate and dangerous interaction of discordant egos.[10]

Though the Supreme Court may have effected some change in judicial attitudes since Mencken's day, police views of the Bill of Rights have changed little. Criticism of the high court by the police heads of Los Angeles and New York in 1964 was typical. A few years earlier Police Chief James F. Lynch of Warwick, Rhode Island, exhibited a similar uncomprehending attitude toward constitutional rights when he described a system his men had for recognizing racketeers. He said, "If he is a real racketeer, he won't let you into his home without a search warrant." [11]

BETTER QUALIFIED POLICE

In the implementation of codes of fair practice, police should be made to understand that the restraints upon them are not for the purpose of aiding suspects but to insure that law enforcement officers make fewer mistakes and avoid mistreating citizens. But before there can be real improvement, police must be better paid and better qualified for their difficult work. They must be better trained in procedures and methods, especially in the gathering of external evidence by investigative means so that they will be less inclined to sweat information out of suspects and to try to get them to convict themselves out of their own mouths. Former Detroit Police Commissioner George Edwards has suggested the establishment of a national police training college and has expressed the view that a fully trained and qualified officer should command a salary of $10,000 a year.

In Chicago, Police Superintendent Orlando W. Wilson, who once taught criminology at the University of California, has pushed his force a step beyond finding solutions of crimes after they have occurred. He has initiated preventive practices designed to reduce crime: by anticipating crime patterns through computer analyses, by having police where they are most likely to be needed, and by a system of aggressive patrolling of streets and alleys by uniformed officers in conspicuously marked cars.

For those cases in which the police engage in lawless practices in spite of the code, the legislature should provide: (1) an external mechanism such as a civilian review board for judging when a breach of the code has occurred, and (2) a system for compensating the person whose rights have been violated, such as allowance for a liquidated damage action against the local governmental unit which employs the offending policeman. The principle involved was upheld by the United States Supreme Court in the Monroe case in 1961 when the tribunal ruled that policemen and other local officials who violated a citizen's constitutional rights could be sued for damages in federal courts.[12]

Unless effective sanctions for police lawlessness are provided, a sizable segment of the population, made up particularly of minority groups, will continue to harbor hostility toward the police, and a largely invisible condition of injustice will remain uncorrected.

POLICE EFFICIENCY

Despite protests of police officials and their sympathizers against the Supreme Court, there is little indication that the imposition of procedural requirements in law enforcement has enabled a significant portion of accused felons to "beat the rap," as the saying goes. The Uniform Crime Reports for 1964 show that, of those charged with crime in our larger cities, 71.1 per cent were found guilty. An additional 13.5 per cent were referred to juvenile courts (with the record not showing the outcome in this category). Acquittals or dismissals occurred in only 15.4 per cent of the cases. Most of the 1964 convictions were secured after the Supreme Court had enunciated the procedural rules in the decisions that have stirred so many alarms. The figures suggest that we have little to complain about as to the effectiveness of police and prosecutors in putting the accused behind bars. Can any organization, least of all a police organization whose work is by its very nature subject to a high probability of error, be certain that its decisions are better than 70 per cent accurate?

If anything, the overall figures on convictions indicate a disquietingly high efficiency in prosecution. As Justice Bernard Botein of the Appellate Division of the Supreme Court of New York has observed, the figures do not suggest that our criminal processes are "the technically-mined booby traps for prosecutors imagined by laymen." He noted that, when convictions after trial are added to convictions after guilty pleas, the rate of convictions reaches the level of 90 per cent of all prosecutions in most jurisdictions and may be as high as 98 per cent in some.[13]

The critics of the Supreme Court usually fail to recognize that seemingly still greater police efficiency may be achieved only at the undesirable cost of restrictions on liberty and at the risk of unwittingly implicating the innocent and allowing mistreatment of the guilty. Various procedural safeguards were designed not, as some seem to think, to frustrate law enforcement but to make sure that the police make as few errors as possible.

Equalizing the Positions of Defense and Prosecution

ASSURING THE ASSISTANCE OF COUNSEL

The procedural safeguard for which the legal profession has a special responsibility is the constitutional guarantee of the assistance of counsel in criminal cases. The bar's obligation is enlarged by the increasing judicial emphasis on this protection in the prearraignment stage.

Before the right to counsel can be really implemented on a large scale, however, lawyers themselves will have to change their attitude toward criminal practice. In 1964 Justice Tom C. Clark of the United States Supreme Court told a law school audience that the practice of criminal law had reached "such a degrading stage" that good lawyers shun it—believing that criminal practice will injure their reputations and destroy their civil practice—and as a result defendants are hard put to find competent counsel from among members of the bar generally. Expressing a similar view the same year, Chief Judge Lumbard of the United States Court of Appeals said that, while everyone professes a belief in effective representation of the indigent, the public and most lawyers have a "Yes-but attitude." This outlook, he said, is signified by the position that, though defendants have a right to counsel, 95 per cent are going to plead guilty anyway and don't need a lawyer and almost all the rest are guilty and any lawyer is good enough for what needs to be done.

The scarcity of attorneys seriously interested in criminal practice is suggested by the fact that in 1964 only 850 of the nation's nearly 300,000 lawyers were members of the National Association of Defense Lawyers in Criminal Cases.[14] This figure must be considered in conjunction with the fact that some 60 per cent of defendants in criminal cases have not been able to afford counsel. And as better provision is made for their legal defense, a great many more qualified defense attorneys will be needed.

Even if the truth about a crime could be best disclosed by a careful matching of legal wits, the fact is that in most cases the contest is not even. A majority of defendants—being unable financially to hire any lawyer or at any rate unable to hire any of the few good lawyers in criminal practice—are thrown against experienced prosecutors, many of whom regard themselves as scourges of criminals rather than as officers of justice. A California court observed some years ago, "It is too much the habit of prosecuting officers to assume beforehand that a defendant is guilty, and then to have . . . the features of a fair trial distorted to secure a conviction."[15] Eager for fame and political advancement, many prosecutors use all of the tricks legitimately available to them under the game theory of justice in order to win court victories which they can later boast about. Meanwhile their opponents in this supposed fight for justice are likely to be young, inexperienced, court-appointed attorneys whose only chance to learn the facts and master the game occurred a short time before the trial. In such a situation the prospect that defendants have of winning justice may unfortunately rest on sheer luck. Only in the last two or three years has the right to counsel, as a result of Supreme Court decisions, begun to measure up in practice to the promise of the Constitution. Not until defenders (adequately paid from tax funds or other sources) are available in all jurisdictions will all defendants be assured of generally effective legal representation in court.

One way of bringing about a change in lawyer education for and attitudes toward criminal practice was advanced recently by Chief Judge Charles S. Desmond of the New York State Court of Appeals. He suggested that law schools expand their criminal law and procedure courses, add a fourth year for problem courses and direct action training in the common branches of law practice, and "step up" their legal aid services. Observing that the right to counsel, fair trial, and due process are meaningless unless good young lawyers take on the difficult task of criminal practice, he urged that schools stop pointing their graduates toward corporation law practice and clerkships to appellate judges as the two admired goals.

The objective of more expert legal counsel on the prosecution side is already being aided by Northwestern University Law School, which, with the help of a $300,000 grant from the Ford Foundation, has launched a program to train lawyers to be legal advisers to police departments, interpreting recent court decisions for them and seeking to bring police practices into line with judicial rulings.

INVESTIGATIVE HELP FOR THE DEFENSE

During the pretrial stage, an accused who has been provided counsel is still at an acute disadvantage if he lacks the investigative resources needed to gather evidence indispensable to his defense. In the Scandinavian countries a defendant is not only entitled to counsel of his own choosing at government expense but also to call on government officials, at government expense, to make all necessary investigations, including searches for witnesses and documents, and to furnish analyses of handwriting, as well as expert testimony on his behalf. Only a few United States jurisdictions with public defender offices provide similar services, even though they may make the difference between conviction or acquittal of an innocent accused.

FREEDOM FOR THE ACCUSED BEFORE TRIAL

An aspect of law enforcement in which the indigent accused is treated with flagrant unfairness is in the operation of the bail system. As the system is still administered in most jurisdictions, the freedom of the accused hinges largely on the discretion of committing magistrates, who often lack the information and the competence to make fair decisions, and on the grace of private bail bondsmen, who are in business for profit, sometimes gained by unscrupulous methods. In jailing accused persons merely because they are unable to raise sufficient money for bail bonds, the state is administering justice in a grossly unequal fashion. The man with some means is freed, a practice that is in keeping with the law's presumption of innocence. But the imprisoned poor man is in effect punished even though his subsequent trial may exonerate him.

In seeking to curb such unjust punishment in Pennsylvania, the Philadelphia Bar Association in 1961 pointed out that the year before in Philadelphia there had been approximately 15,000 commitments of persons to await trial or further hearings. Each person so committed spent an average of about twenty-three days in confinement. Thus, 345,000 days (or about 945 years) were spent in Philadelphia jails in 1960 by persons not convicted. Since about one in five persons is acquitted when brought to trial in Philadelphia, the Bar Association showed that innocent persons spent about 189 years behind bars in this one city in one year.[16]

The jailed defendant is not only punished but he is also hampered in preparing his defense and is stigmatized by imprisonment when he may be innocent. University of Pennsylvania surveys have shown that a defendant is less likely to be convicted if he has been bailed out of jail before trial; and if convicted, the bailed defendant is less likely to be sent to prison.

Besides the injustice done to imprisoned defendants who have not been convicted of any crime, their families are also made to suffer when the breadwinners lose pay checks or even jobs and are thus unable to provide support or to keep up payments on houses and possessions.

The train of evils and abuses of the bail system flows from the fact that the system has lost touch with its original purpose, which was simply to insure that the defendant would appear in court on the day of his trial. Former Supreme Court Justice Arthur Goldberg, in his introduction to the recent book on bail by Ronald Goldfarb, says that "at best it is a system of checkbook justice; at worst a highly commercialized racket." Goldfarb estimates that in 90 per cent of the criminal prosecutions in this country neither jail nor bail is required to assure the defendant's appearance. A recent bail study in Manhattan showed that, of selected prisoners who were released on their own recognizance, only 1 per cent failed to appear in court, whereas 3 per cent of those out on bond failed to show up.

Lawyers can help to correct the injustice of the bail system by working, as the Philadelphia Bar Association did, for legislation to permit the substitution of a summons for arrest in minor criminal cases and by urging the adoption of a plan under which accused persons are released on their own recognizance if, after screening, they are deemed good risks. Another worthwhile reform was contained in federal bail legislation introduced in 1965. It provided that convicted persons should be given credit for time spent in pretrial custody against any fine or prison term imposed at the trial.

CONTROLLING PREJUDICIAL PRETRIAL STATEMENTS

One of the major disadvantages which the defense labors under, especially during the pretrial stage, is police and prosecutor use of the press to aid their side. As far as the prosecuting attorney is concerned, this involves the application of Canon 20, which already bars such methods of appealing to prejudice but which is almost universally ignored. The widespread flouting of Canon 20 in turn calls attention to the way in which the organized bar generally neglects its responsibility to discipline its members. After the New York State Bar Association approved a more stringent version of Canon 20 in 1957, there was some feeling in the bar that district attorneys were being more circumspect in talking to the press. But there were no widely observable actions against indiscreet prosecutors. One way to make Canon 20 more effective was suggested in late 1965 by the Due Process Committee of the American Civil Liberties Union. After studying the whole question, that group recommended the adoption in all courts by rule or statute of a procedure allowing judges to publicly admonish prosecution and defense attorneys responsible for aiding or creating prejudicial publicity. A judge, the committee asserted, could be empowered to summon the offending lawyer before him, either on his own motion or at the request of the opposing counsel, to administer a rebuke in open court and to permit the opposing counsel upon request to issue a statement answering the damaging information previously publicized. In addition, the court could refer the matter to the appropriate bar association committee on ethics if the infraction seemed to warrant such action.

This procedure, as the committee pointed out, should not only have the advantage of a deterrent effect on lawyers but would also enable the judge to employ a curative measure when it is most needed, by labeling the release of prejudicial publicity as wrongful and permitting an "equalizing" statement to be made under controlled conditions.[17]

If the procedure for reprimand should be adopted by statute, it could also be extended to police officials who in effect seek to convict suspects through the agency of the press. Judicial rebuke of the police should be regarded by appropriate municipal officials as a cue to impose administrative discipline such as temporary suspension from duty without pay. This would represent punishment short of a criminal sanction.

Without going into detail on the method of discipline, the New Jersey Supreme Court in the 1964 Van Duyne case said that potentially prejudicial statements by prosecutors should bring discipline by the court under the canons of ethics and that policemen who make such statements should be dealt with by their superior officers.[18]

Such discipline can hardly be applied fairly to either attorneys or police officers, however, without the previous establishment of an information policy for their guidance. A useful set of guidelines, adapted from the United States Attorney General's policy statement of April 1965, has been suggested by the American Civil Liberties Union. Recommended for the guidance of all federal, state, and local officials involved in the enforcement of law and the prosecution of criminal defendants, these guidelines would apply to the release of information to news media from the time a person is arrested or is charged with a criminal offense until the proceeding has been terminated by trial or otherwise. They provide that:

1. At no time shall any official furnish any statement of information for the purpose of influencing the outcome of a defendant's trial.

2. Officials, subject to specific limitations imposed by law or court rule or order, may make public the following information:

a. The defendant's name, age, residence, employment, marital status, and similar background information.
b. The substance or text of the charge, such as a complaint, indictment, or information.
c. The identity of the investigating and arresting agency and the length of the investigation.
d. The time and place of arrest.

3. No judicial, prosecutorial, or police official or employee shall reveal any information about any individual's criminal or arrest record or about a confession of a person in custody unless for a proper purpose. Under no circumstance shall such information be given out for the purpose of publicity.

4. The release of certain types of information generally tends to create dangers of prejudice without serving a significant law enforcement function. Therefore officials should refrain from making available the following:

a. Observations about a defendant's character.
b. Statements, admissions, confessions, or alibis attributable to a defendant.
c. References to investigative procedures, such as fingerprints, polygraph examinations, ballistic tests, or laboratory tests.
d. Statements concerning the identity, credibility, or testimony of prospective witnesses.
e. Statements concerning evidence or argument in the case, whether or not it is anticipated that such evidence or argument will be used at trial.
f. The circumstances immediately surrounding an arrest, including resistance, pursuit, possession and use of weapons, and a description of items seized at the time of arrest.

5. The officials in charge of the custody of an arrested person have a duty to protect him from being photographed or televised while in the custody of the police. Moreover, photographs of a defendant should never be released unless they serve a proper investigatory function.

6. This statement of policy is not intended to restrict the release of information concerning a defendant who is a fugitive from justice.

These proposals would for the most part establish desirable informational standards. But they should not be applied in such fashion as to prevent a defendant or his lawyer from seeking the publication of material that might help to elicit evidence helpful to the defense. For example, an accused mistakenly identified as an offender may want his picture published so that witnesses of the event might come forward and say he was not the person involved. Or he might want an alibi publicized so that unknown witnesses might verify that he was where he said he was at the critical time.

With respect to any information that is a matter of public record, such as that on previous convictions, the guidelines should be understood not to bar the access of the press but only to require officials not to call it to the attention of reporters. Nor should the press be expected to refrain from publishing the details of an arrest when the event was widely observed and is a matter of intense public curiosity, as in the case of the seizure of a suspect after a gun battle.

In general, however, the ACLU guidelines could, if followed, mean much fairer news coverage of criminal cases. But the first problem is to get them adopted in state and local jurisdictions (the United States Department of Justice has already adopted a similar policy). That problem would be made far more difficult if the guidelines were to be enforced by contempt of court action—a method under discussion by the ACLU. Contempt is tactically objectionable because it would impede the effort to achieve the goal. But it is also objectionable in principle because it is subject to abuse, as pointed out in Chapter 8. Enforcement of the guidelines should, therefore, be left to departmental discipline of the police by their superiors and to censure of the police or prosecutor by the judge.

The press, for its part, should be asked to generally respect the guidelines by not publishing forbidden information, except in the kinds of instances noted with respect to the defense. But newsmen should be free to gather information, which would be subject to release when it becomes an appropriate part of the proceedings, or to earlier publication if this is clearly in the interest of preventing a miscarriage of justice. The observance of a future release date should be no less valid for crime stories than for news of other subjects which is routinely delayed by editors.

A LIMITED LIBEL REMEDY

Prejudicial publicity might be deterred not only by internal discipline, but also by applying to policemen and prosecuting attorneys, as well as the press, a recognized legal penalty less severe than a criminal sanction invoked by statutory authority or by the judicial contempt power. This curb could be imposed through the civil suit for libel brought by an accused against a public official who imputed or directly alleged his guilt in an unauthorized statement; or a similar suit could be brought against a newspaper which alleged or imputed the complainant's guilt in published information that did not come from an identified privileged source.

Frank Thayer, in his book on *Legal Control of the Press,* has pointed out that

> Investigations by police officers, officials in the district attorney's office, or the coroner's office, are not privileged communications and so newspaper stories based on such reports or investigations are not accorded qualified privilege, according to the great weight of authority.[19]

Yet it is a fact that pretrial pronouncements of guilt from such sources rarely result in libel suits, the obvious reason being that such suits have seldom been successful. Another probable reason for the scarcity of libel actions is that most victims of such defamation are not financially able to bring suit.

To make the deterrent impact of libel law more effective, the remedy would have to be better defined in judicial decisions or by statute. To prevent libel from being used to curb the publication of information vital to the interests of justice, the decisional law or the statute should make specific the limited circumstances under which actions could be brought. Information authorized for release under approved guidelines for officials should be made privileged (not subject to liability). On the other hand, unprivileged pretrial information which clearly imputes guilt to the accused could be defined as libel per se, that is, defamatory on its face according to community standards and subject to action for damages without the necessity of proving injury.[20]

A Georgia court, in interpreting a statute in that state, once enunciated the relevant distinction between privileged and unprivileged reports when it said,

> While a newspaper is privileged to publish a fair and honest report of a court proceeding, or a truthful report of information received from an arresting officer or police authorities (Civil Code 1910, Sec. 4432), the publication is not privileged, when the newspaper in undertaking to publish only an account of a court proceeding, or the report of information given by an arresting officer or the police authorities, amounting only to a mere charge by the arresting officers or the police authorities of the commission of a crime, goes further and publishes a statement that the person charged with the commission of the crime is in fact guilty of the crime.[21]

This rule could certainly be adapted to cover policemen and prosecutors themselves when they reported pretrial confessions of guilt and made statements to the effect that the accused was definitely the perpetrator of the crime in question. It would apply, for example, to descriptions of the accused in unqualified terms as "the robber," "the blackmailer," or "the murderer."

The rule would not apply, of course, to information from defense or other sources which might be outside guideline standards but which tended to establish the innocence of the accused. In the first place, such information would not be defamatory and thus not within the usual libel rules. But the more important consideration would be that its distribution would be consistent with the objective of curbing only that publicity which flagrantly undermines the law's presumption of innocence.

Providing for libel suits against vociferous prosecution sources and the press should help to protect the private citizen whose case might otherwise be prejudiced during the pendency of his trial by material published through surreptitious cooperation between the press and the prosecution. Max Radin, professor of law at the University of California, many years ago implied a preference for the libel remedy when he said, "our courts are themselves largely to blame for the reckless disregard of the libel law which is a concomitant of 'trial by newspaper' . . . by stretching the privilege of newspaper comment." Radin opposed the use of the contempt power as a check on the press.[22]

Under the United States Supreme Court ruling in the 1964 case of *The New York Times v. Sullivan,*[23] public officials who are involved in criminal cases should not be allowed to collect libel damages unless they prove actual malice.[24] The exception for public officials would safeguard newspapers in seeking to expose malfeasance in office or actual criminal activity on the part of the police, district attorneys, or other officials who would normally be the sources of information about violations of the law. In 1965 a three-judge court in Pennsylvania, acting under the rule of the Sullivan case, wiped out a $135,000 libel verdict awarded two years before to Frederick O. Brubaker, then district attorney of Berks County, for articles in the Reading *Times* alleging the prevalence of prostitution, gambling, and other forms of organized racketeering and suggesting that Brubaker was one of the persons responsible for this situation.[25]

The value of a statute covering libel in the handling of pretrial news of criminal cases would lie in the vehicle it would provide for precisely spelling out the nature of the remedy and the limits of its use, by specifying that it would not apply in the same way to newspaper criticism of public officials and by stipulating that judgments should be only for reasonable actual damages—nominal damages if a timely retraction is published—and not punitive damages.[26] This restriction would be designed to prevent the use of the remedy as a vindictive weapon against the press. Another advantage of the libel remedy is that it would permit the aggrieved party to initiate the action for relief. Finally, the action, if successful, would bring a civil judgment against the offending party rather than a criminal sentence. Such a sanction should nevertheless serve as a deterrent to leaks by public employees and subsequent irresponsible publication by the press. In the process it should be an aid in the maintenance of discipline over police under departmental regulations and over prosecutors under Canon 20.

Improving the Reliability of the Court Proceeding

DUBIOUS LEGAL DOGMA

Even if the police were well trained in investigative techniques and conditioned to respect the rights of suspects and even if the accused were given the assistance of counsel and treated equally in the pretrial stage regardless of their financial resources, the rules and attitudes still customarily prevailing in the courtroom do not inspire confidence that the criminal trial itself could produce justice in most cases. The late Justice Curtis Bok of the Pennsylvania Supreme Court called the court trial "the weakest part of the system."

Lawyers need to reexamine the time-honored and still popular legal dogma that, in the purified atmosphere of the courtroom, practically any pretrial injustice can and will be detected and corrected—assuming, that is, that no contamination is introduced into the courtroom by the press. In its most extreme form this dogma was expressed some years ago by a district attorney in Massachusetts who reportedly remarked: "Innocent men are never convicted. Don't worry about it; it never happens in the world. It is a physical impossibility."[27] While most lawyers would not be so categorical, most lawyers do cling to the notion that the prevailing forms are best simply because they have stood for a long time. Too few lawyers are as open-minded as was the late Justice Holmes when he said of the concept of *stare decisis* (the doctrine of adherence to rules and principles laid down in previous judicial decisions):

> The theory is that each new decision follows syllogistically from existing precedents. But just as the clavicle in the cat only tells of the existence of some earlier creature to which a collar bone was useful, precedents survive in the law long after the use they once served is at an end.

Basic among the still current but nevertheless questionable lawyer concepts is the theory that the truth will be elicited by a trial staged as a fight or game between opposing attorneys in which the judge acts as a kind of referee to see that neither side commits a foul. No citizen who became a defendant would want, we can be sure, to gamble his liberty or life on a sporting contest in which the outcome depends upon how well the two legal antagonists are matched. Yet otherwise intelligent members of the bar continue blithely to accept this notion without realizing how callous it seems to laymen. In a recent book on the trial of Jack Ruby, the authors, a law professor and a practicing attorney, observe casually that the "hard fact is that our adversary system must rely to a great extent not only on both sides being represented with equal skill but also upon their having approximately equal amounts of luck."

DISCOVERY

Luck won't help the defendant if the law denies him access to certain prosecution information that is vital to the preparation of his defense. Although the advance disclosure of evidence, known as discovery, has been in effect for decades in Britain and in some American states and to a marked extent in federal courts, most American courts grant little or no discovery in criminal cases. When a sociologist, Dr. David Dressler, asked a Los Angeles police official a few years ago whether police findings should not be shared with the defense, the official replied, "Do the Dodgers give the Giants their signals?" His response symbolizes the attitude of most American prosecution officials. In England and Canada, before an accused is put on trial, there is a preliminary court hearing in which the prosecution discloses its evidence; the defense has a chance to cross-examine the government's witnesses and to see the documents the prosecution proposes to use.

In recent years an increasing number of states have begun to recognize that the process of discovery, already applied earlier in civil litigation, is even more necessary to fairness in criminal cases. With California, Washington, Pennsylvania, and Texas in the lead, a few states have adopted rules allowing defendants' attorneys to see their clients' confessions, results of scientific tests, lists of witnesses, and other evidence in the prosecutor's files. On July 1, 1966, the federal courts instituted a new rule of discovery allowing a defendant's lawyer to demand copies of any confession made by the defendant, the recorded grand jury testimony of the defendant, any reports of physical or mental examinations or other scientific texts, and any relevant papers, documents, or tangible evidence.[28]

Officials in most jurisdictions, however, still cling to the strange idea that a criminal trial is like a sporting event in which victory may be properly achieved by surprises and other tricks. Some opponents of change have advanced the arguments that discovery may lead to bribery and intimidation of prosecution witnesses (especially in racketeering cases), to perjury on the part of defense witnesses, and to a generally more difficult task for the prosecution. The Supreme Court of Maryland, where more liberal discovery rules are in effect, has observed, however, that it is not impressed with the fear that the procedure "will make the securing of proper convictions more difficult to obtain." Moreover, the dire predictions of the opponents of change have not been borne out in jurisdictions where information essential to preparation of cases has been made available to attorneys in advance. As an answer to fears of bribery and intimidation of witnesses, Justice William J. Brennan, Jr., of the United States Supreme Court noted in a lecture favoring liberalization of discovery that unusual circumstances could be met by giving the judge discretion in the matter.[29]

PROTECTION FROM PRIOR RECORDS

The general failure to make information available to defense lawyers in advance of the trial is not the only practice which impedes the search for truth in criminal cases. Another common rule which interferes with the development of the facts at the trial is the one generally in effect with regard to a defendant's prior record. If a defendant has been previously convicted in an unrelated case, he is reluctant to take the stand in his own defense even if he is innocent, for most American courts follow the rule that, if the defendant chooses to testify, the prosecution may introduce his prior record in order to impeach his testimony. The theory is that the testimony of any witness who is an ex-convict is not trustworthy. Even though the judge admonishes the jury that evidence of the defendant's previous conviction is to be considered only for the purpose of judging the truth of his testimony in the current case, the admonition is not likely to keep the jurors from concluding that, since the accused was proved a criminal in the past, he is probably still a bad man and is probably guilty of the new crime with which he is charged.

Under the rule on prior records prevailing in most American jurisdictions, the accused is damned if he does testify and damned if he doesn't. If he chooses not to take the stand, the prosecutor is not permitted to introduce his previous record unless the earlier crime is in some way linked with the new offense with which he is being charged. Nor is the prosecutor allowed to comment on his failure to take the stand. But there is usually at least one court-wise juror who will advise his associates that the reason for the defendant's refusal to testify is probably that he has a long string of convictions. Thus the silence of the accused is likely to be held against him. A recent analysis showed that, in 99 per cent of all criminal cases tried in federal courts, defendants who did not testify in their own behalf were convicted by juries.[30]

A much fairer rule on previous convictions is in effect in England and in a few American states. Under this rule, the prosecutor may introduce evidence of earlier convictions only if the accused tries to prove that he has a good reputation or if he attacks the credibility of the prosecution's principal witness. If such a procedure were followed, the previously convicted defendant would be in a far better position to take the stand and tell his side of the story without fearing that reference to an unrelated earlier conviction might cause him to be found guilty again. If the jury should bring in a conviction in the new case, the defendant's past record could then be made known to the jury or judge for the purpose of providing guidance in assessing the penalty. This is the rule in murder trials in Pennsylvania under a 1959 statute.

PROTECTION AGAINST FORCED CONFESSIONS

One of the most disputed questions relating to truth as adduced in trials has to do with the reliability of challenged confessions which the prosecution strives to introduce into evidence. The police and prosecuting attorneys lay great stress on the value of confessions in securing convictions. But the United States Supreme Court has been getting ever more insistent that the voluntariness of confessions be established. In 1964 the court invalidated a New York procedure under which the trial judge, except in unusual cases, allowed the jury to consider the confession, instructing the panel to determine its voluntariness and to disregard it if found to be involuntary.[31] Even after the New York procedure was revised by leaving the issue of voluntariness to judges, defense lawyers began to doubt that their clients were any better off. They soon discovered that it was as difficult to convince a trial judge that a confession was coerced as it had been to convince a jury.

Without some protective procedure in the police station, the guarantee against self-incrimination of the accused is not likely to mean much despite the 1964 decision of the United States Supreme Court in *Malloy v. Hogan* holding that the Fourteenth Amendment's due process clause forbids the states to require self-incrimination just as the Fifth Amendment forbids the federal government.[32] In that case Justice Brennan stated that developments in the area of coerced confessions necessitated a reconsideration of prior holdings that the Fifth Amendment's specific privilege against self-incrimination was not included in the Fourteenth Amendment's requirements on the states. Theretofore the cases barring coerced confessions in state courts had been based only on the general requirement of fairness implied in the provision for due process rather than in the specific guarantee against self-incrimination contained in the Fifth Amendment and made obligatory upon the states by judicial application of the Fourteenth Amendment. In the Miranda case in 1966 (see Chapter 27) the Supreme Court further broadened the protection against coerced confessions.

No matter how explicit the guarantee against self-incrimination has been made by the Supreme Court, however, the police will be tempted to go on trying to extract confessions as long as the defendant has little way of proving duress. Following their customary techniques, the police look to the persons who may be connected in some way with the crime: the victim's family or associates, persons seen in the vicinity, men with records suggesting that they are likely to have been involved in offenses of the sort in question. After the investigation has narrowed the focus of suspicion, a routine procedure is used on an arrested individual. Isolated from family and friends, he is subjected to questioning in accordance with highly developed methods well calculated to extract admissions of guilt, which are later blandly described as "voluntary." [33]

In view of the record of increasing disclosures of coerced confessions, the threat to the innocent of admitting challenged admissions of guilt should be obvious. The clear need is to provide some better way of guarding against coerced confessions. The use of improper police pressure on the accused cannot be satisfactorily determined by the weighing of contradictory testimony in the courtroom as to what took place during a secret interrogation in the back room of a police station. The interrogation room is the modern equivalent of the Star Chamber where the accused is at the mercy of his accusers. Confronted at the trial with a battery of police witnesses, detectives, and one or two assistant district attorneys all saying that the defendant made his admissions voluntarily and lacking witnesses to confirm that the accused was forced to confess, the defense is at a decided disadvantage in trying to undo the harm. In the absence of testimony substantiating the claim of duress, neither judge nor jury is inclined to throw out a purported confession, thus taking a step which may let a guilty man go free.

Some jurisdictions have at least devised procedures to avoid leaving the police completely on their own. In Philadelphia the district attorney's office started the practice of sending a representative to the police station as soon as possible after a murder suspect was apprehended in order to observe whether any duress was used in questioning. New York State Assemblyman Bertram L. Podell introduced a bill in 1965 providing that in all cases in which a confession was to be used as a basis for indictment, either a judge or a defense attorney must have been present during the questioning leading to the confession. Another form of safeguard against coerced, and therefore possibly untrue, admissions of guilt would be to bar confessions from evidence unless they are made in open court or have originally been witnessed by a disinterested third party.

PROVIDING EXPERT TESTIMONY

In the effort to make the trial a search for truth rather than a battle for jurors' minds, the legal profession should be devising a better way to present expert testimony. Unlike ordinary witnesses who are not supposed to offer opinions, the expert witness is called upon to express his opinions as derived from specialized knowledge. As scientific knowledge has increased, so-called expert witnesses have been summoned to testify on a wide variety of subjects. The practice has given rise to "experts" who will sell their opinions to any litigant who can pay. Even honest experts may indulge in wishful thinking and subconsciously stretch the probabilities to favor the side that calls them. In cases in which the defense has the means, there is therefore almost inevitably a parade of witnesses on two sides offering conflicting views. The effect is bound to detract from the value of scientific opinion and confuse the jury. One answer might be to have expert witnesses paid by the state and called, not by the prosecution and defense but by the court, with specific instructions to give their opinions without regard to which side might be aided.

SECURING REPRESENTATIVE JURIES

Besides taking steps to improve the reliability of the evidence presented in the courtroom, the bar should also seek to improve the caliber of those who hear the evidence. A potential source of injustice that urgently calls for more attention by the legal profession is the method of selecting prospective jurors. Though legal tradition has affirmed the right to be tried by a jury of one's peers and though the Supreme Court has said that jurors should represent "a cross-section of the community," the system used in many jurisdictions does not insure that veniremen will constitute a true cross-section—one that will provide, for example, juries of their peers to decide the cases of the poor and the disadvantaged who are the defendants in so many criminal trials. Under the varying and haphazard techniques used in different courts, state and federal, the venire may or may not represent a community cross-section. Names for panels may be drawn from voter registration lists, lists of taxpayers, telephone directories, city directories, or lists of householders. In many federal courts the "key man" system is employed. Persons well known to the court—usually men of substance—are tapped, and they in turn suggest their friends. Such methods, which ignore the welfare and relief rolls, exclude from the jury box representatives of that segment of the community from which a large percentage of defendants come.

Since the jury is often regarded as the community's voice in the administration of justice, there is good reason to have that voice speak for the deprived as well as for other elements. An objective system of juror selection which would produce a completely representative cross-section of the entire community has been devised by John F. Kraft, a specialist in public opinion surveys, and Leon Rosenbluth, a consulting statistician. Using racial, population density, sex, economic, and other data on the community, this system provides for the random drawing of jurors' names without relying on such subjective methods as the judgment of a key man or a jury commissioner.[34] Introduction on a wide scale of the Kraft-Rosenbluth method would help to insure that criminal defendants are not judged by persons who know little or nothing about the social milieu in which the majority of the accused in criminal cases are reared.

IMPANELING IMPARTIAL JURIES

Not only would equal justice be better served if the accused were assured of judgment by a jury of his peers but it would also be more surely safeguarded if there were better devices for securing the impartiality which the Sixth Amendment supposedly guarantees and which is also covered by the due process clause of the Fourteenth Amendment.[35] Though it is obvious that a perfectly impartial jury can never be obtained, it is also obvious that insistence on impartiality is practically abandoned in cases of saturation publicity of a prejudicial nature. The criteria for granting a challenge for actual bias, whether formulated by statute or judicial decision, have been narrowly construed in order to minimize the instances in which it will be impossible to impanel a jury. This often means the acceptance of jurors who have absorbed columns of news condemning the defendant but who are deemed by the court to be capable of laying aside any prejudices or preconceptions resulting from their reading.

Sometimes the court may have great difficulty in determining whether prospective jurors are biased. If members of the venire are especially interested in serving in a particular case, they may not admit to prejudice. Alexander Woollcott wrote of the jury selection in the Hauptmann trial:

> In advance it had seemed reasonable to fear it might be necessary to draft the entire citizenry of Hunterdon County in the quest for twelve adults who had neither discussed the case nor formed any opinion about it. One would expect to find such satisfactory aloofness only among congenital idiots or among those who had spent the last few months in the kind of withdrawal from the world usually achieved only by Lamas in Thibet. But as it worked out, nearly every member of the panel seemed eager to serve on the jury and was unblushingly willing to put his or her hand on the court Bible and blandly deny ever having given the case a thought. Thus in our time in New Jersey is justice served quickly—if at all.[36]

But even in those cases in which bias on the part of prospective jurors seems probable as a result of inflammatory publicity which they have admittedly read, challenges are usually not upheld unless the venireman states that he can no longer have an open mind. In the 1954 Sheppard case in Ohio, the news media of Cleveland set records in persistent prejudicial coverage. A campaign for a solution of the crime was pushed with incessant vigor by the city's three newspapers, particularly the Cleveland *Press*. The Cleveland *Press* in front page headlines, editorials, and cartoons berated the slowness of officials, demanded an inquest, condemned the "protection" of "the chief suspect," demanded the arrest and "grilling" of Dr. Samuel Sheppard at police headquarters. Widespread publicity was given to the police suggestion that Dr. Sheppard be given a lie detector test and to his refusal to take one. As the trial approached, the names and addresses of all prospective jurors were published in the papers, leaving them open to telephone calls, letters, and other forms of improper influence in advance of the trial. Extensive quotes from the *voir dire* examination of all prospective jurors were carried.

Paul Holmes, who covered the case for the Chicago *Tribune* wrote later that there

> were three and one-half months of a vicious, all-permeating propaganda buildup against Sam and his family. . . . No rational thought on the subject of Sam's guilt or innocence was possible any more. The large and vocal group of residents—perhaps a majority—who had come to accept Sam's guilt as a kind of axiom which needed no proof amounted to a mob loose in the community, an ominous, ugly mob intent on seeing to it that this man should not escape.

In this atmosphere the jurors were selected. Every juror who ultimately was seated, except one, testified to reading about the case in the Cleveland papers. Most of them had also heard it discussed on the air. Yet all of those who had admittedly been exposed to the extensive publicity, much of it prejudicial, were seated when they said they could give unprejudiced attention to the evidence and base their verdict solely on what they were to hear in court. Defense efforts to get a postponement and a change of venue were repeatedly rebuffed by the trial judge, Edward Blythin.[37] And his action was never overruled by the appellate courts of Ohio.

Once the trial has begun, the problem of protecting the jury from prejudice is not solved. Despite judicial admonitions to jurors against reading or listening to news about their case, there is a strong likelihood that in instances in which it is not locked up the panel will come into contact with any prevalent biased publicity. During four weeks of Dr. Sheppard's trial for murder, the jurors were allowed to go home each night even though the judge had no way of insuring that they would not be exposed to the highly inflammatory coverage of the case by the Cleveland news media. It is hard to believe that people under such circumstances could avoid a subject so prominently featured in the news. Yet jurors in sensationally covered trials are frequently allowed to go their own way in the evening. Though willing jurors admittedly might be hard to find if panels were customarily locked up for the night during lengthy proceedings, this procedure should nevertheless be followed in capital cases receiving an extraordinary amount of publicity.

Presumably because they feel that the courts might be paralyzed if any other attitude prevailed, judges persist in saying that any intrusion of biased material can be cured merely by getting the assurance of the jurors that they will close their eyes and ears outside the courtroom or that they can ignore anything read in the papers and base their verdict solely on the evidence.[38] But as Judge Jerome Frank once remarked, expecting jurors to obey orders to disregard prejudicial accounts is like the expectation of the teacher (in Mark Twain's story) who told the little boy to stand in a corner and not to think of a white elephant.

JUDGE'S ROLE IN AVOIDING BIAS

The simple truth is that judicial warnings to jurors are not enough to insure fair trials. Yet it is also true that those responsible for the administration of justice, while they may not (and should not) be able to control the press, have not been doing nearly as much as they could to protect defendants from the prejudicial influence of the press. Even when police and prosecutors obviously use the press to persuade the public as to the guilt of defendants, their superiors almost never reprimand them and lawyers generally do not criticize the obvious attempt to "try" cases outside the courtroom. When highly publicized cases reach the courtroom, judges exhibit a great reluctance to use the powers they have to offset the effects of prejudicial statements issued by the prosecution and eagerly disseminated by the press. As a result of long experience with such cases, judges have, by a process of rationalization, evolved rules which make it easy to overrule challenges of prospective jurors because of bias, to deny defense requests for postponement of the trial until passions subside, to refuse motions for the removal of the trial to another county or district or for the summoning (as allowed in some states) of a foreign jury.

By allowing prospective jurors to be the judges of their own bias or lack of it, courts have in effect abandoned their own responsibility to insure impartial juries. As one judge said in an all too typical expression of satisfaction with the usual procedure, jurors in "*voir dire* examinations speak eloquently for themselves."

As in the matter of seating jurors in accordance with their own subjective evaluations of their frame of mind, the question of granting a change of venue has also been made subject to elastic rules. Though constitutions, statutes, and rules of court vary as to the kinds of situations in which the removal of criminal cases may be approved, typical provisions give the trial judge discretion to grant a change of venue on the defendant's application. Judges have often rejected as a valid ground for removal the existence of intensive adverse newspaper publicity presuming the defendant to be guilty and advocating severe penalties. This view has prevailed even in situations in which the publicity has caused a large number of the eligible jurors in the community to believe the defendant guilty. The justification has been that newspaper stories alone are an insufficient basis for a juror to decide the case contrary to the evidence, or that finding an impartial jury in any county or district would be difficult in the light of widespread newspaper publicity, or that granting removal on the basis of press reports alone would make impossible the trial of any sensational case in the venue of the crime.

Where hostile feeling has permeated the jurisdiction, thus minimizing the value of a change of venue, the granting of a continuance is designed to remove the trial in time (instead of in location) from the focus of prejudice. But in this situation too, the courts have justified refusals to grant continuances on various grounds that avoid the necessity of facing the issue. Thus the denial of postponement has been upheld on grounds that the defendant failed to move for a change of venue or failed to exhaust his peremptory challenges, that his rights were protected by the *voir dire* examination or by the trial court's instructions.

The pretexts given by judges in order to avoid taking remedial action against prejudicial publicity are many and varied. They have reasoned, for example, that the trial was "quiet and orderly," that residents of a particular county were "eminently fair and tolerant," that "most people are willing to give the defendants a fair trial," that so "strongly is the American system of justice embedded in the minds of our citizens that outraged feelings usually give way to a desire for orderly procedure." Despite the obvious reluctance of trial courts to grant relief, appellate tribunals seldom overthrow their decisions—the usual rule being that the higher courts will interfere only if trial judges have abused their discretion.[39]

The scarcity of appellate cases on prejudicial publicity is often advanced by spokesmen for the press as evidence that no substantial problem exists. Richard W. Cardwell, general counsel of the Hoosier State Press Association, has pointed with pride to the statistics in such cases. After studying the decisions, Cardwell reported that of sixty cases carried to appellate courts in the United States in 1963–1964, seeking reversals of convictions or writs of relief on the general plea of prejudice stemming from pretrial publicity, courts affirmed convictions or denied writs of relief in forty-nine cases and reversed convictions or granted writs of relief in eleven cases.[40] He added that only two of the reversals were on the actual grounds of juror prejudice due to publicity by news media.[41]

Cardwell reported further that of twenty cases carried to appellate courts during 1963–1964 and asking for reversals on the ground that prejudicial publicity during trial made a fair proceeding impossible, only three reversals were granted.[42] Concluding with evident satisfaction that the press of the United States had in effect been vindicated by the courts, Cardwell summed up: out of eighty appellate cases in the country in 1963–1964, there were only five reversals of convictions—two involving pretrial incidents and three involving incidents during trial; no writ of relief was granted on the narrow ground that publicity by news media had made a fair trial impossible.

But Cardwell's argument is misleading. The relatively small number of appellate cases stems not from the absence of a problem but from the obvious and well documented reluctance of the courts to deal with it. If trial judges are given a maximum of discretion and if appellate courts are inclined not to question that discretion, no voluminous record of reversals is likely to be built up. The trial in Boston of eight men charged with the $1,219,000 Brink's robbery is illustrative. Defense lawyers accused FBI Director J. Edgar Hoover and the government of a "shabby form of jury fixing" through news releases announcing the "solution" of the nation's greatest cash haul. Judge Felix Forte, in overruling the defense motion to quash the indictments on grounds of prejudicial statements, observed that "other trials had been presented before an aroused citizenry in the past," and in each case the public had confidence in the jury. He cited the Hauptmann trial and others.[43] However defensible on other grounds the judge's action may have been in this case, his reasoning on prejudicial publicity—as is so often true in cases of this kind—was far from convincing. And his dodging of the real issue was all too plain.

There are, of course, plausible reasons why judges are loathe to bar jurors with opinions on the case or to grant a postponement or change of venue. Prejudicial publicity may be so pervasive that unbiased jurors may be very difficult to find either in the immediate area of the crime or in another county. Or the likelihood of resumption of inflammatory coverage may be so great that postponement doesn't offer much hope of a future calmer atmosphere. Finally, there may be inconvenience and extra cost to the state in granting a continuance or change of venue. Besides these reasons, which are frankly expressed from time to time, there is probably the additional but unvoiced reason that judges are unwilling to antagonize the press. Yet if more judges took the requirement of an impartial jury at face value, they would grant the relief sought by defendants when the occasion called for it; they would rebuke the press for the difficulty of impaneling an unbiased jury, or for the necessity to postpone the trial or transfer it to another location. The lecture might give editors second thoughts and lessen the occasions when such action, involving inconvenience and expense, will be needed.

Before judges can undertake to chastise the press, however, they must feel secure in their positions (through tenure and immunity from popular pressure) and fairly certain of their conclusions as to the existence of bias. Certainly the measurement of neither community nor individual attitudes is simple. As the United States Supreme Court said many years ago:

> Bias or prejudice is such an elusive condition of the mind that it is most difficult, if not impossible, to always recognize its existence, and it might exist in the mind of one . . . who was quite

positive that he had no bias, and said he was perfectly able to decide the question wholly uninfluenced by anything but the evidence.[44]

Yet modern scientific survey techniques are such that it should be possible to determine, by objective means, the extent of public prejudice in highly publicized cases. Though a judge in New Jersey rejected a defense-sponsored community survey as a basis for granting a change of venue, such a test, conducted under court auspices, should be worth considering as a method for guiding decisions of this kind.[45]

Besides seeking more dependable ways to evaluate the extent of community prejudice, the judiciary should strive to find more reliable procedures to prevent the seating of deeply prejudiced individual jurors. A test for this purpose should be within the realm of possibility. If bias in prospective jurors cannot be measured, courts should resolve doubts in favor of the defense by being more receptive to challenges in cases involving sensational pretrial publicity. Fairness to defendants necessitates an expansion of the traditional challenge for cause to allow the exclusion of any juror who has obviously been exposed to a substantial amount of prejudicial coverage of the case.[46] Such a rule, also, might have a chastening effect on the press if it became apparent that prejudicial coverage was forcing the postponement of trials or making it next to impossible to swear in impartial juries. In a 1962 decision the Tennessee Supreme Court actually upheld the dismissal of murder charges against two men because, of 1,400 veniremen (all those available in the county), all but two said they had formed an opinion, were related to the principals, or could not give a fair verdict. A few actions of this kind would focus public attention sharply on the evils of irresponsible news treatment of criminal cases. Yet few judges are likely to take such a step unless they feel unusually secure in their positions, enjoying long terms and not having to face possible popular retribution at the polls.

A judge must be endowed with even greater intrepidity in order to weather the pressures that may result from the granting of a mistrial on grounds of prejudicial newspaper coverage of the court proceedings after the trial is well under way. For a mistrial ruling means that all of the legal activity up to that point has constituted wasted effort and expense which must be repeated.

A judge faced just such a decision at one point in a 1960 trial in a federal district court in Pittsburgh of six defendants charged with illegally exporting firearms to Cuba. During the first week of the three-week trial local papers published conspicuously headlined articles containing derogatory material about the defendants which was not and could not be put in evidence. They were said, among other things, to be members of a "gambling combine." When the judge questioned the panel, which had not been sequestered, nine jurors and two alternates first admitted having read the prejudicial accounts of the trial. But taking the second thought cue of one juror, they all then said they had only glanced at the headlines, obviously realizing that whatever they had done was in violation of the judge's specific instructions.

After eliciting a statement from each juror that he had paid little attention to the papers and could base his decision on his own judgment, the judge let the trial proceed.[47] But he did term the performance of the news media "reprehensible." For this statement Judge Robert T. Foley—who happened to be a visiting judge from Las Vegas—was sternly told by the Pittsburgh *Sun-Telegraph* that that newspaper did "not need a judge from the capital of gambling and nudity" to tell it "how to cover the news." Grandly ignoring the main issue, the *Sun-Telegraph* went on to lecture the judge on freedom of the press and on the reprehensible nature of his "unwarranted criticism against newspapers, which, in the final analysis, are among the staunchest defenders of our Constitution." The defendants were convicted and their appeal on the basis of prejudicial coverage was later rejected by the United States Court of Appeals for the Third Circuit, though not without a vigorous dissent by Judge William Hastie in which he was joined by two other judges.[48]

The Pittsburgh case suggests the difficulties of granting a mistrial motion. Yet a judicial willingness to approve relief of this kind may be the only practical answer to prejudicial coverage once the trial has begun.

REMEDIES GEARED TO NATURE AND TIMING OF PUBLICITY

The answer to the question of whether the press has had an unfair impact on justice depends on the timing, the pervasiveness, and the intensity of prejudicial publicity. All of these factors would have a bearing on whether a judge should grant relief and, if so, what kind and at what stage of the proceedings. The nature of the press influence and the character of the remedy would vary in accordance with whether the publicity occurred: (1) after an arrest or indictment and before the trial, (2) during the trial, or (3) after the trial and before the disposition of an appeal. Publicity during the first period is probably most difficult to deal with. If there is a substantial lapse of time between the arrest and trial, the effect of initial damning news may have been dissipated by the time the jury is being picked.[49] On the other hand, if the case has aroused considerable public and editorial interest, the publicity may be resumed with all of its sensational flavor just as the trial opens. In such a situation, if the prejudicial coverage has been so widespread as to make a change of venue impractical, the granting of a continuance may be the only remedy. Yet even this would do no good unless accompanied by a judicial admonition to which the press was ready to respond.

Publicity in the pretrial period is perhaps subject to more imponderables than at any other time, since the ultimate admissibility in the courtroom of various reported facts and opinions cannot be easily gauged. The source also has a bearing on the credibility of a published statement. The quoted remark of a prosecutor or chief of police would presumably carry more weight with a prospective juror than that of a bystander who had a fleeting glimpse of the crime scene. With so many variables complicating the determination of an after-the-fact remedy by the judge, the need for self-restraint on the part of law enforcement officials and the press in the pretrial stage is clear.

A further complicating, and often ignored, factor in the pretrial stage is the possible effect of publicity on the police and prosecutor as well as on potential jurors. In cases involving high pressure publicity such as the murder of Marilyn Sheppard in Cleveland in 1954, the press may generate a condemnatory drive that moves the whole community, including the police, the prosecuting attorney, and even the judge. In such a case the only authority able to provide a remedy may be an appellate court that is willing to look at the situation in a detached manner.

During the trial period the impact of publicity can be gauged more precisely, both in terms of its focus on individuals (veniremen or jurors) and its admissibility as evidence. By weighing the conditions at the time, the judge can decide by fairly specific criteria whether to approve a postponement or whether, while the jury is being chosen, to exclude certain veniremen who have been exposed to clearly prejudicial accounts. But after the jury has been selected, the case acquires a momentum which the judge is reluctant to check by granting a mistrial even though the formula for determining improper intrusion by the press should be easiest to apply at this stage.

In the posttrial stage, the effect of publicity again becomes difficult to assess. And yet it is no less real. Appellate judges, states' attorneys who prosecute appeals, and members of boards of pardon and parole are not immune to press influence, though there is hardly any appropriate remedy in law for prejudicial coverage at this stage.

The variable and intangible relationships of the press to justice suggest the difficulties of judicially counteracting prejudicial influence from the news media. Thus, while the bar and the bench have an obligation to criticize the press and to make greater use of the range of inadequately applied remedies when they are appropriate, they could exercise their responsibilities to justice more effectively by working harder in those areas where the shape of needed reform is more concrete and clearcut.

REVIEWING FACTS ON APPEAL

Regardless of the care with which its procedures are devised, a trial cannot be a perfect instrument for the discovery of truth. Mistakes from time to time will always be made in deciding what were the true facts of the case. Yet in most states appellate courts may reverse convictions only for errors of law and not because of mistakes as to the facts. Except in a few states, upper court judges do not, in hearing appeals, become a sort of new jury to retry cases. As a general rule, the United States Supreme Court will not concern itself with factual contradictions that have been decided against the convicted petitioner but will draw its own conclusions from the state's version of the facts. The theory behind the general rule in most jurisdictions is that the trial court, as the tribunal which heard all of the evidence, is the best judge of what was believable.

Yet trial courts do sometimes draw inaccurate factual conclusions without violating the formal requirements of law. To avoid the injustices which result in such cases, Professor Borchard suggested a generation ago that appellate courts review the facts as well as the law in felony cases, or at least in capital cases.[50]

Appellate courts might also correct injustices perpetrated in trial courts if there were a change in the prevailing rule against reviewing sentences. In the federal courts and in more than thirty states, no sentence within the statutory limits for a proven offense may be modified by a higher court. United States Senator Roman L. Hruska of Nebraska in 1965 sponsored a bill to allow appellate courts to reduce federal sentences they deemed too harsh. In similar vein the Judicial Conference of the United States recommended that appellate judges be permitted to adjust sentences either upward or downward, with the possibility of increased penalties being designed to discourage frivolous appeals. Given such authority, upper courts could render justice in cases such as that of the purple-heart veteran with no police record who was handed an 11-year sentence for smuggling parrots into the United States from Mexico and that of the embezzler in a Fort Worth trial who drew a 15-year sentence for a first offense while another embezzler with a criminal record got only thirty days for the same crime. Though punishment cannot be equal for all like offenses, these examples suggest the need of a remedy for capricious penalties.

Judges, Prosecutors, and the Rights of the Accused

The criminal law cannot be shaped into a better instrument for justice merely by an improvement of procedures; the bar must also show a far greater interest in the disciplining and upgrading of personnel.

DISCIPLINE OF LAWYERS

In the 1964 Van Duyne case the New Jersey Supreme Court called for the discipline of attorneys under Canon 5 as well as Canon 20. Not only do prosecutors generally ignore Canon 20 with impunity but they are seldom even reprimanded for disregarding Canon 5, which says:

> The primary duty of a lawyer engaged in public prosecution is not to convict but to see that justice is done. The suppression of facts or the secreting of witnesses capable of establishing the innocence of the accused is highly reprehensible.

If the Canons of Professional Ethics—including Canons 5 and 20—are to be more than pious exhortations, then the courts, or the bench and bar in cooperation, will need far more effective machinery for disciplining lawyers. Closer discipline of the legal profession is supposed to be one of the advantages of the integrated bar, a system now in effect in half the states and under which attorneys are required to join the statewide bar association in order to practice. In 1961 the United States Supreme Court upheld the constitutionality of Wisconsin's integrated bar, one of whose purposes was "to foster and maintain on the part of those engaged in the practice of law high ideals of integrity, learning, competence and public service and high standards of conduct." [51] But policing of the profession has not been markedly more effective in those states with integrated bars. The efficacy of the procedure still depends on the zeal and integrity of those applying it. The evidence indicates that the legal profession will have to give far more vigorous support to enforcement before the Canons of Professional Ethics can become really meaningful rubrics.

SECURING BETTER JUDGES

The late Chief Justice Arthur Vanderbilt of New Jersey observed that judges lacking the desirable qualifications for office would "defeat the best system of substantive and procedural law imaginable."

As he described the requisite qualifications, they would be fulfilled by

> . . . judges learned in the law, not merely the law in books but, something far more difficult to acquire, the law as applied in action in the courtroom; judges deeply versed in the mysteries of human nature and adept in the discovery of truth in the discordant testimony of fallible human beings; judges beholden to no man, independent and honest and—equally important—believed by all men to be independent and honest; judges, above all, fired with consuming zeal to mete out justice according to law to every man, woman, and child that may come before them and to preserve individual freedom against any aggression of government; judges with the humility born of wisdom, patient and untiring in the search for truth and keenly conscious of the evils arising in a workaday world from any unnecessary delay.[52]

One of the major obstacles to a better qualified judiciary is the reliance of three-quarters of the states on the elective system for choosing judges. This system, which grew out of the notion of the Jacksonian era that all public officials should be directly answerable to the people, is hardly suitable for the judiciary. Faced with a great number of virtually unknown candidates for the bench, voters are in no position to assess their qualifications. Worse still, the candidates themselves are driven to participation in active politics and into the unjudicial commitments that such participation entails. They campaign along with other partisan candidates and in many states are unofficial but actual party leaders, especially at the county level. This political role for judges not only subjects them to the temptation to make justice a tool for politics but also causes them at times to incur obligations that are grossly incompatible with judicial duty. The campaign expenses of some candidates for the bench have been known to exceed the annual judicial salary.

When they are subject to reprisals from fellow politicians and to retaliation at the polls, judges are not in the best position to dispense justice without fear or favor. The author of a book on lynching observed years ago:

> It can hardly be doubted that political considerations were largely responsible for the neglect and indifference characteristic of of-

ficers and courts in these cases. The members of the mob were nearly all actual or potential voters.[53]

Roscoe Pound once remarked that "the judicial Barnum" had become "a characteristic feature of the American bench" as a result of the choice of judges by direct primary followed by popular election and the consequent necessity for candidates to keep in the public eye in order to insure reelection.[54] Judges elected by the people are unknown in other English-speaking common law countries.

To be independent, to be free to uphold the constitutional rights of hated defendants, to be safe to apply the criminal law without reference to public demands for vengeance, to be better able to resist improper pressure from the press, judges must be immunized from popular pressure. One method is to have them appointed for life by the executive, as in the federal system. Another method is the American Bar Association plan under which judges are chosen initially by the executive from slates of names submitted by judicial commissions made up of judges, lawyers, and laymen. The appointed judge later runs without opposition on a nonpartisan ballot in which the voters simply decide whether or not he is to continue in office for a full term on the basis of his performance on the bench. A failure to win endorsement at the polls would mean that the executive would have to make another appointment, and the new judge would then after a time run on his record. The longer the term provided by law for the judge, the greater will be his feeling of security to dispense justice without fear of retribution.

No matter how well conceived the system for selecting judges may be, it should not fail to provide a better method of removing unfit judges from the bench than most states now have. An act of the legislature should not be required to remove a judge who is incompetent, dishonest, or disabled. Unlike most states, California has effective machinery for judicial discipline. Under a constitutional amendment approved in 1960, California established a nine-member judicial commission with authority to investigate and conduct removal proceedings against any judge for willful misconduct in office, willful and persistent failure to perform his duties, habitual intemperance, or disability of a permanent character seriously interfering with the performance of duties. During the first four years of the commission's operation, over twenty-five California judges resigned or retired as a direct result of action by the disciplinary body.

MAKING PROSECUTORS NONPOLITICAL

The political nature of the prosecutor's office, as it is set up in most American states, has even more adverse implications for justice than the politically chosen judge. The judge's performance at least is not usually measured by his record of convictions, whereas the prosecutor's job often is. In the race for district attorney of King's County, New York, in 1965 the opposing candidates argued over the high rate of acquittals attributed to the incumbent by the challenger. Boasting about convictions is almost standard procedure for district attorneys seeking reelection. Often ambitious to make his office a stepping stone to Congress, the governorship, or some other higher political post, the prosecutor is eager to make a record, even though his primary duty is not to convict but to see that justice is done.

Bent on political advancement and readily accepting the fight theory of justice, the prosecutor utilizes all of the tricks of legal combat to win victories over the alleged criminal enemies of society. While riding roughshod over ne'er-do-well murder and rape suspects, prosecutors, however, have also been known to go easy on racketeers and others with power to influence elections.

The main objection to linking law enforcement and partisan politics is that it often makes the prosecutor oblivious to the procedural safeguards designed to protect the innocent. The blindness of prosecutors to the necessity for observing the guarantees of the Bill of Rights is frequently evident. In recent years individual prosecutors and organized district attorneys have fought proposed federal legislation to curb wiretapping and, in New York, they have opposed bills that would modernize the definition of insanity for defendants and update the rules on entrapment, duress, and conspiracy. Not long after the United States Supreme Court in the Mapp case barred the admission in state courts of illegally seized evidence, the District Attorneys Association of the State of New York sought Governor Rockefeller's support in getting the decision reversed. At a 1964 convention of the National District Attorneys' Association, members complained of Supreme Court decisions broadening the requirement of defense counsel for arrested suspects (the Escobedo case) and overruling the practice of allowing juries to decide when confessions were voluntary (*Jackson v. Denno*).

For years a few reformers have protested against the actual and potential misuse of the great power of the prosecutor's office for political purposes and have suggested ways to gear the office strictly to impartial law enforcement. Professor Borchard suggested that district attorneys be appointed by the state Supreme Court. Roscoe Pound asserted that any program for bettering the administration of criminal justice must seek to take prosecutors out of politics. He proposed centralizing control of them in each state under some sort of director of public prosecutions with secure tenure and concentrated and defined responsibility. To make the system more effective, he recommended the establishment of a ministry of justice in each state to study the workings of the prosecutors' offices, to find out in what ways they fail and why.

Even without the far-reaching changes envisioned by Pound, justice could be made far less political if the prosecutor were appointed by the executive on the basis of his experience and training in the field of criminal law. As a rule, prosecuting attorneys now have no special preparation for their jobs before being elected. Most law schools do not provide such training. In order to qualify for the prosecutor's office, the lawyer should have training in criminal law and, preferably, service under an experienced prosecutor who is himself imbued with the realization that his task is to protect the innocent as well as to convict the guilty. This is the tradition of the prosecutor's office in Great Britain, and it is one that the bar in America subscribes to in principle but does little to promote. A concerted effort by the bar to discourage the use of the prosecutor's office for political objectives would help to remove the temptation for the prosecutor to use the press in the processing of cases and would otherwise serve the cause of justice.

This review of the numerous ways in which the rights of the accused may be jeopardized by weaknesses in both procedure and personnel should not only underscore the responsibilities of the bar, which is pledged to uphold justice, but should also suggest that in the complex interrelationship of the bar, the police, the courts, and the press, no single institution can induce an appreciable change for the better unless there is cooperation by and improvement in the others.

CHAPTER TEN

A FINAL REVIEW

An Ancient Conflict

Because of the intense nationwide attention devoted in the past two or three years to the question of reconciling the needs of justice and the vitality of an unfettered press, the impression has been conveyed that the problem of how to harmonize these sometimes clashing interests is a relatively new one. It is not. Man's quest for justice is as old as recorded history. His recognition of the value of free expression extends back at least to the time of the Greeks of 2,500 years ago. As instruments were developed for promoting justice and for channeling information and comment to the public, it was no doubt inevitable that they would collide. The role of the courts has been to enforce the community's laws, including those made applicable by design or by caprice to speakers and writers. The role of the press has been to scrutinize and report on the community's institutions and public figures, including those connected with the administration of justice. In carrying out their respective roles, both judges and editors have at times trod on each other's prerogatives.

From their earliest days newspapers have experienced suppression by courts. Though courts on other occasions have also been the means of protecting a free press, editors and publishers have learned that the effort to safeguard free expression is a never-ending process. Not until 1931 did the Supreme Court of the United States rule that the due process guarantee of the Fourteenth Amendment forbade the states to abridge freedom of the press, just as the First Amendment prohibited such abridgment by Congress. Even after that historic decision, however, the Supreme Court, under the exigencies of war and public emotion over obscenity, let stand some laws which curbed freedom of speech and press.

If editors historically have had to be on guard against undue restrictions by the courts, judges, on the other hand, have also had to be concerned about interference with justice by the press. The prejudicing of justice by the press is a centuries-old subject of contention, with the dispute in rational moments tempered by the realization that news of law enforcement proceedings can also be an aid to justice. In the United States newspaper prejudgment of the guilt of the accused was evident in the early days of the republic. Over the years the urgency of the problem has increased, not because of a change in the kind of press prejudice, but because of a change in degree created by the growing speed and geographical reach of crime coverage. The newest threat to justice, however, comes not from any intensification of the impact of newspapers but from the potential of the electronic media to produce instantaneous and massive bias against an accused.

For more than 200 years jurists and others have sought ways to limit press prejudice or to immunize the judicial process against it. British courts in the eighteenth century enunciated the rule that editors who impeded the administration of justice by their publications could be held in contempt and punished. In America the contempt power of the federal courts was recognized in the Judiciary Act of 1789. Judges used their contempt power against publications in a number of early American cases. But such an exercise of judicial authority over the press has understandably aroused vigorous editorial opposition. The historic battle over the proper role of contempt seesawed until 1941 when the United States Supreme Court held in the Bridges case that such a judicial curb could be asserted only when there was a "clear and present danger" of press interference with justice—that is, a substantive evil that was "extremely serious" and a degree of imminence that was "extremely high." The effect was to discourage judicial use of contempt as a device for protecting the law enforcement process from intrusions by the press. In the late 1950's the Supreme Court began to convey to the press a message of continuing concern through a series of cases in which it reversed convictions that appeared to have resulted in part from unfair publicity.

Meanwhile various indirect methods have been devised for countering the effect of prejudicial publicity. Veniremen may be excluded from juries when they say they cannot disregard biased accounts which they have read. Postponements and changes of venue may be granted in order to avoid trials in communities where public passions against defendants have been stirred up by the press. But the effect of these methods has been limited by the reluctance of the courts to apply them with any vigor.

Both the bar and the press have voluntarily attempted to deal with prejudicial comment by adopting canons deploring the making or the publication of such utterances as unethical. Any possible mitigating influence from the application of such standards has been minimal, however, for the obvious reason that enforcement of the canons has been indifferent or nonexistent.

A Belated Elevation of Standards of Justice

If progress in dealing with the issue of prejudicial publicity has been halting at best, this sluggish pace is hardly out of step with advances in other areas of justice. Prejudicial publicity, in fact, reflects the grosser pressures on the press from the public. And similar public pressure on the law enforcement process itself produces prejudicial effects on justice from the police, lawyers, judges, juries, and witnesses. Injustice in the press cannot be completely divorced from injustice under law.

Though noble pronouncements on the rights of the accused are part of our ancient legal heritage, standards looking toward the full and effective implementation of constitutional guarantees of fair procedure have been nationally enunciated only in very recent times. Some of the protections for the accused that the original Bill of Rights applied to the federal government have now been imposed upon the states. In 1932 the Supreme Court called upon the states to guarantee the assistance of counsel in capital cases.[1] In 1963 the right to counsel was extended to all serious offenses.[2] In 1936 confessions obtained by duress were barred from state trials.[3] In 1961 evidence obtained by improper search and seizure was ruled inadmissible in state proceedings.[4] The next year the guarantee against cruel and unusual punishment was made applicable to the states.[5] In 1964 the privilege against self-incrimination was applied to state trials.[6] And in 1965 the states were required to guarantee the right of defendants to confront and cross-examine adverse witnesses.[7] Up to that time the high court had not yet, however, imposed on the states the Bill of Rights provisions on double jeopardy, speedy trials, excessive bail and fines, and the requirement that prosecutions be based only on grand jury indictments.

The criminal law still falls considerably short of insuring adequate justice for those who become implicated in its toils. Leadership by the Supreme Court and constant pressure by a forward-looking bar and press are needed to bring the practices of law enforcement officials into line with newly prescribed criteria.

A SLOW RISE IN STANDARDS OF JOURNALISM

Like the standards of justice, the standards of journalism have also been gradually raised during recent years. Newspapers have come a long way since the early days when they were poorly printed and badly edited, when they were vitriolic party organs that published little straight local news, when their contents were influenced far more by advertisers and groups of readers than they are today.[8] In the past generation newspapers have begun to hire more specialists and to publish more sophisticated science and educational news, more interpretive political news. Some papers have begun to take an enlightened attitude toward crime. There are a number of ways in which the press has aided the cause of justice—for example, helping to expose corruption as well as helping to prevent wrongful convictions.

Though the press has improved, it still falls far short, however, of measuring up to its responsibility in the area of criminal justice. It often disregards the law's presumption of innocence in criminal cases and thus prejudices the rights of the accused in numerous ways. It provides a vehicle for the prosecution to "try" cases in print, frequently publicizing "confessions" and prior records without knowing whether this information will be admissible in evidence. It caters to the popular need for scapegoats and to the corollary demand for harsh treatment of the criminals who fill the role. It gives bigger play and more space to news of the kinds of crime that are thought likely to attract reader interest and build circulation, thus focusing public wrath on such cases. Stories about "mad dog" sex killers are emphasized in order to pander to the lowest common denominator of public taste.

No definitive conclusions about the impact of the press on justice are possible—first, because no conclusive experiments or qualitative analyses (that this author is aware of) have been conducted in this field (and reliable ones may not be possible) and second, because no significant statistical data on the extent and nature of press attention to criminal justice is available. But a study of many cases and a review of the literature concerning justice and the press lead this author to the tentative conclusion that the press more often than not prejudges the guilt of the accused in the cases which it covers at some length. Press material prejudicial to the side of the accused is so common that no search is required to find it. The same cannot be said for material which maintains an impartial attitude toward defense and prosecution. This conclusion as to the bias of the press on cases covered is not meant to imply an opinion that the general effect of the press on justice is adverse. The press may exert great restraint on abuse and on corruption in the process of law enforcement by merely existing and being on the alert. Such influence, however, is surely not measurable.

While the press is giving expression to popular taste and prejudice in crime, offenses that are more socially significant are ignored and deep probing of delinquency and its treatment is neglected. Crime reporting, as United States Attorney General Nicholas deB. Katzenbach pointed out in a speech in early 1966, has not improved in the same manner as reporting in some other fields.

There are many ways in which the press could upgrade its performance in covering crime news: by applying to stories about suspects or defendants in criminal cases the stricter standards of objectivity which it applies in other news, by voluntarily subscribing to guidelines designed to curtail the publication of the most prejudicial kinds of information, by employing writers with specialized training for police and court reporting (a foundation could help to set a national standard by establishing with the Associated Press endowed reportorial posts to be filled by specialists in criminology and law), by being more willing to engage in criticism. Louis M. Lyons, former curator of the Nieman Foundation, has observed that the newspaper "is the least criticized institution in our society."

The Presumption of Innocence Ignored

One of the basic principles of criminal law is the presumption of innocence. A defendant is supposed to be considered innocent until the state proves him guilty beyond a reasonable doubt. Yet both the press and the prosecution frequently disregard this principle. Newspapers do so when, upon the arrest of a suspect, they refer to a crime as being "solved," when they identify an arrested suspect as "the gunman," "the holdup man," "the killer"—thus implying that he is the proven perpetrator of the crime before there is an actual guilty verdict. Papers also undermine the presumption of innocence when they publish a suspect's prior police record even though it may prove nothing about his alleged connection with the current crime, when they publicize without qualification a reported confession which may in fact be false. These are only some of the ways by which press, by favoring the prosecution side, helps to shift the burden of proof from the state, where it belongs, to the defense, which is supposed to have the advantage of a legal presumption.

Prosecuting authorities also ignore the presumption of innocence. The police do so when they use and defend methods of interrogation designed to get suspects to incriminate themselves, and when they equate procedural safeguards for the accused with the protection of "criminals." Accused individuals are not "criminals" until they have been convicted in court. The police attitude seems to be reflected in conspicuous omissions from some of the rules drawn up for their guidance. "The Policeman's Code of Ethics," offered for general use by a Louisville, Kentucky, police chief, contains no mention of the officer's duty to remember the law's presumption of innocence.[9] The annual Uniform Crime Reports (compiled from police sources) also contain intimations of police impatience with the law's requirements for the protection of the accused. These yearly documents reveal a tendency to consider clearances by the police as tantamount to the solution of crimes. The "high rate of effectiveness (clearances) by the police," the Reports said one year, "has been offset by a slower pace in court convictions."[10]

Commenting ironically on the gap between legal principle and prosecution practice, Ogden Nash once wrote:

> Our fathers claimed, by obvious
> madness moved,
> Man's innocent until his guilt is
> proved.
> They would have known, had they
> not been confused,
> He's innocent until he is accused.[11]

Equal Justice Denied

Despite the law's noble pronouncements and its sometimes noble fulfillments of its pledges, the machinery of justice is not geared so as to insure for the accused a position of equality with the state. As Professor Abraham S. Goldstein of the Yale Law School has put it, "Both doctrinally and practically, criminal procedure, as presently constituted . . . gives overwhelming advantage to the prosecution." He added that this condition has actually been aggravated by the "modern" approach, which loosens standards of pleading and proof without introducing compensatory safeguards earlier in the process. The effect, he said, has been a "rejection of the presumption of innocence in favor of a presumption of guilt."[12]

With the police armed with the symbols and tools of physical power, with the accused awed by the physical and psychological impact of being taken into custody and questioned, all of the constitutional safeguards together cannot "equalize or neutralize the initial advantage" to the state, in the opinion of Justice Bernard Botein of the Supreme Court of New York. When the powers available to a zealous and ambitious district attorney are added to those of the police, the contest becomes even more unequal.[13]

Apart from the imbalance in resources and power between the state and any individual, inequality is further accentuated by the fact that all defendants in criminal cases are not equally endowed with intelligence and wealth. On the west pediment of the Supreme Court building in Washington are the words, "Equal Justice Under Law." Supreme Court justices, as well as many state judges, take an oath to "do equal justice to the poor and the rich." Yet the criminal process is established and administered in such a way that equal justice cannot be assured.

The poor and the rich do not have equal access to freedom under bail bond. Yet such freedom may make the difference between an ineffective and effective defense. The poor and the rich do not have equal access to counsel. Yet the assistance of counsel may mean the difference between conviction and acquittal, or between severity and leniency. The poor and the rich are not affected in the same way when given a choice between imprisonment and a fine. The wealthy defendant can pay the fine; the impecunious one has to go to jail. The poor and the rich do not have equal access to the costly appellate process, which may mean the difference between serving a sentence or being ultimately exonerated without going to prison. Prison populations clearly reflect that part of the criminal world that isn't smart, rich, or lucky.[14]

The inequality in justice for the rich and the poor is affected not only by the legal advantages that wealth can purchase but also by the differences in the kinds of offenses most often committed by members of the two groups and by society's attitude toward these offenses. Crimes committed by slum dwellers are likely to be carried out by direct physical action—a blow, a shot, a seizing and carrying away of property. People in the upper socioeconomic group may be equally larcenous, but they have opportunities for illegally acquiring property or gaining wealth without using violent means. Government officials may use strategic positions to collect payoffs for favorable actions on business. Business executives may take illegal advantage of their competitors or their customers. Business employees may steal from their employers. The criminologist E. H. Sutherland labeled such offenses "white collar crime"—violations of the criminal law by persons in the upper socioeconomic class in the course of their occupational activity. Such crimes may take the form of violations of the antitrust laws, fraudulent advertising, infringement of patents, unfair labor practices, food adulteration, embezzlement, and income tax evasion.

Professor Sutherland made extensive studies of white collar crime and concluded that people in the business world, judging by the prevalence of their occupational offenses, "are probably more criminalistic in this sense than people of the slums." But despite the extent and cost of white collar crime, he observed that such offenders are relatively immune because of their status. White collar criminals also get less attention from the press.

On the other hand, violent crimes are the ones most conspicuously publicized in the press. They are the most visible offenses both in print and in fact. The people who commit violent crimes are more easily identified and prosecuted than those who commit the devious and indirect offenses that fall in the white collar category. Because of the direct, personal, and exasperating nature of violent crimes, and because of the stimulation of public resentment by the press, the perpetrators of such crimes are likely to be the recipients of a harsher kind of justice than are the relatively fewer white collar criminals who are caught and prosecuted. The poor, whose circumstances lead them more than others to become involved in crimes of violence, are thus for one more reason the victims of unequal justice.

The prevailing prosecution attitude toward the presumption of innocence and the prevailing conditions under which the poor are prosecuted add up to a situation in which the scales of justice are frequently weighted against the accused and especially against the indigent accused. This occurs both as a result of the present organization and motivation of our criminal process and as a result of the usual kind of press coverage of crime news.

The Need for Skepticism

Perfect equality, of course, cannot be guaranteed in any human institution. But if judges, lawyers, policemen, editors, and the public were more conscious of the imperfections in our system, they would be less inclined to press for stern justice. No one has a monopoly on virtue. Members of each segment of society engage in the kinds of transgressions by which they are peculiarly tempted or to which circumstances lead them. Moneyless ex-convicts, ostracized by the community and rejected by employers, turn to holdups and other forms of forceful infractions of the law. Many people in more favored walks of life engage in subtler forms of stealing. Members of all classes indulge in illegal violence against human life, using motor vehicles as weapons. "If criminal law were strictly enforced," remarked Professor Gerhard O. W. Mueller of New York University Law School, "we would lack a sufficient number of unconvicted guards to keep the rest of the population behind bars." No one is so upright or so wise or so certain of the requirements of justice that he can afford to demand a merciless application of the law to criminal defendants.

The imposition of severe penalties will not make the victims of crime whole again. (Compensation of crime victims by the state would help to compensate for the law's failure to provide protection.) Nor is insistence on harsh punishment likely to stem the tide of crime. A far more constructive way for lawyers, editors, and others to tackle the crime problem would be to seek reforms in the penal system so that it does not send up to 70 per cent of its inmates out to commit new crimes. There is an acute need for better preliminary diagnosis of the accused and of the convicted, for better classification and separation of different types of prisoners, for more psychiatric treatment of and more productive use of prisoners, for more halfway houses to ease the transition of released prisoners back into society, for the creation of out-prisoner clinics and the strengthening of the probation and parole system.

Pressure for shortcircuiting procedural safeguards and demands for easy convictions regardless of uncertainties can (as suggested throughout this book) lead to tragic miscarriages of justice.

Judge Learned Hand once said that, "if we are to be saved it must be through skepticism." To remind Americans of dangers of dogmatic certitude, he would have adopted as an inscription for every courthouse in the nation Oliver Cromwell's aphorism: "think that ye may be mistaken." The purpose of the Bill of Rights is to serve not only as a bulwark against arbitrary and deliberate abuses by tyrannical government officials but also against unintended abuses by officials acting on cocksure but mistaken judgments. The English jurist, William Blackstone, said more than 200 years ago: "It is better that ten guilty persons escape than that one innocent suffer." From Blackstone's day to the present, our great judges have recognized the necessity for imposing restraints on government in order to prevent injustice. Justice Oliver Wendell Holmes remarked, "We have to choose, and for my part I think it is less evil that some criminals should escape than that the government should play an ignoble part." Among members of the modern Supreme Court, Justice Hugo Black has led the way in insisting on observance of both the letter and the spirit of the constitutional guarantees of fair trial. Realizing, as one biographer put it, that "man's inhumanity to man may be found in a court house as well as elsewhere," Justice Black has for years argued in favor of applying to the states all of the restrictions of the first eight amendments of the federal Bill of Rights. With the passage of years and changes in court membership, he has gradually gained the support of other justices.

Justice Black would give effect to Bill of Rights safeguards by according them a preferred place in our constitutional system rather than merely balancing them against interests not so explicitly protected.[15] Among the provisions of the Bill of Rights, those in the First Amendment were singled out by Justice Black for preferred recognition early in his Supreme Court career. Other justices too—Holmes, Louis Brandeis, Harlan Stone, and Robert Jackson—have exhibited a readiness to give a preferred place to the First Amendment. Thus freedom of the press, in the view of justices who are most keenly sympathetic to the Bill of Rights, occupies no secondary position among constitutional rights.

The Vital Roles of Justice and the Press

The trend of Supreme Court decisions and the attitudes of justices most concerned for freedom of the press and fair trial imply that government must be required to both uphold justice and keep hands off the press. Both justice and the press are vital to a free society. As Justice Walter V. Schaefer of the Illinois Supreme Court put it, "The quality of a nation's civilization can be largely measured by the methods it uses in the enforcement of its criminal law." The late Justice Curtis Bok of Pennsylvania observed that man

> is not free if he is punished and imprisoned, and if he is not free he is a slave.
>
> Our law cannot stand for slavery. It must stand for the truth and justice, in lower case . . .[16]

The press, when it recognizes its responsibilities, is as essential to truth and justice as are the courts. Most of the deficiencies in justice described in this book were reported in the press. Yet if the press is completely free, it will not always be fair, just as officers of the law will not always be fair, especially if they are completely free of observation by the press. Editors and lawyers must realize that they both hold a public trust and cannot be guided by business motives alone or personal motives alone. To the extent that the press and the bar tolerate injustice, they are both neglecting their trust. Their privileged position under the Constitution obligates them to render more conscientious service to the Bill of Rights than the public demands.

Ideally, there should be no conflict between the press and the courts. Ideally, the press, through the responsible exercise of its freedom, should promote justice and not injustice. The object of the press is to advance the general welfare. The press speaks to and for the public but should champion the individual.

Ideally, the courts, through the responsible, unhampered conduct of trials, should produce justice. This is their function. The courts speak to the individual but they should champion the public good.

But neither the press nor the courts are perfect and neither can function in a vacuum. They are inseparable forums of justice. The public and those directly concerned (editors, reporters, judges, lawyers, and police) must act on the basis of facts and opinions. Facts and opinions, whatever their validity, are transmitted by media of communication. Our system is predicated on the philosophy that social relationships are improved by a maximum of responsible communication. Reasons can be advanced in any context to justify curbs on communication, but they usually run counter to our basic philosophy.

Courts are the agencies by which liberties and, ultimately, the rule of law are upheld. But the press is the chief means for informing the general public of what is going on in the world, including what is going on in the courts and the other agencies of justice. And sometimes it is the only agency to correct a miscarriage of justice, the only agency (in the words of an anonymous wit) "to comfort the afflicted and to afflict the comfortable."

APPENDIX A

LEGAL FOUNDATIONS FOR JUSTICE AND A FREE PRESS

Due Process

ENGLISH SOURCES

Magna Carta, 1215
Petition of Right, 1628
Abolition of the Star Chamber, 1641
Habeas Corpus Act, 1679
Bill of Rights, 1689

UNITED STATES SOURCE

United States Constitution

ARTICLE I

Section 9

The privilege of the writ of habeas corpus shall not be suspended, unless when in cases of rebellion or invasion the public safety may require it.

No bill of attainder or ex post facto law shall be passed.

Section 10

No state shall . . . pass any bill of attainder, ex post facto law.

ARTICLE III

Section 2

The trial of all crimes, except in cases of impeachment, shall be by jury; and such trial shall be held in the state where the said crimes shall have been committed; but when not committed within any state, the trial shall be at such place or places as the Congress may by law have directed.

Section 3

Treason against the United States, shall consist only in levying war against them, or in adhering to their enemies, giving them aid and comfort.

No person shall be convicted of treason unless on the testimony of two witnesses to the same overt act, or on confession in open court.

The Congress shall have the power to declare the punishment of treason, but no attainder of treason shall work corruption of blood, or forfeiture except during the life of the person attainted.

ARTICLE IV

Section 2

The citizens of each state shall be entitled to all privileges and immunities of citizens in the several states.

A person charged in any state with treason, felony, or other crime, who shall flee from justice, and be found in another state, shall on demand of the executive authority of the state from which he fled, be delivered up, to be removed to the state having jurisdiction of the crime.

ARTICLE VI

This Constitution, and the laws of the United States which shall be made in pursuance thereof; and all treaties made, or which shall be made, under the authority of the United States, shall be the supreme law of the land; and the judges in every state shall be bound thereby, any thing in the constitution or laws of any state to the contrary notwithstanding.

FOURTH AMENDMENT

The right of the people to be secure in their persons, houses, papers, and effects, against unreasonable searches and seizures, shall not be violated, and no warrants shall issue, but upon probable cause, supported by oath or affirmation, and particularly describing the place to be searched, and the persons or things to be seized.

FIFTH AMENDMENT

No person shall be held to answer for a capital, or otherwise infamous crime, unless on a presentment or indictment of a Grand Jury, except in cases arising in the land or naval forces, or the militia, when in actual service in time of war or public danger; nor shall any person be subject for the same offense to be twice put in jeopardy of life or limb; nor shall be compelled in any criminal case to be a witness against himself, nor be deprived of life, liberty, or property, without due process of law. . . .

SIXTH AMENDMENT

In all criminal prosecutions, the accused shall enjoy the right to a speedy and public trial, by an impartial jury of the state and district wherein the crime shall have been committed, which district shall have been previously ascertained by law, and to be informed of the nature and cause of the accusation; to be confronted with witnesses against him; to have compulsory process for obtaining witnesses in his favor, and to have the assistance of counsel for his defense.

EIGHTH AMENDMENT

Excessive bail shall not be required, nor excessive fines imposed, nor cruel and unusual punishments inflicted.

NINTH AMENDMENT

The enumeration in the Constitution, of certain rights, shall not be construed to deny or disparage others retained by the people.

FOURTEENTH AMENDMENT

Section 1

All persons born or naturalized in the United States, and subject to the jurisdiction thereof, are citizens of the United States and of the state wherein they reside. No state shall make or enforce any law which shall abridge the privileges or immunities of citizens of the United States; nor shall any state deprive any person of life, liberty, or property, without due process of law; nor deny to any person within its jurisdiction the equal protection of the laws.

Free Expression

UNITED STATES CONSTITUTION

FIRST AMENDMENT

Congress shall make no law respecting an establishment of religion, or prohibiting the free exercise thereof; or abridging the freedom of speech, or of the press; or the right of the people peaceably to assemble, and to petition the Government for a redress of grievances.

APPENDIX B

GUIDELINES FOR THE PRESS AND BAR

Oregon Bar–Press–Broadcasters Joint Statement of Principles (Adopted in 1962)

Oregon's Bill of Rights provides both for fair trials and for freedom of the press. These rights are basic and unqualified. They are not ends in themselves but are necessary guarantors of freedom for the individual and the public's rights to be informed. The necessity of preserving both the right to a fair trial and the freedom to disseminate the news is of concern to responsible members of the legal and journalistic professions and is of equal concern to the public. At times these two rights appear to be in conflict with each other.

In an effort to mitigate this conflict, the Oregon State Bar, the Oregon Newspaper Publishers Association and the Oregon Association of Broadcasters have adopted the following statement of principles to keep the public fully informed without violating the rights of any individual.

1. The news media have the right and the responsibility to print and to broadcast the truth.

2. However, the demands of accuracy and objectivity in news reporting should be balanced with the demands of fair play. The public has a right to be informed. The accused has the right to be judged in an atmosphere free from undue prejudice.

3. Good taste should prevail in the selection, printing and broadcasting of the news. Morbid or sensational details of criminal behavior should not be exploited.

4. The right of decision about the news rests with the editor or news director. In the exercise of judgment he should consider that: a) an

accused person is presumed innocent until proved guilty; b) readers and listeners are potential jurors; c) no person's reputation should be injured needlessly.

5. The public is entitled to know how justice is being administered. However, it is unprofessional for any lawyer to exploit any medium of public information to enhance his side of a pending case. It follows that the public prosecutor should avoid taking unfair advantage of his position as an important source of news; this shall not be construed to limit his obligation to make available information to which the public is entitled.

In recognition of these principles, the undersigned hereby testify to their continuing desire to achieve the best possible accommodation of the rights of the individual and the rights of the public when these two fundamental precepts appear to be in conflict in the administration of justice.

Massachusetts Guide for the Bar and News Media (Approved by a Special Massachusetts Bar–Press Committee in 1963)

I. Guide for Press

Preamble

1. To promote closer understanding between the bar and the press, especially in their efforts to reconcile the constitutional guarantee of freedom of the press and the right to a fair, impartial trial, the following mutual and voluntary statement of principles is recommended to all members of both professions.

2. Both professions, recognizing that freedom of the press is one of the fundamental liberties guaranteed by the First Amendment to the United States Constitution, agree that this fundamental freedom must be zealously preserved and responsibly exercised subject only to those restrictions designed to safeguard equally fundamental rights of the individual.

3. It is likewise agreed that both the press and the bar are obliged to preserve the principle of the presumption of innocence for those accused of wrongdoing pending a finding of guilty.

4. The press and the bar concur on the importance of the natural right of the members of an organized society to acquire and impart information about their common interests.

5. It is further agreed, however, that the inherent right of society's members to impart and acquire information should be exercised with discretion at those times when public disclosures would jeopardize the ends of justice, public security and other rights of individuals.

6. The press and the bar recognize that there may arise circumstances in which disclosures of names of individuals involved in matters coming to the attention of the general public would result in personal danger, harm to the reputation of a person or persons or notoriety to an innocent third party.

7. Consistent with the principles of this preamble, it is the responsibility of the bar, no less than that of the press, to support the free flow of information.

FOR THE PRESS

Newspapers in publishing accounts of crime should keep in mind that the accused may be tried in a court of law.

To preserve the individual's right to a fair trial, news stories of crime should contain only a factual statement of the arrest and attending circumstances.

The following should be avoided:

1. Publication of interviews with subpoenaed witnesses after an indictment is returned.

2. Publication of the criminal record or discreditable acts of the accused after an indictment is returned or during the trial unless made part of the evidence in the court record. The defendant is being tried on the charge for which he is accused and not on his record. (Publication of a criminal record could be grounds for a libel suit.)

3. Publication of confessions after an indictment is returned unless made a part of the evidence in the court record.

4. Publication of testimony stricken by the court, unless reported as having been stricken.

5. Editorial comment preceding or during trial, tending to influence judge or jury.

6. Publication of names of juveniles involved in juvenile proceedings unless the names are released by the judge.

7. The publication of any "leaks," statements or conclusions as to the innocence or guilt, implied or expressed, by the police or prosecuting authorities or defense counsel.

2. GUIDE FOR BROADCASTING INDUSTRY

PREAMBLE

1. To promote closer understanding between the bar and the broadcast news media, especially in their efforts to reconcile the constitutional guarantee of freedom of the press and the right to a fair, impartial trial, the following mutual and voluntary statement of principles is recommended to all members of both professions.

2. Both professions, recognizing that freedom of the press is one of the fundamental liberties guaranteed by the First Amendment to the United States Constitution, agree that this fundamental freedom must be zealously preserved and responsibly exercised subject only to those restrictions designated to safeguard equally fundamental rights of the individual.

3. It is likewise agreed that both the broadcast news media and the bar are obliged to preserve the principle of the presumption of innocence for those accused of wrongdoing pending a finding of guilty.

4. The broadcast news media and the bar concur on the importance of the natural right of the members of an organized society to acquire and impart information about their common interests.

5. It is further agreed, however, that the inherent right of society's members to impart and acquire information should be exercised with discretion at those times when public disclosures would jeopardize the ends of justice, public security and other rights of individuals.

6. The broadcast news media and the bar recognize that there may arise circumstances in which disclosures of names of individuals involved in matters coming to the attention of the general public would result in personal danger, harm to the reputation of a person or persons or notoriety to an innocent third party.

7. Consistent with the principles of this preamble, it is the responsibility of the bar, no less than that of the broadcast news media, to support the free flow of information.

FOR THE BROADCAST NEWS MEDIA

The broadcast news media in news stories originated by them concerning a crime should keep in mind that the accused may be tried in a court of law.

To preserve the individual's rights to a fair trial, news stories of crime should contain only a factual statement of the arrest and attending circumstances.

The following should be avoided:

1. Broadcasting of interviews with subpoenaed witnesses after an indictment is returned.

2. Broadcasting of the criminal record or discreditable acts of the accused after an indictment is returned or during the trial unless made part of the evidence in the court record. The defendant is being tried on the charge for which he is accused and not on his record. (Broadcasting of a criminal record could be grounds for a libel suit.)

3. Broadcasting of confessions after an indictment is returned unless made a part of the evidence in the court record.

4. Broadcasting of testimony stricken by the court unless reported as having been stricken.

5. Editorial comment preceding or during trial, tending to influence judge or jury.

6. Broadcasting of names of juveniles involved in juvenile proceedings unless the names are released by the judge.

7. The broadcasting of any "leaks," statements or conclusions as to the innocence or guilt, implied or expressed, by the police or prosecuting authorities or defense counsel.

3. GUIDE FOR THE BAR

To preserve the individual's rights to a fair trial in a court of law the following guide lines are prescribed for the Bar.

1. A factual statement of the arrest and circumstances and incidents thereof of a person charged with a crime is permissible, but the following should be avoided: a) Statements or conclusions as to the innocence or guilt, implied or expressed, by the prosecuting authorities or defense counsel. b) Out-of-court statements by prosecutors or defense attorneys to news media in advance of or during trial, stating what they expect to prove, whom they propose to call as witnesses or public criticism of either judge or jury. c) Issuance by the prosecuting authorities, counsel for the defense or any person having official connection with the case of any statements relative to the conduct of the accused, statements, "confessions" or admissions made by the accused or other matters bearing on the issue to be tried. d) Any other statement or press release to the news media in which the source of the statement remains undisclosed.

2. At the same time, in the interest of fair and accurate reporting, news media have a right to expect the cooperation of the authorities in facilitating adequate coverage of the law enforcement process.

Kentucky Press Association Statement of Principles for Pre-trial Reporting (Adopted June 1965)

One year ago—concerned over the apparent conflicts which arise from time to time between the First Amendment to the Federal Constitution guaranteeing free press and the Sixth Amendment guaranteeing fair trial—the Kentucky Press Association authorized discussions with other state organizations toward the establishment of a Statement of Principles.

Such discussions have been held. They have been fruitful. The Kentucky Press Association believes that whatever conflicts exist can be kept to a minimum provided that all of those involved in the legal processes and in news coverage take every reasonable step to maintain an unprejudiced atmosphere.

Both Press and Bar stand in strong support of all the Federal and State Constitutional provisions—the rights of the free press, the right of individuals against unlawful search and seizure, the right of an individual to counsel, the right to protection against self-incrimination, the protections against excessive bail or excessive punishment, and the right of all persons accused of criminal acts to swift and public trial by impartial jurors.

It is toward the furtherance of these goals that the Kentucky Press Association has drawn up the following guide lines.

The collaboration of all is solicited—of reporters and editors; of those who serve in law enforcement posts; of officers of the courts; of those who serve as counsel.

And to attain these goals, the Kentucky Press Association warmly invites the endorsement of Bar Associations and of the Kentucky Broadcasters Association.

1. The Danger of "Confessions"

It is the function of police officers and Commonwealth's attorneys to question those suspected of crime. Law enforcement officers have every right to seek as much information as possible from those under arrest, provided these persons are notified of their Constitutional rights, and are not coerced.

The publication, however, of the results of such questioning is not only extralegal, but is often dangerous.

Reporters and editors should bear in mind that in the great majority of cases brought to trial, many purported "confessions" which are published are often not introduced into evidence. The publication of such material, even though issued by law enforcement officers, does not relieve the newspapers of basic legal responsibility. In a great number of cases in recent years, the publication of such matter has resulted in the reversal of convictions by courts of appeal.

It is recommended therefore, that all law enforcement officers and all journalists refrain from using the term "confession" to describe a statement attributed to a person under arrest.

As a general principle, newspapers should follow the policy of stating simply that law enforcement officers have reported that the individual under arrest has made a statement containing damaging admissions.

This procedure may not be adequate in cases involving major offenses and where the degree of public concern is sufficient to justify news coverage in greater detail in order to pacify community unrest. In cases of this type, reporters should make every effort to interview the accused individuals to seek corroboration of the statements attributed to them; or to seek out the accused's counsel for comment. Whatever is published in these instances, however, should be presented in such manner as not to place the newspapers in the role of judge or jury; and should be couched in such dispassionate terms as not to impair the accused person's right to a trial free of prejudice.

In this connection, it is the belief of the Kentucky Press Association that major police departments would be well advised to maintain staff legal counsel. It is not possible for police officers to keep abreast of legal developments, and staff counsel could provide a most valuable service. The weight of legal decisions in recent years makes it clear that reversal is only to be expected in cases where an accused individual has not been notified of his right to counsel, or where notification has not been given that statements made to arresting officers may be used in evidence. The addition of staff legal counsel would provide police departments with up-to-date data or proper procedures and save the law enforcement branch from the disappointments that come from technical failures in complying with both the statutes and the decisions of courts of appeal.

2. THE USE OF PRIOR RECORDS

Under the law an individual must be tried for the accusation at hand —NOT for prior delinquencies. Unless a defendant openly during a trial admits previous arrest and conviction, the record of the past cannot be disclosed to either jury or judge. Only when a verdict has been reached does a report of the individual's past record reach the judge so that he can appraise it in terms of sentencing.

Therefore, when a newspaper transmits information about the prior record of a person under arrest, it is unwittingly bringing into direct conflict the Constitutional rights afforded by the First and Sixth Amendments.

There are cases, however, where a crime is of such a nature and of such importance that restraint in this regard is difficult, if not impossible.

The Lee Harvey Oswald case is not a precise example. There were excesses of another type (these are discussed in Section 3). There was no mention in the published reports of any prior criminal record on Oswald. Had such a record existed it most certainly would have been published. While the principle remains that every accused person is entitled to his Constitutional rights, the assassination of a President is of such unusual nature and the depth of public interest so far-reaching—and the need that maximum information be given the citizenry so compelling—that a violation by the news media under such circumstances would have to be regarded as an understandable departure from the norm.

The problem confronting the news media can best be illustrated by mentioning the name of John Dillinger. Were another Dillinger to develop and the full weight of the Federal Government be brought into play in seeking his capture, the press could not avoid giving all the details of past crimes.

It is not in such cases, however, that the normal difficulty arises. The Kentucky Press Association emphasizes that unless there be clear and overpowering reasons dictated by the public interest, the news media should refrain from publishing prior records of criminal activity.

The news media are urged, however, to seek out such information for its own guidance and for the subsequent protection of society should there be miscarriages of justice.

There have been, and there will be in the future, instances where individuals with long records of violent crime have either been freed or given minor sentences. In such cases, the possession of prior records by the news media will present opportunities after trials for public disclosure and the opportunity thus given the citizenry to seek reforms in the legal procedures.

3. PRE-TRIAL AND TRIAL REPORTING

In cases where there has been unusual news interest, the news media have followed the practice of summarizing such cases immediately preceding the opening of a criminal trial. Careless pre-trial reviewing contains the danger of prejudicing the guarantees of fair trial.

The public is entitled to know when such cases are due for trial and to be given as much information as is proper and reasonable. Every care should be taken in such advance reporting to observe the principles outlined above concerning statements attributed to the accused individual and about prior records of violations.

The Kentucky Press Association believes that law enforcement officers, attorneys, officers of the court, and newspapermen must keep in mind at all times that every citizen is a potential juror. It follows as a fundamental principle for all concerned that pre-trial comment and publication should be as fair, factual and impartial as conscientious men and women can present such information.

. . .

The Oswald case in Dallas brought sharp criticism from many sources, including the Warren Commission and the American Bar Association. The prime fault in that case rested with the ranking officers of the Dallas Police Department and with State's attorneys. Both the Warren Commission and the American Bar held it one thing for police officers to collect evidence; and quite another to release this type of information because it has the effect of conducting a trial in the press, rather than in the courtroom.

There have been other cases (usually sensational in nature) where the conduct of both prosecuting and defense attorneys violated all precepts of fair trial and fair comment. It is the responsibility of the Bar Associations to control such conduct and to enforce proper standards.

. . .

It follows that if newspapers are to exercise restraint in the publication of information about arrests, about prior criminal activity on the part of those accused of crime, and in pre-trial reporting, the public is entitled to fuller coverage of the actual trials.

Newspapers are therefore encouraged to expand trial coverage so that the public can be accorded full information about the nature of criminal activity and the results of the community's law-enforcement procedures.

In covering trials, reporters should use care in one aspect. This concerns statements made in court during times when the jury has been excused. It is proper for a reporter to convey the essence of the courtroom argument, but any prejudicial comment uttered out of the hearing of the jury should be excluded from any published report.

4. THE HANDLING OF JUVENILE CASES

Perhaps more debate goes on concerning the proper method of reporting cases involving juveniles than any other phase of crime reporting. There remains widespread disagreement as to the most effective and ethical means of treating such cases.

The general practice in the Commonwealth is that wherever and whenever possible, the anonymity of juveniles placed under arrest be protected. Under Kentucky law complete discretion in this field is given to the Juvenile Courts, or to the presiding court in those counties where no Juvenile Court exists.

There is as yet no standard method used by the various Juvenile Courts in releasing information for publication. What one County's court considers a serious violation, another County's court may treat as a juvenile prank. The Kentucky Press Association urges some system of uniformity by the Juvenile Courts in releasing information.

The news media is placed in difficult position in cases where gangs of young toughs attack other juveniles or adults and where an 18-year-old may use a gun to commit a crime. Under law, the press is free to report the names of those over 18, but the names of the worst of the violators can be withheld if the Juvenile Court of jurisdiction so decrees. To cover instances such as this, the Kentucky Press Association stands ready to work with the Bar Associations in order that the public interest may be protected adequately.

As a basic principle, all responsible newspapers already cooperate fully with the Juvenile Courts to uphold the State law which protects juveniles for whom rehabilitation is possible.

5. THE USE OF "WANTED" DESCRIPTIONS

From time to time crimes are committed in which law-enforcement officials must issue descriptions of individuals sought in such cases.

The press is urged to collaborate with the law-enforcement agencies in this regard, but is cautioned that there is danger in the use of photographs, sketches and names.

The Federal Bureau of Investigation periodically releases the names and photographs of "most wanted" individuals. In these cases, the FBI is acting under Federal law and is seeking persons under indictment for major crimes.

In state cases, a newspaper assumes full risk in publishing names, photographs or sketches of individuals sought, but not yet under indictment. A case of mistaken identity can result in libel.

There also is inherent danger in the publication of photographs taken by cameras placed in banks and other business establishments. Misidentification of a legitimate customer as a law violator can have serious repercussions for a newspaper.

Consistent with these precautions, newspapers are urged to give every possible assistance to law-enforcement agencies in their search for individuals under indictment.

6. THE PRINCIPLE OF EQUITY

One of the major continuing criticisms against all branches of the news media is that reports of criminal involvement are often given considerable prominence, but that subsequent clearance or acquittal of the individual is accorded only casual mention.

The Kentucky Press Association recommends the principle of equity treatment—that all acquittals, clearances of suspicion, and corrections of serious misstatement of fact be given news treatment as close in importance and position to the original publication as is possible.

7. ESTABLISHING A STANDING COMMITTEE

In the furtherance of these Principles, the Kentucky Press Association stands ready to join the Bar Associations and the Kentucky Broadcasters in establishing a Standing Committee to periodically review these guide lines.

The Kentucky Press Association would envision the function of such a Committee as that of appraising the scope and effectiveness of the Principles and to recommend changes, alterations or additions when desirable or necessary.

8. THE RIGHT OF THE PRESS TO INVESTIGATE

Nothing in this Statement of Principles in any way limits or proscribes the rights of the press to investigate and expose corruption and wrongdoing in the society. The press remains free to search out waywardness no matter where it exists and to focus the searchlight upon the conduct of any who may violate the public trust.

The intent of these Principles is to maintain the fullest flow of information consistent with the obligation of a free society toward those accused of violating the laws.

Every individual, no matter what his rank in life, is entitled to the protections of a fair and impartial trial. To this end the Kentucky Press Association urges its membership to pledge themselves to pursue the precept of the Preamble to the Federal Constitution which calls for the establishment of justice and the insuring of domestic tranquility.

Intelligent communications insures domestic tranquility—in maintaining a community's faith that its law-enforcement machinery is operating faithfully and efficiently—in maintaining public faith that innocent individuals are not being unjustly sought or punished—in upholding faith that justice prevails.

By the same token, intelligent communications calls for a sense of responsibility. Responsibility indicates restraint in the dissemination of pre-trial information concerning those accused of crime—the restraint of intelligent self-interest that dictates that fair and impartial trial is a cornerstone of American freedom—that we follow the advice of Abraham Lincoln, as writen to the editor of The Illinois Gazette on August 11, 1846:

> . . . he who makes an assertion without knowing whether it is true or false is guilty of falsehood, and the accidental truth of the assertion does not justify or excuse him.

It is in this spirit that these Principles have been drawn up and adopted—toward the end that Free Press and Fair Trial may complement each other.

Printed copies of the Statement, through the courtesy of the *Courier-Journal* and *Times* will soon be placed in every state editorial office from the Central Office.

Code on Fair Trial and Free Press (Proposed in 1953 by the Committee on Fair Trial and Free Press of the New York County Lawyers Association)

Whereas in the constitutional history of the American people the two concepts of a fair trial and a free press have been traditionally associated, and should always co-exist, without the necessity of either concept expanding at the expense of the other; and

WHEREAS in recent years the cause of justice has suffered by reason of newspaper and other publicity during or immediately preceding trials, as well as subsequently thereto during the pendency of appeals, so that the efforts of the Courts to secure for the accused his rights to a fair trial have been thwarted and defeated; and

WHEREAS informed opinion of persons in positions of leadership in these two related branches of human activity indicates the necessity of a restatement and clarification of principles the better to secure justice under law as their common objective;

NOW, THEREFORE be it resolved that the Press on the one hand, and the Bench and the Bar on the other hand, do propose for acceptance the following principles:

1. The public is entitled to a complete and truthful factual statement of events occurring in the courtroom; but factual statements should not be elaborated with statements of opinion as to the way a case should be decided, or with statements designed to persuade either jury or judge to decide the case or frame a judgment in a particular way.

2. In certain cases the press should refrain from giving factual statements where to do so would impair public morals, or have a corrupting effect upon young readers.

3. Attorneys should not give interviews to the press in advance of, or during a trial stating either what they expect to prove or whom they propose to call as witnesses; and attorneys for both the prosecution and the defense should not, during the progress of the trial, engage in public criticism of either judge or jury, but should be scrupulous in conforming to Canon 20 of the Canons of Professional Ethics of the American Bar Association.

4. The press should not seek to ascertain and publish in advance the stories which witnesses expect to tell upon the witness stand; nor should they solicit from witnesses or parties and publish articles by them giving what they purport to know about a case, or what they expect to prove or disprove; and this restraint should continue until the final disposition of the case, including appeals if any.

5. The press should not express opinions on the credibility of witnesses, nor advocate that particular witnesses be believed or disbelieved, nor advocate particular rulings on questions as to the admissibility of evidence.

6. Sensational headlines, not strictly warranted by the facts, should be avoided.

7. Where evidence has been excluded by the judge, or where objections have been sustained to a particular question put to a witness, or where an answer has been stricken out, the press should not make public that which has thus been excluded from the jury by the judge.

8. Facts concerning the discreditable acts of a person prior to the commission of the crime for which he is being put on trial should not be published until the trial is over; provided, however, that judgments of convictions which have actually been entered and not reversed on appeal or vacated may be referred to. Nevertheless, allusions to prior convictions are to be discouraged because of their tendency to prejudice a jury.

9. Statements that a prisoner has confessed to a crime should not be made until proof of a confession has been received in evidence at the trial; and neither the police nor the district attorney or other law enforcing officer should give out in advance, statements concerning confessions.

10. After a verdict has been rendered, or the jury has disagreed, the press should not seek to ascertain, or publish, the attitude of particular jurors or the factors which influenced their decision.

11. In criminal cases the press should not, either editorially or otherwise, attempt to influence the judge as to what sentence he should impose.

12. These principles should be scrupulously observed to the end that the verdicts of juries and the judgments of courts shall not be influenced by anything except the evidence actually received at the trial.

[*Note:* The New York County Lawyers Association appointed a Special Committee on Fair Trial and Free Press, consisting of: Hon. William Dean Embree, Chairman, Porter R. Chandler, Esq., Hon. Paxton Blair, W. Randolph Montgomery, Esq., William J. O'Shea, Esq., and Hon. Simon H. Rifkind, and this Committee has adopted the text of the foregoing Code and recommends its promulgation by the New York County Lawyers Association and its favorable adoption by other Bar Associations, by the representatives of press, motion pictures, radio and television and other media of communication.]

Statement of Policy of Philadelphia Bar Association Regarding Release and Publication of Information in Connection with Criminal Proceedings (Approved December 29, 1964)

1. PRE-ARREST PUBLICITY

A. Police and Investigators

News releases regarding criminal matters should be made by the head of the police department or by designated and authorized ranking police officials. They should not be made by the individual officer. It is recognized that under some conditions the appropriate official may not be reached in a reasonable time, and it may become necessary for the ranking officer on the scene to furnish basic and unelaborated data. This should be avoided, however, wherever possible.

When a crime occurs, the news media may be furnished with all pertinent facts relating to the crime itself. It is undesirable to furnish intimate and sordid details about the victims or perpetrators of sensational crimes. It is apparent that such details would serve only to create or satisfy an appetite for sensationalism. The right of the public to be kept aware of conditions in the community and the operations of its public servants must be modified by the right of the victims to privacy and the right of defendants to a fair trial; and even by considerations of good taste.

During the investigation of a crime, information should not be furnished unless the publicizing of certain aspects of the case will help the investigation. For example, it might be necessary to publicize description, photograph, artist's conception, etc., for the purpose of seeking assistance in identifying the criminal or in apprehending the suspect. Broad publicity may become necessary in a fugitive matter. In such cases, it may be necessary not only to publicize the issuance of a warrant and the charges as described therein, but also the fugitive's past criminal history and the fact that he may be armed and dangerous, in order to increase the public interest in his apprehension and at the same time alert the public and law-enforcement officials to the need for exercising caution.

If publicity is given regarding suspects who are picked up, they should not be identified by name unless they are actually charged with the offense. The release of any information, however accurate, which would not be admissible at a future trial of the individual should always be avoided.

The issuance of a search warrant may be released to the news media but one which has been served with negative results should not be the basis of a release. The existence of the warrant, however, is a public record, and it is not proper to hide it. Accordingly, in the event of a press inquiry, the issuance of the warrant, the grounds described therein, and the positive or negative results of the search may be released.

B. Prosecuting Attorneys

Prosecuting attorneys should be bound by the same rules as the police and other investigators during this period. Nothing contained in these rules will preclude the right of the prosecutor to reply to any charges of misconduct on his part that may be publicized by the accused or anyone speaking on his behalf.

C. Judiciary

Judicial officials have no occasion to make comment to the news media during an investigative period. In general, it is improper for a judicial official to make statements with respect to any case which is before him or may later come before him, and it is equally undesirable for him to comment on cases that are before or may come before other judges.

D. News Media

The law imposes only slight limitations upon the news media; accordingly, any restraints must be self-imposed, either by agreement among the news media, or by the policy of a company as not being in the public interest or in good taste. Excesses which may logically result in denying a fair trial to a person accused are not in the public interest for they strike at the public respect for the legal processes of a democratic system.

It is recognized that in certain cases of great news interest there will be conflicting pressures between the needs of the news media and the obligations of the law enforcement authorities to protect both the rights of the defendant and the investigative requirements of the case itself. Under such conditions it is felt that the police and/or prosecutors should refuse and the press should not request:

1. The right to review police reports;

2. The right to invade the police department or the prosecutor's office;

3. The right to demand photographs;

4. The right to receive intimate and sordid details about the victims or perpetrators of sensational crimes;

5. The right to accompany police in the course of an investigation, a raid, a round-up of suspects, etc.

2. POST-ARREST PUBLICITY

A. Police and Investigators

In general, at the time of apprehension, it is proper to make a release. It may restate the facts of the case but should avoid the use of spectacular, inflammatory adjectives and expressions of opinion. The details of arrest may be furnished, including the identity of the subject, his residence, description, his family status, the manner in which the arrest was made, the names of the arresting officers if the police desire to furnish this information, and similar data. Law enforcement officials should release information relative to the issuance of the warrant, the nature of the charges against the accused, and the potential penalties provided by law. They should not mention admissions or a confession.

It is preferable that the release be made promptly after arrest, since this will protect the defendant's right not to be held incommunicado, the public's right to know what has transpired and the right of the news media not to be victimized by preferential treatment. Photographs may be furnished to the news media and the latter may photograph the defendant when he is moved about and exposed to view. The police should not pose the prisoner.

In the course of describing the details of arrest, it may be permissible to refer to the recovery of loot, the presence of weapons and comparable information; and the loot and the weapons may be displayed for photographs. It is not permissible, however, to display and comment upon loot, weapons, or other physical articles if they will not clearly be admissible as evidence at the time of trial. If there is question about admissibility, the advice of the prosecutor should be obtained.

Releases and press inquiries should be handled by the head of the police department or by a designated and authorized police official and not by an individual officer, particularly if that officer is to be called as a witness in court. Interviews with the defendant himself should be prohibited during the period he is in police custody. There should be no release of a criminal record or police history for publication.

B. Prosecuting and Defense Attorneys

From the moment of arrest all practicing attorneys, whether they represent the defendant, the state, or private prosecutor, or whether they have any interest whatever in the pending criminal case, should refrain from:

1. making any statements concerning a pending criminal case;
2. granting any interviews with the press or other media of communications concerning a pending criminal case;
3. engaging in any public discussions whatsoever concerning a pending criminal case;
4. preparing any statement for release by any other person which is intended to influence public opinion and prospective jurors.

It is recognized, however, that administrative officials of the courts and the District Attorney in the conduct of their offices may not keep secret information regarding the administration of justice. Accordingly, information may be released or furnished on request, such as the scheduled dates for hearings, grand jury, trial, etc. Information and opinions regarding the substantive case should not be furnished.

C. Judiciary

At the time of preliminary hearings or thereafter, the presiding magistrate or judge should refrain from inflammatory statements. The expressed views of a judge are more likely to fix the opinion of the prospective jurors than even those of the police and prosecutor.

The courtroom, including the magistrate's court should reflect an air of decorum, and the dignity of the law and the rights of the defendant should at all times be protected. No cameras, radio or TV should be permitted in any courtroom, including the magistrate's court.

D. News Media

At the time of the preliminary hearing or any other appearance in court for pleading, the press and public have access to all information and testimony introduced. At that point, the existence of admissions or a confession, and in some instances, the details thereof may become a matter of public record and hence available to the news media.

Within self-imposed limits of good taste and public interest, the news media may report what takes place in public view in the magistrate's court or what otherwise appears in public records. The existence of a criminal history may be made public in the course of the fixing of bail. At this time, however, there is rarely any need to alert the public and ask for assistance in the location and apprehension of a fugitive, and no valuable public service will be performed by publishing or republishing the defendant's criminal history. At the time of the hearing it is difficult to predict whether a confession will or will not be admissible in evidence at a subsequent trial, and publication of a confession at this stage may be extremely prejudicial. Accordingly, unless the confession is made in open court by the accused himself, it should not be publicized by the media.

3. PUBLICITY DURING TRIAL

A. Police and Investigators

No news releases, statements or comments regarding the evidence should be made by the police. The evidence as produced publicly in court should be permitted to speak for itself.

B. Prosecuting or Defense Attorneys

No statements of any kind should be made for publication by either the prosecutor or defense attorneys during the course of trial.

C. Judiciary

No comments should be made for publication by any member of the judiciary during the course of a trial.

D. News Media

From the commencement of the selection of the jury until the rendering of the verdict, it is most undesirable that any evidence should be published by the news media except that which is presented before the jury in open court. While the jury is sitting, the publication of information, whether accurate or not, which has not been introduced into evidence, may be prejudicial and violative of the defendant's right to a fair trial, and the news media should refrain from its publication. For the same reason, editorial or other comment on pending cases should be avoided until after the verdict.

4. PUBLICITY FOLLOWING TRIAL

A. Police and Investigators

After the jury has rendered its verdict, the police need not refrain from comment. They should, of course, avoid inflammatory statements and contempt of court.

B. Prosecuting and Defense Attorneys

The only restrictions that would be placed on the attorneys with respect to comment would be those involving contempt of court, or statements tending to destroy confidence in our system of justice.

C. Judiciary

The judiciary should likewise exercise self-restraint and avoid inflammatory comment.

D. News Media

No restrictions should be placed on the news media except those which are self-imposed by good taste and sound judgment. The media have the right to express opinions fully, even to the extent of indicating that there has been a miscarriage of justice, and they have full right to express criticism of the judge, jury and other participants. They should, of course, avoid any excess that would constitute contempt of court. They may publicize at this time the defendant's admissions, confessions and criminal record.

Statement of Principles and Standards Pertaining to Publicity Through Communications Media and Its Impact Upon a Fair Trial by an Impartial Jury

To provide ways and means by which, in criminal prosecutions, an accused's right to a fair trial by an impartial jury can be protected against publicity which is potentially biasing and prejudicial in effect, the following principles and standards should govern the conduct of all persons and entities playing any part in such publicity.

1. The impartial jury guaranteed by the Sixth Amendment to the Constitution of the United States is one which decides the case solely on the evidence presented at the trial. Even though having outside information,

a jury can be impartial if it disregards all such knowledge and decides the case solely on the evidence presented at the trial.

2. American justice presumes every accused innocent until proved guilty by evidence beyond a reasonable doubt presented in open court under the safeguards of an adversary proceeding. To publish information tending to how or imply guilt, which is not part of the trial evidence, prejudices and may destroy the accused's protective cloak of presumed innocence.

3. All persons in a just society have the inalienable right to know whether our courts of justice function in conformity with constitutional standards and safeguards. To that end communications media have the right to inform the people whether such constitutional standards and safeguards are observed.

4. Attorneys at law, including but not limited to, prosecutors and their aides, defense counsel and their aides, should comply with the letter and the spirit of the Canons of Legal Ethics governing their conduct with respect to publicity and thus assist news media's adherence to the principles and standards herein stated.

5. News Media, by their activities, can produce and on occasion have produced positive results in the public interest particularly, for instance, where law enforcement agencies would appear to be inert or inactive. The principles and standards herein set forth can be and should be observed and effectively implemented without inhibiting such activities.

6. Except where description, photograph, artist's conception and other indicia or information are deemed necessary and proper, by appropriate authorities, for purposes of apprehension and public safety, no one knowingly should play any part in permitting, allowing or cooperating in the reporting, through any one or more of the communications media of:

(a) Interviews, after an accused is charged with a crime, with persons who have or claim to have any information directly or indirectly concerning or touching on the relationship to the crime of the one so charged. The accused would be an exception, if after consultation with his counsel, he chooses to be interviewed.

(b) The criminal record of any person charged with a crime except on the occasion of first publishing the news of his arrest and then only if, in the judgment of an editor, it is necessary to do so.

(c) Any alleged confession or statement of any person charged with a crime until such confession or statement has been admitted in evidence in the court record of any particular case, then current, except where the person arrested, after consultation with his counsel admits that he voluntarily made the confession or statement reported.

(d) Editorial comment preceding or during trial which would influence judge or jury for or against the defendant.

(e) Any "leaks," statements, announcements of what evidence will be presented in court, expressions of opinion or conclusions, implied or expressed, by police, prosecuting authorities or others interested in the case as to the innocence or guilt of an accused.

7. The basic purpose and spirit of these principles and standards should guide conduct falling within the purview of such principles and standards. Where the responsible news editor or responsible news executive determines that a newly developed state of affairs has arisen which, in his judgment, demands publication of any particular news matter falling within the purview of these principles and standards such a judgment will be made, mindful of the basic purpose and spirit of these principles and standards, and will be made only in such instances when publication would be in the furtherance of an overriding public interest.

[Approved by The Cleveland Bar Association and Cleveland *Plain Dealer* March 22, 1966. Also accepted by the Cleveland chapter of Sigma Delta Chi.]

Statement of Policy Concerning the Release of Information by Personnel of the United States Department of Justice Relating to Criminal Proceedings (Announced April 16, 1965)

The availability to news media of information in criminal cases is a matter which has become increasingly a subject of concern in the administration of criminal justice. The purpose of this statement is to formulate specific guidelines for the release of such information by personnel of the Department of Justice.

While the release of information for the purpose of influencing a trial is, of course, always improper, there are valid reasons for making available to the public information about the administration of the criminal laws. The task of striking a fair balance between the protection of individuals accused of crime and public understanding of the problems of controlling crime depends largely on the exercise of sound judgment by those responsible for administering the criminal laws and by representatives of the press and other media.

Inasmuch as the Department of Justice has generally fulfilled its responsibilities with awareness and understanding of the competing needs in this area, this statement, to a considerable extent, reflects and formalizes the standards to which representatives of the Department have adhered in the past. Nonetheless, it will be helpful in ensuring uniformity of practice to set forth the following guidelines for all personnel of the Department of Justice.

Because of the difficulty and importance of the questions they raise, it is felt that some portions of the matters covered by this statement, such as the authorization to make available federal conviction records and a description of items seized at the time of arrest, should be the subject of continuing review and consideration by the Department on the basis of experience and suggestions from those within and outside the Department.

1. These guidelines shall apply to the release of information to news media from the time a person is arrested or is charged with a criminal offense until the proceeding has been terminated by trial or otherwise.

2. At no time shall personnel of the Department of Justice furnish any statement or information for the purpose of influencing the outcome of a defendant's trial.

3. Personnel of the Department of Justice, subject to specific limitations imposed by law or court rule or order, may make public the following information:

a. The defendant's name, age, residence, employment, marital status, and similar background information.
b. The substance or text of the charge, such as a complaint, indictment, or information.
c. The identity of the investigating and arresting agency and the length of the investigation.
d. The circumstances immediately surrounding an arrest, including the time and place of arrest, resistance, pursuit, possession and use of weapons, and a description of items seized at the time of arrest.

Disclosures should include only incontrovertible, factual matters, and should not include subjective observations. In addition, where background information or information relating to the circumstances of an arrest would be highly prejudicial and where the release thereof would serve no law enforcement function, such information should not be made public.

4. Personnel of the Department shall not volunteer for publication any information concerning a defendant's prior criminal record. However, this is not intended to alter the Department's present policy that, since federal criminal conviction records are matters of public record permanently maintained in the Department, this information may be made available upon specific inquiry.

5. Because of the particular danger of prejudice resulting from statements in the period approaching and during trial, they ought strenuously to be avoided during that period. Any such statement or release shall be made only on the infrequent occasion when circumstances absolutely demand a disclosure of information and shall include only information which is clearly not prejudicial.

6. The release of certain types of information generally tends to create dangers of prejudice without serving a significant law enforcement function. Therefore, personnel of the Department should refrain from making available the following:

a. Observations about a defendant's character.
b. Statements, admissions, confessions, or alibis attributable to a defendant.
c. References to investigative procedures, such as fingerprints, polygraph examinations, ballistics tests, or laboratory tests.
d. Statements concerning the identity, credibility, or testimony of prospective witnesses.
e. Statements concerning evidence or argument in the case, whether or not it is anticipated that such evidence or argument will be used at trial.

7. Personnel of the Department of Justice should take no action to encourage or assist news media in photographing or televising a defendant or accused person being held or transported in federal custody. Departmental representatives should not make available photographs of a defendant unless a law enforcement function is served thereby.

8. This statement of policy is not intended to restrict the release of information concerning a defendant who is a fugitive from justice.

9. Since the purpose of this statement is to set forth generally applicable guidelines, there will, of course, be situations in which it will limit release of information which would not be prejudicial under the particular circumstances. If a representative of the Department believes that in the interest of the fair administration of justice and the law

enforcement process information beyond these guidelines should be released in a particular case, he shall request the permission of the Attorney General or the Deputy Attorney General to do so.

Nicholas deB. Katzenbach
Attorney General

APPENDIX C

THE SHEPPARD DECISION

THE UNITED STATES SUPREME COURT DECISION IN SHEPPARD *V.* MAXWELL—JUNE 6, 1966

On June 6, 1966, the United States Supreme Court issued its decision in the case of Dr. Samuel H. Sheppard, the Cleveland osteopath who was convicted in 1954 of murdering his wife. Though the decision was announced after this book went to press, many of the remedies proposed in the book to alleviate the problems of prejudicial publicity are the same as those advanced by the high court in the 8-to-1 Sheppard decision.

Because the Sheppard case is one of the key cases covered in this book and because the Supreme Court in the Sheppard decision dealt more comprehensively with the issues of justice and the press than in any previous ruling, the complete text of the opinion is published herewith as an appendix.

SUPREME COURT OF THE UNITED STATES

No. 490.—OCTOBER TERM, 1965.

Samuel H. Sheppard, Petitioner, *v.* E. L. Maxwell, Warden.	On Writ of Certiorari to the United States Court of Appeals for the Sixth Circuit.

[June 6, 1966.]

MR. JUSTICE CLARK delivered the opinion of the Court.

This federal habeas corpus application involves the question whether Sheppard was deprived of a fair trial in his state conviction for the second-degree murder of his wife because of the trial judge's failure to protect Sheppard sufficiently from the massive, pervasive and prejudicial publicity that attended his prosecution.[1] The United States District Court held that he was not afforded a fair trial and granted the writ subject to the State's right to put Sheppard to trial again, 231 F. Supp. 37 (D.C.S.D. Ohio 1964). The Court of Appeals for the Sixth Circuit reversed by a divided vote, 346 F. 2d 707 (1965). We granted certiorari, 382 U.S. 916 (1966). We have concluded that Sheppard did not receive a fair trial consistent with the Due Process Clause of the Fourteenth Amendment and, therefore, reverse the judgment.

I.

Marilyn Sheppard, petitioner's pregnant wife, was bludgeoned to death in the upstairs bedroom of their lakeshore home in Bay Village, Ohio, a suburb of Cleveland. On the day of the tragedy, July 4, 1954, Sheppard pieced together for several local officials the following story: He and his wife had entertained neighborhood friends, the Aherns, on the previous evening at their home. After dinner they watched television in the living room. Sheppard became drowsy and dozed off to sleep on a couch. Later, Marilyn partially awoke him saying that she was going to bed. The next thing he remembered was hearing his wife cry out in the early morning hours. He hurried upstairs and in the dim light from the hall saw a "form" standing next to his wife's bed. As he struggled with the "form" he was struck on the back of the neck and rendered unconscious. On regaining his senses he found himself on the floor next to his wife's bed. He raised up, looked at her, took her pulse and "felt that she was gone." He then went to his son's room and found him unmolested. Hearing a noise he hurried downstairs. He saw a "form" running out the door and pursued it to the lake shore. He grappled with it on the beach and again lost consciousness. Upon his recovery he was laying face down with the lower portion of his body in the water. He returned to his home, checked the pulse on his wife's neck, and "determined or thought that she was gone."[2] He then went downstairs and called a neighbor, Mayor Houk of Bay Village. The Mayor and his wife came over at once, found Sheppard slumped in an easy chair downstairs and asked, "What happened?" Sheppard replied: "I don't know but somebody ought to try to do something for Marilyn." Mrs. Houk immediately went up to the bedroom. The Mayor told Sheppard, "Get hold of yourself. Can you tell me what happened?" Sheppard then related the above-outlined events. After Mrs. Houk discovered the body, the Mayor called the local police, Dr. Richard Sheppard, petitioner's brother, and Aherns. The local police were the first to arrive. They in turn notified the Coroner and Cleveland police. Richard Sheppard then arrived, determined that Marilyn was dead, examined his brother's injuries, and removed him to the nearby clinic operated by the Sheppard family.[3] When the Coroner, the Cleveland police and other officials arrived, the house and surrounding area were thoroughly searched, the rooms of the house were photographed, and many persons, including the Houks and the Aherns, were interrogated. The Sheppard home and premises were taken into "protective custody" and remained so until after the trial.[4]

From the outset officials focused suspicion on Sheppard. After a search of the house and premises on the morning of the tragedy, Dr. Gerber, the Coroner, is reported—and it is undenied—to have told his men, "Well, it is evident the doctor did this, so let's go get the confession out of him." He proceeded to interrogate and examine Sheppard while the latter was under sedation in his hospital room. On the same occasion, the Coroner was given the clothes Sheppard wore at the time of the tragedy together with the personal items in them. Later that afternoon Chief Eaton and two Cleveland police officers interrogated Sheppard at some length, confronting him with evidence and demanding explanations. Asked by Officer Shotke to take a lie detector test, Sheppard said he would if it were reliable. Shotke replied that it was "infallible" and "you might as well tell us all about it now." At the end of the interrogation Shotke told Sheppard: "I think you killed your wife." Still later in the same afternoon a physician sent by the Coroner was permitted to make a detailed examination of Sheppard. Until the Coroner's inquest on July 22, at which time he was subpoenaed, Sheppard made himself available for frequent and extended questioning without the presence of an attorney.

On July 7, the day of Marilyn Sheppard's funeral, a newspaper story appeared in which Assistant County Attorney Mahon—later the chief prosecutor of Sheppard—sharply criticized the refusal of the Sheppard family to permit his immediate questioning. From there on headline stories repeatedly stressed Sheppard's lack of cooperation with the police and other officials. Under the headline "Testify Now In Death, Bay Doctor Is Ordered," one story described a visit by Coroner Gerber and four police officers to the hospital on July 8. When Sheppard insisted that his lawyer be present, the Coroner wrote out a subpoena and served it on him. Sheppard then agreed to submit to questioning without counsel and the subpoena was torn up. The officers questioned him for several hours. On July 9, Sheppard, at the request of the Coroner, re-enacted the tragedy at his home before the Coroner, police officers, and a group of newsmen, who apparently were invited by the Coroner. The home was locked so that Sheppard was obliged to wait outside until the Coroner arrived. Sheppard's performance was reported in detail by the news media along with photographs. The newspapers also played up Sheppard's refusal to take a lie detector test and "the protective ring" thrown up by his family. Front-page newspaper headlines announced on the same day that "Doctor Balks At Lie Test; Retells Story." A column opposite that story contained an "exclusive" interview with Sheppard headlined: " 'Loved My Wife, She Loved Me,' Sheppard Tells News Reporters." The next day, another headline story disclosed that Sheppard had "again late yesterday refused to take a lie detector test" and quoted an Assistant County Attorney as saying that "at the end of a nine-hour questioning of Dr. Sheppard, I felt he was now ruling [a test] out completely." But subsequent newspaper articles reported that the Coroner was still pushing Sheppard for a lie detector test. More stories appeared when Sheppard would not allow authorities to inject him with "truth serum." [5]

On the 20th, the "editorial artillery" opened fire with a front-page charge that somebody is "getting away with murder." The editorial attributed the ineptness of the investigation to "friendships, relationships, hired lawyers, a husband who ought to have been subjected instantly to the same third degree to which any person under similar circumstances is subjected. . . ." The following day, July 21, another page-one editorial was headed: "Why No Inquest? Do It Now, Dr. Gerber." The Coroner called an inquest the same day and subpoenaed Sheppard. It was staged the next day in a school gymnasium; the Coroner presided with the County Prosecutor as his advisor and two detectives as bailiffs. In the front of the room was a long table occupied by reporters, television and radio personnel, and broadcasting equipment. The hearing was broadcast with live microphones placed at the Coroner's seat and the witness stand. A swarm of reporters and photographers attended. Sheppard was brought into the room by police who searched him in full view of several hundred spectators. Sheppard's counsel were present during the three-day inquest but were not permitted to participate. When

Sheppard's chief counsel attempted to place some documents in the record, he was forcibly ejected from the room by the Coroner, who received cheers, hugs, and kisses from the ladies in the audience. Sheppard was questioned for five and one-half hours about his actions on the night of the murder, his married life, and a love affair with Susan Hayes.[6] At the end of the hearing the Coroner announced that he "could" order Sheppard held for the grand jury, but did not do so.

Throughout this period the newspapers emphasized evidence that tended to incriminate Sheppard and pointed out discrepancies in his statements to authorities. At the same time, Sheppard made many public statements to the press and wrote feature articles asserting his innocence.[7] During the inquest on July 26, a headline in large type stated: "Kerr [Captain of the Cleveland Police] Urges Sheppard's Arrest." In the story, Detective McArthur "disclosed that scientific tests at the Sheppard home have definitely established that the killer washed off a trail of blood from the murder bedroom to the downstairs section," a circumstance casting doubt on Sheppard's accounts of the murder. No such evidence was produced at trial. The newspapers also delved into Sheppard's personal life. Articles stressed his extra-marital love affairs as a motive for the crime. The newspapers portrayed Sheppard as a Lothario, fully explored his relationship with Susan Hayes, and named a number of other women who were allegedly involved with him. The testimony at trial never showed that Sheppard had any illicit relationships besides the one with Susan Hayes.

On July 28, an editorial entitled "Why Don't Police Quiz Top Suspect" demanded that Sheppard be taken to police headquarters. It described him in the following language:

> "Now proved under oath to be a liar, still free to go about his business, shielded by his family, protected by a smart lawyer who has made monkeys of the police and authorities, carrying a gun part of the time, left free to do whatever he pleases. . . ."

A front-page editorial on July 30 asked: "Why Isn't Sam Sheppard in Jail?" It was later titled "Quit Stalling—Bring Him In." After calling Sheppard "the most unusual murder suspect ever seen around these parts" the article said that "[e]xcept for some superficial questioning during Coroner Sam Gerber's inquest he has been scot-free of any official grilling. . . ." It asserted that he was "surrounded by an iron curtain of protection [and] concealment."

That night at 10 o'clock Sheppard was arrested at his father's home on a charge of murder. He was taken to the Bay Village City Hall where hundreds of people, newscasters, photographers and reporters were awaiting his arrival. He was immediately arraigned—having been denied a temporary delay to secure the presence of counsel—and bound over to the grand jury.

The publicity then grew in intensity until his indictment on August 17. Typical of the coverage during this period is a front-page interview entitled: "DR. SAM: 'I Wish There Was Something I Could Get Off My Chest—but There Isn't.' " Unfavorable publicity included items such as a cartoon of the body of a sphinx with Sheppard's head and the legend below: " 'I Will Do Everything In My Power to Help Solve This Terrible Murder.' —Dr. Sam Sheppard." Headlines announced, *inter alia,* that: "Doctor Evidence is Ready for Jury," "Corrigan Tactics Stall Quizzing," "Sheppard 'Gay Set' Is Revealed By Houk," "Blood Is Found In Garage," "New Murder Evidence Is Found, Police Claim," "Dr. Sam Faces Quiz At Jail On Marilyn's Fear Of Him." On August 18, an article appeared under the headline "Dr. Sam Writes His Own Story." And reproduced across the entire front page was a portion of the typed statement signed by Sheppard: "I am not guilty of the murder of my wife, Marilyn. How could I, who have been trained to help people and devote my life to saving life, commit such a terrible and revolting crime?" We do not detail the coverage further. There are five volumes filled with similar clippings from each of the three Cleveland newspapers covering the period from the murder until Sheppard's conviction in December 1954. The record includes no excerpts from newscasts on radio and television but since space was reserved in the courtroom for these media we assume that their coverage was equally large.

II.

With this background the case came on for trial two weeks before the November general election at which the chief prosecutor was a candidate for municipal judge and the presiding judge, Judge Blythin, was a candidate to succeed himself. Twenty-five days before the case was set, a list of 75 veniremen were called as prospective jurors. This list, including the addresses of each venireman, was published in all three Cleveland newspapers. As a consequence, anonymous letters and telephone calls, as well as calls from friends, regarding the impending prosecution were received by all of the prospective jurors. The selection of the jury began on October 18, 1954.

The courtroom in which the trial was held measured 26 by 48 feet. A long temporary table was set up inside the bar, in back of the single counsel table. It ran the width of the courtroom, parallel to the bar railing, with one end less than three feet from the jury box. Approximately 20 representatives of newspapers and wire services were assigned seats at this table by the court. Behind the bar railing there were four rows of benches. These seats were likewise assigned by the court for the entire trial. The first row was occupied by representatives of television and radio stations, and the second and third rows by reporters from out-of-town newspapers and magazines. One side of the last row, which accommodated 14 people, was assigned to Sheppard's family and the other to Marilyn's. The public was permitted to fill vacancies in this row on special passes only. Representatives of the news media also used all the rooms on the courtroom floor, including the room where cases were ordinarily called and assigned for trial. Private telephone lines and telegraphic equipment were installed in these rooms so that reports from the trial could be speeded to the papers. Station WSRS was permitted to set up broadcasting facilities on the third floor of the courthouse next door to the jury room, where the jury rested during recesses in the trial and deliberated. Newscasts were made from this room throughout the trial, and while the jury reached its verdict.

On the sidewalk and steps in front of the courthouse, television and newsreel cameras were occasionally used to take motion pictures of the participants in the trial, including the jury and the judge. Indeed, one television broadcast carried a staged interview of the judge as he entered the courthouse. In the corridors outside the courtroom there was a host of photographers and television personnel with flash cameras, portable lights and motion picture cameras. This group photographed the prospective jurors during selection of the jury. After the trial opened, the witnesses, counsel, and jurors were photographed and televised whenever they entered or left the courtroom. Sheppard was brought to the courtroom about 10 minutes before each session began; he was surrounded by reporters and extensively photographed for the newspapers and television. A rule of court prohibited picture-taking in the courtroom during the actual sessions of the court, but no restraints were put on photographers during recesses, which were taken once each morning and afternoon, with a longer period for lunch.

All of these arrangements with the news media and their massive coverage of the trial continued during the entire nine weeks of the trial.

The courtroom remained crowded to capacity with representatives of news media. Their movement in and out of the courtroom often caused so much confusion that, despite the loud speaker system installed in the courtroom, it was difficult for the witnesses and counsel to be heard. Furthermore, the reporters clustered within the bar of the small courtroom made confidential talk among Sheppard and his counsel almost impossible during the proceedings. They frequently had to leave the courtroom to obtain privacy. And many times when counsel wished to raise a point with the judge out of the hearing of the jury it was necessary to move to the judge's chambers. Even then, news media representatives so packed the judge's anteroom that counsel could hardly return from the chambers to the courtroom. The reporters vied with each other to find out what counsel and the judge had discussed, and often these matters later appeared in newspapers accessible to the jury.

The daily record of the proceedings was made available to the newspapers and the testimony of each witness was printed *verbatim* in the local editions, along with objections of counsel, and rulings by the judge. Pictures of Sheppard, the judge, counsel, pertinent witnesses, and the jury often accompanied the daily newspaper and television accounts. At times the newspapers published photographs of exhibits introduced at the trial, and the rooms of Sheppard's house were featured along with relevant testimony.

The jurors themselves were constantly exposed to the news media. Every juror, except one, testified at *voir dire* to reading about the case in the Cleveland papers or to having heard broadcasts about it. Seven of the 12 jurors who rendered the verdict had one or more Cleveland papers delivered in their home; the remaining jurors were not interrogated on the point. Nor were there questions as to radios or television sets in the talesmen's homes, but we must assume that most of them owned such conveniences. As the selection of the jury progressed, individual pictures of prospective members appeared daily. During the trial, pictures of the jury appeared over 40 times in the Cleveland papers alone. The court permitted photographers to take pictures of the jury in the box, and individual pictures of the members in the jury room. One newspaper ran pictures of the jurors at the Sheppard home when they went there to view the scene of the murder. Another paper featured the home life of an alternate juror. The day before the verdict was rendered—while the jurors were at lunch and sequestered by two bailiffs—the jury was separated into two groups to pose for photographs which appeared in the newspapers.

III.

We now reach the conduct of the trial. While the intense publicity continued unabated, it is sufficient to relate only the more flagrant episodes:

1. On October 9, 1954, nine days before the case went to trial, an editorial in one of the newspapers criticized defense counsel's random poll of people on the streets as to their opinion of Sheppard's guilt or innocence in an effort to use the resulting statistics to show the necessity for change of venue. The article said the survey "smacks of mass jury tampering," called on defense counsel to drop it, and stated that the bar association should do something about it. It characterized the poll as "non-judicial, non-legal, and nonsense." The article was called to the attention of the court but no action was taken.

2. On the second day of *voir dire* examination a debate was staged and broadcast live over WHK radio. The participants, newspaper reporters, accused Sheppard's counsel of throwing roadblocks in the way of the prosecution and asserted that Sheppard conceded his guilt by hiring a prominent criminal lawyer. Sheppard's counsel objected to this broadcast and requested a continuance, but the judge denied the motion. When counsel asked the court to give some protection from such events, the judge replied that "WHK doesn't have much coverage," and that "[a]fter all, we are not trying this case by radio or in newspapers or any other means. We confine ourselves seriously to it in this courtroom and do the very best we can."

3. While the jury was being selected, a two-inch headline asked: "But Who Will Speak for Marilyn?" The front-page story of the "perfect face" of the accused. "Study that face as long as you want. Never will you get from it a hint of what might be the answer. . . ." The two brothers of the accused were described as "Prosperous, poised. His two sisters-in-law. Smart, chic, well-groomed. His elderly father. Courtly, reserved. A perfect type for the patriarch of a staunch clan." The author then noted Marilyn Sheppard was "still off stage," and that she was an only child whose mother died when she was very young and whose father had no interest in the case. But the author—through quotes from Detective Chief James McArthur—assured readers that the prosecution's exhibits would speak for Marilyn. "Her story," McArthur stated, "will come into this courtroom through our witnesses." The article ends:

"Then you realize how what and who is missing from the perfect setting will be supplied.

"How in the Big Case justice will be done.

"Justice to Sam Sheppard.

"And to Marilyn Sheppard."

4. As has been mentioned, the jury viewed the scene of the murder on the first day of the trial. Hundreds of reporters, cameramen and onlookers were there, and one representative of the news media was permitted to accompany the jury while they inspected the Sheppard home. The time of the jury's visit was revealed so far in advance that one of the newspapers was able to rent a helicopter and fly over the house taking pictures of the jurors on their tour.

5. On November 19, a Cleveland police officer gave testimony that tended to contradict details in the written statement Sheppard made to the Cleveland police. Two days later, in a broadcast heard over Station WHK in Cleveland, Robert Considine likened Sheppard to a perjurer and compared the episode to Alger Hiss' confrontation with Whittaker Chambers. Though defense counsel asked the judge to question the jury to ascertain how many heard the broadcast, the court refused to do so. The judge also overruled the motion for continuance based on the same ground, saying:

> "Well, I don't know, we can't stop people, in any event, listening to it. It is a matter of free speech, and the court can't control everybody. . . . We are not going to harass the jury every morning. . . . It is getting to the point where if we do it every morning, we are suspecting the jury. I have confidence in this jury. . . ."

6. On November 24, a story appeared under an eight-column headline: "Sam Called A 'Jekyll-Hyde' By Marilyn, Cousin To Testify." It related that Marilyn had recently told friends that Sheppard was a "Dr. Jekyll and Mr. Hyde" character. No such testimony was ever produced at the trial. The story went on to announce: "The prosecution has a 'bombshell witness' on tap who will testify to Dr. Sam's display of fiery temper—countering the defense claim that the defendant is a gentle physician with an even disposition." Defense counsel made motions for change of venue, continuance and mistrial, but they were denied. No action was taken by the court.

7. When the trial was in its seventh week, Walter Winchell broad-

casted over WXEL television and WJW radio that Carole Beasley, who was under arrest in New York City for robbery, had stated that, as Sheppard's mistress, she had borne him a child. The defense asked that the jury be queried on the broadcast. Two jurors admitted in open court that they had heard it. The judge asked each: "Would that have any effect upon your judgment?" Both replied, "No." This was accepted by the judge as sufficient; he merely asked the jury to "pay no attention whatever to that type of scavenging . . . Let's confine ourselves to this courtroom, if you please." In answer to the motion for mistrial, the judge said:

"Well, even so, Mr. Corrigan, how are you ever going to prevent those things, in any event? I don't justify them at all. I think it is outrageous, but in a sense, it is outrageous even if there were no trial here. The trial has nothing to do with it in the Court's mind, as far as its outrage is concerned, but—"

"Mr. CORRIGAN: I don't know what effect it had on the mind of any of these jurors, and I can't find out unless inquiry is made."

"The COURT: How would you ever, in any jury, avoid that kind of a thing?"

8. On December 9, while Sheppard was on the witness stand he testified that he had been mistreated by Cleveland detectives after his arrest. Although he was not at the trial, Captain Kerr of the Homicide Bureau issued a press statement denying Sheppard's allegations which appeared under the headline: "'Bare-faced Liar,' Kerr Says of Sam." Captain Kerr never appeared as a witness at the trial.

9. After the case was submitted to the jury, it was sequestered for its deliberations, which took five days and four nights. After the verdict, defense counsel ascertained that the jurors had been allowed to make telephone calls to their homes every day while they were sequestered at the hotel. Although the telephones had been removed from the jurors' rooms, the jurors were permitted to use the phones in the bailiff's rooms. The calls were placed by the jurors themselves; no record was kept of the jurors who made calls, the telephone numbers or the parties called. The bailiffs sat in the room where they could hear only the jurors' end of the conversation. The court had not instructed the bailiffs to prevent such calls. By a subsequent motion, defense counsel urged that this ground alone warranted a new trial, but the motion was overruled and no evidence was taken on the question.

IV.

The principle that justice cannot survive behind walls of silence has long been reflected in the "Anglo-American distrust for secret trials." *In re Oliver,* 333 U.S. 257, 268 (1948). A responsible press has always been regarded as the handmaiden of effective judicial administration, especially in the criminal field. Its function in this regard is documented by an impressive record of service over several centuries. The press does not simply publish information about trials but guards against the miscarriage of justice by subjecting the police, prosecutors, and judicial processes to extensive public scrutiny and criticism. This Court has, therefore, been unwilling to place any direct limitations on the freedom traditionally exercised by the news media for "[w]hat transpires in the court room is public property." *Craig* v. *Harney,* 331 U.S. 367, 374 (1947). The "unqualified prohibitions laid down by the framers were intended to give to liberty of the press . . . the broadest scope that could be countenanced in an orderly society." *Bridges* v. *California,* 314 U.S. 252, 265 (1941). And where there was "no threat or menace to the integrity of the trial," *Craig* v. *Harney, supra,* at 377, we have consistently required that the press have a free hand, even though we sometimes deplored its sensationalism.

But the Court has also pointed out that "[l]egal trials are not like elections, to be won through the use of the meeting-hall, the radio, and the newspaper." *Bridges* v. *California, supra,* at 271. And the Court has insisted that no one be punished for a crime without "a charge fairly made and fairly tried in a public tribunal free of prejudice, passion, excitement, and tyranical power." *Chambers* v. *Florida,* 309 U.S. 227, 236–237 (1940). "Freedom of discussion should be given the widest range compatible with the essential requirement of the fair and orderly administration of justice." *Pennekamp* v. *Florida,* 328 U.S. 331, 347 (1946). But it must not be allowed to divert the trial from the "very purpose of a court system . . . to adjudicate controversies, both criminal and civil, in the calmness and solemnity of the courtroom according to legal procedures." *Cox* v. *Louisiana,* 379 U.S. 559, 583 (1965) (BLACK, J., dissenting). Among these "legal procedures" is the requirement that the jury's verdict be based on evidence received in open court, not from outside sources. Thus, in *Marshall* v. *United States,* 360 U.S. 310 (1959), we set aside a federal conviction where the jurors were exposed "through news accounts" to information that was not admitted at trial. We held that the prejudice from such material "may indeed be greater" than when it is part of the prosecution's evidence "for it is then not tempered by protective procedures." At 313. At the same time, we did not consider dispositive the statement of each juror "that he would not be influenced by the news articles, that he could decide the case only on the evidence of record, and that he felt no prejudice against petitioner as a result of the articles." At 312. Likewise, in *Irvin* v. *Dowd,* 366 U.S. 717 (1961), even though each juror indicated that he could render an impartial verdict despite exposure to prejudicial newspaper articles, we set aside the conviction holding:

> "With his life at stake, it is not requiring too much that petitioner be tried in an atmosphere undisturbed by so huge a wave of public passion. . . ." At 728.

The undeviating rule of this Court was expressed by Mr. Justice Holmes over half a century ago in *Patterson* v. *Colorado,* 205 U.S. 454, 462 (1907):

> "The theory of our system is that the conclusions to be reached in a case will be induced only by evidence and argument in open court, and not by any outside influence, whether of private talk or public print."

Moreover, "the burden of showing essential unfairness . . . as a demonstrable reality," *Adams* v. *United States ex rel. McCann,* 317 U.S. 269, 281 (1942), need not be undertaken when television has exposed the community "repeatedly and in depth to the spectacle of [the accused] personally confessing in detail to the crimes with which he was later to be charged." *Rideau v. Louisiana,* 373 U.S. 723, 726 (1963). In *Turner* v. *Louisiana,* 379 U.S. 466 (1965), two key witnesses were deputy sheriffs who doubled as jury shepherds during the trial. The deputies swore that they had not talked to the jurors about the case, but the Court nonetheless held that,

> "even if it could be assumed that the deputies never did discuss the case directly with any members of the jury, it would be blinking reality not to recognize the extreme prejudice inherent in this continual association. . . ." At 473.

Only last Term in *Estes* v. *Texas,* 381 U.S. 532 (1965), we set aside a conviction despite the absence of any showing of prejudice. We said there:

> "It is true that in most cases involving claims of due process deprivations we require a showing of identifiable prejudice to the accused. Nevertheless, at times a procedure employed by the State involves such a probability that prejudice will result that it is deemed inherently lacking in due process." At 542–543.

And we cited with approval the language of MR. JUSTICE BLACK for the Court in *In re Murchison,* 349 U.S. 133, 136 (1955), that "our system of law has always endeavored to prevent even the probability of unfairness."

V.

It is clear that the totality of circumstances in this case also warrant such an approach. Unlike Estes, Sheppard was not granted a change of venue to a locale away from where the publicity originated; nor was his jury sequestered. The Estes jury saw none of the television broadcasts from the courtroom. On the contrary, the Sheppard jurors were subjected to newspaper, radio and television coverage of the trial while not taking part in the proceedings. They were allowed to go their separate ways outside of the courtroom, without adequate directions not to read or listen to anything concerning the case. The judge's "admonitions" at the beginning of the trial are representative:

> "I would suggest to you and caution you that you do not read any newspapers during the progress of this trial, that you do not listen to radio comments nor watch or listen to television comments, insofar as this case is concerned. You will feel very much better as the trial proceeds. . . . I am sure that we shall all feel very much better if we do not indulge in any newspaper reading or listening to any comments whatever about the matter while the case is in progress. After it is all over, you can read it all to your heart's content. . . ."

At intervals during the trial, the judge simply repeated his "suggestions" and "requests" that the jury not expose themselves to comment upon the case. Moreover, the jurors were thrust into the role of celebrities by the judge's failure to insulate them from reporters and photographers. See *Estes* v. *Texas, supra,* at 545-546. The numerous pictures of the jurors, with their addresses, which appeared in the newspapers before and during the trial itself exposed them to expressions of opinion from both cranks and friends. The fact that anonymous letters had been received by prospective jurors should have made the judge aware that this publicity seriously threatened the jurors' privacy.

The press coverage of the Estes trial was not nearly as massive and pervasive as the attention given by the Cleveland newspapers and broadcasting stations to Sheppard's prosecution.[8] Sheppard stood indicted for the murder of his wife; the State was demanding the death penalty. For months the virulent publicity about Sheppard and the murder had made the case notorious. Charges and countercharges were aired in the news media besides those for which Sheppard was called to trial. In addition, only three months before trial, Sheppard was examined for more than five hours without counsel during a three-day inquest which ended in a public brawl. The inquest was televised live from a high school gymnasium seating hundreds of people. Furthermore, the trial began two weeks before a hotly contested election at which both Chief Prosecutor Mahon and Judge Blythin were candidates for judgeships.[9]

While we cannot say that Sheppard was denied due process by the judge's refusal to take precautions against the influence of pretrial publicity alone, the court's later rulings must be considered against the setting in which the trial was held. In light of this background, we believe that the arrangements made by the judge with the news media caused Sheppard to be deprived of that "judicial serenity and calm to which [he] was entitled." *Estes* v. *Texas, supra,* at 536. The fact is that bedlam reigned at the courthouse during the trial and newsmen took over practically the entire courtroom, hounding most of the participants in the trial, especially Sheppard. At a temporary table within a few feet of the jury box and counsel table sat some 20 reporters staring at Sheppard and taking notes. The erection of a press table for reporters inside the bar is unprecedented. The bar of the court is reserved for counsel, providing them a safe place in which to keep papers and exhibits, and to confer privately with client and co-counsel. It is designed to protect the witness and the jury from any distractions, intrusions or influences, and to permit bench discussions of the judge's rulings away from the hearing of the public and the jury. Having assigned almost all of the available seats in the courtroom to the news media the judge lost his ability to supervise that environment. The movement of the reporters in and out of the courtroom caused frequent confusion and disruption of the trial. And the record reveals constant commotion within the bar. Moreover, the judge gave the throng of newsmen gathered in the corridors of the courthouse absolute free rein. Participants in the trial, including the jury, were forced to run a gantlet of reporters and photographers each time they entered or left the courtroom. The total lack of consideration for the privacy of the jury was demonstrated by the assignment to a broadcasting station of space next to the jury room on the floor above the courtroom, as well as the fact that jurors were allowed to make telephone calls during their five-day deliberation.

VI.

There can be no question about the nature of the publicity which surrounded Sheppard's trial. We agree, as did the Court of Appeals, with the findings in Judge Bell's opinion for the Ohio Supreme Court:

> "Murder and mystery, society, sex and suspense were combined in this case in such a manner as to intrigue and captivate the public fancy to a degree perhaps unparalleled in recent annals. Throughout the preindictment investigation, the subsequent legal skirmishes and the nine-week trial, circulation-conscious editors catered to the insatiable interest of the American public in the bizarre. . . . In this atmosphere of a 'Roman holiday' for the news media, Sam Sheppard stood trial for his life." 165 Ohio St., at 294.

Indeed, every court that has considered this case, save the court that tried it, has deplored the manner in which the news media inflamed and prejudiced the public.[10]

Much of the material printed or broadcast during the trial was never heard from the witness stand, such as the charges that Sheppard had purposely impeded the murder investigation and must be guilty since he had hired a prominent criminal lawyer; that Sheppard was a perjurer; that he had sexual relations with numerous women; that his slain wife had characterized him as a "Jekyll-Hyde"; that he was "a bare-faced liar" because of his testimony as to police treatment; and, finally, that a woman convict claimed Sheppard to be the father of her illegitimate child. As the trial progressed, the newspapers summarized and interpreted the evidence, devoting particular attention to the material that incriminated Sheppard, and often drew unwarranted inferences from testimony. At one point, a front-page picture of Mrs. Sheppard's blood-stained pillow was published after being "doctored" to show more clearly an alleged imprint of a surgical instrument.

Nor is there doubt that this deluge of publicity reached at least some of the jury. On the only occasion that the jury was queried, two jurors admitted in open court to hearing the highly inflammatory charge that a prison inmate claimed Sheppard as the father of her illegitimate child. Despite the extent and nature of the publicity to which the jury was exposed during trial, the judge refused defense counsel's other requests that the jury be asked whether they had read or heard specific prejudicial comment about the case, including the incidents we have previously summarized. In these circumstances, we can assume that some of this material reached members of the jury. See *Commonwealth* v. *Crehan,* 345 Mass. 609, 188 N.E. 2d 923 (1963).

VII.

The court's fundamental error is compounded by the holding that it lacked power to control the publicity about the trial. From the very inception of the proceedings the judge announced that neither he nor anyone else could restrict prejudicial news accounts. And he reiterated this view on numerous occasions. Since he viewed the news media as his target, the judge never considered other means that are often utilized to reduce the appearance of prejudicial material and to protect the jury from outside influence. We conclude that these procedures would have been sufficient to guarantee Sheppard a fair trial and so do not consider what sanctions might be available against a recalcitrant press nor the charges of bias now made against the state trial judge.[11]

The carnival atmosphere at trial could easily have been avoided since the courtroom and courthouse premises are subject to the control of the court. As we stressed in *Estes,* the presence of the press at judicial proceedings must be limited when it is apparent that the accused might otherwise be prejudiced or disadvantaged.[12] Bearing in mind the massive pretrial publicity, the judge should have adopted stricter rules governing the use of the courtroom by newsmen, as Sheppard's counsel requested. The number of reporters in the courtroom itself could have been limited at the first sign that their presence would disrupt the trial. They certainly should not have been placed inside the bar. Furthermore, the judge should have more closely regulated the conduct of newsmen in the courtroom. For instance, the judge belatedly asked them not to handle and photograph trial exhibits laying on the counsel table during recesses.

Secondly, the court should have insulated the witnesses. All of the newspapers and radio stations apparently interviewed prospective witnesses at will, and in many instances disclosed their testimony. A typical example was the publication of numerous statements by Susan Hayes, before her appearance in court, regarding her love affair with Sheppard.

Although the witnesses were barred from the courtroom during the trial the full *verbatim* testimony was available to them in the press. This completely nullified the judge's imposition of the rule. See *Estes* v. *Texas, supra,* at 547.

Thirdly, the court should have made some effort to control the release of leads, information, and gossip to the press by police officers, witnesses, and the counsel for both sides. Much of the information thus disclosed was inaccurate, leading to groundless rumors and confusion.[13] That the judge was aware of his responsibility in this respect may be seen from his warning to Steve Sheppard, the accused's brother, who had apparently made public statements in an attempt to discredit testimony for the prosecution. The judge made this statement in the presence of the jury:

> "Now, the court wants to say a word. That he was told—he has not read anything about it at all—but he was informed that Dr. Steve Sheppard, who has been granted the privilege of remaining in the courtroom during the trial, has been trying the case in the newspapers and making rather uncomplimentary comments about the testimony of the witnesses for the State.
>
> "Let it be now understood that if Dr. Steve Sheppard wishes to use the newspapers to try his case while we are trying it here, he will be barred from remaining in the courtroom during the progress of the trial if he is to be a witness in the case.
>
> "The Court appreciates he cannot deny Steve Sheppard the right of free speech, but he can deny him the . . . privilege of being in the courtroom, if he wants to avail himself of that method during the progress of the trial."

Defense counsel immediately brought to the court's attention the tremendous amount of publicity in the Cleveland press that "misrepresented entirely the testimony" in the case. Under such circumstances, the judge should have at least warned the newspapers to check the accuracy of their accounts. And it is obvious that the judge should have further sought to alleviate this problem by imposing control over the statements made to the news media by counsel, witnesses, and especially the Coroner and police officers. The prosecution repeatedly made evidence available to the news media which was never offered in the trial. Much of the "evidence" disseminated in this fashion was clearly inadmissible. The exclusion of such evidence in court is rendered meaningless when a news media makes it available to the public. For example, the publicity about Sheppard's refusal to take a lie detector test came directly from police officers and the Coroner.[14] The story that Sheppard had been called a "Jekyll-Hyde" personality by his wife was attributed to a prosecution witness. No such testimony was given. The further report that there was "a 'bombshell witness' on tap" who would testify as to Sheppard's "fiery temper" could only have emanated from the prosecution. Moreover, the newspapers described in detail clues that had been found by the police, but not put into the record.[15]

The fact that many of the prejudicial news items can be traced to the prosecution, as well as the defense, aggravates the judge's failure to take any action. See *Stroble* v. *California,* 343 U.S. 181, 201 (1952) (FRANKFURTER, J., dissenting). Effective control of these sources—concededly within the court's power—might well have prevented the divulgence of inaccurate information, rumors, and accusations that made up much of the inflammatory publicity, at least after Sheppard's indictment.

More specifically, the trial court might well have proscribed extrajudicial statements by any lawyer, party, witness, or court official which divulged prejudicial matters, such as the refusal of Sheppard to submit to interrogation or take any lie detector tests; any statement made by Sheppard to officials; the identity of prospective witnesses or their probable testimony; any belief in guilt or innocence; or like statements concerning the merits of the case. See *State* v. *Van Duyne,* 43 N.J. 369, 389, 204 A. 2d 841, 850 (1964), in which the court interpreted Canon 20 of the American Bar Association's Canons of Professional Ethics to prohibit such statements. Being advised of the great public interest in the case, the mass coverage of the press, and the potential prejudicial impact of publicity, the court could also have requested the appropriate city and county officials to promulgate a regulation with respect to dissemination of information about the case by their employees.[16] In addition, reporters who wrote or broadcasted prejudicial stories, could have been warned as to the impropriety of publishing material not introduced in the proceedings. The judge was put on notice of such events by defense counsel's complaint about the WHK broadcast on the second day of trial. [See p. 393, *supra.*] In this manner, Sheppard's right to a trial free from outside interference would have been given added protection without corresponding curtailment of the news media. Had the judge, the other officers of the court, and the police placed the interest of justice first, the news media would have soon learned to be content with the task of reporting the case as it unfolded in the courtroom—not pieced together from extra-judicial statements.

From the cases coming here we note that unfair and prejudicial news comment on pending trials has become increasingly prevalent. Due process requires that the accused receive a trial by an impartial jury free from outside influences. Given the pervasiveness of modern communications and the difficulty of effacing prejudicial publicity from the minds of the jurors, the trial courts must take strong measures to ensure that the balance is never weighed against the accused. And appellate tribunals have the duty to make an independent evaluation of the circumstances. Of course, there is nothing that proscribes the press from reporting events that transpire in the courtroom. But where there is a reasonable likelihood that prejudicial news prior to trial will prevent a fair trial, the judge should continue the case until the threat abates, or transfer it to another county not so permeated with publicity. In addition, sequestration of the jury was something the judge should have raised *sua sponte* with counsel. If publicity during the proceedings threatens the fairness of the trial, a new trial should be ordered. But we must remember that reversals are but palliatives; the cure lies in those remedial measures that will prevent the prejudice at its inception. The courts must take such steps by rule and regulation that will protect their processes from prejudicial outside interferences. Neither prosecutors, counsel for defense, the accused, witnesses, court staff nor enforcement officers coming under the jurisdiction of the court should be permitted to frustrate its function. Collaboration between counsel and the press as to information affecting the fairness of a criminal trial is not only subject to regulation, but is highly censurable and worthy of disciplinary measures.

Since the state trial judge did not fulfill his duty to protect Sheppard from the inherently prejudicial publicity which saturated the community and to control disruptive influences in the courtroom, we must reverse the denial of the habeas petition. The case is remanded to the District Court with instructions to issue the writ and order that Sheppard be released from custody unless the State puts him to its charges again within a reasonable time.

It is so ordered.

Mr. Justice Black dissents.

NOTES

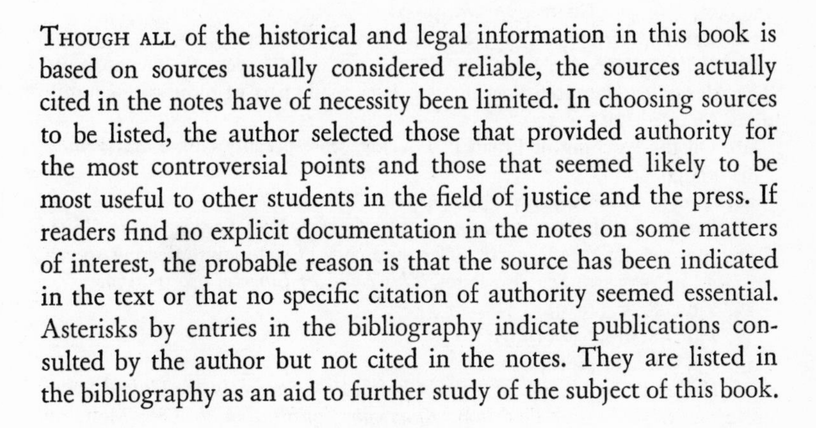

THOUGH ALL of the historical and legal information in this book is based on sources usually considered reliable, the sources actually cited in the notes have of necessity been limited. In choosing sources to be listed, the author selected those that provided authority for the most controversial points and those that seemed likely to be most useful to other students in the field of justice and the press. If readers find no explicit documentation in the notes on some matters of interest, the probable reason is that the source has been indicated in the text or that no specific citation of authority seemed essential. Asterisks by entries in the bibliography indicate publications consulted by the author but not cited in the notes. They are listed in the bibliography as an aid to further study of the subject of this book.

INTRODUCTION

1. See text of Jones speech in 26 New York State Bar Bulletin 206 (July 1954).
2. Darrow quoted in Perry, *The Courts, the Press, and the Public,* 30 Mich. L. Rev. 234 (Dec. 1931).
3. *Report of the Warren Commission* (New York Times ed., Bantam Book), pp. 216, 220, 222, 223, 224.
4. See section page of the St. Louis *Post-Dispatch,* April 26, 1965.
5. American Bar Association, "Report of Special Committee on Cooperation Between Press, Radio and Bar," ABA Annual Report, vol. 62, at 861 (1937).
6. See cases cited in notes 20 through 23, Chapter 4.

CHAPTER I

1. Thayer, *Legal Control of the Press,* p. 7. Other sources for the first two sections of this chapter include: Bowra, *The Greek Experience*; Shotwell, *Way to Freedom*; Chafee, *Freedom of Speech and Press.*

2. Rubinstein and Farley, *Books Which Have Survived,* pp. 24-25.

3. Chafee, *op. cit.,* p. 30.

4. Levy, *Legacy of Suppression,* pp. 9, 10-11, 15-16, 95, 100, 103, 104, 131, 133. Other sources for this section include: Perry and Cooper, *Sources of Our Liberties,* pp. 243, 308; Thayer, *op. cit.,* pp. 8-11; Chafee, *op. cit.*

5. Quoted in Mott, *American Journalism,* p. 6.

6. Levy, *op. cit.,* pp. 176-177, 181-182. Other sources for this section include: Schlesinger, *Prelude to Independence*; Hallgren, *Landscape of Freedom.* On Peter Zenger, see Buranelli, *Trial of Peter Zenger,* pp. iii, 24-25, 30-32, 68-70.

7. Mott, *op. cit.,* p. 144; Perry and Cooper, *op. cit.,* pp. 310, 312, 330, 340, 350, 356, 376, 385; Chafee, *op. cit.,* p. 41.

8. Levy, *op. cit.,* pp. 252-253. See also Mott, *op. cit.,* pp. 142-152.

9. *Ibid.,* pp. 169-170; Levy, *op. cit.,* pp. 297-299; Thayer, *op. cit.,* pp. 24-26. The Alexander Hamilton doctrine was later made part of most state constitutions. Mott, *op. cit.,* p. 170.

10. On the lynching of Elijah P. Lovejoy, see especially Gill, *Tide Without Turning,* pp. 60-74.

11. Quoted in Mott, *op. cit.,* pp. 309-310.

12. Barck and Blake, *Since 1900,* p. 365; Chafee, *Free Speech in the United States,* pp. 326-327, 343ff., 385ff. For a summary of state laws affecting speech, see *ibid.,* pp. 575-597. See also Bates, *This Land of Liberty,* pp. 169-170.

13. 249 U.S. 47 (1919).

14. 250 U.S. 616, 630 (1919).

15. 252 U.S. 239 (1920).

16. Hallgren, *op. cit.,* pp. 371, 372; Chafee, *Free Speech in the United States,* pp. 208-215; Kelly and Harbison, *American Constitution,* p. 680; Mott, *op. cit.,* p. 700.

17. 268 U.S. 652 (1925).

18. 283 U.S. 697 (1931).

19. 297 U.S. 233 (1936).

20. 299 U.S. 353 (1937).

21. 301 U.S. 242 (1937).

22. Thayer, *op. cit.,* pp. 47-48; Gellhorn, *American Rights,* p. 74; Kelly and Harbison, *op. cit.,* pp. 849, 851, 891; Corwin, *Total War and the Constitution,* p. 108.

23. Gellhorn, *op. cit.,* p. 75; Kelly and Harbison, *op. cit.,* p. 891; Corwin, *op. cit.,* pp. 111-115.

24. 322 U.S. 680 (1944).

25. 319 U.S. 583 (1943).

26. See *Terminiello v. Chicago,* 337 U.S. 1 (1949).
27. 341 U.S. 494 (1951).
28. 354 U.S. 298 (1957).
29. 350 U.S. 497 (1956).
30. *New York Times v. Sullivan,* 376 U.S. 254 (1964).

CHAPTER 2

1. On the origins of criminal law, see Trever, *Ancient Civilization,* pp. 33, 34, 35, 37, 38, 102, 186, 187, 188, 189; Wigmore, *Kaleidoscope of Justice,* pp. 5-17, 262, 264, 714, 717, 718, 719, 720, 721, 723, 727-729, 731-732; Barnes and Teeters, *New Horizons in Criminology* (3d ed. 1959), pp. 269-270, 285, 286, 287, 328-329, 330-331; Hibbert, *Roots of Evil,* pp. 7, 8, 265.

2. Vanderbilt, *Judges and Jurors,* p. 52.

3. *Ibid.,* pp. 14-15.

4. Martin, *Break Down the Walls,* p. 109.

5. Howard, *John Howard,* pp. 70, 71, 75, 76, 77, 88, 89, 93, 94. In 1666 at Auvergne 276 criminals were hanged, 44 were beheaded, 32 were broken on the wheel, 28 were sent to the galleys, three were burned. Hibbert, *op. cit.,* p. 34.

6. On the constitutional guarantees, see generally Fellman, *Defendant's Rights*; Perry and Cooper, *op. cit.*; Fraenkel, *The Supreme Court and Civil Liberties*; Corwin, *Constitution of the United States.*

7. *Weeks v. U.S.,* 232 U.S. 383 (1914); *Mapp v. Ohio,* 367 U.S. 643 (1961).

8. Fellman, *op. cit.,* pp. 175-176. See *Chambers v. Fla.,* 309 U.S. 227 (1940).

9. Special Committee of The Association of the Bar of the City of New York and the National Legal Aid and Defender Association, *Equal Justice for the Accused,* pp. 40-41; Fellman, *op. cit.,* p. 113; Perry and Cooper, *op. cit.,* pp. 252, 254.

10. *Powell v. Ala.,* 287 U.S. 45 (1932).

11. *Gideon v. Wainwright,* 372 U.S. 335 (1963); *Escobedo v. Ill.,* 378 U.S. 478 (1964).

12. Fellman, *op. cit.,* pp. 23-24. See *Stack v. Boyle,* 342 U.S. 1, 4 (1951).

13. See *Cummings v. Mo.,* 4 Wall. 277 (1867); *Ex parte Garland,* 4 Wall. 333 (1867); *U.S. v. Lovett,* 328 U.S. 303 (1946).

14. See *U.S. v. Hall,* 26 Fed. Cas. 84, 86 (1809).

15. 3 Dall. 385, 386 (1798).

16. *U.S. v. Provoo,* 350 U.S. 857 (1955).

17. *In re Oliver,* 33 U.S. 257 (1948).

18. Fellman, *op. cit.,* pp. 56-57. See *United Press Assoc. v. Valente,* 308 N. Y. 71, 123 N. E. 2d 777 (1954); *People v. Jelke,* 130 N. Y. S. 2d 662, 680 (1st Dept. 1954).

19. *U.S. v. Coplon,* 185 F. 2d 629 (2d Cir. 1950); *Jencks v. U.S.,* 353 U.S. 657 (1957).

20. *Pointer v. Tex.,* 380 U.S. 400 (1965).

21. *Patton v. U.S.,* 281 U.S. 276 (1930).

22. Note, *Community Hostility and the Right to an Impartial Jury,* 60 Colum. L. Rev. 357-358 (1960). Sometimes it is held that belief in the reliability of the source is the criterion. *Ibid.,* 357, footnote 44.

23. *Glasser v. U.S.,* 315 U.S. 60, 86 (1942).

24. *Ruthenberg v. U.S.,* 245 U.S. 480 (1918); *Thiel v. Southern Pacific,* 328 U.S. 217 (1946).

25. *Ex parte Virginia,* 100 U.S. 339 (1880).

26. *Strauder v. West Va.,* 100 U.S. 303 (1880); *Neal v. Del.,* 103 U.S. 370 (1881); *Norris v. Ala.,* 294 U.S. 587 (1935).

27. *Cassell v. Tex.,* 339 U.S. 282, 287 (1950); *Swain v. Ala.,* 380 U.S. 202, 204 (1964).

28. *Hernandez v. Tex.,* 347 U.S. 475 (1954).

29. 378 U.S. 1 (1964).

30. 380 U.S. 609 (1965).

31. *Counselman v. Hitchcock,* 142 U.S. 547 (1892); *McCarthy v. Arndstein,* 266 U.S. 34 (1924).

32. *Ullmann v. U.S.,* 350 U.S. 422 (1956).

33. See note, *Double Jeopardy: The Reprosecution Problem,* 77 Harv. L. Rev. 1272, 1273 (1964).

34. For a history of the protection against double jeopardy see the dissent by Justice Hugo Black in *Bartkus v. Ill.,* 359 U.S. 121, 150-155 (1959).

35. Fellman, *op. cit.,* pp. 195-196. See *U.S. v. Perez,* 9 Wheat. (U.S.) 579 (1824); *Logan v. U.S.,* 144 U.S. 263, 298 (1892). On the jeopardy rule in mistrials over prejudicial publicity, see *Simmons v. U.S.,* 142 U.S. 148 (1891).

36. *U.S. v. Lanza,* 260 U.S. 377 (1922).

37. *Bartkus v. Ill.,* 359 U.S. 121 (1959); *Abbate v. U.S.,* 359 U.S. 187 (1959).

38. *Kepner v. U.S.,* 195 U.S. 100 (1904). In the 1964 case of *U.S. v. Tateo,* the U.S. Supreme Court held that the government could retry a defendant whose conviction was reversed after he had been improperly coerced into pleading guilty by the trial judge. 377 U.S. 463.

39. *Palko v. Conn.,* 302 U.S. 319 (1937).

40. Fellman, *op. cit.,* pp. 68-69. See *Wales v. Whitney,* 114 U.S. 564 (1885); *Johnson v. Hoy,* 227 U.S. 245 (1913); *McNally v. Hill,* 293 U.S. 131 (1934); *Johnson v. Zerbst,* 304 U.S. 458 (1938); *Bowen v. Johnston,* 306 U.S. 19 (1939). See comment, 113 U. Pa. L. Rev. 1303 (1965); Reitz, *Federal Habeas Corpus,* 74 Harv. L. Rev. 1315 (1961).

41. The states were Virginia, Delaware, Maryland, North Carolina, Massachusetts, and New Hampshire. Perry and Cooper, *op. cit.,* pp. 312, 339, 347, 348, 355, 377, 384, 385.

42. South Carolina and Georgia. Perry and Cooper, *op. cit.,* p. 310.

43. *Weems v. U.S.,* 217 U.S. 349 (1910).

44. *Dye v. Johnson*, 338 U.S. 864 (1949).
45. *Sweeney v. Woodall*, 344 U.S. 86 (1952).
46. *Robinson v. Cal.*, 369 U.S. 824 (1962).
47. Corwin, *Constitution of the United States*, pp. 844-845, 847, 971, 985, 1096-1139.

CHAPTER 3

1. Quoted in Mott, *The News in America*, p. 50.
2. Beirne, *Shout Treason*, pp. 22, 55-56, 57-60, 83, 113, 122, 123, 202.
3. Mott, *American Journalism*, pp. 233, 238, 239, 297.
4. Baskette, "Reporting the Webster Case," *Journalism Quarterly*, XXIV (Sept. 1947), 250-257; Kunstler, *First Degree*, p. 13.
5. Hale, *Greeley*, pp. 321-324.
6. Kennedy, *Profiles in Courage*, Chapter 6; Dickler, *Man on Trial*, p. 111.
7. Berger, *Story of the Times*, pp. 35, 44-45, 47, 48, 50, 51, 52.
8. Mott, *American Journalism*, pp. 381, 488.
9. *Ibid.*, pp. 386, 387, 434, 442, 465; Harris, *Presentation of Crime*, p. 2.
10. Mott, *American Journalism*, pp. 314, 316, 401, 497-498, 499, 500, 600, 601.
11. Bock, "Great News Events," *Editor and Publisher*, vol. 92 (June 27, 1959), Section 2, pp. 188-194.
12. Mott, *American Journalism*, p. 488.
13. Tebel, *American Dynasty*, pp. 53, 54, 56; Mott, *American Journalism*, p. 487; Morris, *Fair Trial*, pp. 296-300.
14. *Ibid.*, pp. 321, 330.
15. Borchard, *Convicting the Innocent*, pp. 286, 288, 291.
16. Mott, *American Journalism*, p. 488.
17. Radin, *Lizzie Borden*, pp. 78, 80, 87, 90, 91, 98, 99, 122, 154, 190, 255, 256; Mott, *American Journalism*, p. 578.
18. Chafee, *Government and Mass Communications*, I, 385. For judge's criticism of newspapers, see *People v. Durrant*, 116 Cal. 223 (1897).
19. Mott, *American Journalism*, pp. 523-524.
20. *Editorials from Hearst Newspapers*, pp. 82, 84, 85.
21. Mott, *American Journalism*, pp. 539-540, 541, 567-568.
22. *Ibid.*, p. 578; Langford, *Murder of Stanford White*, pp. 49, 127, 153, 154, 236, 252.
23. Mott, *American Journalism*, p. 698. See also Kunstler, *op. cit.*, pp. 59, 60, 72.
24. Sullivan, *Trial by Newspaper*, pp. 21-40. This author's judgments are made suspect by his shrill, partisan cry against newspapers, but he offers some useful information.
25. Hays, *Trial by Prejudice*, pp. 302-321; Mott, *American Journalism*,

p. 698. See also Kunstler, *Justice for All,* pp. 24, 34, 35. Harry Golden's book on the Frank case, *A Little Girl Is Dead,* was published too late for use in this study.

26. Wells, *Fremont Older,* pp. 303, 305, 311; Mott, *American Journalism,* p. 573.

27. *Causes of Crime,* National Commission on Law Observance, I, 94-115, 242, 243.

28. Symes, *American Dreyfus Case,* pp. 2, 9, 11-12, 17, 41-42, 43, 44, 45-46.

29. Quoted in Hays, *op. cit.,* p. 248.

30. Painter, *That Man Debs,* pp. 114, 115, 116, 117, 118.

31. Quotations from Coleman, *Eugene V. Debs,* pp. 287, 288.

32. Quoted in Painter, *op. cit.,* p. 137.

33. Quoted in Coleman, *op. cit.,* p. 298.

34. Barck and Blake, *op. cit.,* p. 276; Bates, *op. cit.,* pp. 179-181; New York *Times,* Nov. 11, 1962, p. 123.

35. Fraenkel, *Sacco-Vanzetti Case,* pp. 17-18, 19, 22-23.

36. Moley, *Our Criminal Courts,* pp. 192-193.

37. Weinberg, *Attorney for Damned,* p. 18; McKernan, *Leopold and Loeb* (Signet ed.), pp. vii, viii, 12-13, 16, 20; Kunstler, *First Degree,* p. 74.

38. Mott, *American Journalism,* p. 701; Weinberg, *op. cit.,* pp. 174, 228; Lofton, *Justice and the Press,* 6 St. Louis U. L. J. 479, 482.

39. *New York State Crime Commission Report,* pp. 312-318, 321, 322.

40. Morris, *op. cit.,* p. 424; Mott, *American Journalism,* p. 671; Kunstler, *First Degree,* p. 102.

41. Mott, *American Journalism,* pp. 669, footnote 7, 670, 671.

42. Barck and Blake, *op. cit.,* pp. 799-800; Hays, *op. cit.,* pp. 36, 37, 38; Berger, *op. cit.,* pp. 258, 399.

43. *Ibid.,* pp. 387, 388; Morris, *Deadline Every Minute,* p. 187.

44. Miller, "Reporting the Hauptmann Trial," (unpublished thesis), pp. 139-140, 154; Waller, *Kidnap* (Pocket Books ed.), pp. 293, 294, 295.

45. Morris, *Deadline Every Minute,* pp. 188, 189, 190.

46. Berger, *op. cit.,* pp. 411, 412.

47. St. George and Dennis, *Trial on Trial,* pp. 16, 22.

48. Morris, *Fair Trial,* p. 494; Liebling, *The Press,* p. 143.

49. *Newsweek,* Nov. 1, 1954, p. 56; *Time,* Nov. 22, 1954, pp. 87-88.

50. Breed, "Comparative Newspaper Handling of the Emmett Till Case," *Journalism Quarterly,* XXXV (Summer 1958), 298; Booker, "Till Trial," *Nieman Reports,* Jan. 1956, pp. 13-15.

51. *Editor and Publisher,* Feb. 20, 1960, p. 67.

52. See Lofton, "Too Interested in the Sensational," *The Masthead,* XVI (Spring 1964), 23-26.

53. See *Report of the Warren Commission* (New York Times ed., Bantam Book), pp. 189-194, 220, 221, 222-224.

CHAPTER 4

1. *Roach v. Garvan,* 2 Atk. 469, 471 (Ch. 1742). For a historical account of judicial actions aimed at curbing prejudicial publicity, see McEvoy & Newman, note, *Free Press: Fair Trial—Rights in Collision,* 34 N. Y. U. L. Rev. 1278-1298 (1959).

2. Quoted in Thayer, *op. cit.*, p. 544.

3. Mott, *American Journalism,* p. 173.

4. 7 American State Trials 416 (Lawson ed.).

5. *State v. Morrill,* 16 Ark. 384 (1855).

6. *Ex parte Robinson,* 86 U.S. 505, 510-511 (1873).

7. *Patterson v. State of Colorado ex rel. Attorney General,* 205 U.S. 454 (1907).

8. Train, *Prisoner at the Bar,* pp. 347-348.

9. *U.S. v. Ogden,* 105 Fed. 371, 373 (D.C. Pa. 1900).

10. *Toledo Newspaper Co. v. U.S.,* 247 U.S. 402 (1918).

11. Mott, *American Journalism,* pp. 569, 726; Barrett, *Joseph Pulitzer and His World,* p. 385, says Bonfils received $350,000 from Harry F. Sinclair.

12. *Tribune* quoted in Burch, "Press and Justice," 27 *State Government* 230 (Nov. 1954).

13. Miller, *op. cit.*, p. 141.

14. American Bar Association, "Report of Special Committee on Cooperation Between Press, Radio and Bar," ABA Annual Report, vol. 62, at 851-866 (1937).

15. *Nye v. U.S.,* 313 U.S. 33 (1941).

16. *Bridges v. Cal.,* 314 U.S. 252 (1941).

17. *Pennekamp v. Fla.,* 328 U.S. 331 (1946).

18. *Craig v. Harney,* 331 U.S. 367 (1947).

19. 341 U.S. 50-55.

20. *Marshall v. U.S.,* 360 U.S. 310 (1959).

21. 366 U.S. 717 (1961).

22. *Rideau v. La.,* 373 U.S. 723 (1963).

23. *Estes v. Tex.,* 33 U.S. Law Week 4543 (1965).

24. *Editor and Publisher,* Dec. 15, 1962, p. 53. See Appendix B for guidelines adopted by various organizations.

25. *Report of the Warren Commission* (New York Times ed., Bantam Book), pp. 214, 215, 216, 217, 218, 220, 222-223, 224.

26. New York *Times,* Nov. 17, 1964, pp. 1, 33.

CHAPTER 5

1. Asch, "Opinions and Social Pressure," *Scientific American,* Nov. 1955, pp. 32-33. See also Fitzgerald, *Communicating Ideas to the Public,* pp. 86-87, on bandwagon effects.

2. Moley, *op. cit.,* p. 194. New York County District Attorney Charles S. Whitman, apparently as a result of an editorial in Hearst's New York *American,* ordered his assistants to get an indictment before they finished their investigation in the case of the Flatiron fire many years ago. Haimbough, *Free Press Versus Fair Trial,* 26 U. Pitt. L. Rev. 492 (1965).

3. Haldeman-Julius, *Darrow's Two Great Trials,* p. 45.

4. Hays, *op. cit.,* pp. 353, 354; Haldeman-Julius, *op. cit.,* pp. 70, 74. See also Weinberg, *op. cit.,* pp. 229-268.

5. Bock, *op. cit.,* p. 192.

6. Hohenberg, *The Pulitzer Prize Story,* pp. 67-68.

7. Barrett, *op. cit.,* p. 385.

8. Transcript of television broadcast, "The Open Mind," Station WRCA, New York City, May 18, 1958, p. 6.

9. Douglas, *Vagrancy and Arrest on Suspicion,* 70 Yale L. J. 12 (1960).

10. U.S. Dept. of Justice *Uniform Crime Reports* (1964), p. 108.

11. *Editor and Publisher,* Nov. 26, 1960, p. 60.

12. Mueller, *The Law Relating to Police Interrogation Privileges and Limitations,* 52 J. Crim. L., C. & P. S. 3, 7 (1961).

13. See Lofton, *Justice and the Press,* 6 St. Louis U. L. J. 457-460 (1961).

14. Butterfield, "The St. Louis Post-Dispatch—Pulitzer's Prize," *Collier's,* Dec. 16, 1950, p. 27.

15. Wechsler, "Free Press versus Fair Trial," *Progressive,* March, 1965, p. 19; Zion, "The Suspect Confesses," *New York Times Magazine,* May 16, 1965, p. 30; Ross, "Trial by Newspaper," *Atlantic,* Sept. 1965, pp. 63, 68; New York *Times,* April 27, 1964, p. 21; April 28, 1964, p. 24. For further developments in Whitmore case, see New York *Times,* Jan. 27, 1965, p. 1; Jan. 28, 1965, p. 1; March 20, 1965, p. 23; May 2, 1965, p. 59; May 5, 1965, p. 51.

16. *Blackburn v. Ala.,* 361 U.S. 199 (1959).

17. Borchard, *op. cit.,* pp. xvii-xviii.

18. *Rogers v. Richmond,* 365 U.S. 534 (1961); *Chambers v. Fla.,* 309 U.S. 227 (1940).

19. Borchard, *op. cit.,* pp. xv-xvi. See, e.g., Foster case, described in Wood and Ross, *Nothing But the Truth,* pp. 77-78 (1960). For item on 400 press references to a defendant's conviction in another court, see Washington *Post,* Sept. 19, 1965, p. E3.

20. Frank, *Not Guilty,* pp. 113-114.

21. Lofton, *Justice and the Press,* 6 St. Louis U. L. J. 464-465 (1961).

22. Yankwich, *It's Libel or Contempt If You Print It,* p. 520. See, e.g., Duncan case described in *Editor and Publisher,* May 13, 1961, p. 71.

23. Burton W. Abbott case in San Francisco *Examiner,* July 21, 1955, p. 1. See Webb case related in Moley, *op. cit.,* p. 192.

24. Quoted in Schramm, *Responsibility in Mass Communication,* p. 181.

25. *Press* campaign described in *Editor and Publisher,* Dec. 10, 1960, pp. 9, 65.

26. Chambers, *Witness,* p. 626.
27. Jackson County *Sentinel,* April 3, 1931, quoted in Hays, *op. cit.,* p. 37.
28. Williams, *Due Process,* p. 90; interview with Davis by Lofton, April 11, 1961.
29. Lofton, *Justice and the Press,* 6 St. Louis U. L. J. 468-470, gives extended sources on "Press Comments on the Law."
30. For sources on "Press Influence on the Jury" and on next three sections, see *ibid.,* 475-481. For a report on recent research showing the adverse effect of prejudicial publicity on law school mock juries, see *Journalism Quarterly* (Spring 1966), 113-116. But for a recent report of a study showing only a slightly adverse influence on juries from sensational reporting, see Simon, "Murder, Juries and the Press," *Trans-action,* May-June, 1966, pp. 40-42.
31. Quoted in Ginger, *Six Days or Forever?* p. 129. See Lofton, *Justice and the Press,* 6 St. Louis U. L. J. 482-483, for sources on "Comment on Law and Other Factors."
32. *Bridges v. Cal.,* 314 U.S. 252 (1941); *Pennekamp v. Fla.,* 328 U.S. 331 (1946); *Craig v. Harney,* 331 U.S. 367 (1947).
33. Note, *Community Hostility and the Right to an Impartial Jury,* 60 Colum. L. Rev. 374 (1960).
34. Los Angeles *Times,* May 5, 1938.
35. See note, *Contempt by Publication,* 59 Yale L. J. 535 (1950).
36. Simmons, "The Communist Conspiracy Case: Views of 72 Daily Newspapers," *Journalism Quarterly* (March 1950), 6-9.
37. Quoted in Reynolds, *Courtroom,* p. 295.
38. Barnes and Teeters, *op. cit.,* p. 189.
39. Borchard, *op. cit.,* pp. 250-251, 256.
40. Frank, *op. cit.,* pp. 28-29.
41. See McCormick, *Sprung: The Release of Willie Calloway.*
42. Martin, "Did the Press Kill Caryl Chessman?" *The Progressive,* Dec. 1960, p. 17.

CHAPTER 6

1. Swanson, "What They Read in 130 Daily Newspapers," *Journalism Quarterly,* XXXII (Fall 1955), 417-418.
2. Rosenberg and White, *Mass Culture,* p. 165.
3. Ernst, letter to *Harper's Magazine,* May 1965, p. 6. Whatever their faults in adapting their content to the market for crime, most newspapers seem less zealous than some other segments of the communications industry. A recent study revealed that, of fifty-five general circulation magazines available at a representative Salt Lake City newsstand, seventeen were violence-filled men's magazines and eleven were police and detective magazines. Otto, "Sex and Violence," *Journalism Quarterly,* XL (Winter 1963), 19-20. The men's magazines contained an average of sixty-three incidents of violence, with an average of 4,157 words devoted to this theme. The police and detective magazines

had an average of seventy-seven incidents of violence, with an average of 6,199 words on the subject. In all of the fifty-five magazines there were 2,524 incidents of violence. *Ibid.*, pp. 21-22.

An analysis of 296 paperback books, chosen from another stand in Salt Lake City, showed that 44 per cent had covers falling in the seductive-sadistic-violence categories. *Ibid.*, pp. 20-21, 24. This survey of magazines and books led to the conclusion that the number of magazines specializing in violence and sex had increased markedly in ten years and that the amount of space devoted to these subjects, as well as the number of incidents portrayed, had been rising. *Ibid.*, p. 25.

4. Rosenberg and White, *op. cit.*, p. 147. See also Schramm, *op. cit.*, pp. 299-302.

5. Barnes and Teeters, *op. cit.*, pp. 4-5; Taft, *Criminology* (3d ed. 1956), p. 245. See also Goldstein, *Advantage in Criminal Procedure*, 69 Yale L. J. 1150 (1960).

6. Abrahamsen, *Who Are the Guilty?* p. 287; Allport, *The Nature of Prejudice*, p. 257, *passim;* Reik, *Compulsion to Confess*, p. 293.

7. Menninger, *Psychiatrist's World*, p. 743. Menninger has observed that violence on front pages indicates that the public loves it. New York *Times*, Dec. 13, 1964, p. 76.

8. See McCord, *Origins of Crime*, pp. 170-171.

9. Barnes and Teeters, *op. cit.*, pp. 285-286; Pound, *Criminal Justice*, p. 75; Taft, *op. cit.*, p. 359; McDonald, "Citizen Action," *NPPA Journal*, IV (Oct. 1958), 358. See also Erickson, *Psychiatry and the Law*, 1 Duke L. J. 31 (1961).

10. Blanshard, *The Right to Read*, p. 232; Swanson, *op. cit.*, p. 417. Yankwich, *op. cit.*, pp. 501, 529, quotes an authority as saying in 1926 that crime news was declining. But see Barnes and Teeters, *op. cit.*, p. 185.

11. Stempel, "Content Pattern of Small and Metropolitan Dailies," *Journalism Quarterly*, XXXIX (Winter 1962), 88-89. This press content study analyzing the four largest and the four smallest Michigan dailies found wide and unpredictable variations in the treatment of crime by different newspapers. As revealed by an examination of their issues for the week of October 16-21, 1961, the percentage of space allocated to crime ranged from 3.6 per cent for the Detroit *News* to 6.5 per cent for the Flint *Journal*. Among the small Michigan dailies, the amount of space given to crime during the same period ranged from 2.5 per cent for the South Haven *Tribune* to 5.9 per cent for the Dowagiac *News*. *Ibid.*, pp. 88-89.

12. Otto, "Sex and Violence," *Journalism Quarterly*, XL (Winter 1963), 20, 24. Taken by themselves, the figures from this survey of leading papers may be misleading. The largest circulation papers in various regions of the country are not necessarily representative of the press in general. More than one study has established that there are not only variations between individual big papers but also between small ones. A content analysis of metropolitan

dailies, as reported in 1959, showed vast differences in the treatment of crime among seven New York papers. (New York survey cited in Stempel, "Content Pattern of Small and Metropolitan Dailies," *Journalism Quarterly,* XXXIX (Winter 1962), 88, footnote 1.) Moreover, the survey of ten leading regional newspapers, reported by Otto, showed great discrepancies among the papers studied. The St. Louis *Post-Dispatch* devoted 2.1 per cent of its news space to items dealing with violence; the Detroit *News* gave 8.8 per cent of its space to this type of news; and the New York *Daily News* devoted 33.5 per cent of its news columns to topics of violence. In fact, the *Daily News* figure was considered conducive of such a distorted result that it was not included in calculating the average for the papers surveyed. Otto, "Sex and Violence," *Journalism Quarterly,* XL (Winter 1963), 24.

13. Gottlieb, "Reports of the Heirens Murder Case," *Journalism Quarterly,* XXIV (June 1947), 100, 102. Individually the *Sun* gave slightly more space to OPA news; the *Tribune,* slightly more to bomb tests. On distortion of meaning caused by sensationalizing of crime news, see Mott, *The News,* p. 56.

14. Analysis of Palo Alto *Times,* March 1 through April 25, 1961, by the author. The so-called better papers have not been reluctant to sensationalize crime. In examining the Boston *Evening Transcript* for all of May 1935, the author found crime news prominently played in most issues. Police records and confessions of suspects were regularly reported.

15. For examples of the playing down of news of white collar crimes, see Lofton, *Justice and the Press,* 6 St. Louis U. L. J. 471, footnote 85 (1961). These examples are representative of many others that could be cited. For a definition of white collar crime and comment on the minimizing of, see Caldwell, *Criminology,* pp. 64, 66-67.

16. Patterson quoted in Barnes and Teeters, *op. cit.,* p. 185. See also transcript of television broadcast, *The Open Mind,* Station WRCA, New York City, May 18, 1958, pp. 5, 9, 13.

17. Commission on Freedom of the Press, *A Free and Responsible Press,* pp. 54-55.

18. *New York State Crime Commission Report,* p. 312; Morris, *Fair Trial,* pp. 391-392; Runyon, *Trials and Tribulations,* p. 11.

19. *Editor and Publisher,* Feb. 2, 1957, p. 12; Feb. 23, 1957, p. 46; March 30, 1957, p. 130.

20. San Francisco *Examiner,* July 21, 1957, pp. 1-2; San Francisco *Chronicle,* July 22, 1957, p. 2. For further sources on this case, see notes on Rexinger case in the latter part of Chapter 6.

21. Colegrove, "Attitudes toward Crime News," *NPPA Journal,* IV (Oct. 1958), 313-314.

22. Treuhaft, "Trial by Headline," *The Nation,* Oct. 26, 1957, p. 282.

23. Brown, "A Newspaper's Obligations," *NPPA Journal,* IV (Oct. 1958), 308.

24. Barnes and Teeters, *op. cit.*, pp. 188-189; Harris, *op. cit.*, p. xiii; Münsterberg, *On the Witness Stand,* p. 139; Sutherland, "Crimes, Courts and Newspapers," *Nieman Reports,* April 1956, p. 41.

25. Bennett, "A Cool Look at 'The Crime Crisis,'" *Harper's Magazine,* April 1964, p. 125.

26. Taft, *op. cit.*, pp. 264-265. See also Krasner, "Hoodlum Priest and Respectable Convicts," *Harper's Magazine,* Feb. 1961, p. 58.

27. The authorities cited in note 24 and many others differ with the thesis offered by sociologist Richard LaPiere in his book, *The Freudian Ethic*—that the American public is indulgent toward criminal offenders.

28. New York *Times,* Sept. 3, 1959, p. 14.

29. New York *Times,* Oct. 13, 1959, p. 41.

30. Pittsburgh *Post-Gazette,* Nov. 30, 1959, p. 4.

31. Pittsburgh *Post-Gazette,* Feb. 22, 1960, p. 15.

32. See Raper, *Tragedy of Lynching,* pp. 23, 24, 66, 88, 111, 112, 113, 146, 239, 308, 363, 378. See also the case of *Moore et al. v. Dempsey,* 261 U.S. 86 (1923), in which the U.S. Supreme Court reversed the Arkansas conviction of five Negroes whose trial was held under mob pressure. Justice Holmes said in his opinion for the Supreme Court that the "newspapers had daily published inflammatory articles" while the trial was pending.

33. Breed, *op. cit.*, p. 298.

34. *Guild Reporter,* Sept. 23, 1949, p. 10. See *Shepherd v. Florida,* 341 U.S. 50 (1951).

35. Allport, *op. cit.*, pp. 257-258. For a detailed study of the Cocoanut Grove case, see Veltfort and Lee, "The Cocoanut Grove Fire: A Study in Scapegoating," *Journal of Abnormal Social Psychology,* 1943, p. 38; *Clinical Supplement,* 138-154.

36. Klapper, "Effects of Mass Communication," *Public Opinion Quarterly,* XXI (Winter 1957-58), 458. See also Rosenberg and White, *op. cit.*, p. 472.

37. Klapp, "American Villain-Types," *American Sociological Review,* XXI (June 1956), 337-338.

38. Caldwell, *op. cit.*, p. 66; Barnes and Teeters, *op. cit.*, pp. 42-43.

39. For examples, see short news story in New York *Times,* April 12, 1966, p. 28, under 14-point, one column headline, "Lawyer Indicted in Stealing/ Of $169,258 From 3 Clients"; one column picture in Pittsburgh *Press,* Jan. 6, 1965, p. 17, with the following caption: "SINGER FREED—A New York County grand jury refused to indict singer Fran Warren on charges of possessing narcotics with intent to sell." The question naturally arises as to whether these items would have been treated as so inconsequential if members of the so-called criminal class had been involved.

One writer, in commenting on violations of labor relations laws by shoe manufacturers, observed an unusual press influence on the attitudes of the executives involved. He noted that those "who had violated the law had immersed themselves in a segment of the daily press so hostile to government that violation of the law seemed quite appropriate to them." Here the newspapers "were providing verbalizations that made crime 'all right.'" Cressey, "The Respectable Criminal," *Trans-action,* March-April 1965, p. 15.

40. Reiwald, *Society and Its Criminals,* pp. 271-273.

41. Klapp, *op. cit.,* p. 340.

42. Davison, "On the Effects of Communication," *Public Opinion Quarterly,* XXIII (Fall 1959), 359.

43. United Press International story, Pittsburgh *Press,* July 24, 1961, p. 5; Associated Press story, New York *Times,* July 25, 1961, p. 24; United Press International story, New York *Times,* July 13, 1962, p. 38; Associated Press story, New York *Times,* July 19, 1963, p. 12; New York *Times,* July 21, 1964, pp. 1, 12.

44. Bennett, *op. cit.,* pp. 123, 124, 125.

45. Steffens, *Autobiography,* pp. 285-288. See also *New York State Crime Commission Report,* p. 322.

46. Barnes and Teeters, *op. cit.,* p. 6.

47. Bliven, "The Trenton Murder Case," *New Republic,* May 16, 1949, p. 14.

48. Advertisement by defense organizations, New York *Times,* Nov. 28, 1951, p. 34; New York *Times* news story, Feb. 10, 1956, p. 46.

49. Schrader, "The State of Iowa vs. Robert E. Bednasek," *Journalism Quarterly,* XXVIII (Winter 1951), 17-18.

50. Gottlieb, *op. cit.,* p. 105.

51. *Editor and Publisher,* Dec. 3, 1960, p. 64. See also Bromley, "Free Press vs. Fair Trial," *Harper's Magazine,* March 1951, p. 90.

52. Münsterberg, *op. cit.,* p. 166. On untrue confessions generally, see *ibid.,* pp. 137-171.

In 1966 Joseph F. Shea was acquitted of murder charges in a second Florida trial after earlier being convicted and imprisoned for the same crime following a well-publicized confession. Shea in the second trial repudiated his confession, which he said police had tricked and pressured him into making. (Pittsburgh *Post-Gazette,* Feb. 21, 1966, p. 9.) Gene Miller, Miami *Herald* reporter, had tracked down evidence for six months to help get Shea a second trial and had shown that Shea could not have been at the scene of the murder at the time it was committed. At one time Shea was led to believe he might have committed murder when he was unaware of his actions. (New York *Times,* Jan. 23, 1966, p. 53.) In this case one newspaper helped to undo the harm that might have been done earlier by the press.

Other untrue confessions occurred in New York City in the recent cases of George Whitmore, Hector Cruz, and Santo Sanchez. *New Republic,* Feb. 12, 1966, p. 15.

53. Reik, *op. cit.,* p. 261. See also Rogge, *Why Men Confess.*

54. Borchard, *op. cit.,* pp. 15-22.

55. Münsterberg, *op. cit.,* pp. 75-76.

56. Borchard, *op. cit.*, pp. 112-122.

57. Barnes and Teeters, *op. cit.*, pp. 222-223. See, e.g., Sheeler case in Frank, *op. cit.*, pp. 167-180.

58. *Shepherd v. Fla.*, 341 U.S. 51 note 3 (1951) (concurring opinion). See also *People v. Hryciuk*, 5 Ill. 2d 176, 125 N. E. 2d 61 (1954).

59. Barnes and Teeters, *op. cit.*, pp. 221, 224; Frank, *op. cit.*, p. 181; Douglas, *The Right of the People*, p. 154. See U.S. Commission on Civil Rights, *Justice—1961 Commission on Civil Rights Report*, pp. 1, 6-28.

60. Pittsburgh *Press* editorial, Feb. 14, 1965.

61. American Society of Newspaper Editors, Report of Press-Bar Committee, April 14, 1965, pp. 1, 2, 3.

62. *Editor and Publisher*, June 26, 1965, p. 36. In testimony on Aug. 17, 1965, before a Senate committee considering Senator Wayne Morse's bill to curb prejudicial statements by federal prosecuting officials, Alfred Friendly, then managing editor of the Washington *Post*, told of a 1964 study reporting that, of several hundred thousand criminal trials in the past two years, there were only fifty-one in which prejudicial pretrial publicity was urged as a basis for the reversal of convictions, and only three reversals ensued.

63. Holmes, *Sheppard Murder Case*, pp. 304, 311.

64. Weinman decision in *Sheppard v. Maxwell*, at 231 F. Supp. 37 (S. D. Ohio 1964); Court of Appeals decision at 346 F. 2d 707 (1965).

65. In 1963 the Supreme Judicial Court of Massachusetts reversed a conviction because a Boston newspaper publicized the defendant's criminal record despite a court order not to do so. *Commonwealth v. Crehan et al.*, 188 N. E. 923 (1963). In 1964 the California Supreme Court reversed the second-degree murder conviction of Lee C. Lambright because the jury was exposed during the trial to newspaper stories of legally inadmissible testimony. *People v. Lambright*, 61 Cal. 2d 482 (1964).

66. Block, *The Vindicators*; Borchard, *op. cit.*; Frank, *op. cit.*; Radin, *The Innocents*. On English cases in which innocent defendants were convicted, see Hale, *Hanged in Error*.

67. Borchard, *op. cit.*, pp. xv, xviii, 255, 288; Frank, *op. cit.*, p. 50.

68. Borchard, *op. cit.*, pp. 194-199; Block, *op. cit.*, pp. 4-5, 6.

69. Philadelphia *Inquirer*, Dec. 12, 1946, pp. 1, 3; Dec. 13, 1946, p. 1; Dec. 16, 1946, p. 1; Dec. 21, 1946, p. 1; Dec. 22, 1946, p. 1, 2d section; Dec. 31, 1946, p. 3.

70. Frank, *op. cit.*, pp. 119-129.

71. San Francisco *Examiner*, Oct. 15, 1952, pp. 1, 7; Oct. 17, 1952, p. 1; Oct. 18, 1952, pp. 1, 7; Oct. 19, 1952, p. 1; Oct. 21, 1952, p. 1.

72. Ross, *op. cit.*, pp. 64-65.

73. Martin, "The Innocent and the Guilty," *Saturday Evening Post*, Aug. 13, 1960, pp. 34, 35, 66, 68; Atlanta *Constitution*, Aug. 15, 1956, p. 21; Wood and Ross, *op. cit.*, pp. 77-78.

74. For stories dealing with the Rexinger case, see: San Francisco *Chroni-*

cle, San Francisco *Examiner,* San Francisco *News,* issues from July 21 through Aug. 6, 1957; Treuhaft, *op. cit.,* pp. 280, 282.

75. San Francisco *Examiner,* July 26, 1957; Treuhaft, *op. cit.,* p. 280.

76. 26 New York State Bar Bulletin 206 (July 1954). On the question of whether the public should be simply given what it wants, see the enlightening discussion in Schramm, *op. cit.,* pp. 268-275.

CHAPTER 7

1. Radin, *The Innocents,* pp. 9, 13.

2. New York *Times,* May 9, 1961, p. 35.

3. Southern Regional Council and American Civil Liberties Union, *Southern Justice: An Indictment,* Oct. 18, 1965; U.S. Commission on Civil Rights, *Law Enforcement—A Report on Equal Protection in the South,* 1965; Charles Morgan, "Southern Justice," *Look Magazine,* June 29, 1965; Arensberg, "Mississippi Diary—1964," *Pittsburgh Legal Journal,* Sept. 1965, p. 3; Southern Regional Council, *Law Enforcement in Mississippi,* July 14, 1964; Silver, *Mississippi: The Closed Society,* pp. 91, 93, 95, 96, 100; New York *Times,* Oct. 24, 1964, pp. 1, 29; May 12, 1963, p. 52.

4. *Editor and Publisher,* Aug. 15, 1964, p. 62.

5. Frank, *op. cit.,* pp. 59, 80-83, 92, 121, 131-135, 141, 166, 170, 171, 172, 177, 182.

6. Borchard, *op. cit.,* p. xv.

7. New York *Times,* Feb. 7, 1965, p. 74.

8. Pollitt, *Counsel for the Unpopular Cause,* 43 N. C. L. Rev. 9 (Dec. 1964).

9. New York *Times,* Aug. 29, 1965, p. 4E. Between 1958 and 1962, 313 attorneys were disbarred. Pittsburgh *Press,* Dec. 21, 1964, p. 11. For statistics on 1957-58, see *American Bar Association Journal,* July 1959, p. 689.

10. Pound, *op. cit.,* p. 185. See also Waite, *Criminal Law in Action,* p. 234.

11. Frank, *op. cit.,* pp. 155-156. Borchard, in *Convicting the Innocent,* p. xv, says that in the United States the prosecution technique "is to regard a conviction as a personal victory calculated to enhance the prestige of the prosecutor."

12. Frank, *op. cit.,* pp. 72, 121, 142, 187, 192.

13. *Ibid.,* pp. 152, 195.

14. Borchard, *loc. cit.*

15. Quoted in Wolfram, *Free Press, Fair Trial and the Responsibility of the Bar,* 1 Crim. L. Rev. (N.Y.) 12-13 (1954). For further discussion of the Hogan rule, see 26 New York State Bar Bulletin 220-221 (July 1954); Proceedings of 80th Annual Meeting of N.Y. State Bar Association, pp. 15-16 (1957); note, *Community Hostility and the Right to an Impartial Jury,* 60 Colum. L. Rev. 371, footnote 132 (1960).

16. *Stroble v. Cal.*, 243 U.S. 181, 201 (1952). Justices Black and Douglas also dissented on the ground that the confession was illegally obtained. *Ibid.*, at 203.

17. *U.S. v. Leviton*, 193 F. 2d 848, 865 (1952).

18. *U.S. v. Rosenberg*, 200 F. 2d 666, 670 (2d Cir. 1952). The Supreme Court denied certiorari. 345 U.S. 965 (1953).

19. *People v. Hryciuk*, 125 N. E. 2d 61, 64 (1954).

20. 26 New York State Bar Bulletin 217-218 (July 1954).

21. *Editor and Publisher*, May 13, 1961, p. 71.

22. Williams, *op. cit.*, p. 245.

23. Reynolds, *op. cit.*, pp. 217-218, 246.

24. Darrow, *Story of My Life*, pp. 233, 350.

25. Dissenting opinion in *Craig v. Harney*, 331 U.S. 367, 397 (1947).

26. New York *Times*, Oct. 24, 1964, pp. 1, 29.

27. Raper, *op. cit.*, p. 305.

28. New York *Times*, March 30, 1961, p. 30.

29. Bok, *Star Wormwood*, pp. 42-43.

30. *Editor and Publisher*, April 15, 1961, p. 48.

31. San Francisco *Examiner*, March 2, 1961, p. 33; March 4, 1961, pp. 1, 4; March 5, 1961, pp. 1, 12; March 6, 1961, pp. 1, 13; March 7, 1961, p. 13.

32. New York *Times*, Aug. 3, 1962, p. 1; Oct. 9, 1963, p. 1; April 7, 1964, p. 1; July 3, 1964, p. 38; July 19, 1964, p. 44; Nov. 10, 1964, p. 17; Nov. 14, 1964, p. 14; March 23, 1965, p. 30; May 14, 1965, p. 40. Also see Borkin, *The Corrupt Judge*, concerning fifty-five federal judges who during our history have been investigated by Congress for misconduct.

33. Note, *Community Hostility and the Right to an Impartial Jury*, 60 Colum. L. Rev. 349 (1960).

34. Frank, *Law and the Modern Mind* (Anchor ed.), pp. 188, 189.

35. Broeder, *The University of Chicago Jury Project*, 38 Neb. L. Rev. 749, 750 (1959).

36. Goldstein, *op. cit.*, footnote 37, 1189 (1960); Newman, *Pleading Guilty for Considerations: A Study of Bargain Justice*, 46 J. Crim. L., C. & P. S. 780 (1956); Botein, *Trial of the Future*, pp. 69-70; note, *Guilty Plea Bargaining*, 112 U. Pa. L. Rev. 865 (1964).

37. Hearings Before Senate Internal Security Subcommittee, 84th Cong., 1st Sess. (Oct. 12 and 13, 1955), *Recording of Jury Deliberations*, pp. 65, 68, 71.

38. Carter, "A Double Standard for Murder," *New York Times Magazine*, Jan. 24, 1965, p. 20.

39. Hays, *op. cit.*, pp. 350-351.

40. New York *Times*, Aug. 5, 1963, p. 31.

41. New York *Times*, April 10, 1965, pp. 1, 12. See also Powell speech reported in New York *Times*, Jan. 30, 1965, pp. 1, 24.

42. Gutman, "The Criminal Gets the Breaks," *New York Times Magazine,* Nov. 29, 1964, pp. 36, 123.

43. *Newsweek,* Nov. 16, 1964, p. 97.

44. McCord, *op. cit.,* pp. 170-171.

45. Barnes and Teeters, *op. cit.,* pp. 207-208. See also New York *Times,* Nov. 22, 1964, p. 83.

46. Bennett, *op. cit.,* p. 125. In the spring of 1966 Governor William Scranton of Pennsylvania called a special session of the Legislature to increase the punishment for forcible rape. The House, by a unanimous vote, passed a bill to increase the maximum penalty from fifteen years to life imprisonment. The Senate concurred with little debate as to the value of the change, and the governor signed the measure with a statement expressing satisfaction over the stiffer terms. Pittsburgh *Post-Gazette,* April 27, 1966, p. 8; May 12, 1966, p. 4; May 13, 1966, p. 20.

47. Bazelon, "The Imperative to Punish," *Atlantic,* July 1960, pp. 42, 43, 44, 45.

48. New York *Times,* May 11, 1964, pp. 1, 34.

49. Pittsburgh *Post-Gazette,* May 8, 1964, p. 7.

50. Borchard, *op. cit.;* Frank, *Not Guilty;* Hale, *Hanged in Error.*

51. American Civil Liberties Union Statement, "The Death Penalty and Civil Liberties," July 1965.

52. Barnes and Teeters, *op. cit.,* p. 318. See also Laurence, *A History of Capital Punishment.*

53. Barnes and Teeters, *op. cit.,* p. 319.

54. New York *Times,* March 18, 1965, p. 59.

55. Bok, *op. cit.,* p. 186.

56. Menninger, *Man Against Himself,* p. 463; Menninger, "Verdict Guilty," *Harper's Magazine,* Aug. 1959, p. 60; Menninger, *Psychiatrist's World,* p. 758.

57. Barnes and Teeters, *op. cit.,* pp. 58, 286, 584, 586; Taft, *op. cit.,* pp. 367-368; Martin, *Break Down the Walls,* pp. 233-234. See also Münsterberg, *op. cit.,* p. 233.

58. Pound, *op. cit.,* p. 163. Wigmore on the "sporting theory of justice" referred to in Barnes and Teeters, *op. cit.,* p. 250. See also Frank, *Not Guilty,* pp. 225-236, 243; Morris, *Fair Trial,* p. x.

59. Quoted in Frank, *Not Guilty,* p. 226.

60. Quoted in Barnes and Teeters, *op. cit.,* p. 272. See also Hearings Before Senate Internal Security Subcommittee, 84th Cong., 1st Sess. (Oct. 12-13, 1955), *Recording of Jury Deliberations,* pp. 73, 74.

61. Boston *Evening Transcript,* May 2, 1935, p. 7.

62. Pittsburgh *Legal Journal,* May 10, 1960, p. 2.

63. Barnes and Teeters, *op. cit.,* p. 278. Various studies have revealed a number of unpredictable and unaccountable ways in which juries arrive at their verdicts. One study showed that jurors spent 50 per cent of their time

exchanging personal experiences, 25 per cent on procedural questions, 15 per cent on reviewing the facts in the case, and 8 per cent on the court's instructions. (James, "Status and Competence of Jurors," *American Journal of Sociology,* LXIV [May 1959], 563.)

Another study disclosed that a higher participation by a juror in the group's deliberations helps the participant to influence the others in keeping with his own goals. The same study showed a higher participation on the part of men and on the part of members of higher status occupations. Proprietors, for example, were more vocal than laborers. Strodtbeck, "Social Status in Jury Deliberations," *American Sociological Review,* XXII (Dec. 1957), 715, 716, 717.

64. Los Angeles *Examiner,* Feb. 17, 1961, p. 2.

65. Frank, *Not Guilty,* pp. 219-220; Barnes and Teeters, *op. cit.,* p. 275.

66. Münsterberg, *op. cit.,* pp. 15-17, 20-21, 39-40, 49-51; Frank, *Law and the Modern Mind* (Anchor ed.), pp. 369-370; Seldes, *Freedom of the Press,* p. 162.

67. Frank, *Not Guilty,* pp. 56, 58, 71, 75, 76, 80, 92, 97, 101, 134, 152, 165, 188, 191, 192, 194, 196, 197.

68. Pound, *op. cit.,* pp. 71-72.

69. Frank, *Not Guilty,* pp. 29, 59, 187, 193, 194, 198.

70. New York *Times,* March 22, 1966, p. 25.

71. Frank, *Courts on Trial,* p. 33.

72. Brennan, *The Bill of Rights and the States,* pp. 20-21.

73. Barnes and Teeters, *New Horizons in Criminology* (2d ed. 1951), p. 315.

74. Frank, *Law and the Modern Mind* (Anchor ed.), pp. 266-269.

75. *Durham v. U.S.,* 214 F. 2d 862 (D. C. Cir. 1954); Erickson, *Psychiatry and the Law,* 1 Duke L. J. 38, 39 (1961). See also Bok, *op. cit.,* pp. 142-143.

76. Wechsler, *Sentencing, Correction, and the Model Penal Code,* 109 U. Pa. L. Rev. 473 (1961).

77. Rose and Prell, "Does the Punishment Fit the Crime?" *American Journal of Sociology,* LXI (Nov. 1955), 259. See also Somit, Tanenhaus, and Wilke, *Aspects of Judicial Sentencing Behavior,* 21 U. Pitt. L. Rev. 613 (1960).

78. New York *Times,* July 23, 1965, pp. 1, 32.

79. Banay, "Why the Prison Alarm Sounds," *New York Times Magazine,* July 26, 1959, p. 8. See also Barnes and Teeters, *New Horizons in Criminology* (3rd ed. 1959), pp. 367-372; Martin, *Break Down the Walls.*

CHAPTER 8

1. Letter from Judge Depuy to Lofton, Jan. 6, 1961. For an account of the Adams trial, see Bedford, *The Best We Can Do.* For others who favor

the contempt method, see *New York State Crime Commission Report,* p. 325; Darrow, *op. cit.,* pp. 233, 365; Pound, *op. cit.,* p. 200; Waite, *op. cit.,* pp. 235-236.

2. Griswold, "Responsibility of the Legal Profession," *Harvard Today,* Jan. 1965, p. 12. Statutory curbs on the release of pretrial information were proposed in 1960 by the Georgia Court of Appeals (*Editor and Publisher,* Jan. 16, 1960, p. 9) and by Amory H. Bradford, then vice president and general manager of the New York *Times* (*Editor and Publisher,* Sept. 17, 1960, p. 12). See also Moley, *op. cit.,* p. 198, for 1910 statutory proposal.

3. U.S. District Judge Hubert L. Will of Chicago in 1962 proposed making it a misdemeanor for a news medium to publish information which a jury determines is prejudicial to a case. (Pittsburgh *Post-Gazette,* Sept. 20, 1962, p. 4; *Editor and Publisher,* Sept. 29, 1962, p. 48.) Professor Louis L. Jaffe of the Harvard Law School said in 1964 that publication of a prior record or an illegally obtained confession should be made punishable either as contempt of court or as a crime. (*Editor and Publisher,* Feb. 22, 1964, p. 58.) Professor Telford Taylor of the Columbia University Law School in 1965 proposed legislation to curb the release of prejudicial pretrial information. (New York *Times,* Feb. 7, 1965, p. 80.) A Massachusetts legislative committee in 1964 suggested giving the state attorney general power to maintain surveillance over press coverage of crime news. (*Editor and Publisher,* April 11, 1964, p. 14.) For extensive material on the subject of "Free Press and Fair Trial," see transcript of Hearings Before U.S. Senate Subcommittee on Constitutional Rights, Aug. 17-20, 1965, Parts 1 and 2.

4. Lewis, "British Verdict on Trial-by-Press," *New York Times Magazine,* June 20, 1965, p. 46.

5. Political and Economic Planning Group, *A Report on the British Press,* p. 212.

6. Hohenberg, *op. cit.,* pp. 50-55.

7. Butterfield, "The St. Louis Post-Dispatch—Pulitzer's Prize," *Collier's,* Dec. 23, 1950, p. 48

8. Hohenberg, *op. cit.,* pp. 63-65.

9. *Editor and Publisher,* Jan. 27, 1962, p. 46.

10. Reed, "How to Lynch a Newspaper," *Atlantic,* Nov. 1964, pp. 459-463. In early 1966 Gene Wirges was found guilty of perjury and sentenced to three years. *Editor and Publisher,* Feb. 12, 1966, p. 14: New York *Times,* Feb. 4, 1966, p. 14.

11. New York *Times,* March 31, 1964, p. 19; *Editor and Publisher,* April 4, 1964, p. 63; Oct. 23, 1965, p. 66.

12. The contempt fine was later set aside by the Georgia Supreme Court. (*Editor and Publisher,* Oct. 15, 1960, p. 14.) A separate order by Judge Pye banning photographs on streets and sidewalks surrounding the courthouse was upheld by the Georgia Supreme Court. (*Editor and Publisher,* May 14, 1960, p. 6.)

13. *Congressional Record,* March 19, 1964, p. 5563. See the 1964 case in which the U.S. Supreme Court reversed an Alabama court's contempt conviction of a Negro woman, Mary Hamilton, because she declined to answer when addressed in court simply as "Mary." *Hamilton v. Ala.,* 376 U.S. 650 (1964).

14. New York *Times,* July 20, 1965, p. 55; *Editor and Publisher,* July 31, 1965, p. 12. The outcome of this case had not been decided as this was written.

15. *The Bulletin of the American Society of Newspaper Editors,* April 1, 1965, p. 7. There have, of course, been other cases—not relevant to a discussion of the press role in the pretrial stage—in which the press after the fact has helped to expose that convictions of the innocent have occurred as a result of police suppression of evidence, coercion of confessions, or other misbehavior or negligent conduct. See the Rudolph Sheeler case in Philadelphia. (*Bulletin of the ASNE,* March 1, 1965, pp. 4-5.)

In still other cases newspapers have helped to free wrongfully convicted persons by finding new evidence. See Roy Mundy case in York, Pa. (*Editor and Publisher,* May 7, 1960, p. 50) and Robert Watson case in Tampa, Fla. (*Ibid.,* Sept. 25, 1965, p. 50).

16. *Bulletin of the ASNE,* April 1, 1965, pp. 5-6. In a 1964 New York City case similar to that of Lloyd Cuff in Miami, Gregory Cruz, a 22-year-old clerk, was shot three times by a detective. The police said he was a murder suspect and charged him with felonious assault on a detective, resisting a police officer, and carrying a concealed weapon—a pair of pliers. But they never charged Cruz with murder. Newspaper reporters investigated and found four witnesses who supported Cruz's own story that he had been stopped, searched, and beaten by the detective, who was in civilian clothes and never showed a police identification, and that he (Cruz) had run because he thought the officer was a robber. After the reporters' facts were turned over to the district attorney's office, all charges against Cruz were dropped. Cruz, however, spent three months in a hospital prison ward, unable to support his mother and brother. The detective, John C. Devlin, was suspended for "excessive use of force" (*Bulletin of the ASNE,* March 1, 1965, p. 3) but was otherwise cleared. Cruz later sued the city for $2 million and in a 1965 civil complaint in federal court sued the New York *Daily News* for $1 million in damages for libel, claiming that the paper in an article on Sept. 10, 1964, gave the impression that he was a loiterer who had committed without provocation the heinous crime of viciously and savagely attacking a police officer. (New York *Times,* Sept. 9, 1965, p. 30.)

17. *Bulletin of the ASNE,* March 1, 1965, p. 5. In a 1964 case a *Sun-Times* campaign brought about the closing of eight bars which were operated by the Cosa Nostra but which had remained in business because evidence gathered in police raids was quashed in court. The *Sun-Times* exposed the political alliance the "untouchable" joints had enjoyed. (*Ibid.,* p. 5.)

18. Schramm, *op. cit.*, pp. 90, 91, 96, 98-99.

19. *Editor and Publisher,* March 25, 1961, p. 10. Isaacs, "The Crime of Present Day Crime Reporting," J. Crim. L., C. & P. S., LII (Nov.-Dec. 1961), 405-410.

20. "Editor's Notebook," *Detroit Free Press,* Jan. 17, 1965.

21. Hallam, *Some Object Lessons on Publicity in Criminal Trials,* 24 Minn. L. Rev. 467-468 (1940).

22. Chafee, *Government and Mass Communications* I, 427. Judge Jerome Frank criticized the poor job of American journalism in reporting court actions. (Frank, *Courts on Trial,* p. 1.)

23. Svirsky, *Your Newspaper,* pp. 177, 180.

24. The licenses of 119 physicians were revoked in 1963. (Pittsburgh *Press,* Dec. 21, 1964, p. 11) On newsmen's experience with codes, see Commission on Freedom of the Press, *A Free and Responsible Press,* pp. 74-75; Schramm, *op. cit.,* pp. 282, 292. On lawyers' experience with canons of ethics, see Chapter 7, text at note 9.

25. Butterfield, "The St. Louis Post-Dispatch—Pulitzer's Prize," *Collier's,* Dec. 16, 1950, p. 77.

26. Royal Commission on the Press, 1947-1949, *Report,* p. 177.

27. Freedom of Information Center, *Publication No. 96,* pp. 1, 2; Nelson, "Watchdog of the British Press," *Saturday Review,* Aug. 8, 1964, pp. 42-43.

28. Commission on Freedom of the Press, *A Free and Responsible Press,* pp. 100-102.

29. Blumberg, *One-Party Press?,* p. 21.

30. Hohenberg, *op. cit.,* pp. 60-63.

31. Washington *Post,* Oct. 25, 1964, p. E5; Nov. 8, 1964, p. E5.

32. St. Louis *Post-Dispatch, Sunday Pictures,* Feb. 17, 1963, pp. 22-25. See also articles on prison subjects in Pittsburgh *Press Sunday Magazine,* Feb. 26, 1961, p. 4; July 29, 1962, p. 12.

33. New York *Times,* March 9, 1964, p. 1.

34. See speech by Paul Block, Jr., publisher of the Toledo *Blade,* quoted in *Editor and Publisher,* Nov. 19, 1960, p. 14.

35. U.S. Dept. of Justice, *Uniform Crime Reports* (1964), pp. 1, 101.

36. *Editor and Publisher,* May 12, 1962, p. 11. Michigan Attorney General Frank J. Kelly obtained criminal warrants against a former state legislator and six officials of a state-chartered Peoples Community Hospital Authority after an investigation prompted by a series of articles in the Booth newspapers of Michigan. (*Ibid.,* Feb. 19, 1966, p. 32.) A revival of the Ku Klux Klan in Cleveland in 1965 was exposed by a Cleveland *Press* reporter, Wally Guenther, who joined the organization and then wrote about it. (*Ibid.,* Feb. 19, 1966, p. 58.)

37. *The Bulletin of the American Society of Newspaper Editors,* Dec. 1, 1964, p. 1.

CHAPTER 9

1. Lumbard, "The Adequacy of Lawyers Now in Criminal Practice," *Journal of the American Judicature Society,* Jan. 1964, pp. 179-180.

2. *Editor and Publisher,* Feb. 14, 1959, p. 10; Feb. 28, 1959, p. 14.

3. Goldberg, "Equal Justice for the Poor, Too," *New York Times Magazine,* March 15, 1964, p. 24. See also U.S. Attorney General's Committee on Poverty and the Administration of Federal Criminal Justice, *Report,* Feb. 25, 1963.

4. San Francisco *Chronicle,* May 11, 1961, p. 19.

5. Pittsburgh *Post-Gazette,* Oct. 25, 1965, pp. 1, 13. Robert G. MacBeth, the patrolman involved, was later acquitted in a trial for murder (a degree of homicide with which he obviously should not have been charged). But this did not change the fact that he had unnecessarily drawn his gun in chasing a dice game suspect. (Pittsburgh *Post-Gazette,* March 5, 1966, p. 1.)

6. U.S. Dept. of Justice *Uniform Crime Reports* (1964), p. 107.

7. Bickel, "Fighting Crime," *New Republic,* Sept. 18, 1965, p. 12. For a comment on the British requirement that the police tell suspects of their rights, see Botein, *op. cit.,* p. 66.

8. New York *Times,* Nov. 20, 1965, p. 1.

9. New York *Times,* Nov. 22, 1965, p. 35.

10. Mencken, *Prejudices* (Vintage ed.), p. 140. On guidance for police, see Packer, "Policing the Police—Nine Men Are Not Enough," *New Republic,* Sept. 4, 1965, pp. 17-21.

11. Quoted in New York *Times,* April 19, 1961, p. 6.

12. *Monroe v. Pape,* 365 U.S. 167 (1961).

13. Botein, *op. cit.,* pp. 69-70.

14. McCullough, "Sunset of the Criminal Lawyer," *American Bar Association Journal,* March 1964, p. 225.

15. Quoted in Frank, *Not Guilty,* p. 239.

16. Philadelphia Bar Association Committee on Criminal Justice and Law Enforcement, *Cruel But Not Unusual,* Statement, 1961. See also Goldfarb, *Ransom: A Critique of the American Bail System;* Foote, *Coming Constitutional Crisis in Bail,* 113 U. Pa. L. Rev. 959, 1125 (1965).

17. American Civil Liberties Union memorandum on "Fair Trial and Free Press," Oct. 7, 1965, p. 8.

18. *N. J. v. Van Duyne,* 204 Atl. 2d 841, 852 (1964).

19. Thayer, *op. cit.,* p. 445.

20. *Ibid.,* pp. 238-242.

21. *Augusta Chronicle v. Arrington,* 42 Ga. App. 746, 157 S. E. 394, 395 (1931). On the handling of police news, see Thayer, *op. cit.,* pp. 440-452.

22. Radin, *Freedom of Speech and Contempt of Court,* 36 Ill. L. Rev. 618 (1942). Radin was against the use of the contempt power on the press. (*Ibid.,* at p. 619.)

23. 376 U.S. 254 (1964).

24. See *Garrison v. La.,* 379 U.S. 64 (1964) in which the Supreme Court extended the Sullivan rule, involving civil libel, to the field of criminal libel.

25. *Brubaker v. Reading Eagle Company,* 57 Berks County Law Journal 181 (1965); *Editor and Publisher,* July 17, 1965, p. 13.

26. Riesman, *Democracy and Defamation: Fair Game and Fair Comment II,* 42 Colum. L. Rev. 1282 (1942). David Riesman suggests tailoring the amount of damages to meet different needs and different situations. For example, small publications might be assessed less than large ones. (*Ibid.,* at 1314) Courts might broaden the doctrine of libel *per se.* The plaintiff might be required to give the defendant an opportunity to retract and, if a retraction is made, damages might be limited. The defendant might be required to publish the judgment. (*Ibid.,* at 1315)

27. Quoted in Borchard, *op. cit.,* p. vii.

28. New York *Times,* July 24, 1966, p. E7. Delaware, Florida, Maryland, Michigan, New Jersey, and Ohio also have more liberal discovery rules.

Chief Justice Joseph Weintraub of the New Jersey Supreme Court indicated in 1965 that defense lawyers ought to be able to obtain minutes of grand jury proceedings. (New York *Times,* Sept. 14, 1965, p. 32.)

On the proposed amended federal discovery rule, see 113 U. Pa. L. Rev. 1295 (1965).

29. St. Louis *Post-Dispatch* editorial, March 17, 1963. For another proposal on discovery, see Goldstein, *op. cit.,* p. 1197. See also Vanderbilt, *Challenge of Law Reform,* pp. 59, 91.

30. Botein, *op. cit.,* p. 70. See *Griffin v. Cal.,* 380 U.S. 609 (1965) for the Supreme Court's decision barring prosecutor comment on the defendant's failure to take the stand.

31. *Jackson v. Denno,* 378 U.S. 368 (1964). See *The Supreme Court, 1963 Term,* 78 Harv. L. Rev. 211-213 (1964); New York *Times,* April 14, 1965, p. 33.

32. 378 U.S. 1 (1964).

33. Sutherland, *Crime and Confession,* 79 Harv. L. Rev. 23, 31 (1965). Standard procedures are described in the widely used manual, Inbau and Reid, *Criminal Interrogation and Confessions* (1962).

34. Southern Regional Council and American Civil Liberties Union, *Southern Justice: An Indictment,* Oct. 18, 1965, p. 29.

35. Note, *Community Hostility and the Right to an Impartial Jury,* 60 Colum. L. Rev. 351. See *In re Murchison,* 349 U.S. 133 (1955). In Los Angeles and Ogden, Utah, trial courts have employed a series of test questions aimed at screening out jurors who are unable to decide cases on the basis of reason applied to the evidence. (New York *Times,* Nov. 26, 1960.)

36. Quoted in Miller, *op. cit.,* p. 154.

37. Holmes, *op. cit.,* pp. 67, 69, 74, 213.

38. See *Gicinto v. U.S.,* 212 F. 2d 8 (1954), 348 U.S. 884 (1954); *Reining*

v. U.S., 167 F. 2d 362 (1948), 335 U.S. 830 (1948), in which U.S. Courts of Appeal and then the U.S. Supreme Court denied relief to defendants in whose trials jurors saw newspaper articles that could have prejudiced the outcomes.

39. Note, *Community Hostility and the Right to an Impartial Jury,* 60 Colum. L. Rev. 355 (1960).

40. Pittsburgh *Legal Journal,* Dec. 17, 1965, p. 2.

41. *U.S. ex rel. Bloeth v. Denno,* U.S. Court of Appeals, 2d Cir. (1963) and *Rideau v. La.,* U.S. Supreme Court (1963).

42. *Commonwealth v. Crehan* (Supreme Judicial Court of Mass.), 188 N. E. 923 (1963); *People v. Purvis* (Cal. Supreme Court), 384 P. 2d 424 (1963); *People v. Lambright* (Cal. Supreme Court), 61 Cal. 2d 482 (1964).

43. *Atlanta Constitution,* Aug. 7, 1956, p. 2. In the Brink's case chief defense attorney Paul T. Smith complained to the court that public opinion had been inflamed by stories given to the press by government officials and that these stories had jeopardized the defendants' chances for an impartial trial. He cited and criticized an editorial in the Boston *Herald* which chided citizens for seeking not to serve on the jury and which said in part: "The bulk of them pleaded preconceived opinions in the case. As if responsible men and women could not weigh the evidence and make a reasonable finding on a new basis." Smith brought in volumes of clippings to support his pretrial plea that veniremen be discharged because an impartial jury could not be drawn. But the judge rejected his request. (*Editor and Publisher,* Aug. 18, 1956, p. 58.)

44. *Crawford v. U.S.,* 212 U.S. 183, 196 (1909).

45. David Riesman suggests using public opinion research techniques to determine the effect of published defamatory statements. (Riesman, *op. cit.,* p. 1304.)

Alger Hiss, in requesting a change of venue on grounds of newspaper-fostered prejudice in New York City, attached to his motion a public opinion survey taken by Cornelius Du Bois, Inc. It showed that 45.1 per cent of the New Yorkers questioned said they had formed an opinion on the guilt or innocence of Hiss. This compared to 33.8 per cent of those interviewed in Rutland, Vt., to which Hiss sought to have his second trial removed. But the survey also showed that in New York 21.8 per cent of those interviewed thought Hiss guilty and 12.1 per cent thought him innocent; whereas in Rutland 23.1 per cent thought him guilty and only 5.9 per cent thought him innocent. Thus less coverage of the Hiss case in Vermont and less anti-Hiss newspaper bias did not mean that a trial there would necessarily be more fair. The conservative predisposition of Vermonters may have been more influential than the press in shaping the outcome. Note, *Contempt By Publication,* 59 Yale L. J. 534, 543, footnote 48 (1950).

46. American Civil Liberties Union memorandum "Fair Trial and Free Press," Oct. 7, 1965, p. 9.

47. *U.S. v. Carlucci et al.,* 288 F. 2d 691 (1961).

48. *Ibid.*, at 697.

49. LeWine, "What Constitutes Prejudicial Publicity in Pending Cases?" *American Bar Association Journal,* Oct. 1965, p. 945, footnote 41.

50. See Borchard, *op. cit.,* p. xxi. Though federal district courts sometimes conduct independent factual inquiries in the course of habeas corpus proceedings, this is hardly an adequate remedy. The states, whose courts handle most criminal cases, should themselves provide the remedial machinery.

51. *Lathrop v. Donohue,* 367 U.S. 820 (1961).

52. Vanderbilt, *Challenge of Law Reform,* p. 11. See also *ibid.*, pp. 12, 16, 17-21, 31-32; Pound, *op. cit.*, p. 191.

53. Raper, *op. cit.*, p. 14.

54. Pound, *op. cit.*, p. 191.

CHAPTER 10

1. *Powell v. Ala.*, 287 U.S. 45 (1932).
2. *Gideon v. Wainwright,* 372 U.S. 335 (1963).
3. *Brown v. Miss.*, 297 U.S. 278 (1936).
4. *Mapp v. Ohio,* 367 U.S. 643 (1961).
5. *Robinson v. Cal.*, 369 U.S. 824 (1962).
6. *Malloy v. Hogan,* 378 U.S. 1 (1964).
7. *Pointer v. Tex.*, 380 U.S. 400 (1965).
8. See comments by Paul Block, Jr., publisher of the Toledo *Blade,* as reported in *Editor and Publisher,* Nov. 19, 1960, p. 14.
9. Pope, *Police-Press Relations,* pp. 181-183.
10. U.S. Dept. of Justice *Uniform Crime Reports* (1959), p. 10. See also *ibid.*, 1964, pp. 20, 22.
11. Nash, "You Can't Get There From Here," *Verses From 1929 On,* p. 503.
12. Goldstein, *op. cit.*, p. 1152.
13. Botein, *op. cit.*, pp. 59-62.
14. Jackson, "Who Goes to Prison," *Atlantic,* Jan. 1966, pp. 52, 53. See also Caldwell, *op. cit.,* pp. 65-66; Barnes and Teeters, *op. cit.,* pp. 41-49; Pound, *op. cit.*, p. 64.
15. See Black, "Mr. Justice Black, the Supreme Court and the Bill of Rights," *Harper's Magazine,* Feb. 1961, pp. 63-68; Williams, *Hugo L. Black—A Study of the Judicial Process,* pp. 144, 150, 154. See Black opinions in *Milkwagon Drivers Union v. Meadowmoor Dairies,* 312 U.S. 287, 301-302 (1941); *Marsh v. Ala.,* 326 U.S. 506-509 (1946). See Goldberg, "Freedom and Responsibility of the Press," address before the American Society of Newspaper Editors, Washington, D.C., April 16, 1964, p. 20.
16. Bok, *op. cit.*, p. 227.

APPENDIX C

1. Sheppard was convicted in 1954 in the Court of Common Pleas of Cuyahoga County, Ohio. His conviction was affirmed by the Court of Appeals

for Cuyahoga County, 100 Ohio App. 345, 128 N. E. 2d 471 (1955), and the Ohio Supreme Court, 165 Ohio St. 293, 135 N. E. 2d 340 (1956). We denied certiorari on the original appeal. 352 U.S. 910 (1956).

2. The several witnesses to whom Sheppard narrated his experiences differ in their description of various details. Sheppard claimed the vagueness of his perception was caused by his sudden awakening, the dimness of the light, and his loss of consciousness.

3. Sheppard was suffering from severe pain in his neck, a swollen eye, and shock.

4. But newspaper photographers and reporters were permitted access to Sheppard's home from time to time and took pictures throughout the premises.

5. At the same time, the newspapers reported that other possible suspects had been "cleared" by lie detector tests. One of these persons was quoted as saying that he could not understand why an innocent man would refuse to take such a test.

6. The newspapers had heavily emphasized Sheppard's illicit affair with Susan Hayes, and the fact that he had initially lied about it.

7. A number of articles calculated to evoke sympathy for Sheppard were printed, such as the letters Sheppard wrote to his son while in jail. These stories often appeared together with news coverage which was unfavorable to him.

8. Many more reporters and photographers attended the Sheppard trial. And it attracted several nationally famous commentators as well.

9. At the commencement of trial, defense counsel made motions for continuance and change of venue. The judge postponed ruling on these motions until he determined whether an impartial jury could be impaneled. *Voir dire* examination showed that with one exception all members selected for jury service had read something about the case in the newspapers. Since, however, all of the jurors stated that they would not be influenced by what they had read or seen, the judge overruled both of the motions. Without regard to whether the judge's actions in this respect reach dimensions that would justify issuance of the habeas writ, it should be noted that a short continuance would have alleviated any problem with regard to the judicial elections. The court in *Delaney v. United States,* 199 F. 2d 107, 115 (C. A. 1st Cir. 1952), recognized such a duty under similar circumstances, holding that "if assurance of a fair trial would necessitate that the trial of the case be postponed until after the election, then we think the law required no less than that."

10. Typical comments on the trial by the press itself include:

"The question of Dr. Sheppard's guilt or innocence still is before the courts. Those who have examined the trial record carefully are divided as to the propriety of the verdict. But almost everyone who watched the performance of the Cleveland press agrees that a fair hearing for the defendant, in that area, would be a modern miracle." Harrison, "The Press vs. the Courts," *The Saturday Review* (Oct. 15, 1955).

"At this distance, some 100 miles from Cleveland, it looks to us as though the Sheppard murder case was sensationalized to the point at which the press must ask itself if its freedom, carried to excess, doesn't interfere with the conduct of fair trials." Editorial, The Toledo *Blade* (Dec. 22, 1954).

11. In an unsworn statement, which the parties agreed would have the status of a deposition, made 10 years after Sheppard's conviction and six years after Judge Blythin's death, Dorothy Kilgallen asserted that Judge Blythin had told her: "It's an open and shut case . . . he is guilty as hell." It is thus urged that Sheppard be released on the ground that the judge's bias infected the entire trial. But we need not reach this argument, since the judge's failure to insulate the proceedings from prejudicial publicity and disruptive influences deprived Sheppard of the chance to receive a fair hearing.

12. The judge's awareness of his power in this respect is manifest from his assignment of seats to the press.

13. The problem here was further complicated by the independent action of the newspapers in reporting "evidence" and gossip which they uncovered. The press not only inferred that Sheppard was guilty because he "stalled" the investigation, hid behind his family, and hired a prominent criminal lawyer, but denounced as "mass jury tampering" his efforts to gather evidence of community prejudice caused by such publications. Sheppard's counterattacks added some fuel but, in these circumstances, cannot preclude him from asserting his right to a fair trial. Putting to one side news stories attributed to police officials, prospective witnesses, the Sheppards, and the lawyers, it is possible that the other publicity "would itself have had a prejudicial effect." Report of the President's Commission on the Assassination of President Kennedy, at 239.

14. When two police officers testified at trial that Sheppard refused to take a lie detector test, the judge declined to give a requested instruction that the results of such a test would be inadmissible in any event. He simply told the jury that no person has an obligation "to take any lie detector test."

15. Such "premature disclosure and weighing of the evidence" may seriously jeopardize a defendant's right to an impartial jury. "[N]either the press nor the public had a right to be contemporaneously informed by the police or prosecuting authorities of the details of the evidence being accumulated against [Sheppard]." Report of the President's Commission, at 239-240.

16. The Department of Justice, the City of New York, and other governmental agencies have issued such regulations. E.g., 28 CFR §50.2 (1966). For general information on this topic see periodic publications (e.g., Nos. 71, 124, and 158) by the Freedom of Information Center, School of Journalism, University of Missouri.

BIBLIOGRAPHY

Asterisks indicate publications consulted by the author but not cited in the Notes.

ARTICLES

Arensberg, Charles Covert, "Mississippi Diary—1964." *Pittsburgh Legal Journal* (Sept. 1965), p. 3.

Asch, Solomon E., "Opinions and Social Pressure." *Scientific American* (Nov. 1955), p. 31.

*Ashmore, Harry S., "Has Our Free Press Failed Us?" *Saturday Evening Post* (Oct. 29, 1960), p. 36.

Banay, Ralph S., "Why the Prison Alarm Sounds." *The New York Times Magazine* (July 26, 1959), p. 8.

*Barth, Alan, "Freedom from Contempt." *Nieman Reports* (April 1949), p. 11.

Baskette, Floyd K., "Reporting the Webster Case, America's Classic Murder." *Journalism Quarterly* (Sept. 1947), p. 250.

Bazelon, David L., "The Imperative to Punish." *The Atlantic* (July 1960), p. 41.

Bennett, James V., "A Cool Look at 'The Crime Crisis.'" *Harper's Magazine* (April 1964), p. 123.

*Bickel, Alexander M., "After the Arrest—Interrogation and the Right to Counsel." *The New Republic* (Feb. 12, 1966), p. 14.

———, "Fighting Crime." *The New Republic* (Sept. 18, 1965), p. 12.

Black, Charles L. Jr., "Mr. Justice Black, the Supreme Court, and the Bill of Rights." *Harper's Magazine* (Feb. 1961), p. 63.

Bliven, Bruce, "The Trenton Murder Case." *The New Republic* (May 16, 1949), p. 12.

Bock, Peter E., "Great News Events of the Last 75 Years." *Editor and Publisher* (June 27, 1959), Section 2, p. 188.

Booker, Simeon, "Adventure in Mississippi—A Negro Reporter at the Till Trial." *Nieman Reports* (Jan. 1956), p. 13.

Breed, Warren, "Comparative Newspaper Handling of the Emmett Till Case." *Journalism Quarterly* (Summer 1958), p. 291.

*Brod, Donald F., "The Scopes Trial: A Look at Press Coverage After Forty Years." *Journalism Quarterly* (Spring 1965), p. 219.

Broeder, Dale W., "The University of Chicago Jury Project." *Nebraska Law Review* (May 1959), p. 744.

Bromley, Dorothy Dunbar, "Free Press vs. Fair Trial." *Harper's Magazine* (March 1951), p. 90.

Brown, Sevellon, 3rd, "A Newspaper's Obligations." *NPPA (National Probation and Parole Association) Journal* (Oct. 1958), p. 307.

Burch, A. T., "The Press and the Administration of Justice." *State Government* (Nov. 1954), p. 227.

Butterfield, Roger, "The St. Louis Post-Dispatch—Pulitzer's Prize." *Collier's* (Dec. 16, 1950), p. 26; Dec. 23, 1950, p. 31.

Carter, Hodding, "A Double Standard for Murder." *The New York Times Magazine* (Jan. 24, 1965), p. 20.

Cole, Fay-Cooper, " A Witness at the Scopes Trial." *Scientific American* (Jan. 1959), p. 121.

Colegrove, Albert M., "Attitudes Toward Crime News—A Newspaperman's Viewpoint." *NPPA (National Probation and Parole Association) Journal* (Oct. 1958), p. 313.

"Community Hostility and the Right to an Impartial Jury," note. *Columbia Law Review,* vol. 60 (March 1960), p. 349.

"Contempt by Publication," note. *Yale Law Journal,* vol. 59 (1950), p. 534.

Cressey, Donald R., "The Respectable Criminal." *Trans-action* (March-April 1965), p. 12.

Davison, W. Phillips, "On the Effects of Communication." *Public Opinion Quarterly* (Fall 1959), p. 343.

*Dillon, Hugh R., "Pre-Trial Publicity—A View from Behind the Bars." *Editor and Publisher* (May 8, 1965), p. 18.

"Double Jeopardy: The Reprosecution Problem," note. *Harvard Law Review,* vol. 77 (1964), p. 1272.

Douglas, William O., "Vagrancy and Arrest on Suspicion." *Yale Law Journal,* vol. 70 (1960), p. 1.

*Dressler, David, "Trial by Combat in American Courts." *Harper's Magazine* (April 1961), p. 31.

Erickson, Raymond L., "Psychiatry and the Law: An Attempt at Synthesis." *Duke Law Journal,* vol. 1961 (Winter), p. 30.

Foote, Caleb, "The Coming Constitutional Crisis in Bail: I & II." *University of Pennsylvania Law Review,* vol. 113 (1965), pp. 959, 1125.

*Friedrich, Otto, "A Vivacious Blonde Was Fatally Shot Today, or How to Read a Tabloid." *The American Scholar* (Autumn 1959), p. 467.

*Furlong, William Barry, "Thirty Years Ago." *The New York Times Magazine* (Aug. 9, 1964), p. 25.

*Gerald, J. Edward, "The British Press Council: A Summary and an Evaluation." *Journalism Quarterly* (Summer 1959), p. 295.

*Goettel, Gerald L., "Why the Crime Syndicate Can't Be Touched." *Harper's Magazine* (Nov. 1960), p. 33.

Goldberg, Arthur J., "Equal Justice for the Poor, Too." *The New York Times Magazine* (March 15, 1964), p. 24.

———, "Freedom and Responsibility of the Press." Address Before the American Society of Newspaper Editors, Washington, D.C., April 16, 1964.

*Goldstein, Abraham S., "The Crime of Conspiracy." *The New Republic* (May 15, 1961), p. 8.

———, "The State and the Accused: Balance of Advantage in Criminal Procedure." *Yale Law Journal,* vol. 69 (1960), p. 1149.

Gottlieb, "Radio and Newspaper Reports of the Heirens Murder Case." *Journalism Quarterly* (June 1947), p. 97.

Griswold, Erwin N., "Responsibility of the Legal Profession." *Harvard Today* (Jan. 1965), p. 9.

Gutman, Daniel, "The Criminal Gets the Breaks." *The New York Times Magazine* (Nov. 29, 1964), p. 36.

"Habeas Corpus—Effect of Supreme Court Change in Law on Exhaustion of State Remedies Requisite to Federal Habeas Corpus," comment. *University of Pennsylvania Law Review,* vol. 113 (1965), p. 1303.

Haimbaugh, George D. Jr., "Free Press Versus Fair Trial: The Contribution of Mr. Justice Frankfurter." *University of Pittsburgh Law Review,* vol. 26 (1965), p. 491.

Hallam, Oscar, "Some Object Lessons on Publicity in Criminal Trials." *Minnesota Law Review,* vol. 24 (1940), p. 453.

*Harrison, John M., "The Press vs. the Courts." *The Saturday Review* (Oct. 15, 1955), p. 9.

*Harvey, Joseph M., "Trial by Newspaper." *Nieman Reports* (April 1957), p. 18; (July 1957), p. 3.

*[Hiss Case]—"Eight Out of 12 Vote Hiss Guilty." *Life* (July 18, 1949), p. 37.

Huie, William Bradford, "Approved Killing in Mississippi." *Look* (Jan. 24, 1956).

Isaacs, Norman E., "The Crime of Present Day Crime Reporting." *The Journal of Criminal Law, Criminology and Police Science,* vol. 52 (1961), p. 405.

Jackson, Bruce, "Who Goes to Prison—Caste and Careerism in Crime." *The Atlantic* (Jan. 1966), p. 52.

James, Rita M., "Status and Competence of Jurors." *The American Journal of Sociology* (May 1959), p. 563.

Klapp, Orrin E., "American Villain-Types." *American Sociological Review* (June 1956), p. 337.

Klapper, Joseph T., "What We Know About the Effects of Mass Communication: The Brink of Hope." *Public Opinion Quarterly* (Winter 1957-58), p. 453.

Krasner, William, "Hoodlum Priest and Respectable Convicts." *Harper's Magazine* (Feb. 1961), p. 57.

LeWine, Jerome Martin, "What Constitutes Prejudicial Publicity in Pending Cases?" *American Bar Association Journal* (Oct. 1965), p. 942.

Lewis, Anthony, "British Verdict on Trial-by-Press." *The New York Times Magazine* (June 20, 1965), p. 46.

Lofton, John, "Justice and the Press—Communication Inside and Outside the Courtroom." *St. Louis University Law Journal,* vol. 6 (1961), p. 449.

———, "Too Interested in [the] Sensational." *The Masthead* (Spring 1964), p. 23.

*———, "Trial By Fury." *The Nation* (Nov. 25, 1961), p. 415.

Lumbard, J. Edward, "The Adequacy of Lawyers Now in Criminal Practice." *Journal of the American Judicature Society* (Jan. 1964), p. 176.

McCullough, Dan H., "The Sunset of the Criminal Lawyer." *American Bar Association Journal* (March 1964), p. 223.

McDonald, Miles F., "Citizen Action: An Essential to Correctional Progress." *NPPA* (*National Probation and Parole Association*) *Journal* (Oct. 1958), p. 356.

McEvoy, Andrew T., and Newman, Thomas R., "Notes: Free Press; Fair Trial—Rights in Collision." *New York University Law Review,* vol. 34 (1959), p. 1278.

Marine, Gene, "The Jury Said 'Death'—Second Thoughts on a Murder." *The Nation* (May 19, 1956), p. 424.

Martin, John Bartlow, "The Innocent and the Guilty." *Saturday Evening Post* (July 30, Aug. 6, 13, 20, 1960).

Martin, Melvin, "Did the Press Kill Caryl Chessman?" *The Progressive* (Dec. 1960), p. 12.

Menninger, Karl, "Verdict Guilty—Now What?" *Harper's Magazine* (Aug. 1959), p. 60.

Morgan, Charles, "Southern Justice." *Look* (June 29, 1965).

Mueller, Gerhard O. W., "The Law Relating to Police Interrogation Privileges and Limitations." *The Journal of Criminal Law, Criminology and Police Science,* vol. 52 (1961), p. 2.

*Murthy, N. V. K., "Freedom of the Press and Fair Trial in the U.S.A." *Journalism Quarterly* (Summer 1959), p. 307.

*Nelles, Walter, and King, Carol Weiss, "Contempt by Publication in the United States." *Columbia Law Review,* vol. 28 (1928), p. 525.

Nelson, Helen, "Watchdog of the British Press." *Saturday Review* (Aug. 8, 1964), p. 42.

Newman, Donald J., "Pleading Guilty for Considerations: A Study of Bargain Justice." *The Journal of Criminal Law, Criminology and Police Science,* vol. 46 (1956), p. 780.

*Nolan, John E. Jr., "In the Name of the Law." *Commonweal* (Nov. 20, 1959), p. 231.

*Otterbourg, Edwin M., "Fair Trial and Free Press." *Journal of the American Judicature Society* (Oct. 1953), p. 75.

Otto, Herbert A., "Sex and Violence on the American Newsstand." *Journalism Quarterly* (Winter 1963), p. 19.

Packer, Herbert L., "Policing the Police—Nine Men Are Not Enough." *The New Republic* (Sept. 4, 1965), p. 17.

Perry, Stuart H., "The Courts, the Press, and the Public." *Michigan Law Review,* vol. 30 (1931), p. 228.

*Peterson, Virgil W., "The Crooks Get All the Breaks." *Saturday Evening Post* (Sept. 23, 1961), p. 10.

Pollitt, Daniel H., "Counsel for the Unpopular Cause: The 'Hazard of Being Undone'." *North Carolina Law Review,* vol. 43 (1964), p. 9.

*"Postrelease Remedies for Wrongful Conviction," note. *Harvard Law Review,* vol. 74 (1961), p. 1615.

Radin, Max, "Freedom of Speech and Contempt of Court." *Illinois Law Review,* vol. 36 (1942), p. 599.

Reed, Roy, "How to Lynch a Newspaper." *The Atlantic* (Nov. 1964), p. 59.

Reitz, Curtis, "Federal Habeas Corpus: Impact of an Abortive State Proceeding." *Harvard Law Review,* vol. 74 (1961), p. 1315.

Riesman, David, "Democracy and Defamation: Fair Game and Fair Comment II?" *Columbia Law Review,* vol. 42 (1942), p. 1282.

Rose, Arnold M., and Prell, Arthur E., "Does the Punishment Fit the Crime? A Study in Social Valuation." *American Journal of Sociology* (Nov. 1955), p. 247.

Ross, Irwin, "Trial by Newspaper." *The Atlantic* (Sept. 1965), p. 63.

Schrader, Donald P., "The State of Iowa vs. Robert E. Bednasek." *Journalism Quarterly* (Winter 1951), p. 15.

*Schramm, Wilbur, "Information Theory and Mass Communication." *Journalism Quarterly* (Spring 1955), p. 131.

Simmons, George E., "The Communist Conspiracy Case: Views of 72 Daily Newspapers." *Journalism Quarterly* (March 1950), p. 3.

Simon, Rita James, "Murder, Juries, and the Press." *Trans-action* (May/June 1966), p. 40.

Somit, Albert, Tanenhaus, Joseph, and Wilke, Walter, "Aspects of Judicial Sentencing Behavior." *University of Pittsburgh Law Review,* vol. 21 (1960), p. 613.

Stempel, Guido H. III, "Content Patterns of Small and Metropolitan Dailies." *Journalism Quarterly* (Winter 1962), p. 88.

*Stern, Gerald, "The Two Forums of a Criminal Trial: The Courtroom and the Press," note. *Syracuse Law Review,* vol. 14 (1963), p. 450.

Strodtbeck, Fred L., James, Rita M., and Hawkins, Charles, "Social Status in Jury Deliberations." *American Sociological Review* (Dec. 1957), p. 713.

Sutherland, Arthur E., "Crimes, Courts and Newspapers." *Nieman Reports* (April 1956), p. 39.

Sutherland, Arthur E. Jr., "Crime and Confession." *Harvard Law Review,* vol. 79 (1965), p. 21.

Swanson, Charles E., "What They Read in 130 Daily Newspapers." *Journalism Quarterly* (Fall 1955), p. 411.

Treuhaft, Decca M., "Trial by Headline." *The Nation* (Oct. 26, 1957), p. 279.

Veltfort, Helen R., and Lee, G. E., "The Cocoanut Grove Fire: A Study in Scapegoating." *Journal of Abnormal Social Psychology* (1943), p. 38; *Clinical Supplement,* p. 138.

Vetri, Dominick R., "Guilty Plea Bargaining: Compromises by Prosecutors to Secure Guilty Pleas." *University of Pennsylvania Law Review,* vol. 112 (1964), p. 865.

Wechsler, Herbert, "Sentencing, Correction, and the Model Penal Code." *University of Pennsylvania Law Review,* vol. 109 (1961), p. 473.

Wechsler, James, "Free Press versus Fair Trial." *The Progressive* (March 1965), p. 18.

*West, Rebecca, "Opera in Greenville." *The New Yorker* (June 14, 1947), p. 31.

*Winick, Charles, "How People Perceived the Mad Bomber." *Public Opinion Quarterly* (Spring 1961), p. 25.

*Wright, J. Skelly, "A Judge's View: News Media and Criminal Justice." *American Bar Association* (Dec. 1964), p. 1125.

Wolfram, Harold W., "Free Press, Fair Trial, and the Responsibility of the Bar." *Criminal Law Review* (N.Y.), vol. 1 (1954), p. 1.

Zion, Sidney E., "The Suspect Confesses—But Who Believes Him?" *The New York Times Magazine* (May 16, 1965), p. 30.

BOOKS AND PAMPHLETS

Abrahamsen, David, M. D., *Who Are the Guilty? A Study of Education and Crime.* New York: Rinehart, 1952.

Allport, Gordon W., *The Nature of Prejudice.* Cambridge, Mass.: Addison-Wesley Publishing Company, Inc., 1954.

Barck, Oscar Theodore Jr., and Blake, Nelson Manfred, *Since 1900—A History of the United States in Our Times.* New York: The Macmillan Company, 1947.

Barnes, Harry Elmer, and Teeters, Negley K., *New Horizons in Criminology.* (2nd ed., 1951; 3rd ed., 1959.) New York: Prentice-Hall, Inc.

Barrett, James Wyman, *Joseph Pulitzer and His World.* New York: The Vanguard Press, Inc., 1941.

*Barth, Alan, *The Price of Liberty.* New York: The Viking Press, Inc., 1961.

Bates, Ernest Sutherland, *This Land of Liberty.* New York: Harper and Brothers, 1930.

Bedford, Sybille, *The Best We Can Do.* Great Britain, Penguin Books, 1961.

Beirne, Francis F., *Shout Treason—The Trial of Aaron Burr.* New York: Hastings House, 1959.

Berger, Meyer, *The Story of The New York Times—1851-1951.* New York: Simon and Schuster, Inc., 1951.

Blanshard, Paul, *The Right to Read—The Battle Against Censorship.* Boston: Beacon Press, 1955.

Block, Eugene B., *The Vindicators.* New York: Doubleday & Company, Inc., 1963.

Blumberg, Nathan, *One-Party Press?* Lincoln: University of Nebraska Press, 1954.

Bok, Curtis, *Star Wormwood.* New York: Alfred A. Knopf, Inc., 1959.

Borchard, Edwin M., and Lutz, E. Russell, *Convicting the Innocent—Errors in Criminal Justice.* New Haven: Yale University Press, 1932.

Borkin, Joseph, *The Corrupt Judge—An Inquiry Into Bribery and Other High Crimes and Misdemeanors in the Federal Courts.* New York: Clarkson N. Potter, Inc., 1962.

Botein, Bernard, and Gordon, Murray A., *The Trial of the Future.* New York: Cornerstone Library, Inc., 1965.

Brennan, William J. Jr., *The Bill of Rights and the States.* Santa Barbara, Cal.: Center for the Study of Democratic Institutions, 1961.

*Buranelli, Vincent, *The Trial of Peter Zenger.* New York: New York University Press, 1957.

*Bureau of Municipal Research and Pennsylvania Economy League, *The Magistrates' Courts of Philadelphia* (Revised ed., 1958). Philadelphia, Pa.

Caldwell, Robert G., *Criminology.* New York: The Ronald Press Company, 1956.

Chafee, Zechariah Jr., *Freedom of Speech and Press.* New York: Carrie Chapman Catt Memorial Fund, Inc., 1955.

———, *Free Speech in the United States.* Cambridge, Mass.: Harvard University Press, 1954.

Chafee, Zechariah Jr., Pollak, Walter H., and Stern, Carl S., Consultants; Halleran, Thomas A., Assistant, *The Mooney-Billings Report—Suppressed by the Wickersham Commission.* New York: Gotham House, Inc., 1932. [Chafee says in *Government and Mass Communication,* vol. 1, p. 419, footnote 35, that the Wickersham Commission did not suppress the report but failed to publish it because it was finished too late to be considered.]

Chambers, Whittaker, *Witness*. New York: Random House, Inc., 1952.

Coleman, McAlister, *Eugene V. Debs—A Man Unafraid*. New York: Greenberg Publishers, Inc., 1930.

Corwin, Edward S., *Total War and the Constitution*. New York: Alfred A. Knopf, Inc., 1947.

*Darrow, Clarence, *Crime—Its Causes and Treatment*. New York: Thomas Y. Crowell Co., 1922.

*[Darrow, Clarence], *The Plea of Clarence Darrow, August 22nd, 23rd and 25th, 1924, in Defense of Richard Loeb and Nathan Leopold Jr. on Trial for Murder*. Chicago: Ralph Fletcher Seymour, 1924.

Darrow, Clarence, *The Story of My Life*. New York: Charles Scribner's Sons, 1932.

Dickler, Gerald, *Man on Trial—History-Making Trials from Socrates to Oppenheimer*. New York: Doubleday & Company, Inc., 1962.

*Donovan, James B., *Strangers on a Bridge—The Case of Colonel Abel*. New York: Atheneum Publishers, 1964.

Douglas, William O., *The Right of the People*. New York: Doubleday & Company, Inc., 1958.

*Eastman, Max, *The Trial of Eugene Debs—With Debs' Address to the Court on Receiving Sentence*. New York: Liberator Publishing Co. [no date given].

Fellman, David, *The Defendant's Rights*. New York: Rinehart, 1958.

Fitzgerald, Stephen E., *Communicating Ideas to the Public*. New York: Funk and Wagnalls Company, Inc., in association with Modern Industry Magazine, 1950.

Fraenkel, Osmond K., *Sacco-Vanzetti Case*. New York: Alfred A. Knopf, Inc., 1931.

———, *The Supreme Court and Civil Liberties—How the Court Has Protected the Bill of Rights* (2d ed., 1963). Dobbs Ferry, N.Y.: Oceana Publications, Inc.

Frank, Jerome, *Courts on Trial—Myth and Reality in American Justice*. Princeton, N.J.: Princeton University Press, 1949.

———, *Law and the Modern Mind* (Anchor ed., 1963). Garden City, N.Y.: Doubleday & Company, Inc.

Frank, Judge Jerome, and Frank, Barbara, in association with Harold M. Hoffman, *Not Guilty*. Garden City, N.Y.: Doubleday & Company, Inc., 1957.

*Frankfurter, Felix, *The Case of Sacco and Vanzetti—A Criminal Analysis for Lawyers and Laymen*. Stanford, Cal.: Academic Reprints, 1954.

Gellhorn, Walter, *American Rights—The Constitution in Action*. New York: The Macmillan Company, 1960.

Gill, John, *Tide Without Turning: Elijah P. Lovejoy and Freedom of the Press*. Boston: Starr King Press [no date given].

*Ginger, Ray, *The Bending Cross—A Biography of Eugene Victor Debs.* New Brunswick, N.J.: Rutgers University Press, 1949.

——, *Six Days or Forever? Tennessee v. John Thomas Scopes.* Boston: Beacon Press, 1958.

*Glueck, Sheldon and Eleanor, *Physique and Delinquency.* New York: Harper and Brothers, 1956.

Golden, Harry, *A Little Girl Is Dead.* Cleveland, Ohio: The World Publishing Company, 1965.

Goldfarb, Ronald, *Ransom: A Critique of the American Bail System.* New York: Harper & Row, Publishers, 1965.

Haldeman-Julius, *Darrow's Two Great Trials.*

Hale, William Harlan, *Horace Greeley—Voice of the People.* New York: Harper and Brothers, 1950.

Hale, Leslie, *Hanged in Error.* Baltimore, Md.: Penguin Books, Inc., 1961.

*Hale, William G., *The Law of the Press: Text–Statutes–Cases.* (3d ed., 1948.) St. Paul, Minn.: West Publishing Co.

Hallgren, Mauritz, *Landscape of Freedom—The Story of American Liberty and Bigotry.* New York: Howell, Soskin & Co., 1941.

Harris, Frank, *Presentation of Crime in Newspapers—A Study of Methods in Newspaper Research.* Minneapolis, Minn.: The Sociological Press, 1932.

Hays, Arthur Garfield, *Trial By Prejudice.* New York: Covice-Friede, 1933.

[Hearst Newspapers], *Editorials from the Hearst Newspapers.* New York: Albertson Publishing Co., 1906.

Hibbert, Christopher, *The Roots of Evil—A Social History of Crime and Punishment.* Boston: Little, Brown and Company, 1963.

*Hiss, Alger, *In the Court of Public Opinion.* New York: Alfred A. Knopf, Inc., 1957.

Hohenberg, John (ed. and author of commentaries), *The Pulitzer Prize Story—News Stories, Editorials, Cartoons, and Pictures from the Pulitzer Prize Collection at Columbia University.* New York: Columbia University Press, 1959.

Holmes, Paul, *The Sheppard Murder Case.* New York: David McKay Company, Inc., 1961.

Howard, D. L., *John Howard: Prison Reformer.* New York: Archer House, Inc., 1963.

Inbau, Fred E., and Reid, John E., *Criminal Interrogation and Confession.* Baltimore, Md.: Williams and Wilkins, 1962.

*Joughin, G. Louis, and Morgan, Edmund M., *The Legacy of Sacco and Vanzetti.* New York: Harcourt, Brace & Co., 1948.

*Kaplan, John, and Waltz, Jon R., *The Trial of Jack Ruby.* New York: The Macmillan Company, 1965.

Kelly, Alfred H., and Harbison, Winfred A., *The American Constitution—Its Origins and Development* (Revised ed., 1955). New York: W. W. Norton & Company, Inc.

Kennedy, John F., *Profiles in Courage.* New York: Harper and Brothers, 1956.

*Kirchheimer, Otto, *Political Justice: The Use of Legal Procedure for Political Ends.* Princeton, N.J.: Princeton University Press, 1961.

Kunstler, William, *And Justice for All.* Dobbs Ferry, N.Y.: Oceana Publications, Inc., 1963.

*———, *Beyond a Reasonable Doubt.* New York: William Morrow and Company, Inc., 1961.

———, *First Degree.* Dobbs Ferry, N.Y.: Oceana Publications, Inc., 1960.

*———, *The Minister and the Choir Singer: The Hall-Mills Murder Case.* New York: William Morrow and Company, Inc., 1964.

Langford, Gerald, *The Murder of Stanford White.* Indianapolis, Ind.: The Bobbs-Merrill Company, Inc., 1962.

La Piere, Richard, *The Freudian Ethic.* New York: Duell, Sloan and Pearce, 1959.

Laurence, John, *A History of Capital Punishment.* New York: Citadel Press, 1960.

Lawson, John D., ed., *American State Trials.* 17 vols. St. Louis, Mo.: F. H. Thomas Law Book Co., 1914-1936.

Levy, Leonard W., *Legacy of Suppression: Freedom of Speech and Press in Early American History.* Cambridge, Mass.: Belknap Press of Harvard University Press, 1960.

*Lewis, Arthur H., *Lament for the Molly Maguires.* New York: Harcourt, Brace & World, Inc., 1964.

Liebling, A. J., *The Press.* New York: Ballantine Books, Inc., 1961.

*Lustgarten, Edgar, *Verdict in Dispute.* New York: Charles Scribner's Sons, 1950.

McCord, William and Joan, with Zola, Irving Kenneth, *Origins of Crime—A New Evaluation of the Cambridge-Somerville Youth Study.* New York: Columbia University Press, 1959.

McCormick, Ken, *Sprung: The Release of Willie Calloway.* New York: St. Martin's Press, Inc., 1964.

*MacDougall, Curtis D., *Covering the Courts.* New York: Prentice-Hall, Inc., 1946.

McKernan, Maureen, *The Amazing Crime and Trial of Leopold and Loeb.* New York: New American Library, 1957.

*Machlin, Milton, and Woodfield, William, *Ninth Life.* New York: G. P. Putnam's Sons, 1961.

Martin, John Bartlow, *Break Down the Walls.* New York: Ballantine Books, 1954.

Mencken, H. L., *Prejudices—A Selection.* (Made by James T. Farrell.) New York: Vintage Books, 1958.

Menninger, Karl A., *Man Against Himself.* New York: Harcourt, Brace & Co., 1938.

———, *A Psychiatrist's World.* New York: The Viking Press, Inc., 1959.

Miller, Bruce Moulton, "A Critique of the Reporting of the Bruno Richard Hauptmann Trial." Unpublished master's thesis, Stanford University, 1947.

Moley, Raymond, *Our Criminal Courts.* New York: Minton, Balch and Co., 1930.

Morris, Richard B., *Fair Trial—Fourteen Who Stood Accused from Anne Hutchison to Alger Hiss.* New York: Alfred A. Knopf, Inc., 1952.

Mott, Frank Luther, *American Journalism—A History of Newspapers in the United States Through 250 Years—1690-1940.* New York: The Macmillan Company, 1941.

———, *The News in America.* Cambridge, Mass.: Harvard University Press, 1952.

Münsterberg, Hugo, *On the Witness Stand.* New York: Clark Beardman Co., Ltd., 1941.

Nash, Ogden, *Verses from 1929 On.* Boston: Little, Brown and Company, 1959.

Painter, Floy Ruth, *That Man Debs and His Life Work.* Indiana University Graduate Council, 1929.

*Patterson, Haywood, and Conrad, Earl, *Scottsboro Boy.* New York: Doubleday & Company, Inc., 1950.

Perry, Richard L., and Cooper, John C., eds., *Sources of Our Liberties—Documentary Origins of Individual Liberties in the United States Constitution and Bill of Rights.* Chicago: American Bar Foundation, 1952.

Pope, John Keith, *Police-Press Relations—A Handbook.* Fresno, Cal.: Academy Library Guild, 1954.

Pound, Roscoe, *Criminal Justice in America.* New York: Henry Holt, 1930.

Radin, Edward D., *The Innocents.* New York: William Morrow and Company, Inc., 1965.

———, *Lizzie Borden: The Untold Story.* New York: Dell Books, 1962.

Raper, Arthur F., *The Tragedy of Lynching.* Chapel Hill, N.C.: University of North Carolina Press, 1933.

Reik, Theodore, *From the Works of Theodore Reik: The Compulsion to Confess—On the Psychoanalysis of Crime and Punishment.* New York: Farrar, Straus and Cudahy, 1959.

Reiwald, Paul, *Society and Its Criminals.* Timperley, Altrincham: William Heinemann—Medical Books, 1949.

Reynolds, Quentin, *Courtroom—The Story of Samuel S. Leibowitz.* New York: Farrar, Straus & Company, 1950.

Rogge, O. John, *Why Men Confess.* New York: Thomas Nelson & Sons, 1959.

*Rokeach, Milton, *The Open and Closed Mind—Investigations Into the Nature of Belief Systems and Personality Systems.* New York: Basic Books, 1960.

Rosenberg, Bernard, and White, David Manning, *Mass Culture—The Popular Arts in America.* Glencoe, Ill.: Free Press, 1957.

Rubinstein, Joseph, and Farley, Earl, *Books Which Have Survived.* Lawrence, Kans.: University of Kansas Library, 1955.

Runyon, Damon, *Trials and Tribulations.* Philadelphia, Pa.: J. B. Lippincott Company, 1947.

St. George, Maximilian, and Dennis, Lawrence, *A Trial on Trial—The Great Sedition Trial of 1944* [no place of publication given]. National Civil Rights Committee, 1946.

Schramm, Wilbur, *Responsibility in Mass Communication.* New York: Harper and Brothers, 1957.

*Schwartz, Bernard, *The Supreme Court—Constitutional Revolution in Retrospect.* New York: The Ronald Press Company, 1957.

Seldes, George, *Freedom of the Press.* Indianapolis, Ind.: The Bobbs-Merrill Company, Inc., 1935.

Silver, James W., *Mississippi: The Closed Society.* New York: Harcourt, Brace & World, Inc., 1963.

Steffens, Lincoln, *The Autobiography of Lincoln Steffens.* New York: Harcourt, Brace & Co., 1931.

Sullivan, Harold W., *Trial by Newspaper.* Hyannis, Mass.: The Patriot Press, 1961.

Svirsky, Leon, ed. (By Nine Nieman Fellows, 1945-1946), *Your Newspaper—Blueprint for a Better Press.* New York: The Macmillan Company, 1947.

Symes, Lillian, *Our American Dreyfus Case—A Challenge to California Justice.* Los Angeles: Inter-Religious Committee for Justice for Thomas J. Mooney, 1935.

Taft, Donald R., *Criminology* (3d ed., 1956). New York: The Macmillan Company.

Tebbel, John, *The Story of the McCormicks, Medills and Pattersons—An American Dynasty.* New York: Doubleday & Company, Inc., 1947.

Thayer, Frank, with cooperation on research by Eugene O. Gehl and Harold L. Nelson, *Legal Control of the Press.* (Fourth ed., 1962.) Brooklyn: The Foundation Press, Inc.

*Toland, John, *The Dillinger Days.* New York: Random House, Inc., 1963.

Train, Arthur, *The Prisoner at the Bar—Sidelight on the Administration of Criminal Justice.* New York: Charles Scribner's Sons, 1908.

*Trebach, Arnold S., *The Rationing of Justice: Constitutional Rights and the Criminal Process.* New Brunswick, N.J.: Rutgers University Press, 1964.

Trever, Albert A., *The Ancient Near East and Greece.* Vol. I of *History of Ancient Civilization.* New York: Harcourt, Brace and Co., 1936.

Vanderbilt, Arthur T., *The Challenge of Law Reform.* Princeton, N.J.: Princeton University Press, 1955.

———, *Judges and Jurors: Their Functions, Qualifications and Selection.* Boston: Boston University Press, 1956.

*Von Hentig, Hans, *Crime—Causes and Conditions*. New York: McGraw-Hill, Inc., 1947.

Waite, John Barker, *Criminal Law in Action*. New York: Sears Publishing Co., 1934.

Waller, George, *Kidnap*. New York: Pocket Books, Inc., 1962.

Weinberg, Arthur, ed., *Attorney for the Damned* [Clarence Darrow in His Own Words]. New York: Simon and Schuster, Inc., 1957.

Wells, Evelyn, *Fremont Older*. New York: D. Appleton-Century Co., 1936.

*Wiggins, James Russell, *Freedom or Secrecy*. New York: Oxford University Press, 1956.

Wigmore, John H., *A Kaleidoscope of Justice—Containing Authentic Accounts of Trial Scenes from All Times and Climes*. Washington, D.C.: Washington Law Book Co., 1941.

Williams, Brad, *Due Process—The fabulous story of criminal lawyer George T. Davis and his thirty-year battle against capital punishment*. New York: William Morrow and Company, Inc., 1960.

Williams, Charlotte, *Hugo L. Black—A Study of the Judicial Process*. Baltimore: The Johns Hopkins Press, 1950.

Wood, James Horace [lawyer] as told to John M. Ross, *Nothing But the Truth*. New York: Doubleday & Company, Inc., 1960.

Yankwich, Leon R., *It's Libel or Contempt If You Print It*. Los Angeles: Parker & Co., 1950.

NEWSPAPERS

Atlanta *Constitution*
*Atlanta *Journal*
*Birmingham *News*
*Birmingham *Post*
Boston *Evening Transcript*
*Charleston (S.C.) *News and Courier*
*Chicago *Daily News*
*Chicago *Sun-Times*
Chicago *Tribune*
*Cleveland *News*
*Cleveland *Plain Dealer*
Cleveland *Press*
*Columbia (S.C.) *State*
*Denver *Post*
Detroit *Free Press*
Guild Reporter
*Houston *Post*
Los Angeles *Examiner*
Los Angeles *Times*
*Miami *Herald*
*Milwaukee *Journal*
*Milwaukee *Sentinel*
*Montgomery *Advertiser*
*New York *Daily News*
New York *Herald Tribune*
*New York *Mirror*
*New York *National Inquirer* [weekly]
New York *Times*
Palo Alto (Cal.) *Daily Times*
*Philadelphia *Evening Bulletin*
Philadelphia *Inquirer*
Pittsburgh *Courier* [weekly]
Pittsburgh *Post-Gazette*
Pittsburgh *Press*
Pittsburgh *Sun-Telegraph*
*Pottstown (Pa.) *Mercury*
*Rochester (N.Y.) *Democrat and Chronicle*
*Rochester (N.Y.) *Times-Union*

St. Louis *Post-Dispatch*
San Francisco *Chronicle*
San Francisco *Examiner*
San Francisco *News*
*Toledo *Blade*
*Trenton (N.J.) *Times*
Washington *Post*

PUBLIC DOCUMENTS

*Commissioners' Committee on Police Arrests for Investigation, *Report and Recommendations of*. District of Columbia (July 1962).

*Commonwealth of Pennsylvania, Department of Justice, *Report of the Attorney General on the Investigation of the Magisterial System*. Harrisburg, Pa. (Sept. 8, 1965).

Corwin, Edward S., ed., *The Constitution of the United States of America—Analysis and Interpretation*. Senate Document No. 170. 82d Cong., 2d Sess. Washington: Government Printing Office (1953).

New York, State of, *Report of the Crime Commission*. (Submitted Feb. 28, 1927.) Legislative Document (1927) No. 94. Albany: J. B. Lyon Co. (1927).

Royal Commission on the Press, 1947-1949, *Report Presented to Parliament by Command of His Majesty, June 1949*. London: His Majesty's Stationery Office.

U.S. Commission on Civil Rights, *Justice—1961 Commission on Civil Rights Report*. Washington: Government Printing Office.

U.S. Commission on Civil Rights, *Law Enforcement—A Report on Equal Protection in the South*. Washington: Government Printing Office (1965).

U.S. Congress, Senate. Committee on the Judiciary, *Recording of Jury Deliberations*—Hearings Before the Subcommittee to Investigate the Administration of the Internal Security Act and Other Internal Security Laws. 84th Cong., 1st Sess., Pursuant to S. Res. 58. Washington: Government Printing Office (1955).

U.S. Congress, Senate. Committee on the Judiciary, *Free Press and Fair Trial*—Hearings Before the Subcommittee on Constitutional Rights and the Subcommittee on Improvements in Judicial Machinery. 89th Cong., 1st Sess., on S. 290. Part 1 and Part 2, Appendix. Washington: Government Printing Office (1966).

U.S. Dept. of Justice, *Report of the Attorney General's Committee on Poverty and the Administration of Federal Criminal Justice*. (Feb. 25, 1963.)

U.S. Dept. of Justice, Federal Bureau of Investigation, *Crime in the United States*—Uniform Crime Reports, 1959 and 1964. Washington: Government Printing Office.

[Warren Commission], *Report of the Warren Commission on the Assassination of President Kennedy*. (New York *Times* ed.) New York: Bantam Books (1964).

[Wickersham Commission], National Commission on Law Observance and

Enforcement [George W. Wickersham, Chairman], *Report on the Causes of Crime*. Vol. 1. Washington: Government Printing Office (1931).

REPORTS OF CIVIC AND PROFESSIONAL ORGANIZATIONS

American Bar Association, *Report of the Special Committee on Cooperation Between Press, Radio and Bar, as to Publicity Interfering with Fair Trial of Judicial and Quasi-Judicial Proceedings,* Annual Report of the American Bar Association. Including Proceedings of the Sixtieth Annual Meeting held at Kansas City, Missouri, September 27-30 and October 1, 1937. Vol. 62. Chicago: Headquarters Office (1937).

American Civil Liberties Union Statement, "The Death Penalty and Civil Liberties," New York (July 1965).

American Civil Liberties Union memorandum, "Fair Trial and Free Press," New York (Oct. 7, 1965).

American Society of Newspaper Editors, "Report of Press-Bar Committee," Washington (April 14, 1965).

Chafee, Zechariah Jr., *Government and Mass Communications—A Report from the Commission on Freedom of the Press.* 2 vols. Chicago: University of Chicago Press (1947).

Commission on Freedom of the Press, *A Free and Responsible Press—A General Report on Mass Communication: Newspapers, Radio, Motion Pictures, Magazines, and Books*. Chicago: University of Chicago Press (1947).

*General Council of the Press [British], *The Press and the People—The First Annual Report*. London: Bell Yard, Fleet Street (1954).

New York State Bar Bulletin, vol. 26, no. 4 (July 1954).

Political and Economic Planning [Group], *Report on the British Press—A survey of its current operations and problems with special reference to national newspapers and their part in public affairs.* London.

Southern Regional Council, *Law Enforcement in Mississippi.* Atlanta (July 14, 1964).

Southern Regional Council and American Civil Liberties Union, *Southern Justice: An Indictment.* Atlanta (Oct. 18, 1965).

A Special Committee of the Association of the Bar of the City of New York and the National Legal Aid and Defender Association, *Equal Justice for the Accused*. Garden City, N.Y.: Doubleday & Company, Inc. (1959).

INDEX